Women and

Working-Class

Politics in the

United States,

1900–1965

COMMON SENSE & A LITTLE FIRE

ANNELISE ORLECK

The University of North Carolina Press | Chapel Hill & London

Manufactured in the
United States of America

The paper in this book
meets the guidelines for
permanence and durability
of the Committee on
Production Guidelines for
Book Longevity of the
Council on Library
Resources.

The publication of this
volume was aided by
a generous grant from
the Z. Smith Reynolds
Foundation.

Library of Congress Cataloging-in-Publication Data

Orleck, Annelise.

Common sense and a little fire : women and working-class

politics in the United States, 1900–1965 / Annelise Orleck.

p. cm. — (Gender & American culture)

Includes bibliographical references and index.

ISBN 0-8078-2199-3 (alk. paper). —

ISBN 0-8078-4511-6 (pbk.: alk. paper)

1. Women in the labor movement—United States—History—

20th century.   2. Working class women—United States—

Political activity.   3. Jewish women—United States—Political

activity.   4. Women social reformers—United States—

History—20th century.   I. Title.   II. Series.

HD6079.2.U5075   1995

331.4′78′09730904—dc20   94-24544

                                                            CIP

99   98   97   96   95

5   4   3   2   1

To the memory of my father, Norman Orleck

And to the memories of Rose Schneiderman,
Fannia Cohn, Pauline Newman, and
Clara Lemlich Shavelson

CONTENTS

Illustrations can be found on pages 81–86, 205–14,
and 289–94.

ACKNOWLEDGMENTS

Like the women this book is about, I have been sustained in my work by the support and encouragement of many people. First and foremost there was my sweet family: my father, Norman, who wanted me to be, of all things, a historian; my mother, Thelma, whose friendship, wisdom, and love have buoyed me throughout my life; Ruth, Joe, and Jerry Orleck, and my nephews Larry and Jon, who have cheered me on through the long years of this project's development.

I also owe a great deal to the families of Pauline Newman and Clara Lemlich Shavelson, who graciously opened their homes and lives to me, sharing memories, personal letters, photographs, and thoughtful suggestions. I want to express my appreciation to Elisabeth Burger, Michael Owen, Martha Schaffer, Rita Margules, Evelyn Velson, Julia Velson, and Jane and Adela Margules. I know that it is not the easiest or most pleasant thing to have a stranger rummaging through one's family history. Their patient and generous cooperation has vastly improved this book. Special thanks are due to Joel Schaffer for allowing me to copy and quote tapes of interviews that he did nearly twenty years ago with his grandmother, Clara Lemlich Shavelson, and with her family and fellow activists.

My thinking about working-class women's activism was greatly enriched by conversations with friends, colleagues, and protégés of the four women this book portrays. Rose Nelson Raynes, Sophie Melvin Gerson, Dora Smorodin, Sidney Jonas, and Jack Friedman gave me wonderful interviews. I owe a particular debt to Miriam Stein, who, with her late husband Leon Stein, spent a long, lovely afternoon talking with me about Rose Schneiderman, Fannia Cohn, Pauline Newman, and the stormy life of the International Ladies' Garment Workers' Union.

I am deeply grateful to Susan Ware, who read this manuscript more times than anyone should have to. Her keen critique, insightful suggestions, and diligent editing helped me carve a readable book out of a mass of detail. Thanks are due, too, to Molly Nolan, Marilyn Young, David Reimers, and Daniel Walkowitz, whose thoughtful criticisms also shaped the book's evolution.

My friends and colleagues in the history Ph.D. program at New York University read many of these chapters when they were quite rough-hewn. Fond thanks to Adina Back, Harriet Jackson, Lynn Johnson, Claire Potter, Renqiu Yu, and Nancy Robertson. Their sharp critiques, good food and drink, and unflagging support eased my writing process considerably. Susan Yohn also offered help at a crucial time, reading the manuscript in its entirety when it was no longer a dissertation but not yet a book. It was especially kind of her to do this when she was racing to finish her own book.

Then, of course, there are the archivists, without whom no historian could do her work. The staffs of the Schlesinger Library and the Franklin Delano Roosevelt Presidential Library were extremely helpful. Special thanks to Angie Sierra, Melanie Yolles, and Wayne Furman at the New York Public Library Manuscripts Division for their speed, efficiency, and good humor; and to Peter Filardo and Deborah Bernhardt at New York University's Tamiment Library for their enthusiasm and expert guidance during all the years I camped out in their reading room.

For the last four years I have had the good fortune to be a member of the faculty of Dartmouth College. From the day I arrived, my colleagues in the history department have shown me nothing but kindness, warmth, and encouragement. I could not ask for a better environment in which to do my work. I owe two debts in particular. David Sloane read every chapter of this book carefully and critically at a time when I could no longer discern what worked and what didn't. I have benefited in many ways from his wit, his wisdom, and his friendship. Mary Kelley read this manuscript twice, contributing in important ways to its refinement and evolution. I feel extremely lucky to enjoy her friendship and sage advice. And I am most grateful to her for going above and beyond the call more times than I can count.

The Dartmouth Women's Studies Program has introduced me to wonderful scholars from many disciplines, including Diana Taylor, cultural critic and organizer par excellence. Like so many aspects of my work, the first few chapters of this book were improved by her always-interesting perspective.

The staff of Dartmouth's Baker Library have cheerfully and effectively aided my research. Gregory Finnegan, William McEwen, and Francis X. Oscadal found answers to virtually any question I put to them. Patsy Carter at Interlibrary Loan enabled me to do more of my research right here in the Upper Valley than I could ever have imagined was possible, given that my office window overlooks a field and a pine forest.

Like every other scholar of working-class women's history, I have learned from and been inspired by the work of Alice Kessler-Harris. Ten years ago, when Pauline Newman's personal papers were still closed, Alice let me read her note cards so that I could begin my work. Many years and drafts later, she read the manuscript and offered valuable critiques. My thanks to her both for the work she does and for helping me with mine. I also owe intellectual debts to Xiaolan Bao and Erin Rowland, whose writing on Chinese, African American, and Puerto Rican garment workers taught me much of what I know about what happened to women in the International Ladies' Garment Workers' Union after 1950.

Lauren Lewis, my meticulous research assistant, was indispensable to me in the last stages of preparing this manuscript. Thanks for being so good at all the detail work that I find so daunting. I also want to express my appreciation to Barbara Hanrahan, editor in chief of the University of North Carolina Press, for her diligence and friendly guidance, and to Christi Stanforth, project editor. Her consummate professionalism and good sense of humor made her a pleasure to work with.

Finally, I owe two deeply personal debts. To my dear friend Elizabeth Cooke, with whom I've shared twenty-five years of the most extraordinary, stimulating, and wide-ranging conversations. She has profoundly affected the way I think about everything. And to my partner, Alexis Jetter, for reading, chewing on, and battling with me over every word, every idea, every quote in the pages that follow. This book has been immeasurably improved by her incisive editing, her clear thinking, and her irrepressible sense of humor. Her closeness has sweetened every facet of my life.

This book is far more than it could ever have been without the people mentioned above. Any flaws or errors are completely my own.

ABBREVIATIONS

ACW	Amalgamated Clothing Workers
AFL	American Federation of Labor
ALP	American Labor Party
CAW	Congress of American Women
CLUW	Coalition of Labor Union Women
CP	Communist Party
ELF	Emma Lazarus Federation of Jewish Women's Clubs
ERA	Equal Rights Amendment
FIC	Factory Investigating Commission
HUAC	House Un-American Activities Committee
ILGWU	International Ladies' Garment Workers' Union
ILO	International Labor Organization
IWO	International Worker's Order
IWW	Industrial Workers of the World
NAWSA	National American Woman Suffrage Association
NIRA	National Industrial Recovery Act
NRA	National Recovery Administration
NWP	National Woman's Party
NYWTUL	New York Women's Trade Union League
TUEL	Trade Union Educational League
UCWCH	United Council of Working Class Housewives
UCWW	United Council of Working Class Women
UE	United Electrical Workers
WEB	Workers Education Bureau
WTUL	Women's Trade Union League

This book has its roots in the memories and stories of my grandmother, Lena Orleck, a sharp-tongued woman with a talent for survival and for dominating everyone she met. A child immigrant from the Ukraine, she was less than ten when she began work at the Triangle Shirtwaist Factory, that most famous of U.S. garment shops. She claimed to have led a strike when she was seventeen, to have known "the famous anarchist Emma Goldman" and to have marched in the great early-twentieth-century Fifth Avenue suffrage parades.

But in the early 1970s, when I began to read histories of the immigrant labor movement, I found few echoes of my grandmother's life. The books available at that time contained no hint of the exhilarated activism she had described or the exhaustion she must have felt as a single working mother. Typical was Benjamin Stolberg's *Tailor's Progress: The Story of a Famous Union and the Men Who Made It.* This 1944 memoir of the International Ladies' Garment Workers' Union (ILGWU) contained only brief, sarcastic references to women but showed picture after picture of male union officers. Women were nearly invisible in such accounts, appearing neither as leaders nor as shop-floor activists.[1]

The past twenty years have seen dramatic growth in the literature on American working-class women. Historians have given us insight into their participation in labor unions and women's union auxiliaries, in shop-floor culture and leisure activities. But we still know very little about these women's private lives. What were their dreams and yearnings? What friendships did they form in the shops and in their neighborhoods? How important were racial, religious, and ethnic ties and conflicts? How did they balance long-term intimate relationships with work and activism? And how did these forces shape their political vision?[2]

As a collective biography of four Jewish immigrant women radicals whose political activities spanned the first half of this century, this book explores those questions. Fannia Cohn, Rose Schneiderman, Pauline Newman, and Clara Lemlich Shavelson all came of age amid the women's labor uprisings of the early 1900s and remained active through the 1960s. All four rose from the garment shop floor to positions of influence in the American labor movement. They devoted their lives to the empowerment of working-class women, but they disagreed frequently and fervently about the best strategy for doing so. Using their writings, speeches, letters, and journals, together with oral history interviews, this book explores the tensions between their private lives and their public work, highlighting the links between personal experience and the larger processes of political change.

These four women were certainly not the only working-class women of their generation to devote themselves to political activism. But there were few who remained active for as long as they did, and even fewer who left behind much written evidence of their lives. Scarcity of sources has forced most historians of working-class women to depend on institutional records, social science studies, and journalistic accounts of strikes, boycotts, and protests. I was drawn to Schneiderman, Newman, Lemlich, and Cohn in part because, unlike most women of their class and generation, they wrote a lot—both about the work they did and about their more private, intimate experiences. These rich and varied writings add a vital, and too often missing, dimension to working-class women's history: their own voices.

My ability to interpret these writings was greatly enhanced by interviews that I did with Pauline Newman herself, as well as with friends, colleagues, and children of the four women. Together these sources gave me a strong sense of immigrant working women in the United States as forceful historical actors. I offer this portrayal in contrast to the myriad accounts of poor and working-class women's lives—scholarly, journalistic, and otherwise—which have described in detail the ways that poor women have been victimized but overlooked the ways they have acted as agents of change. Biographies ascribe historical importance to individual lives. Poor and working-class women are rarely deemed worthy of such credit. One aim of this book, then, is to provide four fully fleshed characters to offset the faceless crowds and bit players who have dominated working-class women's history.

This book has several other purposes as well. The four women's shared origins allow me to examine the cultural roots of U.S. working women's radicalism during the first years of the century. Tracing the divergent paths taken by the four over their long careers, this book also suggests the range and evolution of working-class women's politics between 1900 and the 1960s. Finally, it illustrates through four women's lives and work, the longevity, vitality, and impact of working-class feminism, a strain of political thought that has received little attention either from labor or women's historians.

Rose Schneiderman, a 4′9″ capmaker with flaming red hair and legendary speaking power, came to believe that allying with progressive upper-class women and men was the quickest way to improve the lot of American working women. She remained, through her life, a committed and passionate union organizer. But she placed equal importance on building women's alliances across class lines. That led her into the cross-class New York Women's Trade Union League (NYWTUL), which she would guide and lead for more than forty years.

From a fire-breathing stump speaker, Schneiderman evolved into a lobbyist, a fund-raiser, and an administrator. Over several decades of activism, she moved through a range of cultural and political milieus, from the garment shops of Manhattan's Lower East Side to political offices in Albany and Washington, D.C. She counted Franklin and Eleanor Roosevelt among her friends and taught them much of what they knew about working people. She helped shape some of the major pieces of New Deal legislation: the National Labor Relations Act, the Social Security Act, the Fair Labor Standards Act. By the end of her long career, Schneiderman had traveled far from the culture into which she had been born and raised. As her life changed, so too did her sense of which strategy held the most promise for working women.

Schneiderman's best friend, Pauline Newman, was a die-hard union loyalist described by one male colleague as "capable of smoking a cigar with the best of them." An acerbic woman whose unorthodox tastes ran to cropped hair and tweed jackets, Newman loved the labor movement. She referred to the International Ladies' Garment Workers' Union as her "family" and believed that it was, for all its flaws, the best hope for women garment makers. The first woman hired to organize full-time for the ILGWU, Newman remained on the union's paid staff for more than seventy years. But she was a pragmatist who understood that most union leaders were only marginally interested in the concerns of working women; so she agreed with Schneiderman that it was necessary to work for labor legislation and to ally with progressives of all classes.[3]

Newman's career was a balancing act. Torn between the gruff, male-dominated Jewish Socialist milieu of the ILGWU and the more nurturing, "women-centered" Women's Trade Union League, Newman chose, for personal as well as political reasons, to divide her energies between the two. Through the League she and Schneiderman found an alternative family of women who sustained each other, providing emotional as well as political support. But unlike Schneiderman, Newman never left the trade union movement. She kept one foot in each world.

Thorny, emotional, and thin-skinned, Newman's ILGWU colleague Fannia M. Cohn dreamed of liberating workers through education. Skeptical about legislated change, Cohn believed that only through education would women gain the confidence to challenge gender as well as class inequalities. And only through learning, she argued, would men abandon their prejudices against women. Drawing the support of some of the nation's leading scholars, Cohn became the guiding force for a movement that created a vast network of worker education programs: worker universities, night schools, residential colleges, lecture series, and discussion groups. She believed that such programs would both enrich workers' lives and imbue a new generation of leaders with fresh visions of change.

Cohn occupied a unique place in the labor movement, as she does in this study. Unlike the other three women, she was not born into a poor family. Cohn's relatives were cosmopolitan middle-class urbanites who badly wanted her to attend college and graduate school. Cohn, who had been a teenage revolutionary in Russia, turned them down. She chose instead to take a job making kimonos in a Brooklyn sweatshop. At age twenty Cohn gave up her class privileges to live the life of a worker; and, as converts tend to do, she became an uncompromising and zealous advocate for her chosen cause. Cohn argued against cross-class alliances, placing all her hopes in the working-class movement. Ironically, the most ardent and devoted supporters of Cohn and her work were middle-class educators and intellectuals. By contrast, many of Cohn's male union colleagues misunderstood and mocked her.

Clara Lemlich Shavelson, a proud maverick, rejected both mainstream unionism and alliances with women of the upper classes. A brilliant street-corner orator, Shavelson never wavered in her commitment to class-based organizing. She was an organizer and agitator first, last, and always—from her teenage years in the shop to her final days in a California nursing home. Blacklisted by garment manufacturers for her pivotal role in the 1909 shirt-waist strike, then fired from her job as a street-corner suffrage speaker for refusing to curb her politics, Shavelson turned to organizing in her own community. An early member of the Communist Party, Shavelson spent the 1920s, 1930s, and 1940s building neighborhood coalitions of housewives to fight for public housing, better education, and price controls on rent and food.

Shavelson remained closer to her cultural roots than any of the other four. She married and quit work to raise her children. She made her home in a densely populated Jewish working-class neighborhood that, into the 1940s, retained the flavor of the old Lower East Side. Still, Shavelson was no ordinary Jewish housewife and mother. A woman who ate, drank, and breathed politics, Shavelson was constantly active: she spoke on street corners, organized rent strikes and citywide boycotts, lobbied in Washington, and led women's Marxist study groups. And at the end of the day, Clara Shavelson brought her politics into the family kitchen. Long before 1960s feminists popularized the idea of personal politics, Clara Shavelson had made her own home into a site of struggle.

Like most working-class women activists, the four women faced triple-tiered conflicts: with men of their own class, with women of the middle and upper classes, and with each other. Each grappled with these multiple tensions in her own way, often disagreeing fiercely about matters of political strategy. Sometimes these arguments led to painful and acrimonious splits. Fannia Cohn disapproved of the cross-class women's networks that sustained Schneiderman and Newman. As a result she was unable to really trust or become close to either of them. A more dramatic rift resulted from Clara Shavelson's decision to join the Communist Party. Though she viewed it as a necessary political choice, it destroyed her friendship with former ILGWU colleague Pauline Newman, who blamed the Communists for fragmenting the union during the 1920s. Newman never forgave Shavelson for this shift in loyalties, and Shavelson never apologized.

But if these women's careers reflect the bitter infighting that so often fractured working-class women's solidarity during the first half of this century, they also illustrate the sources of its cohesion. For despite their differences, the four activists shared a set of beliefs rooted in their common experiences as Jewish immigrants, as women, and as workers. Schneiderman, Newman, Cohn, and Shavelson were all born in small towns in Eastern Europe between 1882 and 1891. They all moved to New York City at the turn of the century and went to work in the garment trades. They were all involved in the 1909 Shirtwaist Strike, the largest strike by U.S. women to that time. That strike, often called "the Uprising of the Thirty Thousand," and the decade that followed left its mark on a generation of organizers. Pauline Newman would later call her circle "the 1909 vintage," women whose vision of the world was forged in mass strikes—and in fire.

For if the 1909 strike was their lasting inspiration, the 1911 Triangle Shirtwaist Factory fire was their recurring nightmare. It filled them with an urgency that precluded considerations of ideological purity. Newman and Lemlich had worked at the factory, and all four lost friends in the fire, which killed 146 young workers. Memories of the charred victims haunted them throughout their careers, reminding them that women workers could not wait for change. They adopted what they called the "common sense of working women" in their approach toward social change: whatever route was the quickest, which-ever path seemed most promising, they would take.[4]

That pragmatism was matched by a fierce passion and conviction that made them lifelong activists when others of their generation were swept up only briefly in mass protest before retreating to the safety and relative peace of private life. "I'm not a redhead for nothing," Rose Schneiderman liked to say. And, explaining why she loved the soapbox so, Clara Lemlich Shavelson told one interviewer: "Ah! Then I had fire in my mouth!"[5]

Their beliefs were shaped by a deep-seated feminism, though they would never have applied that label to themselves. For they associated feminism with the women of the middle and upper classes, who had the luxury of focusing solely on gender; and they refused to embrace any movement that was blind to class. Their brand of feminism was deeply imbued with class consciousness and a vivid understanding of the harsh realities of industrial labor. They opposed the Equal Rights Amendment, not because they didn't care about equality but because they feared it would endanger laws protecting women workers. If their position on the matter was short-sighted, it was because images of sweatshops and industrial accidents blocked their vision. Memories of the shop floor would always remain central to their politics. For that reason they are best described by a term coined in 1915 by author Mildred Moore. Writing about the Women's Trade Union League, she labeled its members "industrial feminists."[6]

Industrial feminism does not fit neatly into any of the established categories of American feminist history; it contradicts—and offers an important correc-tive to—the popular misconception that feminism was reserved to the middle and upper classes, while working-class, poor, and immigrant women identified more with their class, racial, or ethnic group. The process of political identity formation has never been so simple as that, certainly not in the complex world that early-twentieth-century immigrants found in the United States. Like other working-class women, Rose Schneiderman, Pauline Newman, Fannia Cohn, and Clara Lemlich Shavelson struggled to forge personal politics that balanced the conflicting pulls of gender, class, ethnicity, and family.

The political philosophy that emerged—industrial feminism—was a hybrid vision of working-class activism that was far broader than the bread-and-butter unionism of American Federation of Labor president Samuel Gom-pers. "The woman worker wants bread," Rose Schneiderman said in 1911, "but she wants roses too." Shorter hours, higher wages, safer working condi-tions, medical care, and decent and affordable housing and food were the bread for which industrial feminists fought. Meaningful work, access to educa-tion and culture, and egalitarian relationships were the roses. They pursued that dream through four strategies that became the blueprint for working-class women's activism in the twentieth-century United States: trade unionism;

worker education; community organizing around tenant and consumer issues; and lobbying—for laws regulating wages, hours, factory safety, and food and housing costs.

I use the phrase "working-class women's activism" rather than "labor activism" intentionally. The vision of these four organizers extended beyond the shop floor to the homes and neighborhoods of working-class families. In their view, the home was not isolated from the marketplace, the unions, and the government. They believed that the wives of wage-earning men, organized as tenants, consumers, and voters, could be powerful combatants in the working-class struggle. By tracing the life cycles of four organizers rather than focusing on a particular period, this book charts the continuity of working-class women's activism over sixty years.

Examination of these women's long careers reveals significant unrest in decades when American women and workers are generally thought to have been quiescent: the 1920s, 1940s, and 1950s. Because big labor unions were less active during these years than in the 1910s or the 1930s, and because there was no equivalent to the suffrage movement of the 1910s, the tendency has been to think of these decades as politically dormant. But Schneiderman, Newman, Lemlich, and Cohn did not stop organizing, speaking, or writing during these years. Accounts of the work they did in "quiet" times are filled with vital information about working-class women who continued to protest and strike, scoring victories even without the support of large movements. Studying the sporadic protests of these decades, we can better understand how working-class women held the line against reaction and even made some gains in conservative times.

A closer look at the writings and speeches of Schneiderman, Newman, Lemlich, and Cohn also exposes the roots of late-twentieth-century American movements—the struggle for women's, tenants', and consumers' rights, and for human rights around the globe. Clara Shavelson's support of Nicaragua's Sandinistas began not in the 1970s but in 1927, when Augusto Sandino first led his army against the U.S. Marines. Schneiderman's 1911 cry for bread and roses in many ways foreshadowed the 1960s slogan "The personal is political."

Biography helps us to unravel the tangled interaction between the personal relationships activists build and the political strategies they pursue. Still, the late-twentieth-century historian must be careful when reading the lives of early-twentieth-century women. This study spans more than six decades, during which conceptions of women's roles, of gender, and of sexuality changed dramatically. It is therefore not surprising that several of the women chronicled here were prickly toward feminist historians who came to interview them during the last years of their lives.

I certainly got a taste of that when I visited ninety-five-year-old Pauline Newman. She grilled me with the same white-hot intensity that had served her so well as an organizer and lobbyist. She was not even faintly charmed by my stated desire to write about her life and work. She wanted to get a sense of me, my politics, and my motives before she answered any questions. Her discomfort stemmed in part from her coming of age in an era that held very different views on privacy and relationships than we hold now at the end of the century. But it also reflected understandings of politics, trade unionism, and feminism formed in the 1910s rather than the 1970s or the 1980s. One of the purposes of this study is to show how the meanings of those terms have changed with time.

By choosing to devote themselves to activism, Shavelson, Cohn, Newman, and Schneiderman violated the cultural norms prescribed for women of their generation, class, and ethnicity. They sacrificed the respect accorded to wives and mothers in Jewish culture. They lived without the protections that early-twentieth-century U.S. culture promised to respectably feminine women. Choosing careers as political activists left them vulnerable to charges that they were failures as women. From the earliest days of her union career, Rose Schneiderman's mother warned her that activism would destroy her chances of marriage. Indeed, Schneiderman, Newman, and Cohn never did marry.

Their "singleness" made them outcasts in many ways, but it also forced them to create alternative families and emotional support networks. Even Clara Shavelson struggled to recast the boundaries of conventional family life, for her activism did not fit easily with the traditional roles of wife and mother. These personal experiences colored the women's politics. In their speeches and writings, in the unions, schools, and neighborhood councils they organized, the four activists began to articulate a political vision that called for more than economic reform. They also looked for ways to transform relationships between women, between male and female workers, between husbands and wives.

The life of a political organizer is, by its nature, draining and difficult. No activist could persevere for long without emotional support. When I asked Pauline Newman how she was able to keep the fire of activism going for so long, she told me about her friends—Rose Schneiderman, Mary Dreier, Frieda Miller, and Elisabeth Christman—the women who led the Women's Trade Union League for half a century. Newman, who outlived all the rest, was visibly irritated by the accolades she received at the end of her life. "I did my share," she snapped in a 1984 interview. "That's all." And she would say no more about herself. But she spoke warmly and endlessly about her friends, the women who walked with her on picket lines, lobbied with her in state legislatures, and strategized around the poker table.[7]

Such friendships were key to these activists' vision of social change. They looked toward a world in which social as well as political and economic relations would be transformed so that even a lowly garment worker attached to a sewing machine from dawn until dark could gain education and culture, express herself creatively, and form meaningful relationships with friends, colleagues, and lovers. The unions, workers' schools, and neighborhood councils they organized became testing grounds for these new kinds of relationships. Within these alternative communities men were not foremen or sexual predators but brothers and comrades. Women were not sexual competitors but friends and sisters.

Were these four activists and their vision representative of American working-class women in the first half of the twentieth century? In some very important ways, yes. They were all immigrants. All but Cohn were forced by economic hardship into factory labor as early as nine years of age. None but Cohn was educated beyond the eighth grade, and she had only a high school degree. They were moved to action by the same hunger for education and shock at factory conditions that drew hundreds of thousands of women workers into unions in the early twentieth century. And, finally, their strong class identification tied them to the average woman worker.

Of course, they themselves were not average. All but Shavelson ultimately held paid positions in government or the labor movement that offered them more comfort and prestige than any factory worker could aspire to. They were all Jewish, and their organizing efforts worked best among Yiddish-speaking Jewish women, though they tried, with varying degrees of success, to reach out to working women of other races and ethnicities. Finally, their commitment to political activism and the strength of their class identification proved stronger than that of many women workers. They were political animals who thrived on struggle and debate. That's how they became leaders.

But as leaders they represented a wide range of working-class women, and their political vision encompassed workers across racial and ethnic lines. Through their contributions to the National Industrial Recovery Act of 1933 and the labor laws that followed, they helped transform the relationship between the federal government and workers. By lobbying, demonstrating, and working in state and federal agencies, these women also helped push the U.S. government into the business of regulating the cost and quality of food and housing. The study that follows is, thus, a political as well as a social history of women's activism.[8]

The careers of Rose Schneiderman, Pauline Newman, Fannia Cohn, and Clara Lemlich Shavelson illustrate the extent to which working-class women have participated in all facets of U.S. political life. If they or other working-class women activists have not been given their due as political actors, it is because U.S. political history has been too narrowly defined. This book seeks to expand those boundaries.[9]

Working-class women organized, demonstrated, lobbied, and ran for office during the first half of this century. However, their activism has been discounted as apolitical because many of the issues that moved them to action—rising food prices, poor housing, and inadequate child care and birth control—were considered "private sphere" matters, removed from the centers of power. And their organizing venues—street corners, kitchens, and local food markets—fell outside the lens used by most journalists and political historians, who have focused more on the halls of government than on the hallways of tenements.

Even when working-class women have engaged in inarguably political activities—voting, lobbying, demonstrating in state capitals and in Washington, D.C., organizing unions, striking—their class and sex have rendered them invisible to journalists and political historians. One goal of this book is simply to make these women's activism visible, to challenge the myth that poor women are capable of spontaneous protest but not of sophisticated or sustained political work. The careers of Newman, Schneiderman, Lemlich, and Cohn force a rethinking of that stereotype.

Their collective biography sheds new light on a remarkably broad spectrum of issues in twentieth-century U.S. history: the emergence of an immigrant labor movement; women's cross-class political alliances and their role in shaping reform politics; the women's suffrage movement; the crystallization and evolution of the welfare state; the bureaucratization of labor unions; the rise and fall of the Communist Party; the rise of tenant and consumer organizing; and the impact of McCarthyism on women's political activism. It also offers important insights into the truncated development of the U.S. labor movement.

Industrial feminists struggled to create democratic trade unions in which men and women worked together as equals. This book highlights the contributions these women made to their labor unions and the ways that male labor leaders ignored or discounted them. The expansive vision of the 1909 vintage clashed first with the pure and simple unionism of Samuel Gompers and later with the corporate unionism of David Dubinsky, who ran the ILGWU from the 1930s through the 1960s. As losers in a fierce battle for the soul of the garment unions, industrial feminists were largely written out of U.S. labor history.

But as we approach the end of the twentieth century, with the U.S. labor movement having grown largely moribund and popular opinion of unionism at an all-time low, it is a good time to ponder what happened to American trade unionism. One answer to that question is contained in the story of a generation of women organizers who fought to keep their unions from becoming what most are now: hierarchical bureaucracies governed by remote and conservative leaders who know and care little about the average worker.

The lives of Rose Schneiderman, Pauline Newman, Fannia Cohn, and Clara Lemlich Shavelson illustrate the complex interactions between personal and political matters, between feminism, trade unionism, and twentieth-century U.S. politics. This book examines those links, reflecting on their significance as keys to a revision of U.S. social and political history. It also tells the story of four remarkable women.

1

PART ONE.

THE RISE OF A

WORKING-CLASS

WOMEN'S

MOVEMENT,

1882–1909

PROLOGUE.
FROM THE
RUSSIAN PALE
TO THE LOWER
EAST SIDE:
THE CULTURAL
ROOTS OF
FOUR JEWISH
WOMEN'S
RADICALISM

———————————

Poverty did not deprive us from finding joy and satisfaction in things of the spirit.
—Pauline Newman

During the summer of 1907, when New York City was gripped by a severe economic depression, a group of young women workers who had been laid off and were facing eviction took tents and sleeping rolls to the verdant Palisades overlooking the Hudson River. While rising rents and unemployment spread panic among the poor immigrants of Manhattan's Lower East Side, these teenagers lived in a makeshift summer camp, getting work where they could find it, sharing whatever food and drink they could afford, reading, hiking, and gathering around a campfire at night to sing Russian and Yiddish songs. "Thus we avoided paying rent or, worse still, being evicted," Pauline Newman later recalled. "Besides which, we liked living in the open—plenty of fresh air, sunshine and the lovely Hudson for which there was no charge."[1]

Away from the clatter of the shops and the filth of Lower East Side streets, the young women talked into the night, refreshed by what Newman called "the cool of the evening, glorious sunsets, the moon and stars." They shared personal concerns as well as shop-floor gripes—worries about love, about the future, and about the pressing problems of housing and food.

Their cliffside village meant more to Newman and her friends than a summer escape. They had created a vibrant alternative to the tenement life they found so oppressive, and their experience of it had set them to wondering. Perhaps the same sense of joy and comradeship could help workers transcend the drudgery of the garment shops and form the basis for effective organizing.[2]

At season's end, they emerged with strengthened bonds and renewed resolve to organize their communities around issues that the recent depression had brought into sharp relief: the need for stabilized rent and food prices, improved working conditions, and housing for the poor. Fired up by their time together, inspired by the Socialist shoptalk they'd heard at their jobs and by the militant street actions of Lower East Side wives and mothers, this group would soon spearhead the largest rent strike New York City had yet seen.[3]

The spirit of intimacy and solidarity that pervaded the summer of 1907 would inspire much of Pauline Newman's later organizing. Indeed, it became a model for the vision of change that Newman, Fannia Cohn, Rose Schneiderman, and Clara Lemlich shared. The four were moved to political struggle not simply by the need for better wages, hours, and working conditions but also, in Newman's words, by a need to ensure that "poverty did not deprive us from finding joy and satisfaction in things of the spirit."[4]

That summer taught the young women that their politics were not separable from the quality of their personal lives. Sharing troubles to ease hard times, they forged friendships with other working-class women. On the strength of such bonds they would later build effective political institutions: women's unions, worker education programs, and neighborhood housewives' councils. The effect was strongly reciprocal. For just as shared politics strengthened their relationships with friends and lovers, a desire for fuller lives shaped their political vision.

These marginally educated immigrant women wanted to be more than shop-floor drudges. They wanted lives filled with beauty—with friendships, books, art, music, dance, fresh air, and clean water. "A working girl is a human being," Newman would later tell a legislative committee investigating factory conditions, "with a heart, with desires, with aspirations, with ideas and ideals." That image nourished Newman, Schneiderman, Lemlich, and Cohn throughout their long careers. And it focused them on a single goal: to reshape U.S. society so that "working girls" like themselves could fulfill some of their dreams.[5]

THE LESSONS OF THE PALE:

SEX, ETHNICITY, AND CLASS

The four women profiled in this book moved through strikingly different cultural milieus over the course of long careers that would carry them in different directions. Still, they each bore the imprint of the shared culture in which they were raised, first in Eastern Europe and then in New York City. That common experience gave them a particular understanding of gender, class, and ethnicity that shaped their later activism and political thought.

All four were born in the Russian-dominated pale of Jewish settlement during the last two decades of the nineteenth century. Rose Schneiderman was born in the Polish village of Saven in 1882; Fannia Cohn was born in Kletsk,

Poland, in 1885; Clara Lemlich was born in the Ukrainian village of Gorodok in 1886; and Pauline Newman was born in Kovno, Lithuania, around 1890.[6]

They were ushered into a world swept by a firestorm of new ideas, where the contrasting but equally messianic visions of orthodox Judaism and revolutionary Socialism competed for young minds. The excitement of living in a revolutionary era imbued these young women with a faith in progress and a belief that political commitment gave life meaning. It also taught them, at an early age, that gender, class, and ethnicity were fundamental social categories and essential building blocks for political change. Being born into turbulence does not in itself make a child into a political activist. But the changes sweeping the Russian Empire toward the end of the nineteenth century shaped the consciousness of a generation of Eastern European Jews who contributed, in wildly disproportionate numbers, to revolutionary movements in Russia and to the labor and radical movements in the United States.

Even before the four were born, the tradition-bound world of Eastern European Jewry was tearing asunder. As revolutionary fervor in Russia crested, government officials lashed out at the Jews, stirring ancient religious and social tensions to distract peasants from their burdens. The assassination of Tsar Alexander II in 1881 fueled anti-Semitic edicts, bloody pogroms, and mass expulsions of Jews from their homes in White Russia and the Ukraine. Whole villages disappeared as hundreds of thousands of Jews wandered the countryside in search of new homes.[7]

At the same time, rapid industrialization was robbing Jewish artisans and innkeepers of their traditional livelihoods, leaving a large percentage of the population on the brink of starvation.[8] Tens of thousands of young people left small towns to find work in the garment factories of Kiev, Odessa, Minsk, and Vilna. There they were exposed to the new ideas of Socialism, Zionism, Russian revolutionary populism, and Yiddish cultural nationalism then being debated all over Eastern Europe. Many provincial Jews were radicalized in this way, and when they brought their visions of change back to the Jewish small towns, their younger brothers and sisters were radicalized as well.[9]

Small towns closed to the world for centuries were suddenly opened to Western and urban influences. Sons and daughters were tantalized by tastes of secular knowledge, literature, art, and science. Carried away by visions of revolution, many turned their backs on tradition and joined struggles for social and political change. It was into this turbulent atmosphere that Newman, Schneiderman, Cohn, and Lemlich were born.[10]

The four were exposed to Marxist ideas at a tender age. As Eastern Europe shifted uneasily from feudalism to capitalism in the latter part of the nineteenth century, class analysis became part of the common parlance of young people in Jewish towns and villages. "Behind every other volume of Talmud in those years, there was a volume of Marx," one union organizer recalled of his small Polish town. Clara Lemlich grew up on revolutionary tracts and songs; Fannia Cohn considered herself a committed Socialist by the age of sixteen.[11]

Their awareness of ethnicity was even more keen. As Jews in Eastern Europe, the four learned young that ethnic identity was a double-edged sword. It was a source of strength and solace in their bitterly poor communities, but it also enabled Tsarist authorities to single Jews out and sow seeds of suspicion among their peasant neighbors. Jews living under Russian rule were made painfully aware of their status as permanent "others" in the land where they had lived for centuries.

Clara Lemlich's family lived not far from Kishinev, where in 1903 the Tsar's government openly and unabashedly directed an orgy of anti-Jewish violence that shocked the world. After the massacre, in which scores were killed and hundreds gravely injured, young Clara listened as her elders debated whether to stay and form Jewish self-defense groups or leave Russia for good. In cosmopolitan Minsk, where she had gone to study, Fannia Cohn watched with dismay as the revolutionary populist organization she had joined began mouthing the same anti-Semitic conspiracy theories spewed by the government they despised. Frustration turned to fear when her brother was almost killed in yet another pogrom.[12]

Pauline Newman, even as a child, was anxious about rising anti-Semitism in Russia and across Europe. Tension grew in her household as her father read daily accounts of the treason trials of Major Alfred Dreyfus, a French Jew whose court-martial and Devil's Island imprisonment laid bare French anti-Semitism. After Zionist visionary Theodor Herzl visited their village, Newman's older sisters believed they had found the answer. Jews would never be safe, young Pauline heard them argue, until they created their own Jewish state. She never felt a pull to Palestine, but the memory of anti-Semitism colored her work with women workers of other races and ethnicities.[13]

Sex was just as distinct a dividing line as class and ethnicity. Eastern European Jews had observed a strict sexual division of labor for more than a thousand years. But by the late nineteenth century, as political and economic upheaval jolted long-accepted ways of thinking, sex roles too were being questioned. And so the four girls' understandings of gender were informed both by traditional Jewish conceptions of womanhood and by the challenges issued by new political movements.

In traditional Jewish society, mothers were also entrepreneurs. Clara Lemlich, Pauline Newman, and Rose Schneiderman were all raised by mothers who were skilled businesswomen. Jewish mothers' success in this role grew out of and reinforced a belief that women were innately suited to competition in the economic sphere. In contrast to the image of the sheltered middle-class housewife then dominant in the United States, Eastern European Jewish religious tradition glorified strong, economically sophisticated wives and mothers.

These women, like their American counterparts, were responsible for the home, but that responsibility did not bind them to it. Like women in many preindustrial societies, they often peddled food and wares from town to town and traveled to market to support their families. All contributed financially to their family's upkeep; some were the sole breadwinners.[14]

Clara Lemlich's mother ran a small grocery store. Pauline Newman's mother provided most of the family income by buying fruit from peasants in the countryside and selling it at the town marketplace. Pauline's older sisters worked as seamstresses in a dress shop. And Rose Schneiderman's mother did a little bit of everything: she sewed for neighbors, baked ritual breads and cakes for local weddings, treated the sick with homemade herbal medicines, and tended bar in a nearby saloon when the proprietor was too drunk to do it herself.[15]

But as much as women's entrepreneurship was respected, a far higher premium was placed on study and prayer. And that, religious tradition dictated, could be performed only by men. A woman was expected to be pious, to read the vernacular Yiddish—rather than ancient Hebrew—translation of the Bible, and perhaps to attend women's services at the synagogue. But her primary religious role was as keeper of the home. Formal religious education was offered only to males. A young boy began studying in Hebrew, the language of male religious ritual and scholarship, at the age of three or four and continued at least until his thirteenth birthday. Some girls were given a year to study religious texts translated into Yiddish. The majority received no formal education at all.[16]

Years later, many Jewish women immigrants would describe a lingering sense of deprivation and desire for the education lavished on their brothers. Study, the rabbis had told their brothers, was an exalted process that would bring liberation. Ironically, many Jewish men of that generation remembered their years in *kheydr* (religious school) as an exercise in rote memorization. But it was easy for their sisters to feel jealous with their noses pressed against the glass.

They shared with the young men of their generation a longing for release from the bonds of small-town isolation and religious insularity. But what differentiated them—and would continue to set them apart from their male counterparts in the Jewish immigrant labor movement in the United States—

was that they had to fight for every scrap of education they received. For this reason, they began to see education as the key to independence from all masters.

The link between education and liberation was reinforced for them when, as young girls, they heard Zionist, Yiddishist, and Socialist speakers attack Jewish religious education and gender roles as old-fashioned, narrow, and provincial. The most costly aspect of Jewish backwardness, many speakers argued, was the belief that women did not need to be—-indeed, should not be—educated. If Russian Jews were mired in poverty and ignorance it was because they refused to educate their women.[17]

Many Jewish parents, like the Lemlichs, resisted the kinds of changes called for by urban intellectuals. They feared that once their daughters were exposed to a broader world they would be unable to control them. Worried that young women would abandon religious traditions entirely, anxious elders forbade them to learn Russian—the language of the oppressor—or attend lectures given by Socialists and Zionists. More than a few Jewish daughters, Lemlich among them, got their first taste of rebellion by defying their parents' injunctions against studying the newest political theories.

But other small-town Jewish parents, including those of Newman, Schneiderman, and Cohn, were moved by "enlightenment" arguments, and by their daughters' entreaties, to send them to school. All three saw their parents buck centuries of convention, fighting both religious and secular authorities to educate them. Schneiderman, Newman, Cohn, and Lemlich learned an enduring lesson in their quests for education: those in power limit access to education as a way of preventing change. That realization forever politicized education in their minds.[18]

"Though it was somewhat unusual for girls to study," Rose Schneiderman later recalled, "Mother was determined that I learn Hebrew so I could read and understand the prayers recited at home and in the synagogue." When they moved from the small town of Saven to the city of Khelm, Deborah and Samuel Schneiderman fought successfully to get Rose into a public school, despite quotas limiting the number of Jews who could attend. There she learned to read, write, and speak Russian. Schneiderman's knowledge of Hebrew and Russian made her an educated woman by her mother's standards. But she would always hunger for more, and her desire to emigrate to the United States was linked to her dream of getting a free, public school education.[19]

Pauline Newman's parents helped their daughter get the education she wanted so badly. When the one public school in Kovno denied Pauline entry because her family was Jewish and poor, the bookish child begged the local rabbi to let her attend the all-boy religious school. He refused. But after much lobbying, Pauline, a born negotiator, won his permission to attend Sunday school, where she learned Hebrew. And when her father was hired to teach Talmud to the sons of several wealthy townsmen, he gave eight-year-old Pauline the rare opportunity to sit in on the classes. The arrangement fueled much gossip in the town. "My father laughed at the taunts and kept me in the class," Pauline recalled proudly.[20]

But to her father's chagrin, religious education turned his youngest daughter into even more of a rebel, for Pauline soon concluded that she could not accept the restrictions Jewish law placed on women. "I remember . . . asking my father why the synagogue had two sections—one for men, the other for women—since they all came to worship the same God. The answer my father gave me was too complicated for my young mind to understand. But in later years I often wondered whether this observation conditioned me to resent and to fight all discriminations based on sex. I think it did."[21] A little taste of education whetted the young girl's appetite for more. "Desire . . . to learn, to understand," she wrote later, "became the dominant force in my life." She haunted the small local library, beginning a process of self-education that she would continue for the rest of her life.

Newman found a model for her later attempts at peer education in a Zionist study group formed by her sisters and their friends. Listening to their discussions did not make Newman a Zionist. But she was impressed by the way that studying together helped unite her sisters' friends on behalf of a cause. Remembering the bond that shared study could create, she would later use study groups as a jumping-off point for union organizing.[22]

Clara Lemlich had to struggle against parents, religious authorities, and state authorities to get her education. Like most girls she was taught Yiddish but was offered no further Jewish schooling. Her parents were willing to send her to public school, but they knew that Gorodok's only school was closed to Jews. In protest, they banned the Russian language from their house, which only served to inflame their daughter's passion for Russian culture. Defying her parents, the headstrong child befriended non-Jewish peasant children, who taught her Russian folk songs. She taught those songs to older Jewish girls; in exchange, they taught her how to read Russian and lent her their volumes of Tolstoi, Gorky, and Turgenev.[23]

Before she was in her teens, Lemlich was sewing buttonholes on shirts to pay for her reading habit. Already fluent in written Yiddish, she fattened her book fund by writing letters for illiterate mothers to send to their children in America. When her father found a cache of her books hidden beneath a meat pan in the kitchen, he burned the whole lot, and Clara had to start her collection again from scratch. She began storing her books in the attic, where she would perch on a bare beam to read. One Sabbath afternoon, while her family dozed, she was discovered by a neighbor. Ten-year-old Clara burst into tears, inconsolable until he assured her that he would keep her secret.

The neighbor did more than that. He lent her readings from his own collection, including revolutionary, anti-Tsarist pamphlets that might have brought her parents prison time if they had been found. The tracts of her book-lending neighbor, the only adult in town who encouraged her education, left their mark. By 1903, when the Kishinev pogrom convinced her family that it was time to leave the Ukraine, sixteen-year-old Clara was committed to the Russian revolutionary movement. Clara came to America believing that only revolutionary thought could truly free the mind. It was a belief she would carry for the rest of her life.[24]

Fannia Cohn was also radicalized through education, but not because she had to fight her parents to get it. Cohn's family members, she later said, "distinguished themselves with culture, wealth, and humor." They were cosmopolitans who prided themselves on their progressive views in terms of both politics and treatment of their daughters. In the early twentieth century, Jewish merchant families like the Cohns often educated their daughters as a sign of their enlightenment and sophistication. Cohn was sent to a private school, where she learned to read and write Russian as well as Yiddish. Her parents sought to preserve their status by educating their children to become pharmacists. All but Fannia did.[25]

Fannia's decision to pursue learning for its own sake rather than for a vocation was perhaps sparked by the unfulfilled desire of her mother, who had been denied the opportunity for advanced study because she was a woman. Cohn recalled "being raised by my mother on books" and promising her mother that "I would continue my studies . . . as my mother wanted her children to be no less than professors."[26]

As her mother hoped, Cohn did make education her life's work. But her mother never imagined that study would lead her intense and emotional daughter where it did. For Cohn, as for Lemlich, studying Russian was the first step toward involvement in the Russian revolutionary movement. Much to her family's dismay, Cohn grew deeply enamored of the ideas of populist revolutionaries who idealized, and attempted to mobilize, Russian peasants and workers.

In 1901, at the age of sixteen, Cohn joined the Minsk branch of the Socialist Revolutionary Party, an underground organization that sought to win popular support and foment revolution by assassinating particularly hated government officials. Despite danger of imprisonment, she remained in the organization for three years. But in 1904, after one brother was nearly killed in a pogrom, Cohn decided to emigrate to the United States. Swallowing her revolutionary pride, she accepted the steamship tickets sent by wealthy cousins in New York.[27]

Cohn's strident ethos quickly created tensions with her upwardly mobile family. "When I arrived in New York," she later told a friend, "my cousin's husband suggested that I continue my education and he would finance it. . . . I proudly rejected this offer." Cohn claimed that taking money from her cousin would have "conflicted with my sense of independence. Coming as I did from a revolutionary background I was eager to be with the people." A few years later, her brother invited her to join the family's thriving wholesale drug business, but she declined.

Cohn had made up her mind to give up, once and for all, the comfortable trappings of middle-class life. "I was convinced that to voice the grievances, the hopes and aspirations of the workers, one must share in their experiences." Fannia Cohn chose to look for work in a garment shop. That choice would soon bring her together with other militant young garment workers, including Rose Schneiderman, Pauline Newman, and Clara Lemlich.[28]

IMMIGRANT MOTHERS AND DAUGHTERS
IN NEW YORK CITY, 1890–1907

The four emigrated as part of the mass movement that brought two million Jews from Eastern Europe to the United States between 1881 and 1924. Schneiderman came in 1890, Newman in 1901, Lemlich in 1903, and Cohn in 1904. Like most of their compatriots, they arrived in New York Harbor and settled on Manhattan's Lower East Side, the largest settlement of Eastern European Jews in the United States.[29] The newcomers were tantalized by the exciting diversions that New York life promised: libraries, theater, music, department stores, and amusement parks. But they had neither time nor money to indulge in such pleasures, for all of them soon found themselves laboring long hours to support their families.

Not long after arriving in New York, ten-year-old Pauline Newman succumbed to despair as she walked home from work through the teeming streets of the Lower East Side. She had worked from dawn to dark and was exhausted. As she passed little children playing in garbage and noted the uniformly "tired and drab" expressions on the faces of the working men and women shuffling home, an overwhelming sadness struck her. "Dear God," she recalled whispering to herself, "Will this ever be different?"[30] But that same grim environment offered Newman, Schneiderman, Lemlich, and Cohn glimpses of two new movements for change: Socialist trade unionism, which they would learn about as adolescents on the shop floor, and housewives' food and rent protests, which they watched take shape in the bustling food markets and tenements of the Lower East Side.

Growing up female in the culturally rich and politically charged community that Eastern European immigrant Jews created on the Lower East Side in the early 1900s, the four developed an understanding of class distinctly different from that of their brothers. Older workers, Socialist newspapers, and street-corner speakers taught them the gospel of trade unions. But simultaneously, their mothers taught them that the quality of working-class life was not solely determined by the wages that unionized workers could win at the bargaining table. It rested as well on mothers' entrepreneurial skills and their successful campaigns to block sharp increases in housing and food costs.

Jewish women played as central a role economically in the American ghetto as they had in the shtetls and cities of Eastern Europe. Daughters worked in garment shops with their brothers and fathers, while mothers engaged in a wide range of money-making enterprises. Some Jewish wives worked alongside their husbands in "mom and pop" stores; others ran their own stores. Many Jewish wives became peddlers, dragging their children along with the cart. And almost all of them rented out space in their apartments to boarders, while cooking, washing, and ironing for everyone in the house.[31]

Most immigrant Jewish families lived on the edge. For widows like Mrs. Newman and Mrs. Schneiderman, the boarder's small contribution was all that stood between their families and eviction. Rose Schneiderman's mother, Deborah, struggled for years after her husband died of influenza in 1892, leaving her with three small children and another on the way. The family survived for a while on a daily basket of food sent by United Hebrew Charities. But it was not enough. Reluctantly, Deborah Schneiderman sent her two sons to the Hebrew Orphan Asylum for temporary care. Only the arrival of a boarder fresh from Poland, Rose later recalled, postponed the further breakup of her family: "After Father died, we rented out the living room of our apartment to a young man, a tailor who worked at home, and we kept the bedroom and the kitchen. As long as he stayed, we were able to pay the rent of seven dollars a month."[32]

Deborah Schneiderman supplemented the boarder's contribution by working odd jobs at night, but her meager income was not enough to feed her two daughters. Soon she was forced to send Rose and her sister Jane to the orphanage as well. It took her a year to save the money to bring them home again. She would not have enough to retrieve her sons for several more years.

Despite the family's poverty, Deborah Schneiderman kept Rose in school as long as she could, for she knew how desperately her elder daughter wanted an education. But just as gender and ethnicity had limited Schneiderman's education in Poland, class would thwart her hopes in America. Deborah worked a night job while Rose took care of her baby sister. But she was laid off when Rose was still in eighth grade, and she was unable to find another night job.

So the thirteen-year-old Rose was forced to leave school and find work in a department store. She never got over it. Throughout her long career, Schneiderman felt embarrassed about her limited schooling. From that time forward Rose would be the prime support of her family, a source of some pride. But memories of the orphanage and of being forced to leave school stayed with Rose all her life; and those memories were bitter reminders that, for working women, "women's issues" like child care were hardly peripheral.[33]

Pauline Newman, too, was raised by a single mother. Soon after she was widowed in 1900, Mrs. Newman sailed to New York City with her three daughters; her brother and son had already set up homes there. Nine-year-old Pauline felt uprooted. Decades later, she could still recall the pain she felt on leaving "the lovely land" of her childhood, and her sadness at leaving her father alone "in the ground."

The Newmans arrived in New York with only the clothes on their backs, having become separated from their belongings at Ellis Island. Though Pauline had hoped to continue her education, she and her sisters were immediately sent out to work. Pauline assembled hairbrushes, while her sisters found work as seamstresses, the trade they had learned in Lithuania. Mrs. Newman supplemented her daughters' earnings by "taking in washing."[34]

Though Clara Lemlich's father was still alive and able-bodied in 1903, when the family landed in New York, sixteen-year-old Clara found a job more easily than he did. This was common. Even in shops that produced expensive, high-fashion clothing, employers preferred to hire young girls rather than their more highly skilled elders. Girls accepted lower pay and, employers believed, were less likely to be drawn into labor organizing than boys and grown men. Clara found a job almost immediately, sewing "very beautiful, very costly, very delicate" dresses at a fraction of the wage her father would have earned for the same work.[35]

A 1909 study by settlement house worker Louise More indicated that even in intact two-parent families like Lemlich's, children's earnings were critical to the family's survival. More's study also found that wage-earners handed their paychecks over to the mother, who disbursed the family income on rent, clothes, and food. Watching their mothers battle to improve their families' standard of living, it was clear to working daughters like Schneiderman, Newman, and Lemlich that their homes were not isolated from market forces that determined wages, rents, and food prices. Their mothers saw their homes as directly linked to the larger economy and fought to keep them safe from deprivation.[36]

During the first decade of the twentieth century, Jewish mothers dramatically illustrated their awareness of that link. Five times between 1902 and 1908, when sudden increases in staple commodity prices or housing costs stretched their budgets farther than they could go, immigrant mothers on the Lower East Side and in other Jewish ghettos organized and fought back. Building on informal neighborhood networks, they picketed, boycotted, and marched in protest.

These housewives' predilection for protest was nourished by the unique political culture of Eastern European immigrant Jews. The excitement over new ideas then sweeping Eastern Europe was intensified on the Lower East Side, where Jews from countless villages, towns, and cities lived together in what was, with the possible exception of Beijing, the most densely populated square mile on earth. Lower East Side political organizations and labor unions played an important role in fomenting protest. Jewish immigrant mothers were politically transformed by their husbands, sons, and daughters, who came home from the shops speaking the language of Socialism and trade unionism.[37]

These new ideas were reinforced by what they read in the daily papers. Abraham Cahan's *Jewish Daily Forward*, the favorite paper of New York's Jewish immigrants, offered a daily dose of brass-tacks Socialism and trade union theory. And the message was not aimed solely at men. Yiddish newspapers made a particular effort to appeal to women: editors knew that women made up a sizable part of their readership, so they provided entertainment, poetry, and fiction—often by women writers—as well as sympathetic coverage of both the labor movement and housewives' activism.[38]

The *Forward* provided Newman's first exposure to trade unionism. "One day while I was standing and watching the multitude, I saw a small boy selling . . . the *Jewish Daily Forward*. . . . The first piece that claimed my attention was a story about working men and women of the east side—the conditions under which they worked and lived—the long hours, the terribly low wages, the filthy tenements. All this and more interested me so much that I looked forward to the next day when I could again buy the *Forward*." In its pages, Newman was introduced to the works of Yiddish poets and political theorists, male and female. Soon her aspiration was to write for the *Forward*; before she was eighteen, she was a regular contributor. Newman's early success at publishing thrilled her, and she began to harbor hopes of one day becoming a professional writer. Though her progression from reader to writer was atypical, her devotion to the *Forward* was not. Most Jewish immigrant New Yorkers of her day were nourished on the same daily diet of Socialist fundamentals.[39]

Jewish religious leaders were, at most, lukewarm to Socialism. But in the Jewish Socialism of the time there was a cross-fertilization of Biblical and Marxist imagery that made even men and women from religious homes feel comfortable with Socialist ideas and activism. Immigrant Jewish Socialism had its own language and symbols, a mixture of the ancient prophets and nineteenth-century revolutionaries. Jewish Socialists used Biblical allusions, says former organizer Sidney Jonas, to appeal to "Jewish workers who were deeply imbued with an Old Testament sense of social justice." The Book of Isaiah, with its warnings to the rich and haughty and its prophecies of judgment and cleansing, was particularly popular.[40]

That potent amalgam of Isaiah and Marx animated the speeches of Jewish mothers who organized the kosher meat boycotts and rent strikes that rocked New York's ghettos between 1902 and 1910. These housewives referred to themselves as "strikers" and to those who broke their boycotts as "scabs." They lashed out at the middlemen who profited by selling meat at high prices while poor children went hungry. And they promised just retribution.

But these women did not simply echo the principles they had learned from rabbis, newspaper writers, husbands, and children. They contributed a layer to immigrant working-class discourse that arose out of their own experience as wage-earners, entrepreneurs, and money managers. Feeling neither confused nor helpless, they saw and articulated a relationship between production and consumption that mainstream Socialist theory either ignored or rejected outright. They saw a power in organized consumers that paralleled that of organized producers. Daughters like Clara Lemlich would later try to tap that power by mobilizing women consumers as a wing of the working-class movement.[41]

One housewife leader of the era, Cecilia Schwartz, clearly articulated Jewish women's sense that their homes were directly affected by market forces. In a speech made from her apartment window to a crowd of women who stood below complaining about meat prices, she urged the women to boycott meat. Displaying her mastery of political economy, she rallied her troops: "If we don't buy from the butchers, they won't be able to buy from the wholesale dealers. The result will be that the wholesalers will find themselves with a lot of meat on their hands. They will then sell cheap to our butchers and we will get our meat cheap."[42]

There is evidence of similar activity by Jews dating back to late-eighteenth-century Poland. The first leader of the Hasidic movement, Israel Baal Shem Tov, won much of his early support by criticizing kosher butchers for charging exorbitant prices. Rural Polish Jews of that period expressed outrage at the monopolistic practices of town-based ritual slaughterers, in much the same way that twentieth-century urban immigrants blamed high kosher meat prices on the monopolies held by American meat trusts.[43]

But there the parallels end, for there was no precedent for the scale and duration of the food protests that began in the early 1900s and continued for the next fifty years. When preindustrial Eastern European Jewish values collided with the principles of trade unionism, the result was a new political strategy among housewives that was as volatile as it was effective. The tinderbox atmosphere on the Lower East Side was noted by a *New York Times* reporter, who commented during a 1908 women's meat boycott that "when East Siders don't like something they strike."[44]

The first of these women's food protests began spontaneously in May 1902, when the price of kosher meat rose suddenly by 50 percent. Calling for a boycott of kosher meat, thousands of women marched through the streets of the Lower East Side, entered kosher butcher shops, and threw the meat into the streets. The *New York Times* called it a "riot." Police arrested seventy women and fifteen men and charged them with disorderly conduct. A strike support rally attracted twenty thousand people.[45]

Four days later, Jewish women in Brooklyn and Harlem joined the boycott. In the Williamsburg and Brownsville sections of Brooklyn, four hundred women "patrolled" butcher shops to make sure no one purchased meat. Committees of women visited labor unions, benevolent societies, and fraternal lodges to lobby for the establishment of cooperative meat stores. Two such stores were established and lasted for many years after the strike ended. More immediately, the price of kosher meat was rolled back to within two cents of the prestrike cost.[46]

Though the immigrant housewives may not have been looking to join a movement, the success of the 1902 boycott made them aware that community organizing was a powerful tool. Strikes and boycotts by their nature enhance a sense of group consciousness. The frequency of Jewish housewives' protests in the years following 1902 suggests that these immigrant women saw themselves engaged in a common struggle to protect the quality of life of the Jewish working-class family.[47]

That sense of shared responsibility extended beyond food prices to women's other traditional responsibility—providing shelter. Working-class families commonly responded to rent increases by moving. Rose Schneiderman recalls moving three or four times a year: "It was easier for the poor to move than to pay rent. When you moved into a new place, you always paid a month's rent and you got a concession of a month or six weeks. After that was all used up, if you had the money to pay the next month's rent you stayed on. If not, you moved again."[48]

By 1904 moving was no longer an option. Construction of the Williamsburg Bridge, several parks, and a school had displaced thousands of families and created a housing shortage on the Lower East Side. With no place to go, several hundred East Side mothers decided to stay and fight. They urged tenants to "fight the landlord as they had the czar" by withholding their rents to protest rent increases. Two thousand tenants responded. Within a month local landlords rolled rents back to prestrike levels.[49]

Three years later, tenants on the Lower East Side launched a rent strike that dwarfed all previous subsistence protests. The Depression of 1907 had left an estimated hundred thousand people unemployed on the Lower East Side and their families unable to pay rent. That was the summer Pauline Newman and a group of her co-workers from the Triangle Shirtwaist Factory created a utopian outpost for three months on the Palisades. By the time they returned to their homes and jobs in September, they had decided to fight against evictions and for rent controls.

After five years on the shop floor, sixteen-year-old Pauline Newman had seen enough misery and developed enough political sophistication that she hatched an ambitious plan: to build a rent strike using both women's neighborhood and shop-floor networks. The result was the best organized of the early-twentieth-century housewives' actions, and the largest rent strike New York had ever seen. Newman and her friends began by organizing their peers. By late fall they had assembled a band of four hundred self-described "self-supporting women" like themselves, committed to rolling back rents. These young women soon found a sea of willing converts: the mothers of the Lower East Side.[50]

The young garment workers, who could not work the neighborhood during the day, organized committees of housewives who could. The housewives canvassed from tenement to tenement and convinced the residents to strike for a one- to two-dollar reduction in monthly rents. Assured of legal support by the Socialist Party, the young women promised tenants that they would be represented in court if their landlords tried to evict them. Then, on December 26, 1907, they called for a hundred thousand residents of the Lower East Side to ring in the New Year with a rent strike.

The following day the *New York Times* profiled the group's voluble young leader:

The rent war begun yesterday on the Lower East Side is led by a frail looking woman who is hailed throughout the Grand Street section as the east side

Joan of Arc. . . . The young woman who is recognized as the real leader of the movement is Pauline Newman, who is employed in a shirtwaist factory on Grand Street. Although most of her daylight hours are spent in the shop, she has for a week or more devoted six hours out of twenty-four to visiting the tenements and arousing the interests of the dwellers there. She has organized a band of four hundred women, all of whom earn their own living, whose duty it is to promulgate the doctrine of lower rents.[51]

Newman and her "band of four hundred" fell short of their dream of mobilizing 100,000. Still, by year's end 10,000 families—approximately 50,000 people—had pledged not to pay their rents on January 1. Striking tenants sent the following message to their landlords. (Note the language of the form letter; women, not men, communicated with the landlords.) "We the tenants of _____ having realized our present misery came to the following conclusions. Whereas the present industrial depression has affected us most severely and whereas our husbands are out of work and cannot earn a living, and whereas the rent for the last two years has risen skywards so that even in the so called days of prosperity the rent was a heavy burden upon us. Therefore we resolve to demand of you to decrease the rent immediately."[52]

The rent strike, described by the *New York Times* as "greater than any that has occurred in this city before," had mixed success. By January 7, landlords had won three-day eviction orders for six thousand families. They either paid or moved. Two days later the strike was over. However, according to organizers, some two thousand families had their rents reduced. Most important, the strike attracted the attention of Lillian Wald and Mary Simkovitch, leading figures in the settlement house movement. They called for capping Lower East Side rents at 30 percent of a family's monthly income. The ceiling was not established, but the idea of rent control entered New York political discourse and in the 1930s became law.[53]

Newman, Schneiderman, Cohn and, above all, Clara Lemlich would work to keep community-based women's protest alive in the decades to come. All four women would later try, with varying degrees of success, to build permanent organizations of working-class housewives. All four would argue that the working-class movement must include not only factory workers but also housewives. With a heady mix of ideology gleaned from Isaiah, Marx, and their mothers, immigrant Jewish women in the first decade of the twentieth century laid the groundwork for working-class women's activism for the next fifty years. Rose Schneiderman, Fannia Cohn, Clara Lemlich, and Pauline Newman would sustain and adapt those traditions over their long careers.

1

COMING OF AGE:
THE SHOCK OF
THE SHOPS AND
THE DAWNING
OF POLITICAL
CONSCIOUSNESS,
1900—1909

*We of the 1909 vintage knew
nothing about the economics
of... industry or for that
matter about economics in
general. All we knew was the
bitter fact that, after working
seventy and eighty hours in a
seven day week, we did not
earn enough to keep body
and soul together.*
—Pauline Newman, on
union sentiment among
Triangle Shirtwaist Fac-
tory workers

The 1907 rent strike made headlines in all the New York newspapers and transformed its petite and pugnacious leader, Pauline Newman, into a Lower East Side celebrity. Lauded in the press, courted by radical leaders in the community, the dark-eyed, dark-haired sixteen-year-old found that she liked the spotlight: "The press gave us front page publicity and my own photo was carried under the caption 'leader of the strike.' . . . I became 'famous.' I was invited to speak at meetings which provided an opportunity for self-expression and the art of speaking in public. As my 'fame' grew so did my interest in all things concerning working and living conditions of my fellow workers."[1]

Newman was keenly interested in labor issues well before the 1907 rent strike. Indeed, many of the techniques she used in the strike—such as assembling a core group to mobilize an entire community, and forming local housewives' committees to manage each block—were adapted from union-building strategies she'd observed on the shop floor. Though only sixteen in 1907, Newman was already a seasoned worker; like so many immigrant Jewish women of her generation, including Rose Schneiderman and Clara Lemlich, she had spent her childhood as a laborer in the sweatshops of lower Manhattan. Fannia Cohn did not enter a garment shop until the age of twenty, but she too was profoundly shaped by the experience.

Coming of age in New York's early-twentieth-century garment shops, the four would become determined organizers of their fellow "working girls." Their political commitment was fueled primarily by anger at the filthy and dangerous conditions under which they were forced to work. But it was sustained by affection and loyalty to their fellow workers and guided by the tutelage of more seasoned political hands. The four found emotional support in factory-floor friendships and late-night study groups. And as they began to organize, they were introduced to mentors: older workers, Socialist Party activists, and Progressive reformers. All of these influences helped to create, by the end of the century's first decade, a critical mass of radicalized young women garment workers. Schneiderman, Newman, Lemlich, and Cohn were among the most highly regarded of these. By the time they reached their mid-twenties, the four had distinguished themselves by their eloquence, spirit, and tenacity in fighting to improve not only their own lives but also those of their sister workers.

Pauline Newman first began working in a hairbrush factory in 1901, at the age of ten. Two years later, a relative found her a better-paying job at the most famous of early-twentieth-century garment factories, the Triangle Shirtwaist Factory on Washington Square. Newman spent her girlhood at a sewing machine stitching women's shirtwaists—the contemporary name for man-tailored blouses and dresses.

At an age when most girls in the United States were still in grade school, immigrant working girls like Newman spent twelve- to fourteen-hour days in the harshest of atmospheres. Their bodies and minds reeled from the shock of the shops: the deafening noise, the brutal pace, and the rebukes of foremen. Some children were able to slough off the hardship with jokes and games. Others, realizing that they were destined to spend their youth in dank factories rather than in classrooms or schoolyards, grew sullen and withdrawn.

Newman fought depression by recording what she saw around her. She kept detailed notebooks and submitted poems and articles to the Yiddish language press. Later, she penned descriptions of the shops that she hoped would convince others of the urgent need to regulate factory conditions. Her vivid prose evokes the gloom that many children must have felt:

> Most of the so-called factories were located in old wooden walkups with rickety stairs, splintered and sagging floors. The few windows were never washed and their broken panes were mended with cardboard. . . . In the winter a stove stood in the middle of the floor, a concession to the need for heat, but its warmth rarely reached the workers seated near the windows. During the summer months the constant burning of gas jets added their unwelcome heat and smell to an atmosphere already intolerably humid and oppressive. . . . There was no drinking water available. . . . Dirt, smells and vermin were as much a part of the surroundings as were the machines and the workers.[2]

Rose Schneiderman and Clara Lemlich also spent their youth in factories. Schneiderman began working at age thirteen in a department store, but, lured by higher wages, she became a capmaker at sixteen. Lemlich was a twelve-year-old seamstress in her small Ukrainian village; by sixteen she was a dressmaker in New York. As teenagers, all three hoped to rise to skilled positions in the garment trades. They had heard that garment work offered opportunity for advancement, and they believed that Jewish shop owners and supervisors would be kind and fatherly toward young Jewish workers.[3]

Clara Lemlich, like so many others, was quickly disillusioned by her first job in a New York garment shop: "I went to work two weeks after landing in this country. We worked from sunrise to set seven days a week. . . . Those who worked on machines had to carry the machines on their back both to and from work. . . . The shop we worked in had no central heating, no electric power. . . . The hissing of the machines, the yelling of the foreman, made life unbearable."[4]

The conditions Lemlich described had deteriorated since the turn of the century. With the invention and refinement of the industrial sewing machine, operators were forced to speed up their work: a 1905 garment worker was expected to sew twice as fast as her 1900 counterpart.[5] By the end of the century's first decade, one study of factory conditions in women's trades reported that the "high rate of speed . . . leaves its impression on even the most robust worker." In shop after shop, researcher Annie MacLean found that workers' nerves were noticeably strained: "It appears in heavy eyes with deep dark rings, in wrinkled skin, and old young faces. The high rate of speed that must be maintained through so many successive hours is undermining the health of thousands of girls in this industry."[6]

Among all the torments of the shop, what workers hated most were the petty humiliations imposed by foremen and "foreladies." Without time to think or permission to speak, they felt that they had been turned into machines. Clara Lemlich was furious about being so dehumanized. "And the bosses! They hire such people to drive you!," she wrote bitterly. "It is a regular slave factory. Not only your hands and your time but your mind is sold." In another article, she explained: "For talking, shop girls were immediately fired. . . . At the conclusion of the day's work, the girls were searched like thieves."[7]

Anger drove young women workers like Lemlich and Newman to band together. Untrained and largely unschooled, these young women were drawn to Socialism and trade unionism not because they felt an ideological affinity but because they had a desperate need to improve their working conditions. "I knew very little about Socialism," Lemlich recalled. "[But] the girls, whether Socialist or not, had many stoppages and strikes." Newman too found that for most young women workers, political understanding followed action rather than precipitating it: "We of the 1909 vintage knew nothing about the economics of . . . industry or for that matter about economics in general. All we knew was the bitter fact that, after working seventy and eighty hours in a seven day week, we did not earn enough to keep body and soul together." These assertions reveal much about the political development of the tens of thousands of women garment workers who would soon amaze New York and the nation with their militancy.[8]

Shop-floor culture fed the young women's emerging sense of political identity. Working alongside older men and women who discussed Socialism daily, they began to feel a sense of belonging to a distinct class of people in the world: workers. This allegiance would soon become as important to them as their Judaism. The shops also provided an opportunity for bonding with other women. Slowly, out of their workplace experiences, they began to develop a complex political identity in which class, gender, and ethnicity overlapped. Because most of their fellow garment workers were Jewish *and* female, Newman, Lemlich, Schneiderman, and Cohn felt loyalty not simply to the working class but particularly to the Jewish female working class. Jewish identity would play a less prominent role in their politics in later years, when they branched out and organized many different kinds of women workers. But for the rest of their lives they would remain committed to the melding of gender and class they had first experienced among their fellow garment workers.

Political sophistication was not uncommon among Jewish immigrant girls of their generation. Many had encountered Socialist ideas as children in Eastern Europe, in the Yiddish newspapers of New York's Lower East Side, and at the family dinner table. Still, it took shop work to give those ideas life and urgency. Faced with the harsh realities of factory labor, young women workers began to think and talk about how they could use Socialism and unionism to improve their daily lives.

In Progressive Era New York, they quickly found that they had other potential allies besides working men: middle-class suffragists and reformers who held out the seductive promise of cross-class sisterhood. These educated women flattered the young immigrants with attention and praise and provided money, protection from police brutality, and assistance in gaining positive press coverage. Such women gave Schneiderman, Newman, Lemlich, and Cohn their first real insights into the U.S. upper classes and helped the young leaders broaden their political understanding beyond the bounds of Jewish immigrant culture.

Just as important, they sharpened the young women's consciousness of gender, clarifying the differences between their political vision and that of their Socialist brothers. Each in her own way, Newman, Schneiderman, Lemlich, and Cohn all embraced the ideology of sisterhood propounded by such feminists and suffragists. Each woman's organizing, writing, and thinking over the next half century reflected her own struggle to adapt and apply the insights of feminism to the lives of working-class women. Awareness of gender discrimination, more than anything else in their political education, would set them apart from the Jewish Socialist men who led the emerging garment unions.

Young women workers were moved by the idea of sisterhood. It meshed with the bonding they saw at the marketplaces and in their neighborhoods. Even more profoundly, it captured their own experiences in the sex-segregated shops where they worked. The majority of New York's garment workers were little more than girls, and the relationships they forged with factory friends were similar to those of schoolgirls—intense, melodramatic, and deeply loyal. They were teenage confidantes as well as fellow workers, and they relied on shop-floor rapport to soften the harshness of factory life.[9]

Shared dreams of revolution also intensified their bonds. With her dashing, bespectacled bravado, Pauline Newman captured the imagination of many young co-workers. Sometimes, as this letter from Triangle worker J. A. H. Dahme to the sixteen-year-old Newman illustrates, the lines between political commitment and personal infatuation blurred: "Yes, I understand you— understand you to that depth of thoroughness as only one who has long suffered can! . . . From the deepest deepest place of my bosom let me utter the words, 'We shall be friends in joy and sorrow!' What is there sweeter in life than the sympathy between woman and woman—what purer than the sincerity of hearts—what greater than the harmony of minds? . . . Yours in friendship and socialist comradeship."[10]

Highly emotional herself, Newman did not always know how to respond to such adulation, but she thrived in the loving atmosphere of her shop. The community of young women at the Triangle Shirtwaist Factory was so important to her, in fact, that she stayed there long after she could have found higher-paying work elsewhere. With friends who have worked together for years, Newman later wrote, "you are no longer a stranger and alone." For young immigrant women trying to build lives in a new land, such bonds were powerful and lasting. From these shop-floor friendships would soon evolve the ties of union sisterhood.[11]

SHOP FLOOR LIFE AND "THE SCHOOL
OF SOLIDARITY," 1898–1906

Pauline Newman and her co-workers at the Triangle Shirtwaist Factory literally grew up together. Only twelve when she first came to Triangle, Newman was assigned to a corner known as "the kindergarten," where workers as young as eight, nine, or ten years old trimmed threads from finished garments. They labored, Newman later recalled, "from 7:30 A.M. to 6:30 at night when it wasn't busy. When the season was on we worked till 9 o'clock. No overtime pay." Their only taste of a normal childhood came through the songs and games they invented to help pass the time, the stories they told and the secrets they shared.[12]

By the early twentieth century, New York State had passed laws prohibiting night work for children. But little attempt was made to enforce them. On the rare occasions when an inspector showed up at her factory, Newman remembered, "the employers were always tipped off. . . . 'Quick,' they'd say, 'Into the boxes!' And we children would climb into the big box the finished shirts were stored in. Then some shirts were piled on top of us and when the inspector came—No children." In a way it was fun, Newman remembered. They thought they were playing a game like hide and seek.[13]

But it wasn't really a game. Children who had to help support their parents grew up quickly. Rose Schneiderman was thirteen when her mother begged United Hebrew Charities, an organization run by middle-class German Jews, to find her daughter a "respectable job" at a department store. Retail jobs were deemed more respectable than factory work because the environment was more pleasant and sexual harassment was thought to be less common. Deborah Schneiderman worried that factory work would sully Rose's reputation and make her less marriageable. A job as a fashionable salesgirl, she hoped, would usher Rose into the middle class. The single mother who had fed her children on charity food baskets and had been forced to place them in orphanages was grimly determined to help them escape poverty. Perhaps self-conscious about a childhood that was poor even by Lower East Side standards, Schneiderman latched onto her mother's obsession with respectability. That preoccupation lasted throughout her life, shaping and limiting her political and personal choices.

But then as now, pink-collar jobs paid significantly less than industrial work. Anxious to free her mother from the rigors of maintaining their tenement building, Schneiderman left her job in Ridley's department store for the harsher and more morally suspect conditions of an industrial shop. Making linings for caps and hats, she immediately raised her weekly income from $2.75 to $6. As the sole supporter of her family, the sixteen-year-old hoped to work her way up quickly to a skilled job in the cap trade.[14]

Clara Lemlich's family also relied on her wages, particularly because her father was unemployed. She aspired to the skilled position of draper, one of the highest-paid positions a woman could attain in the dressmaking trade. Despite terrible working conditions, many ambitious young women chose garment work over other jobs because it seemed to offer their greatest chance to acquire skills and command high wages. When these hopes were dashed, some young workers grew angry. That anger was fanned and channeled by older women in the shops who were itching to challenge the authority of the bosses.[15]

That is what happened to Rose Schneiderman, who, like many skilled women garment workers, was blocked from advancement by the unofficial gender hierarchy at her factory. Finding that all the highest-paid jobs in her capmaking shop were reserved for men, Schneiderman asked around about ways to break through those barriers. When she approached fellow worker Bessie Braut with her concerns, Schneiderman was initiated simultaneously into trade unionism, Socialism, and feminism. Schneiderman recalled, "Bessie was an unusual person. Her beautiful eyes shone out of a badly pockmarked face and the effect was startling. An outspoken anarchist, she made a strong impression on us. She wasted no time in giving us the facts of life—that the men in our trade belonged to a union and were, therefore, able to better their conditions. She added pointedly that it would be a good thing for the lining-makers to join a union along with the trimmers, who were all women."[16]

Schneiderman, Braut, and several other workers called on the secretary-treasurer of the United Cloth Hat and Cap Makers to request union recognition for their fledgling local of trimmers and lining makers. Skeptical of young women's ability to organize, the official told them to gather twenty-five signatures from women working at other factories. Schneiderman and her comrades stationed themselves at factory doors with membership blanks in hand and approached women as they came off their shifts. Within a few days they had enough signatures to win a charter for their local, and Schneiderman was elected secretary.[17]

Surprising even herself, the once-shy redhead soon found she could be an eloquent and fierce advocate for her fellow workers. In recognition of her growing reputation, the capmakers elected her to the Central Labor Union of New York. Deborah Schneiderman was disturbed by the turn Rose's life was taking. She warned Rose that if she pursued a public life she would never find a husband. No man wants a woman with a big mouth, her mother said.[18]

In the flush of excitement at the praise and warmth suddenly coming her way, young Rose did not stop to worry. In organizing, she had found both a calling and a world of friends. She had no intention of turning back. "It was such an exciting time," she wrote later. "A new life opened up for me. All of a sudden I was not lonely anymore. . . . It was the beginning of a period that molded all my subsequent life."[19]

Fannia Cohn, too, chose garment work as her path to a career. And like Schneiderman, Lemlich, and Newman, she found a community there. Unlike the others, however, she did not enter a garment factory looking for work that paid well. She was a comfortable middle-class woman in search of a trade ripe for unionizing.

Cohn arrived in New York in 1904 and moved in with her affluent cousins. There was little about her early days in the United States that was comparable to the hard-pressed scrambling for a living that the Schneidermans, Lemlichs, and Newmans experienced. Her cousins offered to support her while she studied, but the independent nineteen-year-old wanted to pay her own way. She soon found a job with the American Jewish Women's Committee, providing aid and information to new arrivals at Ellis Island. Though it was an appropriate job for a middle-class woman of some education, Cohn quickly grew restless and quit after only a few weeks. "It was too much of a charitable nature," she explained to a friend. For a time she toyed with the idea of going to college. But soon, to the chagrin of the cousins who had paid her passage from Russia, Cohn decided that she had only one ambition: to join the working class in its struggle for a better life.[20] "My family suggested that I complete my studies and then join the labor movement but I rejected this as I did not want to come into it from 'without' but from 'within.' I realized then that if I wanted to really understand the mind, the aspirations of the workers, I should experience the life of the worker in a shop."[21] In 1905, Fannia Cohn became a sleevemaker. For a year she moved from shop to shop until, in the "white goods" trade, she found the organizing challenge she was looking for.

Shops that manufactured white goods—underwear, kimonos, and robes— were considered particularly hard to organize. Production took place in tiny sweatshops, not large factories, and the manufacturing process had been broken down into small tasks that required little skill. The majority of white goods workers were immigrant girls under the age of fifteen. And because they came from a wide range of backgrounds—Jewish, Italian, Syrian, Turkish, and Greek—it was difficult for them to communicate with each other, let alone organize. As a result, these workers were among the lowest paid in the garment trades.

At twenty, Cohn was an elder in the trade. With her high school education and fluency in three languages, she was seen as a mother figure by many of the adolescents in the shops. She and a handful of older women workers began to operate as mentors, meeting with the girls in each shop and identifying potential leaders. Cohn taught her co-workers to read, write, and speak in public, hoping they would channel those skills into the union struggle. Cohn had already created the role that she would play throughout her career: an educator of younger workers.[22]

Education was a primary driving force in the metamorphosis of all four young women from shop workers to union organizers. From the isolated towns and restive cities of Eastern Europe, where gender, class, and ethnicity stymied Jewish girls' hopes for education, the lure of free public schooling in the United States beckoned powerfully. Having to drop out of school to work was more than a disappointment for many Jewish immigrant girls; it was their first great disillusionment with the dream of America. And they did not give that dream up easily.

"When I went to work," Rose Schneiderman remembered, "I was determined to continue my studies." Her only option was to attend one of the many night schools then open to immigrant workers in New York. Having carried with her from Poland the ideal of education as an exalted, liberating process, she was disgusted by the mediocre instruction she encountered and felt betrayed by teachers who seemed to be patronizing her. "I enrolled and went faithfully every evening for about four weeks. But I found that . . . the instructor seemed more interested in getting one-hundred-percent attendance than in giving one-hundred-percent instruction. He would joke and tell silly stories. . . . I soon realized I was wasting my time." Schneiderman left the evening school but did not stop studying. She asked older co-workers if she could borrow books that she had discussed with them in the shop. In the evenings, she read with her mother at home. Serializations of Emile Zola's *J'Accuse* and other contemporary writings in the Yiddish evening paper *Abendblatt* gave Rose a taste for literature. "I devoured everything I could get my hands on."[23]

Clara Lemlich was an equally avid reader. At the end of each twelve-hour day stitching shirtwaists, she would walk from her factory to the East Broadway branch of the New York Public Library. There she read the library's entire collection of Russian classics. "I was so eager to learn things," she later recalled. When she tired of solitary study, Lemlich joined a free night school on Grand Street. She returned home late each night, ate the dinner her mother had kept warm for her, then slept for just a few hours before rising again for work.[24]

That zest for learning was typical of Jewish immigrant working girls. In one contemporary study of working women, 12.5 percent of the Jewish women listed reading as their favorite pastime, even though it was not one of the choices presented. A study called "Working Girls in Evening Schools" found that, in New York City, 40 percent of those enrolled were Jewish.

Frustration with the limited and patronizing quality of night school education was also typical. Popular author Anzia Yezierska captured that impatience in a story called "Crazy to Learn," in which an immigrant girl, admonished repeatedly by her night school principal to study something useful, finally cries out in anguish, "Ain't thoughts useful? . . . Does America only want the work from my body?" Night school English classes must have confirmed those fears. While men were taught to identify political leaders, women were taught the names of kitchen utensils. While men were asked to translate the sentence "I read the book," women translated "I wash the dishes."[25]

Not surprisingly, young women like Schneiderman, Newman, and Lemlich turned to radical politics to fulfill their desire for a life of the mind. If no other school was available, then what Pauline Newman called "the school of solidarity" would have to do. Membership in the Socialist Party and in unions, tenant organizations, and benevolent societies provided immigrant women with an opportunity to learn and study that most would never have gotten otherwise. And as Newman put it, "Because they were hitherto deprived of any tutorship, they at once became ardent students."[26]

Pauline Newman was just fifteen when she first knocked on the doors of the Socialist Literary Society. Although women were not yet allowed to join, she was permitted to attend classes. The Literary Society was a revelation to the young worker. There she was introduced to the writings of Shakespeare, George Eliot, and Thomas Hardy and personally met writers like Jack London and Charlotte Perkins Gilman, who came to speak there. Gratitude, however, didn't stop her from joining a successful petition drive to admit women to the society.

For Newman—as for Clara Lemlich, who attended Marxist theory classes at the Socialist Party's Rand School—studying was more than a distraction from work. The "desire to get out of the shop," Newman wrote later, "to learn, to understand, became the dominant force in my life." But unlike many immigrants, who saw schooling as a ladder out of the working class, both she and Lemlich were committed to helping others rise with them. So Newman and Lemlich formed study groups that met during lunch hours and after work to share what they were learning with their friends.[27]

"We tried to educate ourselves," Newman remembered of her co-workers at the Triangle Shirtwaist Factory. "I would invite the girls to my room and we took turns reading poetry in English to improve our understanding of the language." In another interview, she elaborated on these reading lessons:

> We read Dickens, George Eliot, the poets. I remember when we first heard Thomas Hood's "Song of the Shirt" I figured that it was written for us. You know, because it told the long hours of stitch, stitch, stitch. I remember one of the girls said, "He didn't know us. Did he?" And I said, "No he didn't." But it had an impact on us. Later on . . . we got to know Shelley. . . . Very few people know his poem dealing with slavery called "The Masque of Anarchy." He appealed to us . . . because it was a time when we were ready to rise.[28]

Like Newman's Zionist sisters back in Kovno, young women garment workers found that their groups nourished a spirit of rebellion. Reveling in beautiful language and debating difficult ideas made them feel that they had defeated those who would reduce them to machines. Because they had to steal the time to study, the young women approached everything they read with a heightened sensitivity. And when something they were reading struck a chord of recognition, seemed to reflect on their own lives, the catharsis was not only emotional; it was political.

The evolution of Lemlich's study group illustrates how study often led to union activity. Older workers, who were teaching Lemlich the craft of draping, invited her to join their lunchtime discussion groups to learn more about trade unionism. Soon Lemlich and a group of young women waistmakers formed their own study group. Discussion quickly escalated to action, and they decided to form a union.[29]

Skilled male workers in the shirtwaist trade had been trying to establish a union since 1900. But after five years the union had managed to attract only ten members. The problem, Lemlich told her male colleagues, was that women workers had to be approached by an organizer who understood their particular needs as women. They bristled at the suggestion that this young girl might know more about their business than they did. But years later, one conceded that the failure of the first waistmakers' union was due at least in part to their ham-fisted tactics: "We would issue a circular reading somewhat as follows: 'Murder the exploiters, the blood-suckers, the manufacturers. . . . Pay your dues. . . . Down with the Capitalists!' " Few women or men showed up at their meetings.[30]

During the spring of 1905 the union disbanded and reorganized as Local 25 of the ILGWU, with Clara Lemlich and a group of six young women from her waistmaking shop on the executive board. Taking their cue from Lemlich, the new union used women organizers to attract women workers. Lemlich addressed street-corner meetings in English and Yiddish and found Italian women to address the Italian workers. Soon, like Schneiderman, Newman, and Cohn, she realized that she had found a calling.[31]

SOCIALISTS, REFORMERS, AND

NEW YORK SHOP GIRLS, 1905–1909

In the progressive atmosphere of early-twentieth-century New York City, influential people quickly noticed the militant young working women. Older Socialists, trade unionists, and middle-class reformers offered their assistance. These benefactors helped the young organizers sharpen their arguments, provided financial assistance, and introduced them to politicians and public officials. The protégés recognized the importance of this informal mentoring and would later work to recreate such networks in the unions, schools, and training programs they built for young women workers. Schneiderman, Newman, Lemlich, and Cohn were keenly aware that young working women needed help from more experienced and more powerful allies. But they also worried that the voices of women workers might be outshouted in the clamorous process of building alliances. From these early days, they battled to preserve the integrity of their vision.

Pauline Newman found her first mentors in the Socialist Party, which she joined in 1906 at the age of fifteen. Older women, including former garment worker Theresa Serber Malkiel, took her on as a protégé. Newman quickly blossomed under their tutelage. Before long she was running street-corner meetings. Armed with a sonorous voice and the certitude of youth, she would take "an American flag and a soapbox and go from corner to corner," exhorting the gospel of Socialism in Yiddish and English. "I, like many of my friends and comrades, thought that socialism and socialism alone could and would someday fill the gap between rich and poor," Newman recalled. In a neighborhood crowded with sidewalk proselytizers, this child evangelist became one of the party's most popular street-corner attractions.[32]

In 1908, nine years before New York State gave women the vote, seventeen-year-old Newman was nominated by the Socialist Party to run for New York's Secretary of State. Newman used her campaign as a platform for suffrage. Her speeches were heckled by some Socialist men, and her candidacy provoked amused commentaries in New York City newspapers; some writers snickered at the prospect of a "skirted Secretary of State." It was a largely symbolic crusade, but Newman felt that she got people talking about the idea of women in government. The highlight of the campaign was her whistlestop tour with presidential candidate and Socialist leader Eugene V. Debs on his "Red Special" train.

The Socialist Party opened up a new world to Newman, who, after all, had never graduated from elementary school. Along with Debs, she met future Congressmen Meyer Berger and Morris Hillquit and leading Socialist intellectuals. Newman later wrote about the excitement of discussions that carried over from meetings and went into the night as she and her friends walked through Central Park, arguing till the sun came up. Those nights made her feel part of a historic moment.[33]

While Newman was being nurtured by the Socialist Party, Rose Schneiderman found her mentors in the United Cloth Hat and Cap Makers. At the union's 1904 convention she was elected to the General Executive Board; she was the first woman to win such a high-level post in the American labor movement. During the winter of 1904–5, Schneiderman's leadership skills were tested when owners tried to open up union shops to nonunion workers. The largely immigrant capmaker's union called for a general strike. The 1905 strike was a watershed event in Schneiderman's emerging career. Her role as the only woman leader in the union won attention from the press and lasting respect from male capmakers, including the future president of the union, Max Zaritsky, who became a lifelong friend and admirer.[34]

It also brought her to the attention of the newly formed Women's Trade Union League (WTUL), an organization of progressive middle- and upper-class women reformers founded in 1903 to help working women organize. Schneiderman had misgivings about the group because she "could not believe that men and women who were not wage earners themselves understood the problems that workers faced." But she trusted the League's best-known working-class member, Irish shirtmaker Leonora O'Reilly. And she could not ignore the favorable publicity that the WTUL won for the strikers. By March 1905, Schneiderman had been elected to the executive board of the New York WTUL. In 1906, the group elected her vice president.[35]

Schneiderman's entrance into the New York WTUL was an important turning point for both her and the organization. Three years after its founding, the WTUL remained dominated by affluent reformers who had dubbed themselves "allies" of the working class. Despite their genuine commitment to trade unionism, League leaders had credibility problems among women workers. Representatives from most of New York's major unions were on its executive board, but they rarely attended the meetings. Schneiderman had joined the League recognizing that working women lacked the education, the money, and the political clout to organize effectively without powerful allies. Still, she remained ambivalent for a variety of reasons.[36]

The progressive reformers who dominated the League tried to steer workers away from radical influences, particularly the Socialist Party. Yet Schneiderman and O'Reilly, the League's leading working-class organizers, were Socialist Party members and saw unionism as a potentially revolutionary tool. As a result, the pair often felt torn by competing loyalties. Socialists distrusted their work with upper-crust women reformers. Union men were either indifferent or openly hostile to working women's attempts to become leaders in the labor movement. And the League women often seemed to Schneiderman and O'Reilly to act out of a patronizing benevolence that had little to do with real coalition building. The two grew angry at what they saw as attempts by wealthy allies to manipulate them. In January 1906, Leonora O'Reilly announced the first of her many resignations from the League, claiming "an overdose of allies."[37]

There were a few deep friendships between affluent WTUL leaders and working women like Schneiderman, O'Reilly, and Pauline Newman, who joined the League in 1909. Mary Dreier, a reformer who was then president of the New York WTUL, was very close to Newman, Schneiderman, and O'Reilly. Her friendship with O'Reilly was particularly strong and over the years would come to include financial support. Such bonds created hope that intimacy was possible between women of different classes; but cross-class friendships were the exception rather than the rule. Newman later said of Dreier, "Mary was loved, deeply loved by everybody." However, the same could not be said of her sister Margaret Dreier Robins, president of the national WTUL. "Margaret was respected," Newman said, "and admired, but there was no love." Working women like Newman never lost sight of the ways their class background separated them from wealthy reformers. Sisterhood was exhilarating, but outside the WTUL, their lives and political agendas diverged sharply.[38]

This political and social tension heightened working-class activists' emotional dependence upon one another. Schneiderman, Newman, and O'Reilly were a tight trio. After heart disease and an invalid mother confined O'Reilly to her home in Brooklyn, Newman and Schneiderman visited her every Saturday for years. When they weren't in New York, they wrote weekly. Letters between the three are filled with political advice, affectionate banter, and expressions of gratitude. Such relationships were not easy to come by for women whose lives violated the gender norms of both contemporary U.S. society and the immigrant communities from which they came. Pauline Newman continued to mourn O'Reilly for decades after the older woman's death in 1927. As late as 1984, when she was ninety-four years old, Newman could not talk about O'Reilly without tears.[39]

By contrast, these women's relations with most wealthy League supporters were marked by deep ambivalence. Schneiderman's confusion about WTUL beneficence first came to a head in 1908, when League supporter Irene Lewisohn offered to pay both her salary as an organizer and her expenses toward a college degree. It was not an uncommon practice for Progressive Era philanthropists to offer exceptional working women the chance at an education. Historians Charles and Mary Beard would offer the same opportunity to Clara Lemlich in 1911 and Fannia Cohn in 1914. Though it must have been sorely tempting, the three women turned down the offer with much the same argument: they could not attend college while the vast majority of working women were denied a basic education. Schneiderman did, however, accept Lewisohn's offer of a salary so that she could work full-time as the League's chief organizer.[40]

Lewisohn's crucial support of Schneiderman during those early years highlights a tension in the League that was never completely resolved. If Lewisohn had not paid her salary, Schneiderman would never have been able to cover as much ground, speak to as many women, or unionize as many trades as she did over the next few years. But WTUL backers forced leaders to distance the League from radical working-class activism and to stake out a decidedly middle ground in the struggle for women's rights that was then gathering steam.[41]

Schneiderman tried to counterbalance such influences by encouraging male union leaders to play a more active role in the League, but she had little success. She told them that the WTUL could help the labor movement by successfully organizing women workers, whose low wages might otherwise exert a downward pressure on unionized male wages. A *women's* trade union league was needed, she insisted, because women workers responded to different arguments than did men workers. The League could focus on the particular concerns of women, such as the double shift—having to perform household chores after coming home from long days in the factory. Her suggestions were greeted with indifference. Most male labor leaders believed that women were, at worst, unorganizable and, at best, temporary members of the workforce who would soon marry and stop working. In their view women weren't worth expending energy or resources on because they weren't real workers.[42]

Addressing the First Convention of American Women Trade Unionists, held in New York on July 14, 1907, Schneiderman reported that she "was very much surprised and not a little disappointed that the attention of men unionists was so small." She recalled the shocked expressions on the faces of union leaders when she strode into their meetings to ask for field organizers and strike funds to support her attempts at unionizing working women in New York. "They evidently believed a woman would not attend their meetings," she said. She usually came away empty-handed but continued her work without their help, depending instead on the contributions of League supporters. "I would go through barrooms or anything else," she said, alluding to the union men's preference for holding meetings in bars, "to do my duty by the women who are struggling to secure their rights." The truth is, she told her audience, working women needed more than unions. They needed political power. "The time has come," she said firmly, "when working women of the State of New York must be enfranchised and so secure political power to shape their own labor conditions." The convention passed a suffrage resolution, one of the first prosuffrage statements by any organization representing American working-class women.[43]

Schneiderman confronted middle- and upper-class allies with equal frankness. She told the NYWTUL executive board that they were having little success organizing women workers because they approached their task like scholars, not trade unionists. They surveyed conditions in the women's trades, noting which had the lowest salaries, the longest hours, and the worst hygienic conditions. Then they established committees to study the possibilities for unionizing each trade. Finally they went into the shops to explain their findings to the working women. Schneiderman suggested a simpler alternative: take their lead from women workers and respond to requests for aid from women workers who were already trying to organize. It was something they had never thought to do.[44]

Before long, requests for help were pouring in, mostly from immigrant Jewish women. In the dress trade, where Clara Lemlich was working, and in the white goods trade, where Fannia Cohn was organizing, women workers had launched a series of wildcat strikes. "It was not unusual for unorganized workers to walk out without having any direct union affiliation," Schneiderman later recalled.[45]

In April 1907, long-simmering anger over speedups, wage cuts, and the requirement that employees pay for their own thread reached a boiling point. The first sign came when a group of women's underwear makers at the Milgrim shop on Grand Street staged a spontaneous walkout. Schneiderman rushed in to guide the strike. She set up picket lines and initiated negotiations between strike leaders and management. The women won almost all of their demands, including the creation of a permanent grievance committee. Warning them that they would lose these benefits unless they formed a union, Schneiderman urged the strikers to sign up. They did, but they had to affiliate with the League rather than with the ILGWU. The union refused to recognize them, explaining that women had not yet proven themselves capable of organizing. It was a line that Schneiderman, Newman, Cohn, and Lemlich would hear many times over the next twenty-five years.[46]

Foreshadowing its role in the decades to come, the Women's Trade Union League decided to champion women workers ignored by the male-led unions. An underwear makers' union built slowly, claiming three hundred members by the end of the first year. League secretary Helen Marot saw evidence of increasing confidence in the young women. Marot noted at the end of 1907 that finally, after months of allowing a male union representative to run their affairs, "they have one of their own girls who they have elected president."[47]

Schneiderman believed that the Milgrim strike reflected a growing cohesion among young women workers on the East Side. She later described "how different things had been . . . before the strike. The women looked upon each other as enemies because one might get a better bundle of work done than the other. But now, since they had organized and had fought together, there was a kinship among them."[48]

That feeling of militant solidarity spread to Brooklyn, where for two years Fannia Cohn had been struggling against male union leaders' indifference to her campaign to organize white goods workers. Initially the women of Cohn's shop had approached the United Garment Workers (UGW) for help forming a union. UGW officers agreed; however, they insisted that the young women not conduct union meetings unless a male union representative was present, and they never sent one. So when three hundred workers in one shop decided to strike in 1908, they bypassed the UGW and called for help from Schneiderman and the WTUL.

Schneiderman cultivated leadership by placing the workers themselves in charge of their strike. Marot commented, "We have insisted on their managing their own meetings and their strike themselves. . . . This was in marked comparison to the advice of the men who had come to help them. They had started the idea among the girls that they must have a leader. It was interesting to see how the girls took up the idea of being their own leaders and how their interest increased."[49]

The Brooklyn white goods strike raised a new challenge for Schneiderman: how to forge a sense of solidarity between working-class women of many religions and nationalities. The ethnic makeup of the white goods trade was far more diverse than either Schneiderman's cap trade or Lemlich and Newman's shirtwaist trade. Some organizers believed that underwear manufacturers intentionally hired women from many different immigrant groups, figuring that if the workers couldn't talk to each other, they wouldn't be able to organize. Whether or not that was true, Schneiderman decided that the best way to reach immigrant workers was through organizers who literally spoke their language.

She decided to focus first on Italian workers because, after Jews, they comprised the single largest ethnic group in the garment trades. Recognizing the cultural as well as linguistic differences that separated her from Italian immigrant women, Schneiderman tried a strategy she would employ many times over the years to come: to identify and cultivate a leader from within the ranks of the workers. She began working with a Brooklyn priest on ways to approach young Italian women. She also got the League to hire an Italian-speaking organizer who assembled a committee of progressive New York Italians—including prominent women professionals and the editor of a popular evening paper *Bolatino de la Sera*—to popularize trade unionism among Italian women workers.[50]

The strategy proved successful. By 1909 enough workers had enlisted that the ILGWU finally recognized the Brooklyn white goods workers' union. The vast majority of its members were teenage girls; these young women elected their mentor, Fannia Cohn, then twenty-four, to the union's first executive board. Cohn, who stepped off the shop floor to a policy-making position, would remain a paid union official for the rest of her life.[51]

In 1909, Clara Lemlich—then in her twenties and on the executive board of ILGWU Local 25—enlisted Schneiderman's aid in her drive to organize shirt-waist makers. For the past three years, Lemlich had been zigzagging between small shops, stirring up trouble. Her first full-scale strike was at Weisen and Goldstein's Manhattan factory. Like the Triangle Shirtwaist Factory, where Newman worked, Weisen and Goldstein's was considered a model shop. The workrooms were modern and airy—a pleasant contrast to the dark basement rooms where most white goods workers labored. However, the advantages of working in a clean, new factory were offset by the strains of mechanization. In 1907 the workers at Weisen and Goldstein's went on strike to protest speedups.

Older male strikers proved critical to Lemlich's political education. Con-fused by an argument between workers at a strike meeting, Lemlich asked one to explain the difference between Socialist unionism and the "pure and simple trade unionism" of the American Federation of Labor (AFL). When the meet-ing ended, the man took Lemlich for a long walk. He explained Socialism in terms she could use with her fellow workers. "He started with a bottle of milk—how it was made, who made the money from it through every stage of its production. Not only did the boss take the profits, he said, but not a drop of that milk did you drink unless he allowed you to. It was funny, you know, because I'd been saying things like that to the girls before. But now I under-stood it better and I began to use it more often—only with shirtwaists."[52]

Lemlich returned to the picket line with a more sophisticated view of organizing. She became a regular at Socialist Party meetings and began attend-ing classes at the Rand School. Through the Socialist Party she became friends with Rose Schneiderman, Pauline Newman, and other young women orga-nizers. Both individually and in tandem, this group of radical young women organized strikes across the Lower East Side.

In 1909, after being fired from two more shops for leading strikes, Lemlich began working at the Leiserson shop. Brazenly, she marched uninvited into a strike meeting that had been called by the shop's older male elite—the skilled cutters and drapers. Warning them that they would lose if they attempted to strike without organizing the shop's unskilled women, Lemlich demanded their help in organizing women workers. They bridled at her nerve, but ultimately they helped her unionize the women.

Lemlich, who enjoyed the company of men, saw herself marching side by side with them into a better future for the working class. Still, this unusually self-possessed young woman did not hesitate to challenge even much older men if they expressed indifference or opposition to the idea of organizing women. Her political intensity was offset by great warmth and vitality. Curly-haired, dark-eyed, and flirtatious, Lemlich was a popular entertainer at East Side gatherings; she had a vast repertoire of revolutionary songs. But she also had an iron will and an uncanny certainty about what was right and what was wrong. This gave her a personal power that drew both men and women toward her but sometimes exasperated those she was closest to.[53]

Lemlich's reputation as a leader grew rapidly during the fall of 1909 as stories of her bravery spread. During the Leiserson strike, which began that September, she was arrested seventeen times and had six ribs broken by club-wielding police and company guards. Without complaint, she tended to her bruises and returned to the line. By November 1909, when she stepped onto the stage in Cooper Union's Great Hall of the People to deliver the speech that would spark the largest women's strike the nation had yet seen, Lemlich was not the anonymous "wisp of a girl" that news accounts described. She was a battle-scarred veteran of the labor movement, well known among her fellow workers.[54]

Still, it is worth remembering that in this period, the four women activists were just barely adults. Newman, Schneiderman, and Lemlich still lived with their parents. During the Leiserson strike, Lemlich was so fearful that her parents would try to keep her home if they knew about her injuries that she hid her escapades and bruises from them. Later she explained the events to her grandson: "Like rain the blows fell on me. The gangsters hit me. . . . The boys and girls invented themselves how to give back what they got from the scabs, with stones and whatnot, with sticks. . . . Sometimes when I came home I wouldn't tell because if I would tell they wouldn't want me to go anymore. Yes, my boy, it's not easy. Unions aren't built easy."[55]

The first decade of the century was vital both to the political maturation of the four young organizers and to the development of a political movement of immigrant working women. Coming of age in the garment trades, Schneiderman, Newman, Lemlich, and Cohn had to negotiate a confusing array of conflicting pulls to forge individual adult identities. Each handled those conflicts differently. But all four were deeply influenced by their experiences on the shop floor; those years would shape the way they organized and thought for the rest of their lives. Between 1900 and 1909, the four set the foundations for their activist careers, refusing to accept any definition of class struggle that did not include the active participation of women, or any definition of feminism that excluded the working class. Over the next ten years they would demonstrate not only what working women could do for themselves but also what they had to offer the trade union, Socialist, and women's suffrage movements.

PART TWO.
WORKING WOMEN
IN REBELLION:
THE EMERGENCE
OF INDUSTRIAL
FEMINISM,
1909–1920

2

AUDACITY:

THE UPRISING

OF WOMEN

GARMENT

WORKERS,

1909–1915

I read about them now—all
those important people and
Clara Lemlich here, Clara
Lemlich there! What did I
know about trade unionism?
Audacity—that was all I
had—audacity!

—Clara Lemlich in a
1954 interview

THE EMERGENCE OF "INDUSTRIAL
FEMINISM," 1909–1915

Between 1909 and 1915, women garment workers in
northeastern and midwestern cities exploded in an
unprecedented show of labor militancy. The first
eruption came in New York City in November 1909.
After an inflammatory speech by twenty-three-year-
old Clara Lemlich, described by the press as a "phi-
lippic in Yiddish," between 20,000 and 40,000 young
shirtwaist makers struck for better wages and working conditions. The press quickly dubbed this famous strike "the Uprising of the Twenty Thousand." To understand the catalytic impact of this
uprising—the largest women's strike to that time—
we must see it through the eyes of the "girl strikers"
and of young women workers across the United
States, who cheered their New York counterparts
and organized strikes of their own. Clara Lemlich
told one journalist that the shirtwaist makers' uprising had given young women factory workers "a new
understanding of their relation to each other." It was
a moment of crystallization, the sign of a new integrated class and gender consciousness among U.S.
working women.[1]

Flames from the volcanic 1909 uprising licked
industrial cities from New York to Michigan. Within
a matter of weeks, 15,000 women waistmakers in
Philadelphia walked off their jobs. The spirit of militancy soon touched the Midwest. In 1910, Chicago
women led a strike of 41,000 men's clothing makers.
The following year, women workers and the wives
of male workers played key roles in a bitter cloakmakers' strike in Cleveland. Meanwhile, in Mus-
catine, Iowa, young women button makers waged
and won a long battle for union recognition. In
1912, corset makers in Kalamazoo, Michigan,
launched a campaign for better working conditions
that polarized their city and won national press attention. In 1913, a strike of underwear and kimono

53

makers swept up 35,000 young Brooklyn girls and women. Finally, in 1915, Chicago dressmakers capped this period of women's labor militancy by winning recognition of their local union after years of struggle. They elected their organizer, Fannia Cohn, as the first woman vice president of a major American labor union.[2]

Cohn, Rose Schneiderman, Pauline Newman, and Clara Lemlich were at the center of a storm that by 1919 had brought half of all women garment workers into trade unions. Individually and in tandem, the four women participated in all of the major women's strikes between 1909 and 1915, arguably the most intense period of women's labor militancy in U.S. history. This wave of "uprisings" seemed to herald the birth of a working women's movement on a scale never before seen. And it catapulted the four young women into positions of leadership, forcing them, in conjunction with colleagues, to articulate a clearly defined set of goals for the new movement.[3]

Still young and uncertain, the four learned as they went. The 1909 shirtwaist strike would provide a quick lesson in the art of managing sustained mass protest. But at strike's end their strategic expertise still outstripped their ability to articulate a coherent political philosophy. In the passion and excitement of the years that followed, Schneiderman, Newman, Lemlich, and Cohn would begin to mature as political leaders and to forge a vision of political change that originated in their years on the shop floor. Pauline Newman would later describe this new brand of activism as politics of the 1909 vintage, fermented during a brief era of young women's mass protest. That description expresses the importance of the 1909 strike as both symbol and catalyst for a new working women's politics.

"Industrial feminism," the phrase coined in 1915 by scholar Mildred Moore to describe working women's militancy over the previous six years, evokes the same spirit but focuses more broadly. It simultaneously captures the interaction between women workers and feminist activists and recognizes the profound influence that the shop floor had on shaping working women's political consciousness. Industrial feminism accurately depicts the contours of an emerging political movement that by decade's end would propel the problems and concerns of industrial working women to the center of U.S. political discourse and make them players in the Socialist Party, the suffrage movement, and the politics of progressive reform.[4]

Industrial feminism was not a carefully delineated code of political thought. It was a vision of change forged in an atmosphere of crisis and awakening, as women workers in one city after another "laid down their scissors, shook the threads off their clothes and calmly left the place that stood between them and starvation." These were the words of former cloakmaker, journalist, and

Socialist Party activist Theresa Malkiel, a partisan chronicler of women's labor militancy. Once an organizer, later a mentor for Newman, Lemlich, and Schneiderman, Malkiel told readers of the *New York Call* that they should not be surprised by the seemingly sudden explosion of young women worker's discontent. As hard as they might find it to take seriously the notion of a "girl's strike," she warned them, this was no outburst of female hysteria. "It was not . . . a woman's fancy that drove them to it," she wrote, "but an eruption of a long smoldering volcano, an overflow of suffering, abuse and exhaustion."[5]

Common sense, Pauline Newman would later say, dictated the most immediate goals of industrial feminists in the era of women's strikes. Given the dire realities of garment workers' lives, the first order of business had to be to improve their wages, hours, and working conditions. Toward that end the "girl strikers" of 1909–15 followed the most basic tenets of unionism. They organized, struck, and negotiated through their labor unions. But the "long-smoldering volcano" that Malkiel cautioned her readers to heed had been stirred to life by more than dissatisfaction over low wages and poor conditions.

The nascent political philosophy that began to take shape after the 1909 strike was more complex than the bread-and-butter unionism of AFL president Samuel Gompers. Why, young working women reasoned, should unions only negotiate hours and wages? They wanted to build unions that would also offer workers educational and cultural activities, health care, and maybe even a chance to leave the city and enjoy the open countryside.

Such ambitious goals derived largely from the personal experiences of industrial feminist leaders like Cohn, Schneiderman, Lemlich, and Newman. Political activism had enriched the four young women's lives, exposing them to more interesting people than they would have met had they stayed on the shop floor: writers, artists, professors, people with ideas. Through politics they had found their voices and a forum in which to raise them. The personal excitement and satisfaction they found in activism in turn shaped the evolution of their political vision: they wanted to create institutions that would provide some of the same satisfactions to any working woman who joined.

But alone, working women had none of the political or economic clout needed to open up such doors of opportunity. To build a successful movement, the four knew that they would have to win the support of more powerful allies. So they learned to build coalitions. From the time they left the shop floor until the end of their careers, they operated within a tense nexus of union men, progressive middle- and upper-class women, and the working women they sought to organize. These alliances shifted continuously, requiring the four women to perform a draining and politically hazardous balancing act. But each core group contributed an important dimension to the political education of the four organizers.

With their male counterparts and older women in the labor movement, they shared a class solidarity that would always remain at the heart of their politics. That commitment was strengthened in the 1910s, when three of the four worked for the ILGWU as general organizers. Traveling around the country, they met coal miners, loggers, and railroad workers who shared both their experiences of exploitation as laborers and their exhilaration in the economic and political strength that trade unions gave them.

From the middle- and upper-class women who joined them on the picket lines and lent them both financial and strategic support, they learned that trade union activism was not the only way to fight for improved work conditions. These allies would expose Newman, Cohn, Schneiderman, and Lemlich to a world of power and political influence, encouraging them to believe that through suffrage and lobbying, government could be put to work for their benefit.

Finally, as they began to think in terms of forging a national movement, they were forced to develop new techniques to reach women workers of different races, religions, and ethnicities. They learned from the women they sought to organize that just as women workers were best reached by women organizers, so Italian, Polish, and Hispanic immigrants and native-born black and white Protestant women were better reached by one of their own than by Jewish women steeped in the political culture of Eastern Europe and the Lower East Side. Though each of the four women had some success in bridging racial and ethnic divisions, they were forced to acknowledge their limitations. They could not do it all themselves; they had to nurture women shop-floor leaders from different backgrounds.

The work required to remain politically effective in this nexus of often-conflicting relationships yielded some real rewards, both strategically and personally. But sometimes the constant struggling wore on them. Conflicts and tensions were brought into sharp relief as the four exhausted themselves making speeches and giving pep talks to weary workers, when they themselves needed reassurance: although they had achieved recognition by the end of the 1909 strike, Schneiderman, Cohn, Newman, and Lemlich were still poor, uneducated, and young. Newman was only eighteen years old when the strike began, and Lemlich twenty-three. Even the elders in the circle, Cohn and Schneiderman, were only twenty-five and twenty-eight, respectively.

Letters between Newman and Schneiderman from that era reveal their vulnerability to slights and criticisms by male union leaders and female reformers. Life on "the battlefield," as Newman referred to it, was lonely. At an age when other women were contemplating marriage and family, they spent their nights in smoky union halls or the cheap, dingy hotel rooms that unions rented for their organizers. They sometimes questioned their life choices, for the reality of union work was far less glamorous than it had seemed in their shop-floor days. Indeed, Newman would quit several times before decade's end. Ultimately, though, their disillusionment did not drive the four women from the union movement. Instead, it fueled their desire to broaden the vision of U.S. trade unionism. When Schneiderman said "The working woman needs bread, but she needs roses, too," she was speaking from personal experience.[6]

THE SIGNIFICANCE OF THE 1909 SHIRTWAIST UPRISING

On November 23, 1909, New York City awoke to a general strike of shirtwaist makers, the largest strike by women workers the United States had ever seen. Overnight, between 20,000 and 40,000 workers—most of them teenage girls— silenced their sewing machines to protest the low wages, long hours, and dangerous working conditions. Though the magnitude of the strike amazed nearly everyone, including Schneiderman, Newman, Cohn, and Lemlich, the four knew that this was no spontaneous uprising: they had been organizing feverishly for almost three years and had noted a transformation in the working women they talked to, a growing sense of collective identity matched by an increasing militancy.

The "shirtwaist uprising" of 1909–10 marked a turning point in American working women's activism. The 1909 strike has been written about frequently enough that there is no need to recount it in detail here. Instead, this narrative explores the impact it had on the consciousness of participants. In the eyes of its leaders—Clara Lemlich, Mollie Schepps, Pauline Newman, and Rosie Perr—the strike was a culmination as well as a beginning.

They had laid the groundwork through a series of smaller strikes and had trained fellow workers to expect and respond to the violent and divisive tactics used by bosses to break the strike. Certainly, in order to sustain the months-long strike, they needed the help of union men, Socialist Party women, the Women's Trade Union League, and upper-class suffragists. Nevertheless, this was a genuine grassroots protest, sparked, defined, and led by working women. Shop-floor leaders, many still in their teens, were responsible both for the size of the strike and for the singular "spirit of the strikers." They had inspired their allies, not the reverse.[7]

Most accounts have focused on the complicated politics of the coalition that supported the strike. The strikers themselves have tended to recede into the background. If we foreground the strikers, the uprising takes on a different meaning. Seeing these young women as actors, rather than as acted upon, forces a rethinking of the dominant myths of Progressive Era politics. Working women did not simply receive assistance from benevolent reformers and progressive legislators during this period. Through their collective action, they guided the hands and shaped the ideas of those who made public policy.

The young strikers also forced male labor leaders to reassess the role of women in the American labor movement. Most male unionists still clung to the view that women were difficult to organize and were only an ephemeral part of the workforce. But there were certain facts they couldn't ignore. Between 1909 and 1919, half of all women workers in the garment industry would join unions. That was a remarkable percentage for workers in any industry and directly challenged the notion that women workers were unorganizable.[8]

The solidarity and competence of the young women strikers was a direct outgrowth of the shop-to-shop organizing that Lemlich, Schneiderman, Newman, Cohn, and others had been doing since 1906. They had painstakingly cultivated leaders in hundreds of small shops. The result was a base of support so broad that many observers thought the strike seemed leaderless. Writing in the Progressives' weekly magazine, *Survey*, Mary Brown Sumner noted, "These girls—few of them are over twenty years old—are under the domination of no individuals. Into the foreground of this great moving picture comes the figure of one girl after another as her services are needed. . . . Then she withdraws into the background to undertake quietly the danger and humiliation of picket duty or to become a nameless sandwich girl selling papers on the street, no longer the center of interested attention but the butt of the most unspeakable abuse."[9] Years of preparation had created an infrastructure strong enough to withstand and counteract employers who did everything they could to divide the strikers: stirring up ethnic animosities, attacking the women's virtue, and, when all else failed, unleashing physical violence.

Attempts to divide workers by ethnic group had begun well before the general strike. In September 1909, WTUL secretary Helen Marot reported that manufacturers had tried "to stir up race antagonism between the Jewish and Italian girls. . . . The problem . . . seems to me the most pressing we have before us in helping us deal with women workers in New York City."[10] Clara Lemlich complained that one strike she had been organizing was foiled when management "told the Italian girls that the Jewish girls were striking because they hated Italians and didn't want to work with them. That was not true." Lemlich had to work hard to convince workers in her shop that employers intentionally spread such rumors to keep them from unionizing.[11]

She must have succeeded, because in September 1909, Lemlich and her co-workers at the Leiserson factory went out on strike. That same month, Pauline Newman and her co-workers at the Triangle Shirtwaist Factory walked off their jobs. The Triangle management hired prostitutes to infiltrate the picket lines in an attempt to sully the strikers' reputations by association. When the prostitutes offered suggestions about more lucrative work the girls might engage in if they were dissatisfied with their wages, fights broke out and police quickly arrested the picketers.[12]

Many women were beaten either by police or company guards. Clara Lemlich was a frequent target of hired strongmen, both for leading workers out of the shop and for sustaining them on the picket line. "Clara was so badly hurt," one sympathetic article on the strike reported, "that she was laid up for several days. This did not deter her; she went back to her post and, being a logical talker, straightforward and well fitted to gain the confidence of her comrades, she was able to add to the number of strikers." Beatings and mass arrests strengthened the solidarity of the strikers but also worried national ILGWU leaders, who considered calling off the strikes.[13]

But workers were unwilling to squander the momentum they'd gathered. Local 25, Lemlich's union, pushed instead for a general strike in New York's shirtwaist trade, arguing that women workers across the city would rally to support their colleagues at the Triangle and Leiserson shops. Local 25 asked ILGWU secretary John Dyche and AFL president Samuel Gompers to approve the strike. Both resisted the idea, because general strikes were expensive and difficult to orchestrate, and they did not believe that inexperienced teenage girls could sustain one.[14]

So, as they had many times over the past few years, the strikers turned for support to the Women's Trade Union League. At the urging of O'Reilly and Schneiderman, both Lemlich and Newman joined the League to drum up support for a general strike. But New York WTUL president Mary Dreier cautioned them to go slowly. The strikers got an unlooked-for boost when Dreier was arrested on their picket line. An embarrassed judge quickly dismissed all charges and apologized for the arrest. Wide press coverage of the incident heightened popular interest in the walkouts and in police brutality against the strikers. In this charged atmosphere, the ILGWU agreed to hold a general meeting at which Gompers and Dreier, among others, would speak. Elated, Schneiderman, O'Reilly, Newman, Lemlich, and others distributed thousands of circulars in Yiddish, English, and Italian, calling workers to the mass meeting at Cooper Union on November 22.[15]

That evening, young women workers crowded into the Great Hall of the People in New York's Cooper Union. On the platform were Samuel Gompers, Leonora O'Reilly, and Benjamin Feigenbaum of the *Jewish Daily Forward*. As

Clara Lemlich later recalled, "Each one talked about the terrible conditions of the workers in the shops. But no one gave or made any practical or valid solution." Just as Jacob Panken of the Socialist Party was beginning to speak, the impatient Lemlich shouted out: "I want to say a few words." The *New York Call* described what happened next: "Cries came from all over the hall. 'Get up on the platform.' Willing hands lifted the frail little girl with the flashing black eyes to the stage and she said simply: 'I have listened to all the speakers. I would not have further patience for talk, as I am one of those who feels and suffers from the things pictured. I move that we go on a general strike.'" The room was rocked by cheers. Feigenbaum asked the assembled women and men if they would take the ancient Jewish oath: "If I forget thee oh Jerusalem, may my right hand wither, may my tongue forget its speech." That Lemlich's strike speech was delivered in Yiddish, and that most people in the room knew the Jewish oath and could substitute *union* for *Jerusalem*, dramatically illustrates how overwhelmingly Jewish this movement was and how closely linked Jewish imagery and their vision of unionism were.[16]

The following morning, fifteen thousand waistmakers went on strike. Clara Lemlich spoke at fifteen union halls that day. Tens of thousands of young women would walk out in the weeks to come. The Socialist press was beside itself with glee. Four days after the general strike began, one reporter wrote:

> If you go down to the East Side these cold November days, you may see excited groups of women and girls standing at the streetcorners, gathered in public squares and crowded in the doorways. Go to the halls up and down Clinton and Forsythe streets and you will find similar groups multiplied till the overflow blocks the traffic. . . . And these crowds keep no hours. Early in the morning they are already at the streetcorners; late at night the flickering light of the lamppost reveals their animated faces. What is the reason of it all, you may ask? Why is every available hall in lower Manhattan crowded to its uttermost? A hundred voices answer in chorus: "It's the strike of the forty thousand."[17]

The mythology of the waistmakers' uprising, recorded in both contemporary newspaper articles and historical accounts, has Clara Lemlich as "a wisp of a girl, still in her teens," rising up spontaneously to interrupt the cautious speeches of her labor movement elders. That characterization reinforced the stereotype, widely held within the union movement, that Jewish working girls were *fabrente maydlakh* (fiery girls) who lacked the cool heads and foresight needed for rational planning.

In truth, Clara Lemlich was twenty-three years old and had been working and organizing for eight years before that famous evening. Her discipline as an organizer and ability to channel her outrage into a vision of social change had already won her a reputation among fellow workers and Lower East Side unionists. It is likely that many sitting in the audience at Cooper Union that night knew exactly who was climbing up on the stage and had a pretty good idea of what she was going to say.[18]

Pauline Newman was a familiar figure as well. That year the ILGWU had made her its first woman general organizer. Known for her level head and detail-oriented mind, Newman was trusted to run daily shop meetings and to arrange strike rallies. She also dispatched speakers to union and street-corner meetings, to press conferences, and to gatherings of affluent supporters. Clara Lemlich was her star speaker. The two became close friends and planned to spend a few days together in the country once the strike was over. That vacation would be a long time coming.

Day after day, Newman sent Lemlich from hall to hall to encourage the young women who had heeded her strike call. Making speeches until she lost her voice, Lemlich reported only good news, assuring hungry strikers that "if we stick together, and we are going to stick, we will win." While Lemlich urged strikers to hold the line, Newman visited the homes of wealthy women to stir up sympathy and donations for the waistmakers.[19]

Despite their effectiveness, the strike was threatened by the escalation of police violence against the young women picketers. Two weeks after the strike call, Schneiderman and Dreier led ten thousand young waistmakers on a march to city hall to demand that Mayor George McClellan rein in the police. He promised an investigation but did little. One month into the strike, there had been 771 arrests, many made with undue force.[20]

WTUL leaders decided to try a different tack. They called a mass meeting of all the young women who had been attacked by police. The press and wealthy supporters were invited. One after another, adolescent girls rose to the stage to tell their stories. There was an aggressiveness to their tone, a sense that they were entitled to better treatment, and an explicit awareness of their constitutional rights. Some wore banners that proclaimed in Yiddish, "We Are Not Slaves." They spoke bitterly about being beaten but also expressed pride that the ferocity with which they were being physically assaulted was a measure of just how much they threatened employers and police.

Mollie Weingast told a cheering crowd that when an officer tried to arrest her, she informed him that she had a constitutional right to picket. Minnie Margolis demanded that a policeman protect her from physical attack by her boss. When he refused, she took down his badge and precinct numbers. It was, she told the audience, an officer's job to protect her right to protest peacefully. Celie Newman, sixteen, said that police had manhandled her and dragged her into court, where her boss told a judge that she was an anarchist and should be deported. At another meeting earlier that week, seventeen-year-old Etta Ruth said that police had taunted her with lewd suggestions.[21]

Implying that picketers were little better than streetwalkers, employers often resorted to sexual innuendos to discredit the strikers. "It is a question, whether it is worse to be a streetwalker or a scab," one indignant striker responded tartly. Other women noted that starvation wages drove women into prostitution. The workers clearly resented the manner in which middle-class standards of acceptable feminine behavior were used to manipulate them even though they enjoyed none of the advantages of middle-class birth. Then as now, society offered a limited range of cultural images of working-class women. They were either "good" girls who listened docilely to fathers, employers, and policemen, or "bad" women whose aggressive behavior made them akin to prostitutes. By walking on picket lines and going public with their demands, they'd forfeited their claims to femininity and respectability—and thus to protection.[22]

Such women were shown little deference by police and company thugs, who attacked them with iron bars, sticks, and billy clubs. And they received little sympathy in court when they attempted to press charges. One young woman appeared in court with a broken nose, a bruised face, and a head swathed in bandages. Yet the judge dropped her assault charge against police. "You are on strike against God and nature," one magistrate told a worker.[23] Only the League's decision to invite college students and wealthy women onto the picket lines ended the violence. Alva Belmont and Anne Morgan led a contingent of New York's wealthiest women in what newspapers dubbed "mink brigades," which patrolled the dirty sidewalks of the Lower East Side. Fearful of clubbing someone on the Social Register, police grew more restrained.[24]

The socialites' presence generated both money and press for the strikers. The move proved politically wise for the suffrage cause as well, because the constant proselytizing of suffrage zealot Alva Belmont, who often bailed strikers out of jail, got young workers talking about the vote. But rubbing elbows with the mink brigade did not blind workers to the class-determined limits of sisterhood. How far they were from the protected status of more affluent women was made abundantly clear by the violence they encountered at the hands of police and company guards and by the fact that the mink brigades were able to end police brutality simply by joining the picket lines.

Encounters in court and with feminist allies speeded the growth of group consciousness. Telling their stories in court, to reporters, and to sympathetic audiences of college and society women, the strikers grew more confident of their speaking abilities and of their capacity to interpret their world. They became more aware of the distribution of power in the United States. And finally, the violence directed against them intensified their bonds with one another.

For Schneiderman, Newman, and Lemlich, the 1909 shirtwaist uprising sped their maturation as organizers and political leaders. Fannia Cohn was not directly involved, but as she busily labored to organize the sweatshops in the underwear trade, she was energized and inspired by the strike. She would refer to it in her organizing and writing for the rest of her career. The strike breathed new life into a struggling immigrant labor movement and transformed the tiny ILGWU into a union of national significance. Still, it ended with mixed success for workers. Many won pay increases and union recognition; others did not. And the contracts hammered out by ILGWU negotiators left a devastating legacy, for without consulting the strikers, male union negotiators decided that safety conditions were less important than other issues. Their concessions would come back to haunt the entire labor movement two years later, when the Triangle Shirtwaist Factory burned.[25]

THE INDUSTRIAL FEMINIST ALLIANCE, 1910–1915

The shirtwaist uprising focused national attention on the problems of New York's young women factory workers. But there were hundreds of thousands of women workers in other cities and in other trades who were still not unionized. During the next five years, Rose Schneiderman, Clara Lemlich, and Fannia Cohn continued organizing in New York, while Pauline Newman took to the road as the woman organizer for the ILGWU.

The problem of ethnic, religious, and racial difference surfaced quickly as the four began trying to organize women of varied backgrounds. Partly out of pragmatism, partly in response to the anti-Semitism they encountered from more affluent allies, the four came to espouse a form of cultural pluralism. Given the diversity of the American working class, if they were to be successful at building a unified movement of working women, they would have to sensitize themselves to a range of cultures.

Pauline Newman spent the next four years trying to learn how. The ILGWU gave Newman a tremendous territory to cover. With mechanization, mass immigration, and the emergence of a ready-to-wear clothing market, the garment industry had spread rapidly. By 1910, there were garment manufacturing pockets in every major Eastern seaboard city and in population centers as far west as Iowa. Newman was on the road constantly, crisscrossing New England, Pennsylvania, and the Midwest. The WTUL and the Socialist Party asked her to speak to a variety of workers while she was on the road; as a result, she visited not only the inner-city slums where most garment shops were located but also gritty, gray steel towns and bleak, freezing coal-mining camps. She worked with native-born Protestant women, Slavic, Irish, Polish, and Italian women, and Eastern European Jews. She had no real home for four years; she lived instead in hotel rooms and boardinghouses from Philadelphia to Boston to Cleveland to Chicago to St. Louis to Kalamazoo.[26]

It was an incredible education. Newman would later liken it to graduate school. (She had gotten her undergraduate degree, she liked to say, at the Triangle Shirtwaist Factory.) She chronicled her travels in articles for the Socialist press. These published pieces were mostly triumphal polemics lionizing the women workers, whom she called "labor's unknown soldiers." But in letters to friends, Newman confided dramatic mood swings from exhilaration to deep depression. The serious young woman's sensitivity and emotionalism come through on every page. As uncertain about her sexuality as any young adult, she expressed deep confusions about her intense friendships with women and her unsuccessful romances with men. Her emotions were heightened by the loneliness of being on the road for a total of four years, by her battles with male union officials and affluent women allies, and by frustration with women workers who seemed afraid to take any control.

Still, she took pride in one talent that made her particularly useful to the union in its early days of expansion: her chameleonlike ability to appeal to men and women from widely varied class and ethnic backgrounds. Impressed by her fund-raising successes during the 1909 strike, ILGWU officials made Newman their unofficial liaison to women of the upper classes. "She was a great fund-raiser," her grandson Michael Owen says, "which I'm sure is what brought her to everyone's attention. She herself was amazed by it. She was invited into all these rich people's living rooms and would give a talk about what was going on and they would give her a staggering amount of money. She obviously had a gift." Her efforts to appear refined amused some ILGWU colleagues. "She even cultivated this almost British-sounding accent," said Leon Stein, former editor of the union's magazine, *Justice*. "It was great to listen to."[27]

Shortly after the strike, the union sent her to Boston to speak to wealthy women about the new union label campaign intended to pressure department stores to carry only union-made clothing. Dressed in the immigrant-bohemian style she had come to prefer—white shirt, tie, jacket, and skirt—Newman felt that she looked like the self-taught worker-radical she was. She knew she would stand out in a crowd of Boston Brahmins and was nervous about what she should say to church- and clubwomen. In the hope of bridging the chasms of class and ethnicity, she exchanged the shtetl and Old Testament imagery that dominated Lower East Side union rhetoric for parables from the New Testament. And she decided to pepper her speeches with allusions to Dickens, Tennyson, and Shelley. (Her shop-floor study groups and classes at the Socialist Literary Society came in handy.) It worked. Many in her Boston audiences pledged to support the union label. Elated when one church group of three hundred women presented her with roses after a speech, Newman wrote to Schneiderman, "Am getting the women of churches now . . . by quoting Christ. I have learned, Rose, learned a lot."[28]

Of necessity Newman became skilled at adapting her language to each new locale and audience. In Boston, she tried to convince affluent Protestant women to buy only the union label. In Philadelphia, she assisted the immigrant Jewish and Italian waistmakers who, inspired by their New York sisters, were now waging their own bitterly contested strike. As much as her success with the Boston clubwomen exhilarated her, Newman always felt relieved to return to Philadelphia, where she took comfort in the company of the women workers.

Still, union work frustrated her. She felt undercut by the ILGWU's male leaders, who showed little interest in organizing women workers. From the very start of the union, its male officers were caught in a bind. Though they subscribed to a vision of unionism very close to that of the AFL—a muscular fraternity of skilled male workers—their power as a union depended on being able to organize an industry of unskilled women. So they grudgingly encouraged outreach to women workers, but they consistently blocked attempts by female ILGWU members to exert influence over the union's direction.

In the male world of union organizers she felt isolated and beleaguered by crude jokes and teasing. In 1910 she wrote to Schneiderman, "Rose, dear, if I ever had a spark of hope for our Jewish movement [by which she meant the garment unions], I lost it now. . . . They have no manners and no sense. I do not feel at home with them anymore." Some of her colleagues were openly hostile; one accused her of being a publicity seeker for getting her picture in the paper. Needling from her boss, John Dyche, was sometimes affectionate, sometimes not. "Why do you wear a skirt?," he teased her when they crossed paths on her travels. "Getting to be respectable, Paul?"[29]

She craved the affection and emotional support of her New York friends. In the case of Rose Schneiderman, she seems to have wanted something more. After coming home from a date in October 1910, she wrote, "Wanted you here last night on my birthday. . . . Oh but how I wanted you. All evening I kept on saying if only Rose were here. . . . He said 'it must be Robert instead of Rose.' Rose dear, you will have to come here. . . . I want you too much." It is unclear to what degree Schneiderman reciprocated those feelings. In later letters, Newman noted feeling "blue from your silence," and signed "yours, forever or never." One letter definitely suggests some tension. "Our relations of the past (and if there is any on your part now) is sacred to me," Newman wrote. "The reason why I don't want to write to you at present is well known to you." Whatever that reason was, it disappeared over time. The two women remained close friends for the rest of their lives.[30]

Newman's attachment to her women friends nearly broke her when, on March 25, 1911, a raging fire claimed the lives of 146 young workers at the supposedly fireproof Triangle Shirtwaist Factory. Newman had worked there for nearly seven years and knew many of the victims. In the days after the fire she sank into a deep depression, wondering aloud why all the years of work and struggle had not prevented it. Schneiderman and Lemlich also lost friends in the fire. Frantic with fear, Lemlich joined the hundreds of New Yorkers who searched among the charred bodies for relatives. A newspaper reporter described her as convulsed by tears and hysterical laughter when she finished her gruesome task without finding a cousin who she feared was among the dead.[31]

The Triangle fire was both a personal loss and a bitter reminder of the urgency of their cause. It heightened their distrust of upper-class allies who preached sisterhood while counseling patience and moderation. Schneiderman wrote that she was "tired of resolutions being passed but never acted upon." At a memorial held by heiress Anne Morgan in Carnegie Hall to raise funds for families of the victims, Schneiderman issued a famous challenge to sympathetic members of the upper class: "This is not the first time girls have been burned alive in the city. Every week I must learn of the untimely death of one of my sister workers. . . . There are so many of us for one job it matters little if 146 of us are burned to death. . . . I can't talk fellowship to you who are gathered here. Too much blood has been spilled. I know from experience it is up to the working people to save themselves."[32]

Newman read Schneiderman's speech in Philadelphia and wrote to her, "You really gave them hell, [and I] am glad of it. . . . I wonder how Miss Morgan felt after you got through." But Newman was not able to channel her grief into action. She told Schneiderman that the fire had drained her of hope and energy and that she had submitted her resignation to the union. "I could not write, I could not do anything for the last two or three weeks," she admitted. "The Triangle tragedy had a terrible effect on me."[33]

Schneiderman urged Newman to stay on the job. In the wake of such a tragedy, she wrote, they had to redouble their efforts. ILGWU secretary John Dyche, with whom Newman battled incessantly, felt the same way. He refused to accept her resignation. Newman relented, but not with any real joy. She wrote Schneiderman with deep ambivalence and a touch of envy: "Remember Rose that no matter how much you are with the Jewish people, you are still more with the people of the League and that is a relief. Many times I wish that I could shake the Jewish movement for at least a few years. But, ah that *but* . . . I cannot leave them as long as they don't want to accept my resignation."[34]

Newman's bond with the immigrant Jewish Socialists, garment unionists, and self-taught intellectuals who made up the leadership of the ILGWU was powerful, scored as it was by conflict and pain. From early adolescence, Jewish Socialism had been a central part of her identity. She could not simply discard it. For this young woman with little formal education and few family ties, the union had become both an intellectual home and a family. Besides, she knew that choosing the all-female world of the Women's Trade Union League would not make her feel less conflicted. Schneiderman had her own struggle trying to find a comfortable place among the elite Christian women of the League.[35]

The feeling of perennially walking a tightrope drained both women's energy and frayed their nerves. Though expressed in the romantic language of early-twentieth-century women's friendship, their craving for intimacy and under-standing grew out of the hard realities of radical immigrant women's lives. Their choice to devote themselves to political activism had left them few safe spaces emotionally. As young single women, their friendships with men in the labor movement were complicated by a need to appear respectable and a sense that men didn't respect them or their work. As immigrant working-class Jews, they found that opening themselves up to middle-class women was equally fraught with danger.

New York WTUL secretary Helen Marot was a Socialist and someone New-man and Schneiderman considered a friend—until she stunned them both by announcing in early 1911 that "the time has come when the League must spend the greater part of its budget for organization among American girls." (By "American," Marot and others meant native-born Protestants.) Marot acknowledged that Russian Jewish women had provided the impetus for the dramatic upsurge in women's labor activism. Still, she said, Jews were too ideological, and their "difference in attitude and understanding was a heavy strain on the generosity of the American girls." Marot claimed to admire the courage of Jewish women but argued that trade unionism would never gain a foothold among American-born women unless the organizers were "Ameri-can men and women who understood their prejudices."[36]

Schneiderman and Newman knew well the heavy-handedness of some Jewish male union officials. But they did not attribute the men's arrogance to their ethnic origins, nor did they think it fair for Marot to punish Jewish women workers for the sins of their brothers. Marot's next statement on the subject to the executive board of the New York WTUL left little doubt in their minds that prejudice, not concern for "American-born women," was at the root of her decision. "We have realized for several years," she said, "that the Russian Jew had little sense of administration and we have been used to ascribing their failures to their depending solely on their emotions and not on constructive work."[37]

For Schneiderman and Newman, Marot's not-so-subtle stereotyping of Jewish immigrants was a painful betrayal. When Marot announced in the summer of 1911 that she would keep the League's doors open to Jewish women on "a basis approved by American trade unionists," Schneiderman took that as a direct attack on her work as the League's chief organizer. She toyed with the idea of quitting, but she was in the middle of organizing women in the white goods and kimono trades. So she swallowed her anger and stayed on. But Newman never forgave Marot. More than half a century later she told an interviewer that her former friend was a cold woman who displayed neither affection nor emotion.[38]

Clara Lemlich, who would soon have her own problems with middle- and upper-class supporters, somehow managed to stay out of this fight. Life had gotten a bit tricky for Lemlich. Blacklisted by the Shirt and Dress Manufacturer's Association for her role in the 1909 uprising, she'd been forced to use false names to get factory work. But she used her own name when addressing nightly union meetings; in the years after the 1909 strike, the name Clara Lemlich could draw a crowd. Lemlich's Yiddish fire-and-brimstone style riveted women workers. Even Helen Marot was impressed. "The girls were listless and uninterested" until Clara got up to speak, Marot wrote. "[But] they listened intently to Miss Lemlich's speech and were eager for our cooperation."[39]

Recognizing the need for more women organizers, Pauline Newman began to pull herself out the depression that followed the Triangle fire. A little bit of recognition from ILGWU secretary John Dyche helped enormously. In June of 1911, when six thousand Cleveland cloakmakers struck, Dyche wrote Newman and, citing her past successes in organizing women, asked her to consider representing the union there. Pleased that ILGWU higher-ups seemed finally to be acknowledging her work, Newman agreed. "They are beginning to realize that women can do more effective work than men," she wrote Schneiderman from Cleveland, "especially where girls are concerned."[40]

The Cleveland strike forced Newman to use all her skill at reaching out to women of different backgrounds. Since the strikers were Jewish and Italian women, cloak manufacturers attempted to break the strike by farming out garment work to native-born women in Cleveland's outlying areas. Newman was assigned the task of persuading these women to support the strike. Her success convinced her that ethnic divisions were not an insurmountable obstacle in unionizing working-class women.[41]

In Cleveland, Newman tried her hand at community organizing for the first time since leading the 1907 Lower East Side rent strike. Her success affirmed her belief that workingmen's wives and mothers could make an important contribution to the class struggle. In October 1911, Newman told the story in the WTUL magazine, *Life and Labor*. Workers' wives and mothers, she wrote, went door to door building support for the strike. They ignored the threats of private police hired by manufacturers to patrol the neighborhood. According to Newman's account, guards shot one woman who disobeyed their orders not to enter a strikebreaker's home. When another woman rushed to her aid, guards threatened to shoot her too. "You can shoot me if you want," the woman said, "but I must pick up this woman!" While she was dragging her friend's body away, they shot her too. Newman did not reveal her emotions on having seen blood spilled up close. But the twenty-year-old must have been shaken. In a paean to the bravery of the strikers' wives she wrote, "Never shall I forget the heroism of the women."[42]

By lauding such women's exploits in her articles, she hoped to move sympathetic readers to action and to forge links between progressive groups: Socialists, the women of the various WTUL branches, union men and women. Wearying of union work, she began to feel that she might contribute as much to the class struggle as a writer. The final straw came when John Dyche sent a male organizer to join Newman in Cleveland and paid him a higher weekly wage. Newman decided the time had come to quit the ILGWU for a career as writer and freelance organizer. "You, Rose, know that the seven dollars does not bother me but there is a principle involved and for that I am ready to fight," she wrote Schneiderman. "It was an insult and it hurts an awful lot." Besides, Newman calculated, the union owed her a thousand dollars in back pay, approximately three times the annual salary of an average New York shop girl. Writing could hardly be less lucrative.[43]

Needing some comfort and familiarity after two years on the road, Newman moved in with her sisters Fanny and Sarah in Chicago and contributed to the upkeep of their children. During the next few months she worked furiously on her writing, contributing articles to the *New York Call*, the *Ladies' Garment Worker*, *Progressive Woman*, *Life and Labor*, the *Chicago Daily Socialist*, and the *International Review*. Josephine Conger Kaneko, editor of the Socialist Party magazine *Progressive Woman*, worked with Newman on her writing and encouraged her literary aspirations. Interestingly, for some of her pieces Newman adopted a pseudonym: Norma Mizer Paul, which used her initials in reverse.

Perhaps this was to deflect criticism from several of her male union colleagues, who felt that she liked publicity a little too much. Newman supplemented her income doing odd jobs for the WTUL and the Socialist Party.[44]

Despite insisting to Schneiderman that she wanted to "give my lungs and mouth a chance to rest," she accepted a winter 1912 assignment from the Socialist Party to do a speaking tour of the Illinois coal belt. Through the coldest months she toured ice-bound mining towns, exhorting impoverished families "to awaken and find the solution to their problem in Socialism." Horrified by the conditions she saw, she realized that some in the rural working class endured worse conditions than did urban factory laborers. "Those who keep the world warm are freezing," she wrote to Schneiderman. "Think of it! Those who supply coal for all the people have no coal to warm their two or three little rooms."[45]

Satisfied by her work, Newman was fairly content to remain based in Chicago. But Schneiderman urged Newman to return to a place where she had a support network and colleagues who appreciated her. Newman was more than open to the suggestion. "The loneliness kills me," she wrote Schneiderman. "I am tired, I want to do something else, and the thought that I may never be able to accomplish it is enough to make me feel miserable for the rest of my life!" But she bristled at Schneiderman's suggestion that she help the ILGWU organize New York's white goods workers. Newman replied tartly, "The International does not give a hang whether a local lives or dies. Much less would they care to employ me. . . . I am glad of not having to depend upon them for my living. Will at all times be in a position to find work without that ignorant and inefficient bunch."[46]

When Schneiderman expressed concern over Newman's feud with Dyche, Newman explained that it was not simply over tactics and equal pay but also over sexual harassment. "I had . . . many times to struggle against him and be annoyed by his love, so-called; you don't know how many times I felt like exposing him." But she had no faith that the male union hierarchy would take her complaint seriously. "I do not even think that I will go up before the General Executive Board," she wrote. "I can't expect any justice of the ignorant, stupid and conservative fools."[47]

Her disillusionment with radical men was sharpened by a brief romance that year with Socialist Party organizer Frank Bohm in Chicago. Bohm provided virtually the only intimacy she had had during her lonely years on the road, and Newman was somewhat smitten. Older and more worldly, Bohm recommended books and promised to try to get her a scholarship to the University of Wisconsin. During the autumn of 1911, she went as far as going to a hotel room with Bohm, but at the last minute decided against having sex.

Later, she was not sure she'd made the right decision. "I, like so many, will live with memories that blur and burn."[48]

Ultimately she was glad she'd cut off the relationship. Bohm's "etitude [*sic*] toward women," Newman wrote Schneiderman, "is not worse or better than the average etitude of a Socialist man toward a woman. I . . . am told lately that he believes in promiscuity and I am inclined to believe that he does. . . . While I am free in everything, I am puritanical in sex and home questions and it just sickens me to think of anyone who is not a strict monogamist." Whether Newman recoiled from Bohm because of her sexual "puritanism," her annoyance with the lack of respect she felt from Socialist men, or because she wasn't attracted to him is unclear. But she apparently had no other romances with men. As time passed, she recognized that her deepest affinities were with women. In February 1912, she wrote Schneiderman, "I feel that there is not a person today whom I love more than I do you. . . . I really don't know whether I could love to a greater extent than I—but you know it, enough said."[49]

By that time, Schneiderman had reached a crisis point in her battle with League leaders over how much time she was devoting to Jewish women workers. In early 1912 Schneiderman tendered her resignation. Newman applauded the decision: "So you have decided to give up the League! Really at such moments one feels like saying, 'What is the use of working sincerely for an organization, giving them the best that is in you, when it is not even appreciated.' "[50]

Over the next few years, Schneiderman and Newman would resign repeatedly. Newman bounced between jobs with the union, the WTUL, and the Socialist Party. Schneiderman traded places with her for a time, leaving the WTUL to organize for the ILGWU. But she, like Newman, tired of union leaders' seeming indifference to attempts at organizing women. And she resented not being given credit for her work. When the union sent a male organizer to lead a strike she had labored to build, she resigned and returned to the WTUL.

Both felt on most solid ground with other working-class women who shared their vision. But they did not always get along with them, either. Newman was not above backbiting. Of Chicago WTUL organizer Bessie Abramowitz, an Amalgamated Clothing Workers (ACW) organizer who later married powerful labor leader Sidney Hillman, she wrote, "Her own people of the trade laugh at her." And with a decided lack of prescience, she called another Chicago WTUL organizer, Mary Anderson, future director of the U.S. Women's Bureau, "of very little use to the labor movement." These women would continue to work with Newman for nearly fifty years. But it is perhaps here that we find the root of long-standing tensions between the Chicago and New York branches of the WTUL.[51]

Newman had no intention of returning to the ILGWU, but when a large strike at the Kalamazoo Corset Company ran into trouble, Dyche asked Newman if she would consider traveling to Michigan for the union. "I tell you Rose," Newman gloated, "It feels fine when you can say to a secretary of the International to 'go to hell with your job' and after have the same man beg you to work for them again!" She had her work cut out for her. As she stepped off the train in Kalamazoo, Newman was handed a court injunction against the strike. To the joy of the strikers who had come to meet the new organizer, she tore it up in a typical act of bravado. However, when the union called the other organizers away, stranding Newman in the most all-American town she'd yet seen, she felt more than a little lost.[52]

This was a new situation for her. She was comfortable running strikes that pitted immigrant workers against immigrant owners. But this was, in her words, "an entirely American element." On top of that, the strike was proving hard to control. Management refused to negotiate. Scores of women were being arrested daily. And organizers had left her to manage, as the strike's central issue, a matter that made her profoundly uncomfortable: sexual harassment in the shop.[53]

Seeking to stir up public outrage, strike organizer Josephine Casey had laid out the strike's goals in a letter to the *Detroit Times*: "We are fighting to purify the factory, to bring about the dismissal of the foreman and those male employees who have been continually insulting the girl employees and who have been dragging not a few of them down to ruin. The time has passed when an employer can expect to hold girl employees who are subjected to indignities." Calling for the dismissal of a foreman for sexual harassment, or for any other reason, was a nervy thing to do; few strikers to that time had made such demands.[54]

Sexual harassment of female factory workers was commonplace. References to sexual harassment of working women abound in the literature of progressive scholars, and it was acknowledged as a problem by both social reformers and women labor leaders. However, even reform-minded observers argued that it was up to the worker to find her own solution. A 1913 advice book entitled *Vocations for Girls* suggested unrealistically that young women receiving unwanted physical attention or suffering from "unsanitary surroundings, deadening work and low companionship . . . should promptly seek other employment."[55]

An aggravating factor for working women was that some male workers and employers felt that female factory workers were fair prey. One woman cigar maker told a state investigator, "Many men who would not, under any circumstances, offer the slightest insult or disrespectful remark or glance to a female in the streets[,] . . . in the shops, will whoop and give . . . cat calls and a peculiar noise made with their lips which is supposed to be an endearing salutation."[56]

In an age when sexual matters were rarely discussed in public, neither labor leaders nor reformers expected unions to tackle the issue. So Josephine Casey's assertion that ending sexual harassment was a legitimate union demand sparked widespread controversy. Leonora O'Reilly supported Casey's strategy. She said the corset company so underpaid its women workers that "the wages of sin it offers to the young girls who will 'pay the price' are alluring." But Newman, in spite of her own experience with John Dyche (or, perhaps, because of it), was upset that the strike had come to rest on this issue.[57]

She warned ILGWU superiors that "attacking the company" was the wrong strategy because it would anger the owners and make them unwilling to negotiate. And in a letter to Schneiderman, she virtually dismissed the issue's importance: "Rose dear, you know as well as I that there is not a factory today where the same immoral condition does not exist! You remember . . . factories where you have worked and so do I and both of us know that [in] the cloak factories and all other shops in the city of New York or Chicago, every one of the men will talk to the girls, take advantage of them if the girls will let them. The foremen and the superintendent will flirt with the girls. . . . It is nothing new for those who know it exists everywhere." Her proposed solution reflects a willful refusal to acknowledge the unequal power relations that made sexual harassment so prevalent on the shop floor: Newman concluded tersely that the problem could be handled "by educating the girls."[58]

The issue clearly made her uncomfortable. Newman was twenty-one years old, unmarried, and the only woman then employed by any U.S. union as a general organizer. Her job entailed wandering from city to city, living out of hotels filled with sometimes predatory men, and attending late-night meetings in rough neighborhoods. Any hint of sexual vulnerability would have destroyed her viability as a union representative, making it impossible for her to work with male organizers or with young women still living in their parents' houses. Only by cultivating an image of toughness and invulnerability could she maintain her position within the union, not to mention her own emotional stability.

Newman felt she needed to project a powerful image of women workers generally. In writings and speeches, Newman liked to lionize women strikers, to laud them for their bravery and stamina. To politicize the issue of sexual harassment meant acknowledging that bringing women into the union movement introduced muddy issues like sexuality onto the morally clear battleground of class struggle. That may have contributed to her decision not to report John Dyche's harassment of her. And that was perhaps why she suggested that unions simply teach women workers to defend themselves, for she must have known that was not a realistic solution for a woman factory worker facing a male employer.

Ultimately, as Newman had feared, the strike was broken by management's refusal to negotiate. It seems conceivable that part of the blame lay with Newman, who balked at pushing the women's demands. But she insisted that the ILGWU leadership was at fault because they were ill-equipped to deal with native-born manufacturers. As a last resort, Newman organized a boycott of the corset company. Her success restored her confidence in her organizing skills, but it didn't do the women workers much good. Their employer went out of business.[59]

Chagrined and homesick, Newman was ready to return to New York. Her decision was sealed in the spring of 1912, when she received a pained letter from Schneiderman, whose companion Rose Rishon had just moved out of the house they had shared with Schneiderman's mother and sister. "Poor Rose!," Newman comforted, "I am sorry. For if there is anyone who can feel with you it is me. . . . I often think that a person of my temperament should not be destined to roam about alone. . . . Being absent from those you love is hell—at least to me!"[60]

Newman returned to New York early in 1913, broke and out of work but relieved to be home. Schneiderman helped her get an inspector's position on the Joint Board of Sanitary Control, a factory inspection commission established in the settlement of the 1909 strike. The ILGWU also paid Newman to write the "Woman's Sphere" column for its magazine, the *Ladies' Garment Worker*. The battle-weary, twenty-two-year-old columnist cast herself as a seasoned adviser to innocent young women. She warned them sternly to stay away both from "Prince Charmings" and cheap romance novels, to save themselves for mature love and real literature. The didactic tone of her columns reflected the gap that had opened up between her and the average shop-floor worker.[61]

If Newman had hoped to stay out of the fray for a while, that desire faded quickly once Schneiderman enlisted her in the League's long-fought campaign to organize a general strike of white goods and kimono makers. Newman initiated an investigation by the Joint Board of Sanitary Control and found the conditions bleak. Many of the shops were set up in dark basement rooms—poorly ventilated, unsanitary firetraps. The trade seemed ripe for union organizing.

But there were myriad obstacles. The shops were small and scattered. A large number of the workers were girls under the age of sixteen, most of them new immigrants, who lacked both confidence and a command of the English language. The trade employed girls of so many different nationalities that the workers could hardly speak to one another. Fannia Cohn had led a general strike of kimono workers in Brooklyn during the summer of 1910. But the strike had not had the support of the ILGWU and had thus been a failure. By 1913, Cohn, Schneiderman, Newman, and several other organizers were pleading with the ILGWU leadership to help them organize a citywide white goods strike.[62]

But the ILGWU's executive board had begun to focus on crushing, not fanning, grass-roots militancy. The objects of their attention were the women of Local 25, Clara Lemlich's union. Disgusted by the bureaucratization that had occurred since the 1909 uprising, these women had just unseated their local officers and replaced them with a more responsive and sexually integrated group. Flush with their new power, they began agitating for another general strike to revive the spirit of labor militancy in the shirtwaist and dress trades.[63]

ILGWU president Abraham Rosenberg was not pleased. When the ILGWU needed militant rank-and-file members to spur organization, he and others in the union leadership were willing to tolerate fiery women organizers like Lemlich. But once a trade was organized they had no more use for shop-floor militancy, which they felt got in the way of the union's capacity to negotiate with employers. That was true enough. Union officials' leverage with employers depended on their ability to control their rank and file.

But militancy, once stirred, was not always easy to contain. On January 5, 1913, thousands of women waistmakers and male tailors literally smashed down the doors of the New York Hippodrome after being told by the ILGWU leadership that they could not vote on whether a general strike would be called in their trades. Inside the Hippodrome, a select group of rank and file were about to vote. To prevent a riot, the crowd was allowed to enter the meeting hall. After a loud and clamorous meeting, the decision to strike was made at a peak of emotional intensity. But the ensuing strike was anticlimactic.[64]

Rather than allowing the strikers to set their own demands, ILGWU president Rosenberg and secretary John Dyche secretly negotiated a deal with several large employers that undercut both the shop-floor militants and small manufacturers. Management agreed to allow a short strike to placate the workers and crush small competitors; the union agreed to end the strike quickly if employers signed a protocol in the dress trade guaranteeing minimum wage standards. As the two sides had arranged, the strike was called off after only three days.[65]

When the settlement was announced to one group of Italian strikers at

Cooper Union, four thousand women rioted. Outraged that a deal had been struck in advance of the strike and without the knowledge of the rank and file, they called the protocol a "frame-up" and protested by sitting down on Third Avenue and stopping traffic. In another meeting on nearby St. Mark's Place, the settlement was met with jeers and stomping of feet. Though a majority would ultimately agree to support the protocol, it was only a bare majority, and a sullen one at that. Nearly half the women strikers delivered a no-confidence vote to ILGWU leaders. The leaders, women shop-floor militants said angrily, preferred to deal with employers rather than with their own members.[66]

That elitism would become characteristic of the ILGWU leadership. The male officers, sitting atop a largely female rank and file, perceived themselves to have little in common with the workers they were supposed to represent. They ignored the loud cries of protest against the protocol, asserting that there was no real discontent among the workers, only a plot by the rival Industrial Workers of the World to destroy the union. (The IWW was an anarcho-syndicalist industrial union with great appeal among Italian workers.) They would make similar charges over the next half century, writing off every shop-floor movement for democratization of the union as a power play by the Communist Party.[67]

The women militants were angry not only because their drive to democratize the union had been crushed but because the protocol was a mixed blessing. It facilitated organizing (Local 25 shot up to twenty-three thousand members after it was signed), guaranteed a minimum wage for every job in the trade, and gave the Joint Board of Sanitary Control greater power to ensure safe, healthy working conditions in the shops. But it also institutionalized a sex-based division of labor in which only men could be hired to fill the highest-paid positions and only women could be placed in the lowest-paid jobs. Further, the protocol guaranteed men higher wages than women even in jobs open to both. Union recognition and a guaranteed minimum wage unquestionably improved the day-to-day conditions under which most shirtwaist and dressmakers labored. But it drastically limited the power of the average worker.[68]

While they were crushing militancy among the already-organized shirtwaist makers and dressmakers, the leaders tolerated it among the still-unorganized white goods workers, recognizing reluctantly that there was no other way to bring them into the union. After long years of union indifference in the face of painstaking shop-floor organizing, particularly by Rose Schneiderman and Fannia Cohn, the young white goods workers were ready to rise.[69]

The ensuing strike was in many ways reminiscent of the 1909 uprising. Once again, a group of supposedly "unorganizable" young women workers surprised everyone—that is, everyone except the women who'd organized them—by launching a mass strike involving almost thirty thousand workers. As in 1909, the young strikers captured the attention and support of middle- and upper-class women reformers in New York. Here again, the galvanizing issue was police violence. Rose Schneiderman, chief organizer of the strike, asked New York's mayor, "Red Mike" Hylan, to deputize fifty women trade unionists to arrest strongmen hired by employers to break into meetings and attack the strikers. Hylan refused, claiming that it would be scandalous for New York City to deputize women.[70]

As they had four years earlier, some of New York City's most affluent women stemmed the violence. A group of Barnard College women announced that they would walk picket lines daily to monitor physical abuse of strikers by police and hired guards. Progressive feminist Fola La Follette, daughter of Senator Robert La Follette, mobilized a group of suffragists to accompany strikers to jail. During one night in jail La Follette collected enough evidence to convince her father to sponsor a congressional resolution calling for an investigation of conditions in the garment trades.[71]

The bulk of the young strikers lived at the poverty level and had little money to pool for strike funds, so many went hungry during the strike. Rose Pastor Stokes, the former cigar maker who married millionaire J. G. Phelps Stokes and converted him to Socialism, opened five lunchrooms around the city where strikers could eat free of charge. And in a gesture that reminded the city how young these labor militants were, society sisters L. C. and Joanna Hartshorn hosted huge chocolate cake parties for thousands of white goods workers. The girl strikers, many of whom were not yet fifteen, were thrilled at a chance to put on their best dresses and attend a party.[72]

Also reminiscent of the 1909 strike, elite feminists flocked to the picket lines to convince strikers of the importance of the vote. The Women's Political Union, a suffragist group, sponsored regular entertainment for white goods workers; held at Cooper Union, these events infused classical music with a women's rights message. On one occasion Madame Carrigues, a Colorado suffragist and philanthropist and founder of the Carrigues Grand Opera Trio, taught her young audience to sing "the women's Marseillaise."[73]

New York progressives sought to use the strike to dramatize the need for industrial reform. The National Consumer League's Frances Perkins published a letter in the *New York Times* urging union leaders and employers to remember the Triangle Shirtwaist Factory fire when negotiating the strikers' safety demands. The unquestioned publicity high point for progressives came when former president Theodore Roosevelt decided to visit the strikers. The *New York Times* reported the aging warrior's act of benevolence with obvious relish. Facing a room full of teenage girls, TR raised his hand for silence. "Now young ladies," he intoned, "I want to know all about your lives; how you work and how you manage to be cheerful. Just gather around me and tell your stories!" Roosevelt's words were translated into Spanish, Italian, Turkish, and Greek, reflecting the variety of nationalities employed in the trade.[74]

As Roosevelt sat on a desk and swung his feet, the girls pressed around him and told their personal stories: a sixteen-year-old Spaniard talked about working thirteen-hour days; a seventeen-year-old Italian told him about the exorbitant sums girls were required to pay for their own sewing machines; and a fifteen-year-old Jewish girl said she made only $3.50 a week because she was penalized for not working on the Sabbath. "This is crushing the future motherhood of the country," Roosevelt concluded. "It must be stopped. It is too horrible for words." When one teenager ended her story with a plea that the girls be allowed to sing at work, Roosevelt muttered under his breath: "The brutes, to prevent them from singing if they can be cheerful under such conditions." His visit greatly increased sympathetic publicity of the strike.[75]

Such publicity portrayed the strikers as children in need of protection and moved New York progressives to work harder for the passage of labor laws that would protect them. But like their older sisters in the shirtwaist trade, the teenage white goods workers saw the strike a bit differently. They had begun to feel capable of protecting themselves. Newman described the strike as these young women's first lesson in "the school of solidarity." "With what enthusiasm they took up the first lessons of the class struggle! Picketing, getting arrested, remaining nights in jail, arguing with their employers, defying the police, and getting back at the hired thugs; presiding at shop meetings, calling the roll, and learning to rely upon themselves. Young and inexperienced as these girls are, their strength of character is simply remarkable. They have learned in the past five weeks to do their own thinking . . . and to use it for themselves and their class."[76]

In the illustrated pages of the *Ladies' Garment Worker*, Newman introduced readers to young women like seventeen-year-old Minnie Labetsky, whose employer offered to bring her mother to America if she would cross the picket line. "I would rather die than go back to work, to scab," Minnie reportedly vowed. (A smiling photo of Minnie accompanies her story.) Then there was Newman's personal favorite, Lillie Lavy, "pet of the strikers," a poet who struck a decidedly bohemian pose for her photo. Lavy wrote picket-line poetry that decried the gap between rich and poor. "Who knows but that girls like Lillie, if given a chance, would surprise the world by showing themselves capable of serving society better by writing or painting than by making corset covers," Newman wrote.[77]

Demonstrating their newfound confidence, these workers rejected the instructions of union leaders and turned down a partial settlement offer. Instead, as one witness reported, "girls of sixteen and seventeen developed remarkable powers of oratory as they sprang to the platform to urge their sisters to stand out for full union recognition." Two-thirds voted against accepting any settlement that stopped short of that. Then they returned to the picket lines to continue the fight.

Six weeks into the strike, a protocol agreement modeled on that of the shirtwaist and dress trade was signed. Again the workers greeted the victory as a mixed success. Fannia Cohn's union, Local 41, joined the rebellious waistmakers in Local 25 as the strongest voices for women's militancy in the ILGWU. These two locals, forged under extreme circumstances on the picket line and in the face of serious police brutality, became the first unions in the country to create joint grievance and wage scale boards on which women workers negotiated with management. Cohn represented her local on the boards. This new women's leadership promised to work to get more women into executive positions in the union. Fannia Cohn would be the first woman to achieve that rank.[78]

In 1915, Cohn was hired by the ILGWU to try to unionize Chicago's dressmakers. She led a successful strike and, in August 1915, won a charter for the city's first dressmakers' union. This feat, which Rose Schneiderman had failed to accomplish, moved a Chicago reporter to call Cohn "one of labor's shrewdest diplomats." The Chicago Dressmakers' Union voted to send their organizer to the 1916 ILGWU convention. There, at age thirty-one, Fannia M. Cohn became the first woman vice president of a U.S. union. Her election was the outgrowth of a movement by shop-floor militants to elect the first woman to the union's General Executive Board.[79]

Perhaps sensing that there might be resentment about the fact that the first woman to hold such high office in the U.S. labor movement was a daughter of the middle class, Cohn would later insist that she was drafted. She described a scene of jubilation after her election in which women delegates danced around her holding hands and singing revolutionary songs. "The only silent and confused observer was I," she wrote, "because I . . . realized the responsibility that was mine. I . . . then solemnly resolved that never, never would these women and men resent the confidence they placed in me." But Mary Goff, who knew Cohn from the white goods strike, recalled her colleague as neither passive nor confused at the 1916 convention. Goff believed that Cohn wanted the vice presidency badly and says she campaigned hard for it. These conflicting reminiscences illuminate the complicated relationship that existed even then between Cohn and the union to which she would devote her life.[80]

After almost a decade of intensive strike work, Cohn, Schneiderman, Newman, and Lemlich began to turn their energies from street-level organizing to institution building. But memories of those years of mass strikes stayed with these organizers as they and their movement matured. In later years, bitter infighting would tear apart both the labor and women's movements within the United States, pitting former industrial feminist allies against one another. But even as they parted over strategy, women of the 1909 vintage would remain bound together by that shared vision forged in the turbulent years after 1909. For the four women, political organizing would always be—as Rose Schneiderman put it in 1912—a struggle for both bread and roses. During the second half of the 1910s they would see the realization of one important step toward that goal, as working-class women joined the struggle to win the vote for American women.

Above: The Newman family in Lithuania, ca. 1900. Nine-year-old Pauline Newman is in front, holding a book. (Courtesy of Elisabeth Burger)

Left: Clara Lemlich in her midteens, relaxing with a book in the Ukraine, ca. 1902–3 (Courtesy of Evelyn Velson)

Fannia Cohn, the young revolutionary, in Minsk, ca. 1903– 4 (Fannia Cohn Papers, Rare Books and Manuscripts Division, New York Public Library)

Rose Schneiderman in New York. This picture was taken during the capmaker's general strike of 1905. (Rose Schneiderman Collection, Tamiment Institute Library, New York University)

The New York Herald *ran this photograph in recognition of the "girl leaders" of the 1907 Lower East Side rent strike. Pauline Newman, age sixteen, is on the far right. (Courtesy of Elisabeth Burger)*

This drawing ran in the New York Evening Journal *during the autumn of 1909, on the eve of the shirtwaist makers' "uprising." Clara Lemlich is in the front row, the first woman from the right who is wearing a hat. (Tamiment Institute Library, New York University)*

During the 1909 shirtwaist makers' strike—the largest strike of women in the United States to that time—hundreds of young women garment workers hit the streets to sell copies of a special edition of the New York Call, *the city's Socialist newspaper. The Socialist Party had donated the paper free of charge to the strikers to help them raise money for the strike fund. (International Ladies' Garment Workers' Union Archives, Cornell University)*

Clara Lemlich, shirtwaist maker, spark of the 1909 uprising (Courtesy of Martha Schaffer)

Meeting at the New York Women's Trade Union League during the 1909 strike. Standing: second from left, *Helen Marot;* fifth from left, *Rose Schneiderman.* Seated: second from right, *Leonora O'Reilly, on the telephone (Tamiment Institute Library, New York University)*

On March 25, 1911, at the Triangle Shirtwaist Factory, 146 young workers died in one of the worst industrial fires ever. Clara Lemlich, a former Triangle employee, was one of hundreds of New Yorkers who searched among the bodies of the victims to see if any of the dead were relatives or friends. (Tamiment Institute Library, New York University)

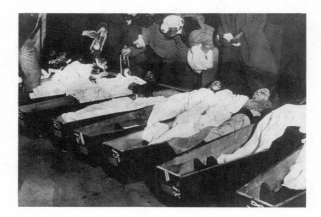

84

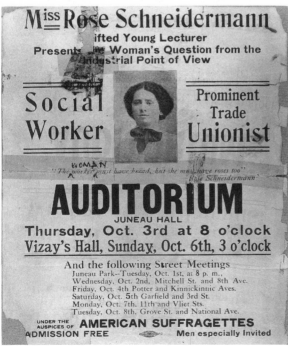

*Above: Rose Schneiderman
was the most popular speaker
employed by Harriot Stanton
Blatch's wage earners' suffrage
organization, the Equality
League of Self-Supporting
Women. Here, Blatch is
introducing Schneiderman at a
rally. (Rose Schneiderman
Collection, Tamiment Institute
Library, New York
University)*

*Left: Handbill announcing a
speech by Rose Schneiderman
for the American Suffragettes,
1914 (Rose Schneiderman
Collection, Tamiment Institute
Library, New York
University)*

Pauline Newman entertains the strikers, 1912, Kalamazoo, Michigan. (International Ladies' Garment Workers' Archives, Cornell University)

Halloween Party, New York Women's Trade Union League, 1913. Rose Schneiderman is the woman standing on the right; Pauline Newman, in mustache, is the woman seated on the left. (Courtesy of Elisabeth Burger)

COMMON SENSE: NEW YORK CITY WORKING WOMEN AND THE STRUGGLE FOR WOMAN SUFFRAGE

Surely . . . women won't lose any more of their beauty and charm by putting a ballot in a ballot box once a year than they are likely to lose stand-ing in foundries or laundries all year round.

—Rose Schneiderman

Man as a class has ruled women. He wants to make her think that it is good for her that he rules her, but it is too late. We are here, Sena-tors. We are 800,000 strong in New York State alone.

—Clara Lemlich

For the vast majority of the young women who participated in the strikes of 1909–15, political ac-tivism was a passing involvement, inflamed by the passion of youth and soon discarded in favor of career or family responsibilities. For some, like waistmaker Fannie Zinsher, who was portrayed in the press along with Lemlich and Newman as a leader of the 1909 strike, involvement in trade unionism would be remembered as a youthful indis-cretion. "I was very young at the time," Zinsher wrote many years later, "and it was my first and last experience in the industrial field. All I remember is that it was a very trying experience and now it seems like a nightmare of long ago."[1]

But for other young women organizers, like Clara Lemlich, Fannia Cohn, Rose Schneiderman, and Pauline Newman, those militant years were revela-tory. The excitement of picket lines, street-corner meetings, and strategic debates was addictive. De-spite the attendant difficulties and frustrations, ac-tivism became a way of life. But as the years wore on, the four began to look beyond the immediacy of strikes and protests, toward longer-term and larger-scale changes. In the aftermath of the Triangle fire, few things seemed more pressing than enacting laws to ameliorate the gravest hazards of industrial labor.

Toward that end, Schneiderman, Newman, Lem-lich, and Cohn joined the campaign for women's suffrage in the 1910s. Without the vote, they argued, American working women would remain dependent on others to pass laws that concerned them. With it, they could make their first strides toward taking control of their own lives. Years of community and labor movement activism had made the four keenly aware that the interests of working women were distinct from those of working men and of women reformers. And because economic and political power imbalances put working women at a disadvantage when they allied with either group, their own unique concerns were rarely voiced. The attraction of suffrage was simple: well-orchestrated use of the vote promised to increase their power and independence in relation to employers, to the state, and to their often-manipulative allies.

The simple but powerful allure of the vote drew working women into the suffrage movement in great numbers during the second decade of the century. With their militancy and youthful energy, they revitalized a movement that had gone stale, helping to provide the surge that finally pushed woman suffrage over the top in 1920. Their interest in the vote and in legislative solutions to working women's problems was piqued during the 1909–15 strikes by exposure to wealthy suffragists like Alva Belmont and to the middle-class suffragists in the Women's Trade Union League. But their attraction to suffrage predated their participation in cross-class women's alliances, and their reasons for seeking the vote were their own. Asserting their difference and their equality, they argued that working women were the real experts on working women and should be given a voice in making the policies that affected them. That, they insisted, was just common sense.

As early as 1907, Rose Schneiderman had articulated a working woman's suffrage position at the First Convention of Women Trade Unionists. "It is the belief of the Trade Union Women . . . that the time has come when working women . . . must be enfranchised and so secure political power to shape their own labor conditions." But winning the vote was only the first stage in a more fundamental transformation.[2]

Industrial feminism posited a reciprocal relationship between economic and political rights. As Schneiderman saw it, the vote was an essential tool if working women were to free themselves "from the drudgeries and worries which come with long hours and low wages." But "industrial citizenship"— decent wages, safe conditions, reasonable hours—would be only the first victory in working women's battle to win their larger "right to citizenship." Schneiderman envisioned that right as a complex entitlement that included "the right to be born well, the right to a carefree and happy childhood, the right to education, the right to mental, physical and spiritual growth and development."[3]

This assertion of their entitlements as women, as workers, and as citizens created conflicts between working women and their allies. There were clashes with middle- and upper-class feminists who sought to dictate working women's politics and with men in the labor and Socialist movements whose votes women were forced to campaign for. Painful and draining, these conflicts were also fruitful because they helped working-class suffragists to clarify the issues of greatest concern to the working women they represented: good wages, safe conditions, and shorter hours; an end to sex-based pay differentials and segregation of the labor force; equal access to education; and greater power within the labor unions. Tying these goals to the attainment of woman suffrage, Schneiderman, Newman, Lemlich, and Cohn fleshed out the contours of the industrial feminist vision.

The early 1910s were a time of tremendous expansion and excitement in the suffrage movement. A restrained and refined style of campaigning was beginning to give way to a more outrageous and colorful one, featuring parades, street-corner rallies, and civil disobedience. The surge of energy and militancy that culminated in the passage of the Nineteenth Amendment in 1920 has often been attributed to the influence of British suffragists. British women's penchant for headline-grabbing activities, such as hunger strikes, and their flamboyance on speaking tours through the United States did generate great excitement among American suffragists. But there was another vitally important source of fresh energy that has been almost entirely overlooked in analyses of the U.S. woman's suffrage movement: working-class women, who brought to the movement both a new perspective on suffrage and a provocative, street-smart campaign style.[4]

Their suffrage agitation, shaped by their lives as women and as workers, was the very opposite of genteel. Custom-tailored by and for their own class, it was gritty, sarcastic, and confrontational. That tone is captured in snapshots that provide an important counterpoint to the silk-stocking image of the women's suffrage movement: Rose Schneiderman bringing tears to the eyes of hardened union men on her suffrage swing through the industrial cities of Ohio; Clara Lemlich on a soapbox outside factory doors, enlivening weary women workers with a stump speech or relishing her verbal duels with jeering men coming off their shifts; Pauline Newman addressing immigrant housewives on Lower East Side street corners or holding heartfelt, late-night talks about suffrage with cold and ragged Illinois coal-mining families.

Time and again they assured listeners that fighting for women's suffrage was not a distraction from the class struggle but a part of it. Even Fannia Cohn, who was not as passionate a suffragist as the others, made this case. Although Cohn was more interested in changing consciousness than in changing laws, she argued for suffrage to enhance the power of the working class.[5]

But there were limitations to their empowerment argument. While working-class suffragists ceaselessly hammered away at themes of class and gender in their speeches, they virtually ignored questions of ethnicity and race. They may have followed this strategy in part because they believed that the vote could unite working women across ethnic lines; thus they avoided such potentially divisive issues as ethnicity, religion, and race. Perhaps, too, they sought to downplay their immigrant backgrounds in the interest of seeming more American. Whatever their reasoning, it is striking that these immigrant women failed even to raise the questions of ethnicity and race in their suffrage campaigns. This omission is surprising given their own experience with anti-Semitism. It is astonishing given that high-profile U.S. suffragists were then demanding the vote to counteract the influence of "all the riff-raff of Europe that is poured upon our shores."[6]

In the end, industrial feminists' avoidance of race in their suffrage arguments must be seen as a willful narrowness of vision. Afforded the luxury to ignore race, they did. The matter could not simply have escaped their notice. Racist justifications for giving women the vote were at least as common as xenophobic ones. Indeed, the National American Woman Suffrage Association (NAWSA), the country's largest suffrage group, had adopted a policy intended to appease its southern members: during an era when southern states actively blocked blacks from voting, NAWSA declared that each state should have the power to decide who could vote. Working-class suffragists must have been aware of those policies as well as contemporaneous struggles by African American women, who sought the vote in order to combat Jim Crow segregation laws and to pass a federal antilynching bill.[7]

Still, their failure to address these issues was probably more a question of focus than a conscious political decision. For white working-class women like Newman, Schneiderman, Lemlich, and Cohn, commitment to suffrage was deeply rooted in their personal experience as workers and as residents of overcrowded slum neighborhoods. Their paramount concern was to improve the intolerable conditions under which they lived and labored. Despite their own experiences with anti-Semitism and xenophobia, most working-class suffragists in New York seemed to identify class and gender, not their immigrant Jewish or Catholic backgrounds, as the primary sources of their oppression. And they were not wrong. Xenophobic and anti-Semitic comments were not, after all, comparable to the codified racist legal structure of Jim Crow.

When working-class suffragists encountered explicit racism, they often confronted it squarely—as at the 1909 national WTUL convention, when a San Francisco delegate called for a resolution to ban Asians from the United States. In response, Rose Schneiderman rose to deliver a blistering denunciation of racism. "The movement we stand for is the brotherhood of man, and we are not going to exclude certain people from that brotherhood on the account of color, degree or caste." Schneiderman responded, too, when African American women asked Local 25 to help them get jobs in the garment industry after the 1909 strike. In addition to helping individual women, she prodded the League to declare its intent to reach out to African American women in large numbers. She wasn't the League's only civil rights advocate; Leonora O'Reilly was an active member of the National Association for the Advancement of Colored People (NAACP).[8]

But neither Schneiderman nor other working-class white suffragists argued for the vote as a weapon to improve the condition of black Americans. And it was not until suffrage was won that they or the League made a serious effort to unionize blacks. Industrial feminists would become more vocal on the issue of race by the end of the decade. Indeed, after 1920 they would lead the way among white trade unionists in their efforts to reach out to black women workers. But during the early 1910s, their suffrage arguments were limited by a shop-floor and community experience that was overwhelmingly white.[9]

There were other limitations to the working-class suffrage argument. Skeptical suffragists like Fannia Cohn believed that suffrage was, by definition, a surface-level reform. Certain problems were difficult to legislate away, she warned, and would still have to be addressed after the vote was won: women's lack of self-confidence; the assumption by employers and union leaders that women would leave jobs after they married; sexual harassment on the job; and sexism in society and in the labor movement. The vote was just a small first step.

Still, by the early 1910s, most working-class women organizers had come to see the vote as essential to their empowerment. Clara Lemlich explained why:

The manufacturer has a vote; the bosses have votes; the foremen have votes, the inspectors have votes. The working girl has no vote. When she asks to have a building in which she must work made clean and safe, the officials do not have to listen. When she asks not to work such long hours, they do not have to listen. The bosses can say to the officials: "Our votes put you in office. . . . Never mind what they say[,] . . . they can't do anything." That is true. For until the men in the Legislature at Albany represent her as well as the bosses and the foremen, she will not get justice; she will not get fair conditions. That is why the working-woman now says that she must have the vote.[10]

NEW YORK CITY GARMENT WORKERS IN THE
WOMAN SUFFRAGE MOVEMENT, 1907–1920

Prior to the early twentieth century, most U.S. working women had responded ambivalently at best to the arguments made by middle- and upper-class suffragists. It was therefore surprising to just about everyone when a working-class suffrage movement appeared in New York in the 1910s. A variety of factors account for its rise. Perhaps most important was the emergence for the first time of a solid core of working-class suffrage organizers, among whom Schneiderman, Newman, Lemlich, and O'Reilly were the most prominent. In the eyes of working people, these well-known trade unionists lent immeasurable credibility to the campaign for women's suffrage.

The new working-class suffrage movement was further catalyzed by the militancy of young women garment workers between 1909 and 1915 and by the unusually sympathetic interaction the women's garment strikes promoted between workers and middle-class feminists. This convergence created both strength and discord. Middle- and upper-class women provided money to pay wage-earning women to agitate for women's suffrage, and they helped working women establish political contacts. But they were surprised and offended when the organizers they had helped used the language of class struggle to argue for their right to vote. From its inception, the working women's suffrage movement spoke in a distinctly different voice from that used by more affluent suffragists. That voice has been largely drowned out in histories of the women's suffrage movement. Only by restoring it can we gain an accurate understanding of the decade before the vote was won.

As suffrage historians have illustrated, middle-class arguments for suffrage changed dramatically between the Seneca Falls Equal Rights Convention of 1848 and the passage of the Nineteenth Amendment in 1920. Mid-nineteenth-century suffrage claims were based on notions of innate and inalienable human rights. In that egalitarian spirit, Elizabeth Cady Stanton and Susan B. Anthony attempted to bring working women into the suffrage movement as early as the 1860s.

After the Civil War they began seeking support from trade union federations, including the National Labor Union (NLU). Their overtures sparked a debate about suffrage among unionized women shoe workers in New England, but no real cross-class alliance developed. A few members of the women shoe workers' union, the Daughters of St. Crispin, argued that laboring women needed the vote. But male NLU members overwhelmingly opposed women's suffrage. And many women workers echoed the sentiments of the stitcher "Tryphosia," who wrote to the *Lynn (Massachusetts) Record* in 1874 that class unity was too important to endanger by suggesting that working women were not effectively represented by their husbands, fathers, and brothers.[11]

By the late nineteenth century there was little pretense of cross-class solidarity in the suffrage movement. Important middle-class suffrage leaders, including Stanton, had grown increasingly elitist in their views. Stanton called for educational restrictions on who could vote. Some younger suffrage leaders, like Carrie Chapman Catt, strayed even farther from the old arguments for innate equality, echoing racist diatribes about the "menace" of "the ignorant foreign vote." At the same time, wealthy suffragists like Alva Belmont, Anne Morgan, and Mary Putnam Jacobi suggested that elite women might use the vote to increase the influence of "the better sort" in city, state, and federal governments. Such arguments further alienated working women from the U.S. suffrage movement.[12]

There was, however, one philosophical strain of the suffrage movement that attracted them: the reform-oriented feminism of women like settlement house pioneer Jane Addams, National Consumer League secretary Florence Kelley, and New York WTUL founders Mary and Margaret Dreier. These Progressives were sympathetic to young women workers and shared their commitment to industrial reform. Their arguments were pragmatic and specific: women voters, they believed, could enact a wide range of social and political changes, from prohibiting child labor to abolishing war. That vision encouraged working-class women to think not only about voting and lobbying but about working within government.

The alliance was tricky, however, for the lives of even sympathetic middle-class reformers were so far removed from the average working woman that the gap between them sometimes seemed unbridgeable. At times Florence Kelley's arguments sounded nearly identical to those of Schneiderman or Newman. As early as the 1890s she had insisted that working women deserved the vote because they had "the right to a voice in their own affairs." But she was also capable of referring to the questionable political judgment of "the ignorant, illiterate, debased foreign women."[13]

Such characterizations convinced working-class suffragists that they needed to speak for themselves. Their message was simple: through careful wielding of the vote, they could finally force legislators and employers to heed their concerns. The advantages of enfranchisement seemed painfully obvious to wage-earning suffragists like Pauline Newman. Decades later, remembering how irritated she felt when male Socialists and trade unionists would ask her why she was bothering with such a paltry goal, Newman grew annoyed all over again. "I was a woman, I worked and I had a brain," she recalled tersely. Radical men could afford to dismiss the vote; they already had it. Just because they were struggling to attain the same privilege, Newman argued, in no way diminished working women's commitment to Socialism or to gaining more power in and through their unions.[14]

Newman and Schneiderman had begun actively campaigning for women's suffrage well before "mink brigade" suffragists like Alva Belmont began proselytizing working women during the 1909 shirtwaist strike. Newman had used her 1908 run as the Socialist Party's candidate for secretary of state of New York to raise consciousness among Socialists about women's suffrage. And Schneiderman had begun talking to working women about the vote as early as 1907, when she was drawn into the suffrage movement by WTUL member Harriot Stanton Blatch.[15]

Blatch, one of Elizabeth Cady Stanton's daughters, had spent twenty years in England, where she came to believe that the poor should have a voice in improving their own living and working conditions. She opposed her mother's support for educational restrictions and was offended both by anti-immigrant suffrage arguments and by the notion that wealthy women should use the vote to take care of the "little daughters of the poor," as Anne Morgan called them. Insisting that the poor could offer more realistic solutions to their problems than the rich, Blatch founded the Equality League of Self-Supporting Women to attract working women to the suffrage movement.[16]

Rose Schneiderman quickly became the Equality League's most popular speaker, and Leonora O'Reilly became its first vice president. These two Socialist firebrands, both known for their eloquence, infused Blatch's organization with verve and helped transform New York suffragism from a parlor project into a militant streetwise movement. Schneiderman also brought the first factory workers into the ranks of the Equality League, which had been dominated by influential intellectuals like Charlotte Perkins Gilman and Florence Kelley. By convincing her Capmakers Union local and other women's unions to affiliate, she hoped to alter the deeply middle-class character of the organization.[17]

Schneiderman's success with the Equality League brought her to the attention of the American Suffragettes. Formed by actresses, teachers, writers, and social workers, the American Suffragettes were generally less affluent than the members of the Equality League. Schneiderman became a featured speaker at American Suffragette street meetings. At her suggestion, they became the first suffrage organization to distribute literature in Yiddish to the women of the Lower East Side.[18]

But tensions inevitably developed between the two classes of working women involved in suffrage agitation. By 1910, the Equality League included both trade union women, who wanted to pass labor legislation, and inspectors and administrators for city and state government, who framed and enforced those laws. To a lesser extent, these same tensions divided the American Suffragettes. Professional women—who were, by and large, well educated, economically comfortable, and native-born—had a different view of sexual equality than did factory workers.

These differences foreshadowed the bitter divisions that would emerge after suffrage was won, when the National Woman's Party (NWP) called for an Equal Rights Amendment. Such conflicts stemmed largely from class-based power differentials: professional and upper-class women sought equal access to the power, money, and prestige that their husbands and brothers already wielded. Working-class women wanted to use the vote to redistribute that power to the working class as a whole.

The speeches and writings of working-class suffragists echoed the philosophy of one of their mentors, former cloakmaker Theresa Malkiel. In 1908, Malkiel described the Socialist woman's view of suffrage: "The ballot, though an absolute necessity in her struggle for freedom, is only one of the aims toward her goal. We cannot renovate a garment by turning over one of the sleeves—the whole of it must be turned inside out. And this renovation is possible under a Socialist regime only."[19]

This view, which put the vote in the service of Socialism, was simply not acceptable to most members of even the sympathetic suffrage organizations. More than most mainstream suffragists, Harriot Stanton Blatch appreciated the contribution of working-class women to the early-twentieth-century women's movement. She believed that "it is the women of the industrial class . . . who have been the means of bringing about the altered attitude of public opinion toward women's work in every sphere of life." But she was not comfortable with the class-based politics of many trade union suffragists. Fearful of losing her wealthy supporters, Blatch decided to keep the Equality League free of the taint of Socialism. The American Suffragettes, too, decided to ban "socialist propaganda." Schneiderman continued to speak at Suffragette and Equality League meetings, but she had to be careful about what she said. By 1910 it was clear that factory workers would have no real say in creating policy in either organization. Indeed, during the early 1910s Socialist suffragists like Schneiderman, Newman, Lemlich, and O'Reilly were hard-pressed to find a forum for their arguments.[20]

Socialist Party leaders, though officially in favor of women's suffrage, considered the vote a bourgeois issue. Hoping to defuse the hostility and promote a rapprochement between suffragism and Socialism, Pauline Newman and other Socialist suffragists convened a party conference in December 1909. At issue was whether Socialist women should cooperate with mainstream suffrage organizations. In the months leading up to the conference, a debate raged in the *New York Call*, New York's Socialist daily. Anita Block, editor of the Women's Page, summed up the view held by Socialist suffragists: "It is very true that . . . a stronger bond exists between working women and men of their own class than between them and idle women of the leisure class. But these arguments do not do away with the fact that women are deprived of the vote as a SEX, regardless of class, and that Socialist women can never effectively help their CLASS till their SEX has been enfranchised."[21]

Still, Block believed that Socialist suffragists needed to carve out a course independent of mainstream suffrage organizations. Schneiderman and O'Reilly disagreed. Let working women freely choose their political allies, Schneiderman urged. They had too few resources, she insisted, to cut themselves off from potential supporters. As trade unionists, she and O'Reilly felt that pragmatic considerations had to supersede ideological purity.

But many Socialists feared that cooperation with "bourgeois suffragists" would give working women the false sense that the vote was all they needed, draining vitality from the class struggle. Block warned, "Freedom from sex slavery does not mean freedom from wage slavery." There is no record of how Pauline Newman voted; but given her party activism over the next few years—she organized Socialist Party suffrage meetings across the Northeast and Midwest from 1909 to 1913—it seems reasonable to assume that she sided with those who called for separate, Socialist-controlled suffrage work. Schneiderman and O'Reilly's faction was soundly defeated. Forced to choose, they would ultimately join the ranks of the mainstream suffrage movement.[22]

More immediately, the two women decided that the time had come to create a suffrage organization run by and for factory workers. On March 22, 1911— three days before the Triangle Shirtwaist Factory fire—they founded the Wage Earners' League for Woman Suffrage. Waistmakers Clara Lemlich and Mollie Schepps and laundry worker Maggie Hinchey were co-founders. O'Reilly, the group's senior member and a street-corner speaker par excellence, was elected president of the Wage Earners' League, and Clara Lemlich became its vice president. As stated in the founding document, the league's goals were threefold: "to urge working women to understand the necessity for the vote, to agitate for the vote, and to study how to use the vote when it has been acquired." Through their speeches and pamphlets, the league's organizers sought to give working women some quick civics lessons and to encourage their participation in the political process.[23]

Hoping to prevent the silencing of working women that had occurred in other suffrage organizations, the league's founders agreed that only workers could be full voting members. Other women could join, but they would have no say in shaping the league's campaigns, its literature, or its speeches. Also, the officers decided to focus their attentions on factories and immigrant neighborhoods. As a result, the league came to have a thoroughly working-class membership. However, the organization's few non-working-class members provided most of its budget and thereby wielded considerable control over its politics. They pressured Wage Earners' League officers to affiliate with the National American Woman Suffrage Association rather than their more obvious ally—the Socialist Party Women's Committee. Forced by both Socialist and mainstream suffragists to choose sides, the Wage Earners' League aligned with those who offered financial support.

While the Wage Earners' League and its affluent allies were hammering out their tenuous alliance, the Socialist Party Women's Committee began its own campaign to convert working women to suffragism. This effort was spearheaded by Theresa Malkiel and Pauline Newman. Shortly after the party's suffrage conference, Malkiel began to build a network of Socialist suffrage clubs around New York City. By the spring of 1911 there were active branches throughout Manhattan, the Bronx, Brooklyn, and Queens. The clubs, which held dances, musical performances, and rallies, had an active membership numbering in the thousands. But as Malkiel herself dispiritedly admitted, most of the women who joined these clubs were already members of the Socialist Party. Malkiel and Newman were discouraged that their message did not seem to be reaching unaffiliated working women.[24]

The Wage Earners' League had more success in that regard, largely because its leaders were talking up suffrage to the same women workers they were then unionizing. The group's success was also a tribute to the grit and explosive speaking style of its chief organizer, Clara Lemlich. Lemlich, who had been bouncing from job to job since the 1909 strike, had been hired as a full-time organizer at the behest of Jessie Ashley, a wealthy Socialist Party activist who was also, despite party proscriptions, treasurer of NAWSA. In 1911, Ashley argued in *Woman's Journal* that "if the working girls ever become really alive to their situation, they will throw themselves into the fight for the ballot in overwhelming numbers and on that day the suffrage movement will be swept forward by the forces that command progress." To hasten that day, Ashley gave historian Mary Beard money to pay the salary of a working-class suffrage organizer. Beard knew just who she would approach.[25]

During the 1909 strike, attracted by her fervor and her speaking ability, historians Charles and Mary Beard had offered Lemlich tuition for college. Torn between her desire for an education and her commitment to the movement, Lemlich refused. After the strike, when she was blacklisted by employers, Lemlich organized intermittently for the ILGWU and for the WTUL. But she could not find a full-time job. In early 1911, Mary Beard made Lemlich another offer: to advocate for suffrage in New York's union halls and immigrant neighborhoods. Lemlich eagerly accepted.[26]

Despite their high hopes, relations between the two women quickly soured. Even Beard's early enthusiasm for Lemlich displayed a trace of the condescension that would soon bring them to loggerheads. "She seems to me to be keen about it," Beard wrote to Leonora O'Reilly, "and does everything that's suggested and does it well, I think. Of course, we don't want to spoil her." Within a few months, Beard had come to regret hiring the hot-headed former shirtwaist maker. Less than one year after she had sought Lemlich out, Beard unceremoniously fired her.[27]

In a letter to O'Reilly, Beard explained her decision. She had, she said, overestimated Lemlich's ability. Now she was worried that if she waited any longer to fire her, Lemlich would not be able to find seasonal work in the garment factories. Sadly, Beard concluded, Lemlich was not cut out for greater glory than she could find behind a sewing machine.

> I am anxious to be fair to the girl and do all I can for her but it seems to me that she can't swing her job. She seems to be unequal physically to the nervous strain of organizing or speaking and you know her mental makeup without my going into that. I do not see how her future is to be a success as a speaker. If she goes on hoping until November after her factory season has begun, she may be left helpless upon my hands. . . . It has been my dream to develop working women to be a help in the awakening of their class, but Clara can't make good along the lines she has attempted this winter it seems to me. She has no initiative.[28]

Lemlich was, as might be expected, very bitter about the experience. She never singled out Beard in describing to her daughter the ups and downs of her suffrage campaigns. But Martha Schaffer recalls that her mother was still angry decades later about the patronizing attitudes of the more affluent suffragists she worked with:

> She had a hard time with some of the suffragettes because at the time of the strike and for years after that she felt that she was being manipulated by these "very rich ladies." She felt that they didn't talk about her union with the respect that they should have. They said the same things that the men did. "Oh, if they were handling it it would have been much better." And they'd say to her, "You're not so very educated. We're college born and bred. Let us tell you how to run your strike." And she was very militant about this. She was very upset about this. And she'd tell them, "Just because we're poor doesn't mean that we're dumb."[29]

Given Lemlich's uncompromising politics and prickly nature, it seems likely that her problems with Beard originated in a battle of wills. Perhaps Beard asked Lemlich to tone down the Socialist rhetoric in her speeches and the militant garment worker refused. Or maybe Beard tried to tell Lemlich how to talk to women workers and Lemlich blew up. Holding her own was a matter of principle to the former waistmaker. Her feelings were complicated by discomfort at having to depend on the largess of affluent women. Lemlich had proudly refused the Beards' offer back in 1910 to send her to college, yet she was never able to shake a sense of shame about her minimal education. As a result, she bristled at any insinuation—whether real or imagined—that affluent women's superior education gave them the right to tell her how to organize women of her own class.

Lemlich had a distorted view of how much power and privilege someone like Mary Beard, a college professor's wife, actually enjoyed. However, it is not hard to understand why. Though Beard was by no means a "very rich lady," as Lemlich described her, she nevertheless had the power to hire and fire the veteran organizer. Lemlich would continue to organize women for the rest of her life, but after her suffrage experience she decided to work only with women of her own class.

Working-class suffragists could not as easily dismiss the condescension of Socialist and trade union men, because their votes were needed to pass statewide women's suffrage referenda. At best, labor union and Socialist men were ambivalent about woman suffrage. At worst, they were openly hostile. Pauline Newman remembers Socialist men disrupting her street-corner suffrage speeches by yelling, "Why don't you go home and wash the dishes?" And devout union men pelted Clara Lemlich with rotten tomatoes when they saw her talking up suffrage to women workers outside their factories.[30]

Though the Socialist Party, the AFL, the New York State Federation of Labor, and the ILGWU all officially supported woman suffrage, individual leaders denounced working-class organizers for wasting time that should be devoted to the class struggle. Rose Schneiderman received this letter from Socialist Max Fruchter shortly after the founding of the Wage Earners' League. Fruchter admired Schneiderman and thought she was squandering her talents on a frivolous distraction.

> You cannot possibly serve two Gods—you cannot fill efficiently two places in two movements—you cannot at the same time be the chief of a great clerical force and do . . . routine work. You either work for Socialism and as a result for equality of the sexes or you work for woman suffrage only and neglect Socialism. Then you act like a bad doctor who pretends to cure his patient by removing the symptom instead of removing the disease. . . . You are approaching a dangerous place; bewildered you are misled by the phosphoric light of a paltry reform. . . . It is time to return to the solid unyielding highway of class consciousness.[31]

Schneiderman, Lemlich, Newman, and other working-class suffragists responded to such arguments with one of their own: that Socialists and trade unionists could not afford to ignore sex-based political inequality. As long as women were denied the right to vote, they insisted, the working class would be denied its full share of political power. Until that changed, it would be severely crippled in its attempts to win the most basic human rights. Rose Schneiderman recalled, "My theme in all my suffrage speeches was that I did not expect any revolution when women got the ballot, as men had had it all these years and nothing of great importance had happened. But women needed the vote because they needed protection through laws. Not having the vote, the lawmakers could ignore us."[32]

Despite such practical arguments, working-class women did sometimes see suffrage as a panacea. Perhaps they became caught up in the excitement of a seventy-year-old movement about to bear fruit. Or maybe it was a sense of pride deriving from their own successful strikes. But as this 1911 leaflet illustrates, the Wage Earners' League was not above suggesting that all manner of social ills might be cured if working women got the vote:

Why are you paid less than a man?
Why do you work in a fire trap?
Why are your hours so long?
Why are you all strap hangers when you pay for a seat?
Why do you pay the most rent for the worst houses?
Why do your children go into factories?
Why don't you get a square deal in the courts?
BECAUSE YOU ARE A WOMAN AND HAVE NO VOTE.
VOTES MAKE THE LAW
VOTES ENFORCE THE LAW
THE LAW CONTROLS CONDITIONS
WOMEN WHO WANT BETTER CONDITIONS MUST VOTE[33]

This leaflet, like everything the Wage Earners' League published, consciously appealed to housewives as well as to wage-earning women. Organizers hoped that involvement in the women's suffrage movement would be an education for all working-class women, including those who were not involved in the labor movement. In a handbill to publicize Suffrage Week, September 1–9, 1911, the organization spoke directly to working-class housewives, trying to spark their interest in the larger good.[34] The handbill asked women: Would you ensure child welfare for "all children everywhere" or only your own children at home? Do you want "pure food from cow to kitchen" or in the kitchen only? Would you bring about clean streets and lowered cost of living "by direct action on laws and lawmakers" or by indirect influence? Don't you think "equal pay for all women who toil" should be a given rather than a privilege? Can you bring about the "abolition of white slave traffic" by "fighting it [or] by ignoring it"? Do you want "sanitary conditions for homes, factories, shops" or for your home only? Do you want peace in the home or "throughout the world"?[35]

It is difficult to know how effective such leaflets were; there is no record of the response to them. What is clear from officers' records is that the Wage Earners' League did not have the money to print more than an occasional leaflet or handbill. Unable to match the flamboyant displays of some of New York's more affluent suffrage organizations, the working-class suffrage movement won new adherents largely on the strength of its talented speakers. Too poor to rent meeting halls, the group capitalized on the crowded street corners of New York neighborhoods and relied on relatively small outdoor meetings as its primary organizing tool. Immigrants were comfortable with street meetings; they provided free entertainment as well as information, and they were much more conducive to audience participation than formal theater settings.

During 1911 and 1912, Clara Lemlich, Leonora O'Reilly, and Mollie Schepps spoke regularly outside factories as shifts were changing. At night they went into workers' neighborhoods, where their words would reach housewives coming home from their shopping. O'Reilly, who Newman said "sounded as though she had tears in her voice," and Lemlich, whose Yiddish was described by one reporter as "eloquent even to American ears," knew how to get even harried mothers to stop and listen. They told wrenching stories about the misfortunes and humiliations of poor women and painted dazzling visions of the change that would be possible if those same women were given the vote.[36]

As prosuffrage enthusiasm built among working women, the leaders of the Wage Earners' League began to feel that they had enough support to pull off a mass meeting. With funding from the Collegiate Equal Suffrage League, another group of middle-class allies, Wage Earners' League officers planned a rally to protest the New York State legislature's failure to pass a resolution endorsing women's suffrage. The rally was structured in an interesting way. Rather than giving a series of random speeches, O'Reilly, Lemlich, Schneiderman, and several other working-class speakers would each take on an argument made by one of the state senators who had spoken against suffrage.

The handbill promised an entertaining evening as the league's best speakers answered the "sentimentality of New York Senators" with the "common sense of working women." Setting the tone for the event, the leaflet sought to generate anger and excitement: "They forgot all about the 400,000 working women in New York City. They forgot the 800,000 working women in New York State. Come just to show the gentlemen we have arrived."[37]

Wage Earners' League supporters leafleted the factory districts in the weeks preceding the event. The result was an overflow crowd, composed almost entirely of working women. On the night of April 22, 1912, Cooper Union's Great Hall of the People—where, two and a half years earlier, the waistmakers had begun their uprising—was once again filled with thousands of cheering women. The speakers were witty, sarcastic, and impassioned. Though they focused on different issues, each speaker ultimately returned to the theme that was at the heart of every working-class argument for suffrage: women's need for independence. The working woman could not and should not, they argued, depend on anyone else to protect her. She had to watch out for herself, and the vote would enable her to do that.[38]

That night, industrial feminists laid out the "commonsense" argument for suffrage in all its dimensions, while aggressively debunking antisuffrage views that were based on what they considered romantic nonsense about women. Several of the senators had waxed poetic about the need to protect women from the vote, saying it would disturb marital harmony, sully female moral purity, and rob women of their femininity. Speakers warned that such flowery notions disguised an ironclad trap used to keep working women powerless and voiceless.

Shirtwaist organizer Mollie Schepps, who had entered the public eye as a leader of the 1909 strike, challenged one senator's claim that "there is nobody to whom I yield in respect and admiration and devotion to the sex." Reminding the audience of the brutal treatment the striking waistmakers had received at the hands of New York City police and judges, Schepps retorted, "This is the kind of respect, admiration and devotion we receive from our admirers . . . when we fight for a better condition and a decent wage."[39] There are some, Schepps continued, who claim that if women's salaries were made equal to men's, women would be more likely to work outside the home, thus degrading the sanctity of marriage. "If long, miserable hours and starvation wages are the only means men can find to encourage marriage," she observed dryly, "it is a very poor compliment to themselves."[40]

Clara Lemlich answered the legislator who claimed that "we want to relieve women of the burdens and responsibilities of life." Not every woman worker has the option of being financially supported, Lemlich began. In New York City alone, she asserted, there were tens of thousands of single working women, divorced women, and widows with children. The senators don't even pretend to care about their burdens, she declared. "Have men relieved women of their burdens and responsibilities? I don't think so." Terrible factory conditions degrade relations between men and women far more than women's suffrage ever could, she argued, by forcing women into bad marriages: "Many a girl who has worked years at a machine trying to live decently, at last sees the only way to get out of the factory is to think of marriage. Now how do you like such a marriage? She is ready to give herself to any man who will make the offer!" Even in good marriages, Lemlich insisted, few working-class women could be described as free of burdens or responsibilities. Indeed, many of them have to work in factories in addition to taking care of their homes. "I am sorry to say that there are thousands of working girls who are soon disappointed, because many girls, thousands of girls, right after they are married have to go back into the factory because their husbands are not making enough to keep them; out she goes to the factory to help carry the man's burdens as well as her own. When she has children she has to be the mother to the children, the housekeeper if you please, and go to the factory as well."[41]

As for the senators' concern about the potentially deleterious effect of suffrage on female purity, Lemlich observed archly that the low wages that force women into prostitution have a far worse effect on their morality:

There are two moralities, one for men and one for women. Have you noticed when a man comes across a fallen woman what he does to take the burden off her back? Does he claim that he is responsible or acknowledge at least that men are responsible? Does he help her? No, he takes advantage of her if possible. If she becomes a woman of the streets and is arrested, the judge fines her and the woman who has no other means of getting money has to go out and sell herself again in order to pay the court. That is man's protection of unfortunate woman every time.

Men in power used this dual moral code to oppress working women both as a class and as a sex, Lemlich concluded. But working women were no longer willing to accept this: "Does this Senator, think that we . . . do not know that every class that ever lived on another always told the slaves that it was good for them to be slaves? . . . It is too late. We are here Senators. We are 800,000 strong in New York State alone." Using concerted protest and the vote, Lemlich said, working women could address economic injustice and cut through the cant about femininity that denied their experience and their dignity.[42]

Rose Schneiderman expanded Lemlich's class-based attack on popular notions of femininity. Rising to her full height of 4'9", her red hair glowing under the stage lights, Schneiderman lashed into the senator who had stated, "Get women into the arena of politics with its alliances and distressing contests—

the delicacy is gone, the charm is gone, and you emasculate women." The pragmatic Schneiderman had no patience for such romanticized nonsense. She won cheers with an open question: "What does all this talk about becoming mannish signify? I wonder if it will add to my height when I get the vote. I might work for it all the harder if it did. It is just too ridiculous, this talk of becoming less womanly, just as if a woman could be anything else except a woman."

Schneiderman was not challenging the idea of difference. On the contrary, she believed in difference. She had always argued that union organizers in female-dominated trades needed to tailor their approach to women. She felt that women had distinct skills and values to contribute to the working-class movement and to American society at large. However, she disdained the coercive use of femininity, which required working women to be strong and sexless in the factory but helpless and modest outside it. "It seems to me that the working woman ought to wake up to the truth of her situation; all this talk about women's charm does not mean working women. Working women are expected to work and produce their kind so that they too may work until they die of some industrial disease." The benefits upper-class women derive from adhering to standards of femininity, Schneiderman said bluntly, will never accrue to the working woman. Working women needed to define their own hard-headed notions of femininity, she told her audience, because they could not afford to indulge in romantic fantasies that were intended to enslave them.

> Senators and legislators are not blind to the horrible conditions around them. . . . It does not speak well for the intelligence of our Senators to come out with statements about women losing their charm and attractiveness . . . [when] women in the laundries . . . stand thirteen hours or fourteen hours in terrible steam and heat with their hands in hot starch. Surely . . . women won't lose any more of their beauty and charm by putting a ballot in a ballot box once a year than they are likely to lose standing in foundries or laundries all year round.[43]

The speeches made by Lemlich, Schneiderman, Schepps, and others reflected a maturation and expansion of industrial feminism as a political philosophy. The speakers demanded access to political power and offered a uniquely working-class critique of prevailing proscriptions on feminine behavior. To them the vote was a symbol of what Schneiderman called working women's "right to citizenship." In dissecting the arguments of those who wished to prevent them from voting, they offered a keen analysis of the intersections of class and gender and of the ways that both were manipulated to abridge their rights as citizens.

Ironically, at its moment of greatest visibility, the Wage Earners' League disappeared. There is no further record of its existence. Soon after the Cooper Union meeting, Rose Schneiderman left on a paid speaking tour for another suffrage organization. Three months after the meeting, Mary Beard fired Clara Lemlich, and there is no indication that she looked for a replacement. Other funding for the group may have evaporated due to the lack of a full-time organizer. Whatever the cause of its demise, the Wage Earners' League seems to have sunk without a trace, its former leaders branching out to work for other suffrage organizations.

During the summer of 1912, NAWSA president Anna Howard Shaw hired Rose Schneiderman to tour Ohio's industrial cities and build support among working men for a statewide suffrage referendum. Perhaps, Newman wrote to Schneiderman, "the 'cultured ladies' . . . are beginning to see the necessity of having a working girl tour a State rather than some Professor."[44] Schneiderman spoke to workers in union halls, on street corners, and in theaters from Toledo to Youngstown. "My argument to them," she later recalled, "was that if their wives and daughters were enfranchised, labor would be able to influence legislation enormously." The Ohio suffrage movement had never seen anything quite like her. A local suffragist described Schneiderman's electric effect on crowds. "We have had splendid speakers here before, but not one who impressed the people as she did. Strong men sat with tears rolling down their faces. Her pathos and earnestness held the audiences spellbound."[45]

They may have cried, but they didn't give her their votes. The 1912 Ohio referendum was soundly defeated, at least in part because it did not win a labor vote. Schneiderman was demoralized. "When my leave was over," she wrote, "I was not sorry to go back to the [Women's Trade Union] League and the White Goods Workers. I had had a very interesting time and had met some wonderful women, but propagandizing is a lonely job, especially for women." It was an irony of the referendum movement, and of the woman suffrage movement generally, that no matter how successful women organizers were at raising consciousness among women, they would win the ballot only if men voted for it. Schneiderman returned to New York, where she, Newman, and O'Reilly began to lay the groundwork for a new alliance between working women and mainstream suffragists.[46]

A 1914 article by Leonora O'Reilly suggests the distance that the debate over cross-class cooperation in the suffrage movement had come in five years. Writing in the *New York Call*, where Socialist women had battled so furiously in 1909 over the question of cooperating with "bourgeois suffragists," O'Reilly laid out a vision of working-class suffragism that clearly reflected a cross-fertilization of middle-class reform ideology and trade unionism:

Abolition of Child Labor
Abolition of the White Slave Trade
Construction of Schools Instead of Armories
Public Playgrounds and Recreation Centers
Abolition of War
The Full Fruit of their Labor for those Who Labor.[47]

The child of this hybrid philosophy was the Industrial Section of the New York Woman Suffrage Party (WSP); this division of the party was founded in 1914 by Schneiderman, O'Reilly, and Pauline Newman.

Unlike the Wage Earners' League, this new group was to be an official arm of the WSP. The relationship meant that all bills would be paid, but it also meant tighter control of political expression. Hoping to prevent the sort of battles that had gotten Clara Lemlich fired by Mary Beard, the founders of the Industrial Section sent Pauline Newman to remind WSP president Carrie Chapman Catt that all three of them were Socialists. According to Newman, Catt was unfazed. "In a way," she said quietly, "we all are." Catt's sympathetic reply notwithstanding, few of the major figures in New York's suffrage movement were comfortable with the trio's politics. Relations between the Industrial Section leaders and the founding mothers of the WSP were almost always strained.[48]

That same year, disputes over class, ethnicity, and politics were also shaking the New York WTUL. In 1914, native-born hat trimmer Melinda Scott defeated Rose Schneiderman in a campaign for the presidency of the New York group. Schneiderman's effectiveness as a suffrage speaker was cited by some upper-class League members as a reason not to vote for her. They insisted that she was too badly needed in the suffrage movement to be spared for the job of League president. Pauline Newman believed that those claims disguised the real objections to Schneiderman: her Judaism and her Socialist politics.[49]

Leonora O'Reilly agreed with Newman. The older Irish activist had never found cooperation with upper-class women smooth or easy. When Mary Beard fired Clara Lemlich two years earlier, O'Reilly had said nothing. Now, furious at the way suffragists in the League were treating Schneiderman, O'Reilly resigned from the Industrial Section. "Paul," she wrote Newman, "I had my shock . . . and I am through. . . . I feel that we ought not to give our time and our brains unless we have our say."[50]

In December 1914, Schneiderman resigned once more from the WTUL. This time the League's executive board decided to let her go. Registering disapproval of the Socialist content of her speeches, the board concluded, "If as VP she felt it important to speak on subjects the League does not stand for . . .

there was no other way open than to accept the resignation." Schneiderman left the League and was soon hired by the ILGWU to fill Newman's old job as general organizer.[51]

But before hitting the road for the union, Schneiderman accepted one more assignment for the suffrage movement. In December 1914, she represented working women at a suffragists' meeting with President Woodrow Wilson at the White House. There is no record of what the other women said to Wilson that day, but Schneiderman was typically blunt. To illustrate the urgency of women workers' situation, Schneiderman compared the ravages of factory labor to the butchery then taking place on the World War I battlefields. There is "an industrial war going on," she told the president. "The horrors in Belgium are more spectacular than they are here, perhaps," but only in terms of degree.

To illustrate her point, Schneiderman described the Triangle fire, still fresh in her mind. She cited the statistics on numerous industrial accidents during the previous two years and vividly described recent bloody labor/management confrontations in which workers in Lawrence, Massachusetts, Ludlow, Colorado, and New York City had been starved, beaten, and killed. Simply to ensure their own safety, she concluded, "working women need to vote." Wilson does not seem to have been moved; it took him over two more years to throw his support behind women's suffrage.[52]

While Schneiderman switched allegiances, Newman, as was her wont, kept one foot on each side of the line between Socialists and bourgeois suffragists. Though she was a founding member of the Industrial Section, she warned Socialist Party leaders not to "leave this thing to the Suffrage Association." Perhaps bored by staying in one place, Newman embarked on a barnstorming tour through upstate New York, speaking to Socialist audiences about suffrage and reporting her progress regularly in the *New York Call*. Introducing herself as speaking both for the Socialist Party Women's Committee and for the WTUL, Newman repeatedly stressed one of the central themes of the wage earners' suffrage movement: the link between political and economic power. "Woman suffrage should not be regarded as an end in itself. It is only a means to an end. . . . At this time when she is first beginning to wake up to the fact that she is an industrial factor in society, and is, as a consequence, taking her place in the labor movement, when she is beginning to realize her economic power, she will . . . use the ballot to back up that economic power . . . [and] slowly but surely achieve the end—economic freedom."[53]

Simultaneously, Newman's old partner in Socialist suffrage work, Theresa Malkiel, launched the Socialist Party's first full-scale campaign in New York City. There Malkiel organized three hundred Socialist women, who distributed

125,000 prosuffrage leaflets to East European Jews, Italians, and Poles. This focus on immigrant communities was geared to bring new women into the party. Besides, urban immigrant votes were considered essential to passing a suffrage referendum in New York State, as native-born men in rural districts were expected to vote heavily against it.[54]

Six months before the November 1915 New York suffrage referendum, the WTUL began an all-out campaign to win labor votes in New York. They also targeted New Jersey, Massachusetts, and Pennsylvania, where similar referenda were coming up. Maggie Hinchey and Melinda Scott toured the industrial cities of New Jersey, speaking on street corners, at factory gates, and in union halls. Leonora O'Reilly wrote personally to every major labor leader in New Jersey, explaining why woman suffrage was good for the trade union movement. Clara Lemlich crisscrossed New York City, leading street meetings in Jewish immigrant neighborhoods across Manhattan, Brooklyn, and the Bronx. Finally, Schneiderman, who was then on the road for the ILGWU, used her position as general organizer to speak with union men in Massachusetts and Pennsylvania.[55]

To their dismay, male voters rejected woman suffrage in all four states. Despite the intensive campaigning by Clara Lemlich and others, only two of New York City's districts had approved suffrage; one was the Lower East Side, where the editorials of the strongly prosuffrage *Jewish Daily Forward* probably were more important in getting out the vote than were WTUL organizers. The vote went as expected in upstate farm districts, and the referendum was soundly defeated. The negative vote left Rose Schneiderman angry and disappointed with union men, who clearly had not turned out to vote for woman suffrage.[56]

Her disillusionment was deepened by her three-year stint as general organizer for the ILGWU. At every turn, she told Newman, the union sabotaged her best efforts. In 1916, she informed ILGWU president Benjamin Schlesinger that she had completed preparations for a general strike of Boston waistmakers that she believed was winnable. "I worked for months," Schneiderman wrote later, "holding shop meetings after work, then visiting women in their homes at night." Three days before the strike was supposed to begin, Schlesinger assigned a male organizer to lead it. Schneiderman was furious and sent in her resignation. She wrote Newman, "They have got to be taught . . . that a woman is no rag, and I propose to do it. Think of doing all that worrying and planning and when the task is almost done to send a man in and give him the credit for building the thing up. . . . You know Paul . . . to take the thing out of one's hands after all the hardship and heartache is more than I can stand."

Schlesinger did not accept Schneiderman's resignation, but she knew she could not continue working for the ILGWU. Accustomed to the closeness of her New York community, she was far less able than Newman had been to tolerate the loneliness of being a woman in a man's world. At the end of 1916, when Leonora O'Reilly decided to step down as chair of the Industrial Section to work on behalf of the Irish Revolution, she offered her old friend the post. Schneiderman jumped at the chance to come home.[57]

As chair of the Industrial Section, Schneiderman swallowed her bitterness over the previous election and pulled out the stops in an attempt to win labor votes for woman suffrage in 1917. She spoke to union men in New York City and upstate, visited union halls, and held spontaneous street meetings in working-class neighborhoods. As O'Reilly had, Schneiderman argued that political disfranchisement made union women weaker negotiators, thus hurting the unions. This time Schneiderman got help from the highest-ranking woman official in the labor movement, ILGWU vice president Fannia M. Cohn.

In the months leading up to the referendum, Cohn published a series of articles in union publications arguing that men who opposed woman suffrage hurt the labor movement. "Our brothers on election day will pronounce judgement on their sisters with whom they work side by side.... If you make a difference between women and men politically, employers too make a difference between them on the economic field. . . . But who benefits from this difference being made between men and women—the employers or the workers? . . . Working men refusing to give working women equal political rights are in league with the employers against their sisters."[58]

Like other working-class suffragists, Cohn reminded working men that the interests of their class extended beyond the shop floor or the union hall. Just as upper-class women appealed to the men of their class in terms of class interest, so did a relentlessly class-conscious Cohn. "Giving the wives and daughters of the workers the vote," she wrote, "means giving them the weapon with which they will sooner or later help them to overthrow the present unjust system."[59]

Assuming that some part of their resistance to women's suffrage must stem from ignorance, Schneiderman and the WTUL created a "Suffrage Correspondence Course" to educate male trade unionists about the working women of New York State. The lessons all ended with reviews explaining why they needed the franchise. Lesson 8, for example, noted that in 1910, "of the 3,291,714 women in New York State over fifteen years of age . . . only 1,793,588 were married, and 1,498,156 were unmarried or widowed. A large part of these have to work in order to live and many of them have children or fathers and mothers or sisters and brothers to support." These women, the lesson concluded, required the vote to look after not only their own interests but also those of dependent family members.[60]

Schneiderman followed up on the correspondence course by sending personal letters to the leaders of every union in the state, detailing the conditions of women in their industry. This letter went out to officers of the restaurant workers' union: "There are fifteen thousand restaurant workers in this State without any protection whatsoever. They are waitresses, cooks, kitchen girls and pantry hands. They work any number of hours for small wages and commonly seven days a week, which means 84 hours a week. Women have been known to work 122 hours a week. . . . Give the women working in restaurants the vote in order that when they appear before legislative bodies they will be listened to with respect and have their just demands recognized."[61]

After the 1915 debacle, working-class suffragists were unsure, right up to election day, of how labor men would vote. The night before the 1917 election, Schneiderman and her fellow organizers "distributed what seemed . . . millions of circulars at Brooklyn Bridge and other places to people going home from work." Partly because of the intensive campaign among industrial workers, partly because of the nationwide momentum that had converted President Wilson to the cause, the men of New York State this time voted to extend suffrage to women.[62]

To attract the votes of newly enfranchised women, several state parties nominated women candidates for public office the following year. Pauline Newman was one of these candidates. Ten years after her first campaign, the Socialist Party nominated Newman for Congress. She headed a 1918 Socialist Party ticket that included male candidates for the New York State senate and assembly. Though she lost, Newman ran well ahead of her ticket and was pleased with the turnout. She would periodically run for office again; ten years later, she even joined the race for county sheriff.[63]

Schneiderman was excited about tapping the power of working women's votes toward a slightly different end: to defeat the most intransigent opponents of legislation protecting women workers. In 1918, she led campaigns to challenge several New York State legislators who had been particularly hostile to bills regulating wages, hours, and working conditions. The tiny woman with the big voice toured New York City neighborhoods, making speeches from the back of a horse-drawn truck as it moved slowly down the streets of each legislator's district. On each side of the truck hung hand-painted banners denouncing particular incumbents.[64]

One such banner read, "Working women ask you to defeat Albert Ottinger [a Republican state senator]. He voted against giving working women in industry a wage that would give them a chance to live in decency and health." Ottinger and three other targeted state legislators were defeated; two were replaced by women who strongly supported social welfare legislation.[65]

The following year, recognizing Schneiderman's fifteen-year role in galvanizing the New York labor movement, the newly formed New York State Labor Party nominated her to run for the U.S. Senate. The Labor Party, created at the 1919 convention of the New York State Federation of Labor, also ran attorney Dudley Malone for governor. Although Schneiderman never expected to win, her candidacy was taken seriously by the mainstream press. The *New York Times* reported the nomination on page 2, under the headline "Woman for Senator is named by Labor."[66]

Unfortunately for Schneiderman and the Labor Party, divisions over gender, ethnicity, and politics within the labor movement badly hurt the campaign. Schneiderman later found that campaign donations by women who specifically wished to support her were channeled secretly into Malone's campaign by Labor Party officials. As for Malone, his campaign ran aground when a strong movement led primarily by Irish Catholics in New York City's largest labor body—the Central Labor Unions Council—resulted in the council's rescinding its endorsement of Malone in favor of Lower East Side favorite Alfred E. Smith, the state's former and future governor.[67]

Nevertheless, the 1920 Senate campaign marked the start of a new phase in Rose Schneiderman's career. No longer just a daughter of the Lower East Side, she had become a credible political leader who felt comfortable speaking to the president of the United States and who was conversant on international as well as domestic issues. Indeed, internationalist goals were becoming increasingly important to Schneiderman. Since attending the Paris Peace Conference the previous year—where she and former shoemaker Mary Anderson were the only women trade union delegates—Schneiderman had become interested in forging bonds with European women workers.

At Versailles she had met and befriended Labor Party leader Margaret Bondfield, who would later become England's first woman Minister of Labor. Excited by their new friendship, the two women laid plans for an international conference of working women, which was held in Washington, D.C., in November 1919. It was the first in a series of such conferences and the beginning of a new era in working women's politics, when industrial feminists from both sides of the Atlantic would meet regularly to discuss shared goals.[68]

The domestic goals of Schneiderman's campaign for Senate are also worth noting, for they indicate the extent to which industrial feminism had matured. The platform on which Schneiderman ran was a broad one, emphasizing the relationship between economic and political power, between the home and the workplace. She and other Labor Party candidates proposed a host of government initiatives to cut the cost of living and enhance the quality of life for workers. Her platform called for publicly owned farmers' markets and milk distribution stations; municipal sales of coal, bread, ice, and milk; creation of a public utility to construct nonprofit housing; and state insurance protection for those facing unemployment, illness, and old age. And in a stance unusual for the labor movement of that era, her platform also called for equal economic, political, and legal rights regardless of race, color, or creed.[69]

It was an ambitious plan of action for a woman who had never gotten beyond the eighth grade, and it reflected the extent to which she had both shaped and been influenced by a broad Progressive vision of reform. But the very breadth of this platform highlighted growing divisions between former allies in the suffrage movement that would burst into open warfare after the Susan B. Anthony Amendment granted U.S. women the vote.

When militant suffragist Alice Paul formed the National Woman's Party in 1920, she set as her major goal an Equal Rights Amendment to the federal constitution. Paul was unresponsive to working-class organizers' arguments that such an amendment might nullify legislation protecting women workers. She was equally uninterested in requests by African American feminists that the suffrage battle be continued until southern blacks—men and women— could safely and easily exercise their right to vote. Paul had decided that sex discrimination would be the sole focus of the NWP. Attempting to deal with issues of class and race, she said, would dilute the party's strength as an advocate for gender equality. This felt like a betrayal to many black and working-class suffragists, for it left all but white women of the middle and upper classes out in the cold.[70]

Industrial feminists were moving in the opposite direction. As the NWP narrowed its political focus, Schneiderman and other working-class leaders were broadening theirs. After a decade of mostly sidestepping the issue of race, Schneiderman and Cohn now began to address it seriously. In the 1920 campaign, Schneiderman and other Labor Party candidates called for a federal antilynching bill and full civil rights for African Americans. During the next two decades, Schneiderman and Cohn would help to found the first interracial trade union committee to fight for full inclusion of African Americans in the labor movement. Toward this end, they would form coalitions with black labor leaders like A. Philip Randolph and would lead the way among white trade unionists in trying to organize black women workers.[71]

After 1920, a wide range of issues would divide former allies in the suffrage movement. While woman suffrage was still a distant goal, it had been possible for women of different races, classes, and political views to unite temporarily. But once suffrage was won, disagreements over policy and direction quickly emerged. These divisions did not fall only along lines of class or racial difference; white working-class feminists divided bitterly.

A few, like Josephine Casey and Maggie Hinchey, would fight for an Equal Rights Amendment, thus placing themselves in open conflict with their former industrial feminist colleagues. Others joined opposing camps in the internecine battle between Socialist and Communist trade unionists. Cohn, Newman, and Schneiderman continued working within the union and political party system, although they would not always work together or on the same goals. But Clara Lemlich, who sought more sweeping and radical social change, shifted her allegiance to a new organization: the Communist Party USA. These women's divergent choices created lasting enmities that made it more difficult for them to combat the intense political backlash of the early 1920s.

Despite this backlash, industrial feminism would by no means become moribund in the years after 1920—quite the opposite. The period between the wars would see working-class women's ideas more fully integrated than ever before into the mainstream of progressive U.S. politics. Rose Schneiderman, Pauline Newman, Fannia Cohn, and Clara Lemlich would play a large part in that development. Over the next quarter century they and their middle-class allies would frame and lobby for labor laws that became the underpinnings of the New Deal welfare state. They would also contribute to the creation of new government agencies, worker's schools, and women's neighborhood councils and unions that would institutionalize key pieces of the industrial feminist vision and leave a permanent imprint on U.S. society and politics.

3

PART THREE.

THE ACTIVISTS

IN THEIR PRIME:

THE MAINSTREAMING

OF INDUSTRIAL

FEMINISM,

1920–1945

By 1920 Rose Schneiderman, Pauline Newman, Fannia Cohn, and Clara Lemlich (now Clara Lemlich Shavelson) were no longer idealistic young factory workers dreaming of a brighter future. Schneiderman was thirty-eight years old, Cohn was thirty-five, Lemlich was thirty-four, and Newman was thirty. All of them were feeling a little frayed at the edges from a decade of full-time organizing. They had reached that stage of life when most people begin to crave permanence and some measure of security. After years of organizing, public speaking, negotiating, and formulating political strategy, the four women now sought ways to stabilize their personal and professional lives.

All four yearned for love and emotional support; nevertheless, they were consumed by their political careers and had no desire to give up political activism. They enjoyed the heat of battle far too much to do that. Finding that they had no choice but to politicize their desires, they constructed support networks that met both their emotional and strategic needs. Like many women trying to balance the personal and professional, they turned for intimacy to people who shared their work and their political goals. This was partly because all four were dyed-in-the-wool activists for whom personal and political fulfillment were intertwined. But forming alternative communities was also a way of finding loved ones who would not pressure them to act like "normal" women and devote themselves exclusively to home and hearth. Thus, choices of the heart interacted with and shaped the political trajectory of each woman's life.

As president of both the national WTUL and its New York branch during the 1920s and 1930s, Schneiderman immersed herself in a cross-class world of women. Newman made a somewhat different choice: as health education director for the ILGWU and vice president of the New York and national Leagues, she performed an emotional and political balancing act between the male-dominated union and the women's community of the WTUL. Cohn used her position as secretary of the ILGWU Education Department to establish contacts and build friendships with middle-class educators. Shavelson married, bore three children, and moved to a working-class enclave on the far edge of Brooklyn, where she immediately began trying to radicalize her neighbors.

Both Schneiderman and Newman would continue to organize women workers on a grassroots level throughout this period, but it was no longer their primary political activity. During the 1920s and 1930s they would become ever more deeply involved in lobbying for and framing legislation; they spent as much time working for government agencies as they did organizing trade unions. Government work gave them far greater power than they had been able to achieve through many years of organizing. But it also limited their independence; for as newly "respectable" administrators, they came to fear association with radical movements.

Fannia Cohn was uncomfortable with the choices Newman and Schneiderman made. Though she would work with them and with the WTUL on various projects between 1920 and 1945, she distrusted the idea of a cross-class women's movement. She did not share their reform visions or put great store in legislative strategies for change. Emotionally she needed the badge of working-class militancy that affiliation with a labor union gave her. So she stuck with the ILGWU through lean and fat times, through anti-Communist purges and her own marginalization. From shortly after her election as union vice president in 1916 until the end of her career, Cohn would devote herself to building a nationwide system of trade union–sponsored schools for workers.

By the 1920s and 1930s Cohn would come to be lauded for her educational work by some of the leading educators in the nation. But by eschewing cross-class women's groups, Cohn was left without a female support network. While she found love and a measure of intimacy from others dedicated to the cause of worker education, she did not establish herself in a primary relationship with either a man or a woman. That state of being single, or of being "married to the union," as her colleagues liked to say, left her open to whispers and cruel jokes by male colleagues.

Clara Lemlich, who married printer Joe Shavelson in 1913, was largely cut off from the other three in the years between the two World Wars. She lived with her husband and three children in a working-class family neighborhood at the outer edge of Brooklyn. But it was not marriage, family life, or geography that separated Shavelson from her old industrial feminist allies; it was the unshakeable allegiance she formed to the Communist Party during the early 1920s. Shavelson's activism in the Party made Schneiderman, Newman, and Cohn distrust her as they distrusted all CP organizers, whom they blamed for the divisive battles that nearly destroyed the labor movement during the 1920s.

Despite these differences, the four continued to share an important credo of industrial feminism: the belief that a reciprocal relationship existed between the working-class mother in her home and the wage earner in the shops. So even as they maintained their distance from the Communist Party, they strongly supported the idea of organizing the wives and mothers of union men into tenant and consumer councils. After an arm's-length rapprochement between Communists and Socialists in the mid-1930s, the four would even find themselves working on the same side again—trying to channel the housewife militancy they had seen in their youth into permanent unions of working-class wives and mothers. In this endeavor Clara Lemlich Shavelson outshone all others. A maverick in the CP, as she had been in the union and in the suffrage movement, she had a talent for debate and street-corner oratory that remained red-hot into her sixties.

As a married woman and a mother who left the workplace to raise her family, Clara Lemlich Shavelson more than any of the others would enjoy the comforts of social acceptance. But Shavelson's choices created their own problems. As an industrial feminist whose views of gender were shaped during a period of young women's strikes and nationwide suffrage activism, Shavelson found herself more than a little ambivalent about accepting the traditional roles imposed by marriage and motherhood. Refusing to choose between marriage and politics, Shavelson instead tried to build a movement that politicized the social position of wife and mother. That created tensions in her home. Her husband and children were proud and supportive, but it was not easy either to have or to be an activist mother.

In the years between the attainment of woman suffrage and the end of the Second World War—against a political climate that swung pendulumlike from the conservative backlash of the 1920s through the militant utopianism of the 1930s to the patriotic fervor of the 1940s—the four activists and their allies labored to institutionalize many of the industrial feminist goals first articulated in their young years on the shop floor. They were instrumental in the creation of new government agencies, the passage of labor laws, the development of worker education programs, and the organization of a nationwide network of women's consumer and tenant councils. These institutions had a lasting impact on many facets of U.S. political culture. Still, little attention has been paid to working-class women's part in building them. Tracing the careers of Schneiderman, Newman, Cohn, and Lemlich in the years between the two World Wars can help us understand why. Throughout those years they were forced to navigate obstacles of class, gender, and ethnicity that obscured their contributions even as they were making them. Though their ideas and actions were important to the development of industrial unionism, the welfare state, adult education, and tenant and consumer consciousness, these women never attained the recognition they deserved in their unions, in government, in education, or in the major political parties.

The four women responded to the challenges and obstacles they encountered in very different ways. Their choices reflect the range of options experienced by activist working-class women prior to the Second World War; but they also highlight the lingering impact of the particular background that these four shared. Despite the different choices they made, despite bitter political and personal conflicts with each other, through their middle years Schneiderman, Newman, Cohn, and Lemlich continued working toward shared goals, the basic goals of industrial feminism: organizing working-class women into unions; legislating improved conditions; and offering education to women who had been denied it.

When asked to explain their goals and their politics, all four liked to hark back to the formative experiences of their youths. Pauline Newman captured that feeling of nostalgia and inspiration in her reading of a verse by Louis Untermeyer at a WTUL birthday party for Rose Schneiderman:

> Open my ears to music; let
> Me thrill with Spring's first flutes and drums;
> But never let me dare forget
> The bitter ballad of the slums.

For Newman, Untermeyer's poem was more than sentimental fluff. As she moved farther from the shop floor and the militancy of young adulthood, she began to measure herself and other activists against that standard: whether or not they had forgotten the "bitter ballad of the slums."

By the 1920s, the four women had traveled far from the ghetto environs where they grew up. There was less time for stump speeches and grassroots organizing as they became caught up in the nitty-gritty work of institution building, political negotiation, and compromise. All four retained the fire of their early years, even as they evolved politically and culturally. It kept them going long after most others of their generation had given up their activism for more private pursuits. But while it enabled them to accomplish a great deal, their drivenness took a toll on their relationships and on their ability to find peace of mind. That tension between personal and political issues strained and animated the four women's middle years.

KNOCKING AT
THE WHITE
HOUSE DOOR:
ROSE SCHNEIDER-
MAN, PAULINE
NEWMAN, AND
THE CAMPAIGN
FOR LABOR
LEGISLATION,
1910–1945

*Imagine me, Feigele Shapiro,
sleeping in Lincoln's bed!*
—a New York City
dressmaker invited to
stay at the White House

CROSS-CLASS WOMEN'S FRIENDSHIPS AND THE
CONTROVERSY OVER LEGISLATING CHANGE

By the end of World War I, Rose Schneiderman and
Pauline Newman were feeling worn out by years of
constant organizing. Neither woman wanted to
abandon union work. But after an exhausting decade on the stump—traveling from city to city, attending late-night meetings, making speeches,
teaching the fundamentals of trade unionism to new
groups of young women workers, and battling lack
of interest among male union leaders—they were
drawn by the idea of lobbying for legislation. Union
organizing could be excruciatingly slow. It often
took years to make any progress. They knew that
laws regulating work hours, wages, and safety conditions would improve the lives of many more women
than would ever join unions; so they began to devote
increasing amounts of time to the pursuit of legislative change.

For Schneiderman and Newman, this shift in
political perspective was reinforced by their personal lives. By their mid-thirties it had become clear
that the two were not going to marry. Instead they
had become part of an unusually tight circle of
women friends who shared their politics and their
lives. Comprising working-class women, educated
middle-class reformers, and one or two women of
wealth, this network of friends would run the national WTUL and its New York branch for the next
three decades. Drawn together after the Triangle
Shirtwaist Factory fire of 1911 by a shared interest in
industrial reform, this cross-class circle emerged
from the First World War well positioned to promote their goal of transforming the state into an
advocate for women workers.

Some of the women in this network had known
each other since the early years of the century. The
friendship between Newman and Schneiderman
had deepened and solidified in the years since 1905,

when they first met. Both women were very attached to Mary Dreier, former president of the New York WTUL, whom they had known since 1906. Leonora O'Reilly, who grew ever more frail in the years after World War I, rounded out this intimate circle. These women were politically bound to a parallel network in the Chicago WTUL that included glovemakers Agnes Nestor and Elisabeth Christman and former bootmaker Mary Anderson, who in 1920 became the first director of the Women's Bureau of the U.S. Department of Labor. However, the two groups were not always friendly.

The lack of intimacy between the working-class women who led the New York and Chicago branches of the WTUL contrasted sharply with the deep love and loyalty that sustained the cross-class New York circle. These women became both an alternative family to one another and a highly effective political network. For Newman and Schneiderman, involvement in this network would change their lives and redirect the course of their careers. Four women were particularly important in this regard.

Schneiderman met Maud Swartz in 1912 at a suffrage rally. Swartz was a red-haired, sharp-tongued Irish-born printer with a genius for administration. The two women became close friends almost overnight. Within a few years Swartz and Schneiderman had become partners in both their personal and political lives. During the late 1910s and through the 1920s, they ran the national WTUL and its New York branch together. It was as a couple and a political team that they became friends, during the early 1920s, with a woman of wealth who would dramatically enhance their influence and help make Rose Schneiderman a national figure.

Eleanor Roosevelt was the wife of Woodrow Wilson's assistant secretary of the navy when she met Schneiderman and Swartz at the First International Conference of Working Women in 1919. In the years that followed, as Roosevelt launched a career of her own in New York reform politics, she became an active member of the New York WTUL, one of its most successful lobbyists and most dedicated financial backers. She also became very close to Swartz and Schneiderman. At her invitation they began to visit Hyde Park during the mid-1920s. There they gave Franklin D. Roosevelt his first lessons in the politics of labor.

Equally important in the political lives of Schneiderman and Newman was a middle-class reformer named Frances Perkins. The three met while working together for a state commission formed in the aftermath of the Triangle fire to investigate factory safety. Perkins forged lasting friendships with Schneiderman and Newman. As a state labor official in the 1920s, and later as U.S. secretary of labor, she provided a sounding board and influential support for

WTUL women's ideas about revamping government's relationship with both employers and workers. Perkins, who greatly respected Swartz and Schneiderman, helped win high-level government appointments for both women during the 1930s.

Rounding out this circle was a disillusioned economics professor named Frieda Miller, whom Pauline Newman met in 1917 when both were working for the Philadelphia WTUL. They were immediately and deeply drawn to one another. Soon the two women were living together and running the organization as a team. They would continue to share home and work for more than half a century. Largely as a result of Perkins's advocacy, Miller would ascend to important state and federal positions, ultimately succeeding Mary Anderson as director of the U.S. Women's Bureau. And through Miller's intercession, Newman became a frequent government consultant, a recognized expert on industrial women workers. Newman also became unofficial liaison between the ILGWU and government agencies.[1]

Both Schneiderman and Newman would continue to organize women workers on a grassroots level throughout this period, but it was no longer their primary political activity. Their increasing involvement in lobbying for and framing legislation gave them influence far beyond what they might have had if they had remained street-level organizers. It also created a dependence on middle- and upper-class allies that limited their freedom of action and blunted their radical vision. Their middle years were marked by this contradiction.

Their shift from full-time organizing to a mixture of organizing and government work has usually been interpreted as marking the end of their careers as organizers. They saw it differently. Labor legislation attracted them, but they did not see it as a substitute for organizing. They believed legislation could spur unionization of trades previously considered unorganizable. Schneiderman described this position: "We only began to stress legislative activities when we discovered . . . a stepping stone cause and effect relationship in the American labor movement. If we organized even a handful of girls and then managed to put through legislation which made into law the advantages they had gained, other girls would be more likely to join a union and reap further benefits for themselves."[2]

By the 1920s, these labor organizers had come to accept several cold realities: the hostility of most male union leaders to organizing women; the sex-segregation of the labor force; and an outmigration of manufacturing jobs from the cities, which forced many urban women into service-sector employment. Given these circumstances, they argued that the only way to organize the most-exploited, lowest-paid, and least-skilled women workers—in whom labor unions had historically shown the least interest—was to legislate minimum standards and to ally with government officials who had some power to enforce those standards.

A growing feminist scholarship on the welfare state has illustrated the importance of middle- and upper-class women's contributions to the creation of the twentieth-century U.S. welfare system. The activities of Rose Schneiderman, Pauline Newman, and the women who made up the inner circle of the NYWTUL between the wars add an important layer to the new scholarship by illustrating the part working-class women played.[3]

The careers of Rose Schneiderman and Pauline Newman make an excellent case study of the problems raised by working-class women's enthusiasm for the U.S. welfare state. For a largely disfranchised group, there were dangers in calling for expansion of the state apparatus. What the state gives in times of working-class strength, it can take away when the political climate is less sympathetic to workers—as it did in the 1920s and the 1980s. For working-class women, this double-edged sword was particularly sharp; their influence with the increasingly powerful state of the post–World War I era was tied to the fortunes of both the larger working-class and women's movements. Also, gendered social welfare programs employing a moral carrot and stick often became the means for establishing greater government control over the lives of poor and working women.[4]

Still, the idea of working with a benevolent state was seductive. Legislating change by forging bonds with sympathetic women of other classes and with male politicians like Al Smith, Robert Wagner, and Franklin Roosevelt gave Schneiderman and Newman a sense of power that they did not have in the male-dominated labor movement. To their amazement, they found that it was easier for working-class women to articulate and win entitlements from an expanding state than from male colleagues in their own unions. Ironically, as big labor drew closer to government in the 1930s, these women's access to key figures in the Democratic Party would give them more clout with male union leaders than anything they had done as organizers.[5]

As in the suffrage movement, the arguments and the legislative goals they articulated were quite distinct from those of their middle- and upper-class counterparts. They sought empowerment, not charity. They viewed wage, hour, and safety standards as bases on which working women could step up to greater economic and political power, not as admissions of weakness or invitations to greater government regulation of working-class women's lives. Unlike many of their middle- and upper-class counterparts, League spokeswomen did not argue for labor legislation on the grounds of women's frailty or their role as potential "mothers of the race." They stressed instead that working women had a right to equal opportunity with working men.[6]

They knew from first-hand experience that women workers had different needs than men, but they felt that working-class women were distinguished by their political and economic disadvantages, not by their biological functions. Schneiderman and Newman justified legislated standards for women workers in the same way that later advocates of affirmative action programs would—as a means of equalizing opportunity. Women were not inherently weaker than men, but they *were* segregated into the least-skilled, lowest-paid sectors of the workforce. And they were discriminated against in labor unions. Given those disadvantages, working women had to maximize the new power they had as voters—power they had fought for self-consciously and with a specific goal in mind: to win for themselves the shorter hours and higher pay that they knew might take years to achieve through union activism.[7]

Though they did not accept the idea that women were or should be slaves to their biology, their arguments for labor legislation did call for a recognition of real-life differences. In seeking to protect women from workplace exposure to chemicals that could cause birth defects or could affect a woman's ability to bear children, Schneiderman and the League asserted not that all women workers would or should become mothers but that work should not preclude motherhood. Conversely, they argued, women's potential motherhood should not be used as an excuse for not giving them equal economic opportunity with men.

There were pitfalls to their approach. In the end, the League's identification of women workers as future mothers reinforced the idea—central to many social reformer's arguments for protective legislation—that women's relationship to the state must be defined by their biological potential as "future mothers of the race." But if Schneiderman and Newman were shortsighted, it was because visions of sweatshops and industrial accidents blocked their view. They were not thinking about long-term implications for women's rights. For working women, they argued, the first step toward full citizenship had to be made through immediate improvements in wages, hours, and safety conditions. Without basic economic rights, abstract arguments about individual women's freedom and the need for sexual equality were little more than a cruel joke.[8]

Years of organizing had left Schneiderman and Newman with considerable expertise in industrial labor conditions and anger at the abuses working women were forced to endure. They felt that equal rights feminists who opposed all legislation for women workers on principle must be either reactionary or unfeeling. That belief would lead them into a long and divisive battle with former suffrage-movement allies who in the 1920s, under the banner of Alice Paul's National Woman's Party (NWP), decided to fight all labor legislation that did not apply equally to men and women. Schneiderman and Newman challenged the women who supported the Equal Rights Amendment, arguing that they did not and could not speak for women in the shops. But ironically, by positioning themselves as women who *could*—as professional representatives of American working women—the two distanced themselves from the shop floor.[9]

By the early 1920s their lives diverged sharply from that of the average garment worker. Much of their new political influence stemmed from their involvement with a circle of women friends and lovers far more privileged and educated than themselves. Membership in this network would allow Schneiderman and Newman to stand at the center of the movement that permanently changed government's relationship to U.S. workers. It also gave them an emotional home, with beloved friends and partners who cushioned them from the censure they experienced as Jewish working-class women who never married and who lived their entire adult lives in the political limelight.

These women supported each other professionally and personally, followed each other into appointed government positions, worked together, vacationed together, and sometimes lived together. The friendships in this network are central to the story of the evolving relationship between government and workers in the first half of the twentieth century. They are also essential to understanding the evolution of Schneiderman and Newman as political leaders.

Through their friends, Schneiderman and Newman got the chance to participate in the building of the U.S. welfare state—a remarkable opportunity for two self-educated immigrant former shop girls. Between 1919 and 1947, they were able to help realize many of the goals first articulated on the shop floor, through passage of legislated minimum wage, maximum hours, and safety standards for workers across the United States. They sat on government commissions, testified at congressional hearings, and wrote memos that made their way to the desk of the president. Given the general lack of respect accorded working-class women, Schneiderman, Newman, Swartz, Christman, and Anderson welcomed the attention and honor that went along with government work and felt that they were opening opportunities for other working-class women.

But the career trajectories of the women in the network reveal the limits that class, ethnicity, and gender placed on politically active working-class women in those years. Of all the working-class women in the network, only Mary Anderson, a Norwegian immigrant, was appointed to an executive position in the federal government. Schneiderman and Swartz were appointed to high office in New York State, but only during her few years with FDR's National Recovery Administration (NRA) was Schneiderman able to directly shape federal policy. Perkins and Miller, by contrast, were granted executive powers—first on the state level, then the federal. Their ethnic, educational, and class backgrounds made them more acceptable appointees. And Pauline Newman, one of the most widely read and intellectually creative members of the network, was limited always to an advisory role. There are many possible reasons for this, but Newman's blunt aggressiveness and fondness for masculine dress may have had something to do with it.

Schneiderman and Newman's positions in this nexus of state power crippled the two old-time firebrands in their dealings with the radical movements of the 1920s and 1930s. As these movements captured the imaginations of a new generation of working-class women, Schneiderman and Newman came to be seen as a conservative "old guard" in the WTUL. And, indeed, they would use their power within the organization to outmaneuver and chastise younger members who attempted to build links with the emerging Congress of Industrial Organizations (CIO) and the Communist Party.[10]

By the 1930s, Newman and in particular Schneiderman felt they had something to lose by aligning themselves with radical activists and organizations. In 1926, Schneiderman became president of both the national WTUL and its New York branch. By the late 1920s, she had become a national figure. With her appointment in 1932 to a post in the first Roosevelt administration, she was hailed in the national press as "the leader of nine million American working women." Still, as an unmarried working-class woman with only an eighth-grade education, Schneiderman felt vulnerable in the world of power she had entered. Nervously, she began to distance herself from her Socialist past and to cultivate an image of moderation. "Red Rose" began to describe herself as mild and nonthreatening.

Her lifelong desire for respectability constrained her behavior in ways that affected both the personal and the political. She never felt comfortable enough to fully immerse herself in her relationship with Maud Swartz. Though they were involved for nearly a quarter century, Schneiderman would never live with her partner; she chose instead to keep up a home with her mother. She played politics just as carefully. She had long expressed her support for the strategy of organizing workers on an industrywide rather than a craft basis, as the AFL insisted on doing. However, when the battle between the AFL and the new CIO heated up in the mid-1930s, Schneiderman waffled. She was fearful that the AFL would withdraw funding; they had always been stingy and ungracious in their support of the WTUL. And she was nervous about being associated with the Communist Party organizers who had been welcomed into the CIO unions. As a result, she refused to embrace the new, more egalitarian labor federation. Her lack of boldness on that score would damage the local Leagues and weaken her effectiveness as president of the national League. Many trade unionists began to see her more as a careful government official than as a militant labor leader.[11]

Newman, less personally reticent than Schneiderman, managed during those years to construct a complicated life that fulfilled her politically as well as emotionally. Her romantic relationship with Frieda Miller was far more open and complete than that of Schneiderman and Swartz. The two lived together, raised a child, and were accepted as a couple by friends and colleagues, male as well as female. Newman was extremely active in the WTUL during this period. She also retained a paid position in the ILGWU, as education director for the Union Health Center. Through her connections to Miller and Schneiderman, she achieved a measure of influence in Albany and in Washington, D.C. This political clout gave her prestige in the ILGWU that her organizing successes never had. Through this complex arrangement Newman found the freedom and flexibility her restless intellect required. Living in two worlds consumed her energies and gave her a large network of colleagues who loved and respected her.

Still, she often found herself in awkward positions. Whatever political influence she had depended absolutely on the intercession of more powerful loved ones. Through Schneiderman she gained access to Eleanor Roosevelt. Frieda Miller and Frances Perkins appointed her to numerous state and federal labor committees. But this situation made her dependent, for professional advancement, on her closest friends. Her story illuminates the emotional complexities of membership in a support network bound by love as well as politics. Power imbalances created personal tensions. As the less privileged partner in a cross-class relationship, as Schneiderman's leading ally in the WTUL, and as a politically marginal officer in her union, Newman must have felt frustrated at times.

Relationships between the women of the NYWTUL circle during the years between the Triangle fire and the Second World War provide a window onto the inner world of coalition building. They offer insights into the particular nature of women's politics, in which personal bonds so often overlap with political networks. Both love and respect cemented these women's friendships. Still, they were not untroubled by class and ethnic tensions. Examining the forces that sustained and frayed this network sheds light on the links between women's friendships and their activism, illuminating the sticky emotional dynamics beneath the surface of political change.

THE NYWTUL, A NEW CROSS-CLASS NETWORK, AND A SHIFT TOWARD LEGISLATIVE ACTIVISM, 1911–1919

In the five years after the 1909 strike, tensions over class and ethnicity splintered the cross-class alliance that had run the New York Women's Trade Union League in its first decade. These tensions came to a head in 1914 when Rose Schneiderman made a play to take over the League. She lost her bid for the presidency to Melinda Scott, who was favored by those allies who believed the League had devoted too much energy to Jewish women. This letter, which Schneiderman wrote to Newman after the election, evokes a sense of the bitterness she felt toward middle-class "uplifters" at the League, particularly Helen Marot. "Never you mind, Helen's day will come. Some day she will stand with the mask torn from her face and then everybody shall know that all her radicalism is not worth a pinch of snuff and that she is a fraud from head to foot. . . . There is more trade unionism in my little finger than there is in her whole make up." Schneiderman assured her friends that it was they "who have made the League go," and that if they leave the League, "it will die a natural death." The League did not die after 1914, and Schneiderman did not leave it. After a three-year hiatus from League work, she ran successfully for the presidency of the New York WTUL; it was a position she would retain for thirty-two years.[12]

During this period, working-class women would come to dominate the executive boards of both the national WTUL and its New York branch. The League remained dependent on financial and political support from middle- and upper-class women; however, the women who supported the League between the wars were a different breed than earlier allies. They made no attempt to run the organization, nor did they try to speak for working women. The task of representing working women to government agencies, to male union leaders, and to the press was left to the League's working-class leadership: Schneiderman, Newman, Maud Swartz, Mary Anderson, Agnes Nestor, and Elisabeth Christman.

The relationships that anchored the post-1917 cross-class women's alliance at the League differed sharply from the troubled relations of the prewar years. There was a presumption of equality in these friendships that made them durable. The equation had changed partly because the League's working-class leaders were no longer "working girls" who needed mentoring; they were adult women who had already achieved some recognition for their accomplishments. But this spirit of egalitarianism also reflected the character of the League's new allies. Frances Perkins, Frieda Miller, and Eleanor Roosevelt were decidedly less condescending toward working-class women than were many of the middle-class women who had run the League in its first years. Of that earlier group of allies, only Mary Dreier became part of the postwar League network.

There was a genuine intimacy that bonded the women of the second WTUL alliance. In part it arose out of the tragic circumstances under which the network was forged. The urgency with which Newman, Schneiderman, Mary Dreier, and Frances Perkins argued for legislative reform after 1911 was fueled not by any intellectual interest in restructuring government but by shared memories of a single night of horror: March 25, 1911, the night the Triangle Shirtwaist Factory burned. The fire and the factory investigations that followed left an imprint on the women that recast their political priorities and cemented their relations with one another.

The Triangle fire had convinced Schneiderman and Newman that fighting for enforceable safety laws had to become their top priority. The friends both had lost in the fire haunted them for years afterward, spurring them to fight for improved working conditions in every way they could. Frances Perkins, who shared that commitment perhaps more than any other middle-class reformer, was equally branded by·the blaze that day, because she was part of the small horrified crowd that watched it happen.

Perkins, then thirty-one years old and secretary of the New York Consumer's League, was having tea with a neighbor in her Greenwich Village apartment when she heard fire engines. She ran from her house to the site of the Triangle factory. For the next few excruciating hours, she watched as scores of terrified young women jumped from eight and nine stories up, their bodies hitting the pavement with such force that they shattered the cement. The air was thick with smoke and the spray of blood. The high wail of screams and the crash of breaking bones assaulted the ears of those who waited helplessly below. In little more than an hour, 146 workers, almost all young women in their teens and early twenties, were dead. By nightfall their bodies lay piled on the sidewalks. It was a nightmare not easily forgotten.[13]

And one that Perkins never tried to forget. Perkins' conscience was seared by what she saw that afternoon. The fire created in her a sympathy for working women rare among middle-class reformers; that spirit of sympathy and respect suffused her friendships with Schneiderman and Newman. Half a century later, when she was in her eighties and they were in their seventies, Perkins, Newman, and Schneiderman spoke, as they had almost every year since 1911, at a memorial for victims of the fire. Perkins described the impact that long-ago afternoon had on her career: "Out of that terrible episode came a self-examination of stricken conscience in which the people of this state saw for the first time the individual worth and value of each of those 146 people who fell or were burned in that great fire. . . . Moved by this sense of stricken guilt, we banded ourselves together to find a way by law to prevent this kind of disaster." The memory stayed with Perkins throughout her career, as she worked to pass labor laws first in New York and then as secretary of labor from 1932 to 1945. Those laws, she said, were based "upon the sacrifices of those who we faithfully remember with affection and respect, [who] died in that terrible fire. . . . They did not die in vain and we will never forget them."[14]

Perkins and Rose Schneiderman met for the first time at a memorial for the victims of the fire, held at the New York Metropolitan Opera House less than two weeks after it happened. As various reformers droned on before an increasingly restive audience, Perkins saw Schneiderman begin to tremble. Then the red-haired labor leader rose to speak. Perkins was struck first by how frail she seemed and then by her command of the audience. Schneiderman was at her most impressive: "The old Inquisition had its rack, its thumbscrews and its instruments of torture with iron teeth. We know what these things are today; the iron teeth are our necessities, the thumbscrews are the high-powered and swift machinery close to which we must work, and the rack is here in the firetrap structures that will destroy us the minute they catch on fire. . . . The life of men and women is so cheap and property is so sacred. There are so many of us for one job it matters little if 146 of us are burned to death." A policeman who had come to the meeting wary of Schneiderman's subversive reputation later recorded his feelings upon listening to that speech: "She herself can make you weep. She is the finest speaker I ever heard." That meeting marked the start of a fifty-year friendship between Schneiderman and Frances Perkins.[15]

Perkins got to know Pauline Newman later that year, after both were hired as investigators for the state Factory Investigating Commission (FIC), which was created to probe the conditions that had led to the Triangle fire. The two women worked closely with Schneiderman, who served as a consultant to the FIC, and Mary Dreier, the only woman commissioner. The group was determined to educate New York's elected officials about dangers in the industrial workplace. They found two willing listeners in commissioners Al Smith and Robert Wagner—the leaders of the New York State Assembly and Senate.

"We used to make it our business," Perkins later wrote, "to take Al Smith, the East Side Boy who later became New York's Governor and a presidential candidate, to see the women, thousands of them, coming off the ten-hour night shift on the rope walks in Auburn. We made sure that Robert Wagner personally crawled through the tiny hole in the wall that gave egress to a steep iron ladder covered with ice and ending twelve feet above the ground, which was euphemistically labeled 'Fire Escape' in many factories." Perkins attributed the two men's lifelong commitment to labor legislation to that "firsthand look at industrial and labor conditions" that she and Newman provided.[16]

With the help of these influential new friends in Albany, the WTUL women, Perkins, and the famous industrial reformer Florence Kelley managed to push through the state legislature a bill establishing a maximum of fifty-four hours per week for women workers in New York stores and factories. Rose Schneiderman and six other working women told of the "physical and moral exhaustion" that long hours created in New York's working women. Perkins tirelessly twisted arms in the legislature, and through her work she met a young state senator who was to change the course of her career—a callow aristocrat named Franklin D. Roosevelt.[17]

The moment the maximum-hours law was in place, Schneiderman and Newman began to lobby for a minimum-wage bill. Unless such a bill was passed quickly, they told legislators, women workers would face salary cuts as a result of the new hours restrictions. The women were not well received. Stung by the rudeness of many of the politicians she encountered, Schneiderman was reminded that the state could be a capricious friend. Even supporters of the fifty-four-hour bill were edgy about the idea of a minimum wage. Unionists worried that wage regulation would undercut organizing, thus turning a minimum wage into the maximum wage. And employers saw minimum-wage laws as government-forced redistribution of their profits, an unprecedented form of intervention into the realm of business.

In 1914, the FIC opened hearings on establishing a minimum wage for women workers in New York. Helen Marot, whose feud with Schneiderman and Newman had culminated in her resignation as League secretary a year earlier, testified against the idea. She echoed AFL president Samuel Gompers's argument that wage laws infringed on unions' prerogative to negotiate wages. Furthermore, she said, "If women need State protection on the ground that they do not organize as men do," said Marot, "then also do the mass of unskilled, unorganized men." She concluded, in an obvious swipe at her former WTUL colleagues, that no true trade unionists would waste time lobbying when they could be out organizing.[18]

Pauline Newman, representing the ILGWU, agreed that male as well as female workers needed a minimum wage. But she contended that the suffering of American working women required immediate amelioration. She described the living conditions of working women she had met in her years as investigator, first for the FIC and, since 1913, for the Joint Board of Sanitary Control, a permanent labor/management investigating team created by the FIC.

> I have a paper here which shows how a girl lives on $4 a week. She has to give up eating meat for at least two or three weeks if she wants to buy a pair of shoes. Now what right have I, even as a trade unionist, to say to this girl you wait and someday you will be conscious of your own power, some day you are going to be organized, some day you are going to gain higher wages through your own efforts. . . . Can they wait? From personal experience I say they cannot, and the sooner the minimum wage is fixed the better for all concerned.

It was impossible, she concluded, "for any human being of intelligence to say that a minimum wage is not a necessity."[19]

Rather than argue the principle of a minimum wage, Newman suggested that the FIC address the question of how that "minimum" should be determined. Her testimony suggests just how much transformative power she and Schneiderman attached to some of the legislation they lobbied for. Newman saw minimum-wage legislation as a matter of human rights. Building on Schneiderman's bread and roses metaphor of two years earlier, Newman argued that a minimum wage should provide more than subsistence. A working girl's earnings had to be sufficient to allow her to aspire to a better future. To have an enjoyable quality of life—including books, flowers, air, and light— was a right, she insisted, not a luxury. A majority of New York working women were making under eight dollars per week. Other experts were then calling for an eight- to nine-dollar-per-week minimum. Newman proposed that New York's minimum wage be set at 50 to 90 percent higher.

> A working girl is a human being with a heart, with desires, with aspirations, with ideas and ideals and when we think of food and shelter we merely think of the . . . necessities. . . . Have we thought of providing her with books, with money for . . . a good drama? . . . Have you thought about a girl providing herself with a good room that had plenty of air, proper ventilation in a somewhat decent neighborhood. Do you think of all these things when you think of a minimum wage? . . . Let us not think of a piece of bread. Let us think of the working woman as a human being who has her desires to which she is entitled.[20]

Newman was intentionally challenging the various scholars and industrial experts then engaged in a national debate over what constituted a "living wage" for women workers. Between 1912 and 1923, thirteen states and the District of Columbia established minimum wages for women workers. These laws were not intended to encourage a young woman to live independently of her family. They sought to provide just enough so that she could survive in rather grim fashion without having to turn to prostitution to supplement her income. Newman rejected the very idea of a "living wage." The whole point of a minimum wage, in her political vision, was to guarantee women workers economic independence and a modicum of comfort. Only then, Newman argued, could a young woman pursue her aspirations. It was the minimum to which she was entitled as a human being.[21] However, Newman's view was a far cry from what even the most sympathetic legislators had in mind. New York legislators rejected the very idea of mandating a minimum wage. Foreshadowing later U.S. Supreme Court decisions, opponents claimed that wage regulation of any kind represented unconstitutional restraint of trade.[22]

Despite its defeats, the WTUL–Consumer League coalition played an important part in shaping New York State industrial policy in the years leading up to World War I. In 1915, the FIC suggested guidelines for a state industrial code and for the creation of new state agencies to regulate industrial and labor conditions. The first New York State Industrial Code was passed into law that year, and a state Industrial Commission was appointed to enforce those regulations. Three years later, when Al Smith was elected governor, a state Labor Department was established to oversee labor policy.

By 1918, the structures had been created that would put the power of state government behind the movement to improve industrial labor conditions. Schneiderman, Newman, Dreier, and Perkins had been instrumental in creating this change. Perkins's role was acknowledged by Smith, who appointed her to the Industrial Commission in 1919. For the first time, Schneiderman and Newman had a friend in government. It made the idea of trying to legislate change more attractive than ever before.[23]

INTIMATE COMRADESHIP ON THE
LEGISLATIVE BATTLEFIELD, 1912–1926

In the course of their work during the 1910s, Schneiderman and Newman met two women who would become their companions and political partners. These relationships realigned the two activists' careers and recast the future of the WTUL.

At a 1912 rally of the Woman Suffrage Party's New York City group, Rose Schneiderman heard an unlikely orator speaking in Italian to a Lower East Side immigrant audience—Maud O'Farrel Swartz, an auburn-haired Irishwoman with a sharp tongue and a perfect Italian accent. She greatly impressed

Schneiderman, who came to the stage after the rally to introduce herself. It was the beginning of a twenty-five-year friendship.

Maud Zaza O'Farrel was born in County Kildare in 1901, one of fourteen children of an impoverished flour miller. With more daughters than he could afford or, according to Swartz, even remember the names of, her father consigned her at a young age to the care of nuns. Her memories of childhood were painful and bitter. She grew up in German and French convents, completely cut off from her family. When she was eighteen, she was hired out as the governess for an English family in Italy. Four years later she emigrated to New York.[24]

Fluent in German, French, Italian, and English, she had no trouble finding work as a governess. However, according to Schneiderman, the strikingly beautiful young woman faced sexual harassment by her male employers. "Every time she got a job as a governess," Schneiderman noted, "she had to give it up because her employer was . . . too attentive." Finally O'Farrel decided to support herself another way. She found work as a proofreader in a printing plant. The job paid eight dollars a week, just enough to cover rent on a single tenement room.[25]

In 1905, at the age of twenty-six, O'Farrel married Lee Swartz. The marriage was brief and unhappy. About the only thing she took away from it was the name she would carry for the rest of her life. Though Swartz left her husband shortly after the marriage, she never sought a divorce, perhaps because of her Catholic upbringing. By the time she met Schneiderman she was used to living on her own.[26]

There is very little hard evidence that has survived about their friendship, since almost all of their personal papers have been lost or destroyed. We will never know for certain whether the two became lovers or what the nature of their intimacy was. We do know that Swartz and Schneiderman became partners in work and in their travels, that they were invited places together and gave gifts together. Schneiderman gives no more specific description of her feelings for Swartz than to say that "she was a wonderful companion." Euphemistic or not, that probably provides an emotionally accurate sense of their relationship.[27]

Swartz's interest in labor union activism grew as her friendship with Schneiderman deepened. In seven years at the printing plant, Swartz had never belonged to a union. But within a year of meeting Schneiderman, she joined the "Big Six" Typographical Union and became an activist in the New York WTUL. In 1914, the national League gave her a scholarship to attend its training school for women organizers in Chicago.[28]

In 1916, Swartz left her proofreading job to take a full-time position as secretary of the New York WTUL; Schneiderman was elected president of the NYWTUL the following year. Thereafter the two ran the organization together. Their complementary skills made them a formidable team. With Schneiderman's powers of persuasion and Swartz's gift for administration, they soon became a dominant force in the national League as well as its New York branch.

In 1917, Pauline Newman met the woman who was to become her lifelong partner. Newman was in Philadelphia, where she had been sent by Rose Schneiderman to organize a new branch of the WTUL. There she encountered a disillusioned academic named Frieda Miller. The granddaughter of a Wisconsin mill owner, Miller was then working as a research assistant in the economics department at Bryn Mawr College. Later she would claim that she was drawn to the League because she had become "disgusted with academic life" and because she "wanted to do something more socially beneficial than writing an academic dissertation." Ready to commit herself to meaningful work, Miller happily abandoned her post at Bryn Mawr for a new job as secretary of the fledgling Philadelphia WTUL. There Newman and Miller set up an arrangement paralleling that of Schneiderman and Swartz in New York. Newman, the trade unionist, was the impassioned voice of the organization; Miller, the more polished and educated of the two, managed logistics and helped develop policy.[29]

Newman's personal relations with Miller were markedly different from Schneiderman's with Swartz. Schneiderman dressed and acted in ways she thought of as "mild" and conventional. Newman was outspoken and passionate and dressed as she pleased. She wore her hair short and had a taste for tweeds and ties. She did not seem to care much about what others thought of her. Perhaps as a result, people were strongly drawn to her.

Schneiderman, who was still very involved with her mother and siblings, put constraints on her own emotions and her relationship with Swartz. But Newman was largely cut off from her family, and she craved the intimacy of a romantic relationship. She quickly fell in love with the mill owner's granddaughter. Miller—as attracted, perhaps, to images of shared struggle as she was to the dark-eyed trade unionist who embodied that vision—returned Newman's love. But from the start, and throughout their relationship, Miller seems to have been less certain about what she wanted the relationship to be than the intense, emotional Newman.[30]

"We had a lot in common," Newman later said, describing their attraction in self-consciously tame phrases. "She was immensely interested in social questions; she was deeply interested in literature, poetry, and music." Common

interests were undoubtedly what enabled women from such different backgrounds to stay together over the decades to come. But this was no simple
friendship, and Newman knew that from the start. Confused, she wrote to
Schneiderman for advice.[31]

Schneiderman's reply of August 11 sheds light both on Newman's early
feelings about Miller and Schneiderman's own more complicated response to
Maud Swartz. She encouraged her younger friend to take risks in pursuit of
"joy," confessing that she had never been able to do so.

> What is to be done Paul? There must be thousands of women who feel like
> us, eurning, eurning [*sic*] all the time for warmth and tenderness from a
> loved one, only to be worn out and settled down to the commonplace
> everyday grind. You ask whether one should grasp at the possibility for joy
> held out to one—Why not?
>
> I always feel that whatever I have done, could not be done in any other
> way because of the kind of personality that I am, and not for any other
> consideration. . . . What I mean is that if any of my love affairs did not go
> further than they did it was [not] because of the possible circumstances that
> might follow but because it just did not happen. That is all. If the craving for
> the utmost fulfillment of love would have been stronger they would have
> been fulfilled.[32]

Perhaps Newman's "craving" for love was stronger, or maybe she felt less
bound by convention than Schneiderman. Whatever the case, she took the
risk of loving Miller. When Miller was stricken in the flu epidemic of 1918,
Newman nursed her back to health. Sometime during the dangerous days of
Miller's illness, the relationship between patient and caretaker deepened. By
October 1918, Schneiderman's letters to Newman sent love to them both.[33]

The tight comradeship between the two former garment workers now
opened up into a group of four that provided love, support, and political
advice for each other for the rest of their lives. That support was essential over
the next few years—a roller-coaster period during which the Women's Trade
Union League grew closer to government than ever before but at the same
time faced furious battles both with Bolshevik-hunting politicians and with
former allies in the suffrage movement.

World War I brought the WTUL into a new relationship with the federal government, for in an effort to keep wartime production functioning smoothly,
federal officials began to consult League leaders on how best to meet the needs
of working women. In 1918, responding to requests from a variety of women's
organizations led by the WTUL, the U.S. Department of Labor created the
Woman in Industry Service (WIIS) to monitor women working in factories

under U.S. defense contracts. Under the supervision of its director—Mary Van Kleeck, a longtime WTUL member—the WIIS conducted nationwide studies to establish safety, minimum-wage, and maximum-hour standards for women war workers. To insure that working women's voices would be heard and strikes prevented, she pushed successfully for the appointment of Chicago WTUL activist Elisabeth Christman as liaison between women workers and the federal government.[34]

At the end of the war, President Woodrow Wilson created a permanent agency within the U.S. Labor Department to deal with the concerns of women workers. The new Women's Bureau would, he promised, have the power to enforce safety, wage, and hour standards in factories working on government contract. He appointed Mary Anderson, a former bootmaker and longtime member of the Chicago WTUL, to head the U.S. Women's Bureau. For the first time in U.S. history, a woman who had been a worker sat in the director's chair of a federal government agency, and the WTUL had a friend in Washington.[35]

The WTUL was also gaining influence in New York State. In 1918, with the help of newly enfranchised women workers, Alfred E. Smith was elected governor of New York. After appointing Frances Perkins as the first woman member of the state's Industrial Commission, he consulted with Mary Dreier on the establishment of a permanent Women's Bureau in the New York State Department of Labor. Smith appointed Nell Swartz, former head of the New York Consumer's League, to head the bureau. A stalwart fighter for minimum-wage and maximum-hour laws, Swartz would become a valued member of the New York WTUL network.[36]

But the romance with Albany was stormy. In the heat of wartime patriotism, Schneiderman and her allies were branded subversives and "Bolshevists." At a 1918 hearing on a bill to roll back the fifty-four-hour maximum for women war workers, Republican assembly leader Elon Brown called Schneiderman and Swartz, who had testified against the bill, "unpatriotic . . . parasites." James Holland of the New York Federation of Labor, who supported the bill, branded Schneiderman "Red Rose" and called the WTUL a "tail to the Socialist kite." The charges stuck. In the published report of the state's Joint Legislative Committee to Investigate Seditious Activities, Rose Schneiderman was cited five times for her activities as a pacifist, Socialist, and advocate of "free-speech, so-called."[37]

In an attempt to distance Governor Smith from such unsavory associations, Smith's chief aide, the politically savvy Jewish reformer Belle Moskowitz, deleted Schneiderman's name from a list of people invited to a discussion on postwar labor policy for New York State. Moskowitz claimed that "it might be unfortunate if she were invited" because Schneiderman was not "practical."

But Moskowitz's caution could not save Smith; a postwar Red Scare was in full swing, and it cost him the 1920 gubernatorial election. It also cost advocates of labor legislation dearly: in the four years before Smith was reelected, New York legislators repealed maximum-hour codes for women as well as other protections.[38]

Pauline Newman and Frieda Miller were finding an equally hostile political climate in Pennsylvania. In an atmosphere of recrimination and Red-baiting, several women's organizations that were allied with the Philadelphia wtul demanded that the League tone down its rhetoric in exchange for their continued support. Newman was furious at what she considered blackmail. In a state where the legislature was far less sympathetic than New York's, she found herself increasingly isolated. In an article for the national wtul publication *Life and Labor*, she complained,

> To expect labor or social legislation from the Pennsylvania Legislature is as easy a task as getting the moon to play with. . . . As long as Chambers of Commerce and Manufacturers' Associations direct our government it is nothing but a farce to try to get something done. It is only the realization that someone has got to keep the issue of human legislation before the people at large that prompts an organization like this to devote its time, money and energy to going to the legislature every two years, reminding it that, like Banquo's ghost, the will of the people will not be brought down.[39]

Their problems with right-wing politicians and manufacturer's associations were compounded when former allies from the suffrage movement launched an unexpected attack on labor legislation. In 1920, the National Woman's Party, led by Alice Paul and funded by former "mink brigade" member Alva Belmont, began to campaign for a constitutional amendment banning all discriminations based on sex. The Women's Trade Union League and its middle-class political allies in the National Consumer's League and the National League of Women Voters warned the nwp that a blanket amendment would threaten laws protecting women workers.[40]

Newman and Schneiderman felt angry and betrayed. The early 1920s were vulnerable years for advocates of labor legislation. In a climate of political backlash, state legislators across the nation were launching assaults on women workers' hard-won gains. Hoping to avoid a divisive battle, the wtul, the National Consumer's League, and the League of Women Voters convened a meeting with the nwp leadership to hammer out wording for an Equal Rights Amendment that would not endanger wage, hours, and safety laws. A precedent had been set in Wisconsin earlier that year with the passage of a state era that explicitly protected existing labor legislation for women.[41]

Despite this encouraging model, hope of compromise quickly faded. The National Woman's Party announced that it would fight any "restrictions upon the hours, conditions and remuneration of labor" that did not "apply to both sexes." Before their part in the negotiations was concluded, Rose Schneiderman and Mary Dreier were called away to fight the forces arrayed against a New York State bill proposing a forty-eight-hour maximum for women. Their opponents now included some of the same women who had worked with them four years earlier in the campaign for a New York women's suffrage referendum.[42]

On April 9, 1923, the U.S. Supreme Court struck the blow that WTUL activists had most feared. In *Adkins v. Children's Hospital of Washington, D.C.*, the court decided that because "contractual, political, and civil" gender differences in the United States "had come almost, if not quite, to the vanishing point," the legal principle of freedom of contract must now apply to women as well as men. To Alice Paul those words were cause for rejoicing. To Schneiderman and Newman the decision threatened everything they had worked for.[43]

Both sides escalated their rhetoric. When one Washington department store cut saleswomen's wages by 50 percent and several hotels immediately reduced the wages of their maids by more than 50 percent, Schneiderman issued a national challenge. "Women needn't accept any wage cuts," she argued, "if they stand together like men."[44] Meanwhile, the National Woman's Party celebrated. On the seventy-fifth anniversary of the Seneca Falls Equal Rights Convention of 1848, Alice Paul announced to a cheering NWP gathering that at last some progress was being made on the road to legal equality between the sexes.[45]

The NWP embrace of what many working women felt to be a crushing defeat deepened increasingly bitter divisions between former suffrage movement allies. Rose Schneiderman accused the NWP of being nothing more than a tool of the manufacturers. She questioned their commitment to women's rights. For middle-class women to gain their rights at the expense of working women, she charged, was hardly an advance for sisterhood. For their part, the NWP alternately accused the WTUL of being Bolshevik pawns and of "talking like clubwomen." At the 1926 Women's Bureau Conference on Women in Industry, Josephine Casey, who had organized with Schneiderman and Newman in the early 1910s, said the League women were growing tired and conservative. "They spend the time they should use in organizing in lobbying state legislatures. No wonder the women's unions are deteriorating."[46]

If working women are slow to organize, Schneiderman retorted angrily, it is because they work such long hours, for such low wages, and under such stressful conditions that they have no time or energy for unions.

The . . . woman who has to support herself and who sometimes has other responsibilities in the way of dependents . . . usually works nine or ten hours a day, perhaps earning just enough to keep body and soul together, has to make her own clothes and attend to her personal life—and this after a nerve-racking, exhausting day at the factory. How much time is left for her to give to social questions! It is only after she is freed from . . . long hours and low wages that she can improve the calibre of her citizenship.

Former telephone worker Mabel Leslie put it more concretely: "We who have worked in industry know that it is conditions we face not theories, and we know that our hours will not be shortened nor our wages increased by wiping out what little support we have now on the statute books."[47]

The battle over the Equal Rights Amendment would rage on for decades, becoming in Schneiderman's words a "perennial headache consuming time, energy, paper, postage and much language." But as the 1920s wore on and antiradical hysteria faded, it became clear that the momentum of government change was behind the advocates of labor legislation. This was due in large measure to structural changes in state and federal governments. A series of state factory investigating commissions created after the pattern of the New York FIC had pressured state legislatures and executives to enact greater regulation and to create permanent agencies to deal with labor problems. Newman and Schneiderman had stood at the forefront of those battles in New York State, as lobbyists and as industrial experts. They had also provided advice to allies in other states. No longer strangers to the legislators and government officials they lobbied, by the early 1930s they found themselves in a position to exert real influence—both in New York and in the nation's capital.

THE ROOSEVELTS AND THE LURE OF
STATE POWER, 1919—1937

By 1924, when Al Smith was reelected governor of New York, Schneiderman, Newman, Elisabeth Christman, Leonora O'Reilly, Maud Swartz, and Agnes Nestor were becoming known in Albany as experts on women's labor issues. Though the respect with which they were now being treated was partly a result of their two decades of organizing and lobbying, there was another reason for their increased political influence: their association with Eleanor Roosevelt.

Eleanor Roosevelt had first encountered the NYWTUL network in October 1919, when the WTUL hosted the first International Congress of Working Women (ICWW) in Washington, D.C. Roosevelt, whose ambitious husband was then assistant secretary of the navy, was intrigued by the congress, which she described as "a very advanced and radical gathering." She invited the U.S. delegation—which included Schneiderman, Cohn, Newman, Maud Swartz, Leonora O'Reilly, and national WTUL president Margaret Dreier Robins—to lunch. That lunch marked the beginning of Eleanor Roosevelt's education in women's labor issues and of a forty-year friendship with Schneiderman.[48]

Two years later, back in New York and just beginning to explore possibilities for a political life separate from her husband's, Roosevelt accepted the invitation of longtime society friend Dorothy Whitney Straight to attend a fund-raising tea for the financially strapped New York WTUL. A year later Roosevelt decided to join the League. That decision was not unexpected behavior for a woman from New York's social elite; some of New York's wealthiest women were League backers. But Eleanor Roosevelt offered far more than financial support. She became one of the League's most dedicated and politically active members.[49]

Unlikely as it was that a woman of Eleanor Roosevelt's class and lineage would become active in a labor organization run by immigrant Socialist women, it seems almost inevitable given the particular web of social and political relationships in which she was embedded by the early 1920s. Frances Perkins, who had known Franklin Roosevelt since his days as a state legislator and who came back into his life when he was recovering from infantile paralysis, had remained in close touch with Schneiderman and Newman. Among Eleanor's New York society friends were several women, like Dorothy Whitney Straight, who were great admirers of Rose Schneiderman. And then there were Eleanor's newest associates, politically active women couples including English professor Marion Dickerman and Democratic Party organizer Nancy Cook. They too had recently become members of the NYWTUL.

One of the key figures in bringing all of these worlds together and in acquainting Roosevelt with the New York League was Mary Dreier, League president from 1906 to 1914. Dreier and her sister Margaret had been converted to the cause of industrial reform by Leonora O'Reilly back in 1899. As a result of their friendship with O'Reilly, the two decided to devote the better part of their considerable inheritances to the infant Women's Trade Union League. After her 1905 marriage to social worker Raymond Robins, Margaret moved to Chicago, where she ran the national WTUL until 1922. But Mary remained in New York, dedicated her life to the NYWTUL, and formed close friendships with O'Reilly, Schneiderman, and Newman. (O'Reilly's premature death from heart disease in 1927 was a profound loss to them all and drew Dreier, Schneiderman, and Newman closer together.)[50]

Well before Roosevelt came onto the scene, Dreier had cultivated some of the earliest ties between the NYWTUL and state government. In 1910, her life partner Frances Kellor was appointed director of the newly created New York Bureau of Industries and Immigration; she was the first woman appointed to an executive post in New York State government. The following year Dreier herself was appointed to the Factory Investigating Commission. In 1917, when both existing and pending labor legislation came under attack in New York State, Dreier organized the Women's Joint Legislative Committee (WJLC) to lobby on behalf of New York's major women's organizations.[51]

The WJLC institutionalized what had until then been an informal alliance between the WTUL, the National Consumer's League, the League of Women Voters, the YWCA, and several other progressive women's organizations. This was the nexus that Eleanor Roosevelt entered in 1921 when she decided to become active in New York women's politics. Roosevelt eventually served as chair of the WJLC. The WJLC also drew Marion Dickerman and Nancy Cook into the WTUL. In 1919, Mary Dreier asked Dickerman to run as the WJLC candidate against New York State assembly speaker Thaddeus Sweet, who had been one of Rose Schneiderman's most vitriolic attackers during the war. Sweet was near the top of the list of politicians targeted by the WJLC for defeat after New York women won the vote. The campaign against Sweet was unsuccessful, but it marked the beginning of a long association between Dickerman, her partner Nancy Cook, and the New York WTUL.[52]

Cook, in turn, drew Roosevelt into the League. Eleanor Roosevelt had met Cook in 1922 through the New York State Democratic Party. Their friendship blossomed rapidly and with great intensity. The two women began to attend WTUL meetings together, and Roosevelt found herself, against all odds, becoming friends with two immigrant working-class women: Rose Schneiderman and Maud Swartz. Before long, Roosevelt began inviting them to the scrambled egg suppers that she liked to cook for friends at her house on Sixty-fifth Street in Manhattan. And after 1925, they came regularly to the cottage at Val-Kill that FDR had constructed for Eleanor, Cook, and Dickerman.[53]

A special closeness developed between ER and Schneiderman that would continue until Eleanor's death. It was a remarkable bond—this friendship between a scion of one of the country's oldest and most aristocratic families and an immigrant daughter of the Lower East Side. But Roosevelt was anxious to experience what lay beyond the narrow confines of the privileged world in which she had been raised, and she made an effort to understand the lives of working women. Schneiderman reciprocated by showering ER with warmth and affection.

ER took on the cause of working women as her own, developing quickly into one of the League's most effective representatives. She lobbied for WTUL-sponsored legislative reforms both on the floor of the state legislature and in Democratic Party back rooms. Through her husband, she had greater access to those smoky rooms than most other women in the state. At the 1924 Democratic state convention she was able to push through planks endorsing an eight-hour day, minimum-wage legislation, and a constitutional amendment banning child labor. Drawing on her considerable influence with state Democratic Party leaders, Roosevelt helped make the New York State Democratic Party of the 1920s a standard-bearer for women workers.[54]

In this work she both learned from and taught Schneiderman and Newman, who had been lobbying state legislatures for over a decade. Perhaps most importantly, she helped grease the wheels for them. The same legislators who had been so rude just a few years earlier now began to recognize them as political actors to be reckoned with. Doors that had been closed began to open. Worn out by battles with both conservatives and radical feminists who opposed labor legislation, they reveled at finding themselves in a major-party mainstream.

They also enjoyed their new position as the dominant figures in both the national WTUL and its New York branch. In 1923, in recognition of her administrative talents, Maud Swartz was elected national WTUL president. The sharp-tongued Swartz quickly ran afoul of several important League activists, in particular the League's whirlwind secretary, glovemaker Elisabeth Christman. Swartz's decision to move the offices of the national League from Chicago to New York sparked fears that the New York WTUL women were trying to eclipse the role of the Chicago WTUL and its mainstays, Christman and Agnes Nestor. Not wanting to alienate the indispensable Christman, Swartz stepped down as WTUL president in 1926. Whatever Christman's problems with Swartz, they clearly did not extend to Schneiderman. When national League officers voted for a new president later that year, Christman joined them in awarding Schneiderman an easy victory. In 1923, after Newman and Miller returned to New York, where Eleanor Roosevelt had become the League's most visible new member, the WTUL's center of gravity permanently shifted to New York.[55]

Tired of the irreconcilable conflicts in the Philadelphia WTUL—and anxious to be closer to Schneiderman, Swartz, and other NYWTUL friends—Newman and Miller had resigned their Philadelphia posts in 1923 and set sail for the Third International Congress of Working Women, held in Vienna. There they met up with Schneiderman, printer Jo Coffin, Fannia Cohn, Elisabeth Christman, and Agnes Nestor, the U.S. delegates to the conference.[56]

But that conference was not the primary reason for their trip to Europe. They had much more pressing personal business. Miller, much as she loved

Newman, seems to have been torn about committing herself solely to a woman. For some time during her first years with Newman she had been conducting a secret relationship with a married man. In 1922 she became pregnant, and that affair came to an end. There is no record of what Newman or Miller were feeling at that time—whether there was talk of Miller marrying the father of her child, whether the pregnancy precipitated a crisis between the two women. But Miller's daughter, Elisabeth Burger, says that in the end the two agreed to continue to live together and to raise the child as theirs.[57]

However satisfying that emotional resolution may have been, Miller still feared that people would want to know how she had conceived. In an effort to protect her reputation, and perhaps that of the child's father also, Miller and Newman concocted a story that they would stand by for the rest of their lives: they were traveling to Europe several months before the conference, they told everyone, so that Miller could adopt an orphan. It is not clear whether she had already given birth by the time the rest of the WTUL crew arrived, whether she kept it a secret from them or whether close friends like Schneiderman and Swartz knew. But in any case, when they returned to New York, friends and reporters alike were told that Miller had adopted an orphan girl she named Elisabeth. Amazingly, Elisabeth herself was not told that Miller was her biological mother until she was seventeen years old.[58] And it was not until many years later that Newman helped Burger to track down the identity of her father. Such remarkable secretiveness between mother and daughter reveals two key strains in Miller's personality: a powerful need for privacy in sexual matters and a consuming concern with propriety and the opinions of others. It is all the more remarkable, given her emotional makeup, that Miller was so comfortable raising her daughter with another woman. But neither she nor anyone else seems to have made much fuss about the decision.

Miller and Newman brought their baby back to New York, rented an apartment in the West Village, and set up a household. By all accounts they were as excited and happy about it as any young family. There is no indication in letters or other sources that they feared hostile responses, although they did choose to live in Greenwich Village, the most tolerant of all environs for a lesbian couple in that era. Nancy Cook and Marion Dickerman, among others, lived nearby. So did Democratic Party activist Molly Dewson and her partner, Polly Porter.[59]

Elisabeth Burger recalls of her childhood that "from time to time I had the sense that my situation was different, but only from time to time. And only in terms of the fact that I had no father and also my father was never mentioned. I went to a fairly nonconventional school . . . and so people didn't stereotype. Conventional ways of living were not stressed."[60]

As unusual as this family was for the 1920s and 1930s, friends and colleagues seemed to take it at face value. Both women kept pictures of Elisabeth on their desks at work. And virtually every letter written to Newman or Miller sent love to the other woman and to their child. For Miller, who was raised by her grandmother and maternal aunt, this all-female household probably felt comfortable and familiar. But the two adult women in the household were not related by blood and, for all anyone knew, had adopted a child to raise together. Their acceptance by both men and women in the labor movement and in government is an interesting commentary on the social space accorded to some female couples in the years before gay rights became a political issue.[61]

When they first returned to New York, only Newman had a job, working with Dr. George Price to build a new ILGWU health center. The prospect was alluring, because she greatly admired Price, whom she had come to know when they worked together on the Joint Board of Sanitary Control in 1913. He was a warm and charismatic man whom she thought of as a visionary figure in the new field of union-sponsored health care. Anxious for Newman to accept, Price helped find Miller a job as inspector for the Joint Board—the same position Newman had held more than a decade earlier.

Since she left Bryn Mawr, Miller's life had followed the direction of Newman's career. But once they returned to New York, that pattern would change for good. As Miller was welcomed into the city's well-established network of educated women activists, her career began to follow a trajectory of its own. While Newman worked for the ILGWU, the WTUL, and in various temporary government appointments, Miller stepped onto a fast track that would carry her to top labor posts in Albany and Washington, D.C. She would take Newman with her—as consultant, negotiator, and advisory board member on a variety of councils and committees. But a permanent shift occurred in the late 1920s, as the spotlight of public attention moved from Newman to Miller.

Naturally, this change began to subtly alter the tenor of their cross-class, interethnic relationship. As their daughter Elisabeth would later put it, "Pauline's strengths were not really stressed much" in her growing-up years, though Newman was home with the child more often than the peripatetic Miller was. From the late 1920s on, while Newman stayed in New York, Miller would divide her time between their home in New York and offices in Albany or Washington. Miller—whom Elisabeth identified with even before she knew that Miller was her biological mother—was both primary decision-maker and primary role model for the child. "There was a kind of accepted feeling," Burger remembers, "that my mother was the more polished, educated one of the two and that was to be my model."[62]

The partnership between the two women remained strong and loving, and whenever they were apart they wrote voluminous daily "Fried-Paul" letters filled with details of their work and travels. Still, as Miller climbed the political ladder through the 1930s and 1940s, Newman's political influence came to rest as much on her association with Miller as on her own work. That can't have been an easy position for a woman of Newman's ambition and intellect.

But if she was unhappy about this situation, she has left no trace of such feelings. She had constructed a delicate equilibrium between Frieda and Elisabeth, the ILGWU, and the Women's Trade Union League—a balance that kept her from feeling trapped in any one social-political-emotional nexus. If she began to feel impatient with playing second fiddle to Schneiderman and Miller, she retreated to her own bailiwick at the ILGWU's Union Health Center. She clearly valued that job and the freedom it afforded her; she stayed with it for the next sixty years.

Miller's political ascendancy marked a new and important phase in the League's relations with government: a period of nearly complete identification with the Democratic Party and the political career of Franklin D. Roosevelt. It began in the mid-1920s, even before Franklin Roosevelt was elected governor of New York. And it continued through his years in the White House, when the women of the WTUL would see their vision of industrial reform written into law across the United States.

The two people most important in shaping Franklin Roosevelt's understanding of labor issues were Rose Schneiderman and Maud Swartz. His friendship with the two dated back to the mid-1920s, when Eleanor first introduced them. Though she had invited them many times to Val-Kill and even Campobello, ER was reluctant to ask Swartz and Schneiderman to Hyde Park, the sanctuary of Franklin's mother Sara. Sara's animosity toward Eleanor's political friends had worsened since ER had started doing such unseemly things as speaking to chambermaids at union meetings and walking picket lines with various groups of women factory workers. And Schneiderman was, on top of everything else, Jewish. In the casually anti-Semitic, ruling-class atmosphere of Hyde Park, Schneiderman would certainly stand out. Still, in 1926 Eleanor took the risk, because she believed that the two red-headed labor organizers had important insights to offer her husband.[63]

He bonded with them immediately; even Eleanor was surprised by the quick rapport they developed. Frances Perkins had noted a change in FDR since his struggle with infantile paralysis. "He had become conscious of other people," Perkins wrote, "of weak people, of human frailty." Perhaps that can partly explain his openness to a couple of immigrant Socialist working women. In any case, the convalescing politician spent hours deep in conversation with Swartz and Schneiderman, drawing them out on every aspect of their expertise. Sometimes he picked them up in his specially fitted car and drove them from New York City to Hyde Park, questioning and talking the whole way. Like so many others, the two were thoroughly seduced.[64]

"One of FDR's great talents," Schneiderman later recalled,

> was in getting people to talk about the things they knew. . . . Maud and I were delighted to tell him all we knew about the theory and history of the trade union movement. . . . We told him about the sweat shops and the tuberculosis rate in the printing industry before the unions were organized. . . . We told him about the prevailing thirteen-hour day. . . . We told him about wages of four and five dollars a week, of how the trade unions were the first to get children under ten out of the factories. . . . We told him everything we had learned in our years in the labor movement.

And FDR apparently took it all in.[65]

Frances Perkins would later argue that FDR's ideas about the labor movement and about government's proper relationship to workers were crystallized and fleshed out during the conversations he had with Swartz and Schneiderman from 1925 to 1928. "These intelligent trade unionists made a great many things clear to Franklin Roosevelt," Perkins wrote, "that he could hardly have known any other way. . . . Relying on the knowledge he had gained from these girls he appeared to have a real understanding of the trade-union movement." Both Perkins and Roosevelt would continue to consult the two women as they worked out the theory and the details for what became the New Deal labor policies.[66]

It was a reciprocal relationship. Without the Roosevelts' friendship, the WTUL would likely have folded by the end of the 1920s. Eleanor Roosevelt's contributions through the 1920s and 1930s, and those she convinced friends and relatives to make, kept the League afloat during very lean times. In 1931, Schneiderman wrote to Eleanor a letter that was both a thank-you and a request for more: "It seems so natural to turn to you for help. . . . There are times . . . when only your cooperation will have any effect."

ER cooperated generously. From 1925 through the 1940s, the Roosevelts hosted annual Christmas parties complete with presents for the children of League members. These parties gave the Roosevelt children their first exposure to poor and immigrant youngsters. ER also began donating royalties from her published works to help pay WTUL bills. And while FDR was governor, she marshaled wealthy contributors to help the League pay off the mortgage on its Lexington Avenue headquarters.[67]

In 1929, in honor of the NYWTUL's twenty-fifth anniversary, Eleanor and Franklin Roosevelt invited three hundred League members to celebrate at

Hyde Park. The Roosevelts chartered a boat for their guests, and Schneiderman and Swartz came up a night early to help prepare. On June 8, 1929, Newman, Miller, Christman, the rest of the NYWTUL executive board, and 250 working women steamed up the Hudson River for their date with the governor and his wife. It was sufficiently unusual for industrial workers to be spending an afternoon with the governor at his home that the *New York Times* ran a story on page 1. No other American labor organization, the *Times* commented, had ever celebrated in such a setting.[68]

FDR's mother Sara, who had gradually warmed to Schneiderman over the years, personally welcomed the WTUL members to her home. And ER presented Schneiderman, as the League's president, with a check for $30,000 to pay off the mortgage on the NYWTUL building. League members staged a song and dance pageant written by Mary Dreier. They reenacted the 1909 shirtwaist uprising, the Triangle Shirtwaist Factory fire, and other important events in WTUL history, creating a remarkable tableaux against the grand backdrop of the governor's Hudson River estate.

Then, in a speech that showed just how far she had come from the anger and distrust she felt in the aftermath of the Triangle fire, Schneiderman heralded the importance of cross-class alliances, calling for the creation of an American Labor Party that included both workers and friends of labor like the Roosevelts. FDR's speech seemed to validate Schneiderman's faith that a new era had begun. In his first pass at what would become the Social Security Act of 1935, he announced the formation of a commission to study ways to enact an old-age pension law for workers, an issue he had come to champion after his discussions with Swartz and Schneiderman. Writing to thank him, Schneiderman effused, "I wish there were a million more like you and Eleanor."[69]

Admiration and affection for the Roosevelts colored Schneiderman's and Newman's political views from then on, moving them away from the Socialist Party and into the left wing of the Democratic Party. In some measure this was due to the Roosevelts' charisma. The two women were also undoubtedly attracted to power; there was more than a little awe in the way these usually unflappable women spoke about their friendship with the famous couple.

But the root of the Roosevelts' appeal for the League women was that both Franklin and Eleanor seemed to genuinely like and appreciate them. FDR would take Schneiderman rowing on the Val-Kill. He spent afternoons chatting and laughing with her, as if they were the most natural of friends. When he drove her upstate they indulged in impromptu roadside hot dog roasts. She and Swartz shared in family evenings at Hyde Park when FDR would sit by the fire in his bathrobe reading aloud. They went on camping trips with Eleanor and the children. It was all very casual and surprisingly intimate. At the same time, Eleanor came weekly to the League clubhouse to read aloud or lead discussions on current events, after which she chatted informally in the kitchen while making hot chocolate for "the girls."[70]

The Roosevelts' genuine willingness to learn from women so different from themselves contrasted sharply with the condescension working-class League members had felt from earlier wealthy supporters, like Anne Morgan and Alva Belmont. Ironically, the Roosevelts achieved with charm what the former could not through coercion. During the 1909 strike and for years afterward, Schneiderman and Newman had resisted elite women's attempts to turn them away from Socialism. Now they left the Socialist Party willingly, for it was through the Roosevelts that the women of the WTUL became players in Albany and Washington.

The heyday of the WTUL's political influence began in 1928, when, shortly after his election as governor of New York, FDR made Frances Perkins the first woman Industrial Commissioner in the country. Perkins brought the network further inside by making Frieda Miller director of the state's Bureau of Women in Industry.[71] Through the 1920s, Schneiderman and Newman had ridden each week to Albany on the Monday Empire State Express and then waited endlessly to speak to legislators or Labor Department administrators. Now their old friend Frances Perkins was running the state's Labor Department. They were frequent dinner guests at the executive mansion. The First Lady of the state debated publicly on behalf of WTUL legislative initiatives. And the governor wrote personal notes to thank Schneiderman for her "splendid and effective help." With the strong support of the governor, the NYWTUL network made New York State a laboratory for labor reforms that would later be enacted on a national level.[72]

Three years later, the Roosevelt administration broke another barrier by appointing Maud Swartz as the first trade unionist to become secretary of labor for New York State. Eleanor Roosevelt had pushed hard to make it happen. Swartz wrote to "thank you Eleanor for all the good words and kind acts you have put in to make this appointment possible." Over the next six years Swartz remade the office, transforming it from a purely bureaucratic one into a whirlwind of activity. She became organized labor's voice in state government, establishing a precedent for the office that would carry on for many years.[73]

Not surprisingly, when Franklin Roosevelt campaigned for the presidency in 1932, the WTUL worked hard to mobilize the working-class vote. His lopsided victory, Rose Schneiderman assured him, "shows clearly that we are ready as a nation to take forward steps in the reconstruction of our social order." Roosevelt took a symbolic step toward that reconstruction when he appointed the first woman to a cabinet position: Frances Perkins, who became secretary of labor. In turn, Perkins invited Schneiderman to Washington, appointing her as the only woman on the National Recovery Administration's Labor Advisory Board, which was created by the National Industrial Recovery Act of 1933 (NIRA). For the next decade, though still technically president of the national WTUL and the NYWTUL, Schneiderman became, essentially, a government administrator.[74]

The NRA job recognized the role that Schneiderman had been carving out for herself since the First World War. Schneiderman had become an expert on wages, hours, and working conditions in the industries where women workers predominated. Her new job tested her knowledge. Because she was the only woman among them, her Labor Advisory Board colleagues expected her to write the codes for every industry with large numbers of women workers. She was to set minimum wages, maximum hours, and safety standards for millions of women workers across the country.

Schneiderman described her years in Washington as "the most exhilarating and inspiring of my life." She had traveled far from the shop where she once sewed hats. She was a presidential appointee, with a staff and an office in the nation's capital. And she was part of a politically savvy network of women with whom she had worked for over twenty years in the struggles for woman suffrage and labor legislation. To participate in the shaping of a new federal government structure was a remarkable experience for all of them, but for none so much as the Polish-born Jew whose formal schooling had ended when she was thirteen years old.[75]

Her appointment to a post in FDR's administration brought her greater visibility than any other woman labor activist of her day. By January 1934, the *New York Times* was calling Rose Schneiderman the "leader of nine million women workers in the United States." Her closeness to the president and First Lady also increased her influence with male labor leaders, who were far more impressed by her appointment to the NRA board than they had been by anything she'd done as an organizer. During her NRA years, Schneiderman could boast the friendship and cooperation of several union presidents. Among them were Max Zaritsky of the capmakers, who had long been an admirer of hers, and also two union men who were not known for their appreciation of women's leadership qualities: the ILGWU's David Dubinsky, and the Amalgamated Clothing Workers' president, Sidney Hillman.[76]

In part they were attracted by her contrasts. Over the years Schneiderman had begun to present herself as increasingly demure. She wore dresses and pearls and carefully applied red lipstick. She cultivated an acceptable feminine style. Compared to the rougher, pushier Cohn, Newman, and Shavelson,

Schneiderman displayed a comforting softness around her male union colleagues. But underlying her sweet exterior was a steely core. She was intriguing, because beneath the lipstick was a mouth Schneiderman was unafraid to use.

David Dubinsky liked dealing with Schneiderman in this period because she could make things happen. During the summer of 1933, Schneiderman engineered an NRA dressmaker's code that breathed fresh life into his destitute union, which was still reeling from the 1929 crash. In a 1934 speech to the ILGWU officers, Dubinsky mused on Schneiderman's access to power. "Rose has a lot to say in Washington. If anybody does not do the right thing, Rose Schneiderman knows the address of the White House." A man who prided himself on paying back debts, Dubinsky never forgot that Schneiderman had done him a huge favor early in his presidency of the union. In the years to come, he would prove to be an important personal and professional ally.[77]

Schneiderman was excited by wielding the stamp of federal power. After years of frustrating, bloody, and unsuccessful attempts to organize southern textile towns during the late 1920s, Schneiderman told ER during the summer of 1933 that she found her role in shaping a cotton textile code "thrilling." "The code, though not an ideal one, will go far toward making life and work for the tens of thousands of textile workers more humane and secure. The fact that children under sixteen will now be outlawed from the industry will not only help make room for adult men and women but will also set a standard for other industries." Compared to the painstaking and often fruitless work of organizing, the NRA seemed to be ushering in change at a breathtaking pace and on a vast scale. What "thrilled" Schneiderman was the prospect of bringing improved wages, hours, and conditions to the majority of women workers who did not belong to unions. She summed up her feelings in a letter to ER: "I hope in my humble way to be of service to the millions of women who will benefit by the NRA."[78]

But Schneiderman quickly recognized that the NRA was not all it promised to be for women workers, and she found that her ability to rectify its inequities was limited. She had been on the job for only one month when she announced angrily to the press that NRA officials had put in place lower minimum-wage scales for women workers. In fields dominated by women, she railed, men were being guaranteed a higher wage. She called for new NRA codes that would set a single wage for men and women. In a rare instance of cooperation, the National Woman's Party joined the WTUL, the National Consumer's League, the YWCA, and the National League of Women Voters in a letter of protest to NRA head Hugh Johnson. Eleanor Roosevelt supported them. But no change was made.[79]

Schneiderman also condemned the NRA for its failure to deal equitably with

African American women. Although she tried to use her position to change that situation, she won fewer battles than she lost. Her signal NRA victory came in negotiating a code in the handkerchief industry that forced manufacturers to lift their ban on hiring black women in skilled positions; however, she was unable to block a line of the laundry code that allowed southern employers to pay black women less than half of what they paid white women. And she was unable to bring domestic workers under the protection of the NRA, though she argued that the government had no reason not to "accept and treat the domestic worker . . . like any other wage earner." Because domestic labor was one of the few fields open to black women, exclusion of domestic workers from the NRA codes meant that most black working women received no benefit from the NRA.[80]

Realizing that women workers in Puerto Rico (whose residents had been made U.S. citizens in 1917) also labored without protection under the NRA, Schneiderman traveled there in 1934 to gather information for a code covering the island's needleworkers. What she found was a subcontracting system that harked back to the early years of the century in New York, a system based on homework and starvation wages. She encouraged Eleanor Roosevelt to observe the terrible conditions for herself. "Your coming at this time will be of inestimable value. . . . It will do more good than any one of us can do."[81]

Roosevelt agreed to take a "working vacation" with her friend, journalist Lorena Hickock, and Schneiderman. The trip was to provide a respite from the glare of the capital's lights. (Throughout this period Roosevelt and Schneiderman were always reminding each other of the need to take vacations.) The group toured villages and spoke with home workers as young as nine years old. On their return, they filed recommendations with the NRA for a one-dollar minimum wage for all Puerto Rican garment workers. But they were unable to prevent passage of a code that Schneiderman slammed as "not worth the paper it was written on . . . a farce, a travesty," because it allowed home workers to be paid less than half the wage of factory workers. The result of the code was an increase in homework and a decline in the number of factory jobs. Many women factory workers lost their jobs.[82]

Discouraged, Schneiderman attributed the failure of the code to "lack of compliance." She did not acknowledge, then or later, the myriad ways that employers could and did harm women workers while fully complying with NRA regulations. Most common among these, in the United States as well as Puerto Rico, was using speedups in combination with layoffs to balance the cost of increased wages. The NRA codes offered no protection against such measures.[83]

Such problems with the codes were made moot in June 1935, when the

Supreme Court struck down the NIRA, declaring it unconstitutional. An angry and deflated Schneiderman returned from Washington, from the spotlight of national press attention and the apex of her career, to the more familiar terrain of New York and the Women's Trade Union League. There, too, she found an organization in the throes of transition.

During the years that Schneiderman was in Washington, Mary Dreier had taken over the New York WTUL, while Elisabeth Christman ran the national League. The NYWTUL annual report for 1933–34 reported that Section 7a of the NIRA, affirming workers' right to organize, had been a boon to their organizing efforts. The new slogan "the president wants you to join a union" gave confidence to some of the most exploited of women workers—black and Hispanic service workers and new immigrants. During the mid-1930s the NYWTUL did more successful organizing than at any time in the past decade. But years of severe economic depression had nearly dried up financial contributions. The national League was so strapped for funds that it had not held a convention since 1929.[84]

Rose Schneiderman's closeness to the president and First Lady made the League more visible nationally and more credible as a voice for working women than at any time in its history. Unfortunately, the Roosevelts were also the only thing standing between the League and bankruptcy. In late 1932, the financial situation was so dire that Eleanor Roosevelt had to donate $300 weekly, for three months running, just to pay salaries and bills at the NYWTUL. She agreed to chair the League's Financial Committee and, along with Schneiderman, did intensive fund-raising over the next few months. But Schneiderman's departure from organizing and lobbying had left a big hole in the League staff and hurt the League's ability to attract donors.[85]

To pick up the slack, Pauline Newman, Maud Swartz, Frieda Miller, and Mary Dreier became more involved in organizing than they had since the early 1920s. They found that the terrain of the trade union movement had changed dramatically since their last stint as organizers. An impending split between craft unions devoted to the American Federation of Labor and industrial unions committed to the new Congress of Industrial Organizations threatened the League's unquestioned alliance with the AFL. As a new idealism swept the nation during the early 1930s, a younger generation of women was breathing fresh life into the New York WTUL. But they were also challenging the political wisdom of old-timers like Newman and Schneiderman.

Partly out of respect for the Roosevelts, and partly in anger over the internecine battles that had almost destroyed many labor unions in the 1920s, Schneiderman and Newman were wary of associating the League with any insurgent union movements, Communist or otherwise. The result was that in the eyes of some of the younger League members, like WTUL secretary Bert Paret, education director Elsie Glick, and chief organizer Eleanor Mishnun, the two women began to appear conservative and stuck in their ways.[86]

Mary Dreier, as one of Newman's most trusted and intimate friends, tried to press Pauline on some of the contested questions, especially the League's allegiance to the AFL. "It seems to me," she wrote Newman in 1934, "that the League Executive Board members are afraid to act with independent judgement in cases . . . when the AF of L has not acted." Dreier worried that by limiting the freedom of younger League activists to work with CIO unions, if they chose, the League might lose them, making it the province only of older women. "We have so few who have enthusiasm and youth and courage and if sometimes we do not agree it does seem to me that we need not be such trimmers. . . . I have great hopes from B. Paret, Elsie and Eleanor but I know there won't be any health in us if we prevent their normal reactions to injustices from finding opportunity for expression."[87]

Newman was unmoved. "I think I have given more of myself to the League in the last two years than ever before," she replied. In terms of organizing, this claim was certainly true. She had been out in the field organizing beauty parlor workers, hotel chambermaids, and laundry workers with a fervor unseen since her tour for the ILGWU twenty years earlier. Maud Swartz too had been "involved at every turn." Newman said, "I don't think that either Paret, Mishnun or anyone else can say that they lack co-operation of the 'old-timers.' In the organization work Eleanor knows that she is free to call upon me at any and all times—and she does, too. . . . Bert and Elsa [sic], too, know that they get all the co-operation they want from me."

Newman further suggested that the younger women were naive in their attraction to the Communist Party. "I can understand," she wrote, "how our young members may be caught in a net of fine phrases, how high-sounding motives may thrill them." But having recently watched the ILGWU be torn apart by Communist "tactics," she wrote, she had "only contempt for them—a contempt based upon knowledge and experience. . . . Conservative? Be it so. I do not think however, that such an attitude should necessarily 'discourage any one who comes to us with enthusiasm and ardor.' " It is unclear here whether Newman was saying that her views should not discourage young women who had the courage of their convictions, or that if they really cared about organizing women they would follow orders and get down to work. But in any case, a battle ensued. Schneiderman and Newman won, and several promising young women organizers decided to leave the League.[88]

Most of these women avoided confrontation, citing marriage as their reason for resigning. But some made clear that they were leaving for political reasons. WTUL educational director Elsie Glick was one of these. A Socialist trained in the ILGWU educational programs, Glick battled with Schneiderman to eliminate what she considered "fluff" courses like pottery and dancing from the NYWTUL school curriculum. She wanted to teach only "serious" courses meant to prepare women for union leadership—courses in economics, political theory, and trade union fundamentals. She believed that the League could not afford to spend precious resources on frivolities in such dire times. Schneiderman, however, did not consider "cultural" courses frivolous. In difficult times, Schneiderman argued, enjoyable courses were important for relieving both physical and emotional tensions. She put her foot down, and Glick left the League.[89]

Some younger women chose to stay despite their differences with the old guard. Eleanor Mishnun contributed greatly to the League's major organizing success of the 1930s, a union of New York laundry workers. Another who devoted herself to NYWTUL work from the mid-1920s through the 1940s was Mabel Leslie, who had come to the New York League from the militant Boston telephone worker's movement. And there were other talented young women who worked for the League over the next decade.

But the moment passed quickly for the group of younger women who had hoped to radicalize and modernize the New York WTUL. After unsuccessfully challenging the "old-timers" who for the past fifteen years had been taking the League in the direction of accommodation, both with the AFL and with government, women like Glick saw no choice but to leave. Those who stayed, like Mishnun, felt obliged to curb or sever ties with the Communist Party and the CIO. As a result, the WTUL came to be identified almost exclusively with older women, particularly Rose Schneiderman, and with the AFL. This ultimately hurt the organization. In the late 1930s and early 1940s, when the CIO mobilized a new generation of women labor activists, the WTUL seemed to many of them old-fashioned and hidebound. These were women who might have joined, but didn't, in a time when the League really needed some fresh blood and new ideas.

Ideological differences can partly explain the failure of Schneiderman and Newman to open up the WTUL to change in the 1930s. But a generation gap and differences in sexuality played their parts as well. Schneiderman and Newman simply did not understand some of the young women who were fighting to change the League. Clearly these younger members cared about organizing women, or they would not have joined the WTUL at all. But their politics had been forged in the 1920s and even the 1930s, very different eras from that which had formed the 1909 vintage. Many of these young women, like Elsie Glick, were more class- than gender-focused. Older activists' vision of building a community of women, of creating organizations that nurtured friendship as well as collegiality, seemed to them quaint, archaic, and irrelevant. For most of them the League was a political commitment, largely separate from their personal lives. It is possible that many of them never intended to stay for more than a few years. It made sense to them to leave the League when they married.

For the women who had sustained the NYWTUL since 1914, on the other hand, League work, friendship, and romantic partnership were so thoroughly interwoven as to be virtually inseparable. They experienced their network of colleagues and friends as a fulfillment of the industrial feminist vision of intimate comradeship. And they hoped through the League school and programs to generate similar feelings of emotional closeness in a younger generation of working women—"a comradeship that goes beyond the classroom and perhaps even reaches out to fill the void of insecurity and loneliness that is today the greatest underminer of labor solidarity." They were extremely pleased when young women workers responded with pleasure or excitement to League classes, lobbying trips, and social gatherings. But they were completely unprepared when younger women challenged their leadership or suggested different paths. The League's veterans, now in their forties and fifties, had been working for decades to build an organization that reflected their vision. When younger women tried to reshape it during the mid-1930s, they found themselves unable to let go.[90]

This unwillingness to yield the reins was motivated partly by fear of losing their own fairly comfortable positions. By the mid-1930s members of the League network had become thoroughly entrenched in the state and, to a lesser extent, federal bureaucracies. The experience of sitting behind government desks and the joy of being friends with the Roosevelts blunted the edges of their radical analysis. With so much they still wanted to do, they felt they would have to be crazy to give up their hard-won positions. What they did not see—what so few could see then—was that FDR's gift for making formerly marginal people feel like insiders did not alter his politician's understanding of the realities of U.S. power relations. The heady feeling of being inside for the first time skewed the perceptions of many politically savvy activists. Schneiderman and Newman were not alone.

"Please always come to lunch or to see me," Eleanor Roosevelt wrote Schneiderman in 1933 upon hearing that the latter had been in Washington without calling. "I always feel badly when I miss my friends." People who have that kind of access to the White House rarely feel inclined toward revolution. As far as Schneiderman was concerned, the best hope for change lay with her dear friends then residing at 1600 Pennsylvania Avenue. In a letter urging

Eleanor Roosevelt not to work herself into exhaustion, she wrote, "You and the President are the country's dearest and most precious possessions and your well being is of the utmost importance."[91]

These cozy relations between the League and the Roosevelts were epitomized by the following anecdote from 1936. When the WTUL announced its first national convention in seven years, Eleanor Roosevelt invited Schneiderman and Newman to bring a group of working women to stay at the White House. Her invitation won the League front-page coverage in newspapers across the country. Describing the arrival of seven Alabama textile workers, six New York garment workers, a waitress, and a stenographer to spend a week at the White House, reporters could barely restrain their amusement.

"A waitress, a stenographer and a dressmaker from New York, and a textile worker from Alabama have unpacked their bags in the Lincoln room of the White House," the *New York Times* chuckled. When a reporter asked Nell Morris about the prospect of breakfasting every day for a week with the First Lady, she replied, "I think it's the most wonderful thing that ever happened to a Southern girl. It's an honor to the state of Alabama." Dressmaker Feige Shapiro was more serious. This, she told reporters, was a historic moment— the first time industrial workers had been invited to sleep at the White House. It was a stunning illustration of how easily the Roosevelts won the hearts of disfranchised Americans simply by being gracious.[92]

When the young WTUL activists arrived at the White House on the evening of April 30, 1936, they were greeted by President Roosevelt. He ushered them into a firelit parlor, offered them supper, and told them to enjoy the main-floor sitting room until they were ready for bed. Eleanor Roosevelt assured them that the icebox in the kitchen would be left unlocked all night in case they felt like coming down for a midnight snack. She told them she'd see them at breakfast the following morning at seven. Pauline Newman, worried that some of "the girls" might oversleep, played the authoritarian older sister to the Roosevelts' relaxed parents: she warned them that anyone who didn't show up for breakfast on time would not get to finish out the week in the White House. No one needed to be coaxed.[93]

New York dressmaker Feige Shapiro joked that the most awesome thing about the whole experience was the size of Lincoln's bed. She had never before slept in a bed where her "toes didn't touch the end." Shapiro later told the authors of the *Jewish Woman in America* that she was taking it all in stride until she woke up from a dream in the middle of the night and looked around at the room where she was staying. Suddenly it hit her where she was; she exclaimed aloud, "Imagine me, Feigele Shapiro, sleeping in Lincoln's bed!"[94]

Pauline Newman was still excited decades afterward: "It was the first time that happened. Working girls were the guests of the White House . . . millinery workers, and clerical workers, garment workers and textile workers who never dreamed of being guests of the White House [were] having breakfast with Mrs. Roosevelt every morning." Looking back on that week, forty years later, she wondered if the White House would ever be so open again. That week in the White House is an apt symbol for the Roosevelt administration's relationship with working women.[95]

Franklin Roosevelt offered a greater opportunity for working women to participate in state policy formulation than any president before him. The key labor bills to come out of FDR's first two terms were all influenced by the political alliance between the Roosevelts, Frances Perkins, and the WTUL network. Schneiderman helped to work out the specifics of wage, hour, and safety regulations for the NRA codes. When the NIRA was declared unconstitutional, Swartz, Schneiderman, and Newman consulted with New York senator Robert Wagner (whom they knew from their work on the Factory Investigating Commission) on the framing of the National Labor Relations Act. Schneiderman provided crucial input on the first Social Security Act, arguing that benefits should be extended to employees of small as well as large businesses. Finally, there was the 1938 Fair Labor Standards Act, which created wage, hour, and safety standards for all workers, regardless of sex.[96]

Those bills, we now know, brought far more limited changes than working-class activists like Schneiderman had hoped for in the heady early days of FDR's first administration. The invitation to sleep in Lincoln's bed, like much of what Franklin Roosevelt offered poor and working Americans, proved to be more symbolic than substantive. Still, Newman's reflection, four decades later, that no other president had opened the White House in the way Roosevelt did is worth recalling here, for it highlights the reason why so many Americans, including working women and African Americans excluded by much of the New Deal legislation, expressed an abiding loyalty to Roosevelt.

What FDR didn't accomplish in the New Deal has come to be seen by many historians as more significant than what he did. Schneiderman and Newman, like so many Americans at that time, felt differently. FDR had done more for working women than any president before him. In addition—and the impression this made was inestimable—he had treated them with respect. That same feeling on the part of African Americans, union men, and other working people created the emotional basis for a new Democratic Party coalition that would hold firm from the 1930s through 1968.

Rose Schneiderman, Maud Swartz, and Pauline Newman had been able to educate FDR, Frances Perkins, and Eleanor Roosevelt on the need to bring about real and permanent changes in government's relationship to labor.

Their work researching and framing bills on the state level created a framework for the striking new federal labor policies enacted between 1932 and 1940. Schneiderman and the League women had spoken out forcefully against administration policies that they felt fell short of their stated goals. It is true that they never criticized Roosevelt directly, in part because they believed that the partial victories won during FDR's first two terms represented important gains for workers, and in part because they were reluctant to challenge the man who'd made them insiders. But then, that could be said of many people in the 1930s. Even the Communist Party wisely displayed deference to Roosevelt's popularity among workers. Some would say Schneiderman and the League women compromised too much; but it is not clear what other choice they had.

NEW YORK STATE'S NEW DEPARTMENT OF LABOR, 1933–1943

At the same time they were working to institutionalize longtime legislative goals on the federal level, they continued to battle in New York State for more progressive and more complete labor laws. During all their years of fighting for government intervention in the workplace, Rose Schneiderman and Pauline Newman had contended that legislation was not a replacement for organizing but, rather, a catalyst. Government protection offered the lowest-paid, least-skilled women workers the support they absolutely needed before they could begin to organize themselves into unions. During the 1930s, using their influence in the National Recovery Administration, the New York State Department of Labor, and New York City government, the women of the NYWTUL network sought to prove that assertion in a two-front campaign to improve the wages and working conditions of New York's growing legions of service workers: waitresses, beauty parlor operators, laundresses, hotel maids, and domestic workers, many of whom were Latina and African American.

These women had been utterly ignored by the major unions because of both their gender and their race. A decade of organizing by Schneiderman and Newman had not improved conditions much.[97] But now, with Schneiderman and Mary Dreier on the NRA Regional Labor Board, Maud Swartz on the state Compliance Board, Pauline Newman on the New York City Compliance Board, and Frieda Miller running the state Women's Bureau, New York State became their laboratory. Using their power to enforce labor laws, they organized women who had long been seen as unorganizable and, within a few years, improved conditions for some of the most exploited of New York's workers.

Rose Schneiderman had been trying to organize New York's laundresses since 1905. She had begun in earnest in 1921, arguing that the shops they worked in were among the most dangerous and unhealthy workplaces in the city. Many of New York's commercial laundries were located in the basements of industrial buildings, where poor lighting and ventilation intensified a dank atmosphere permeated by fumes from cleaning chemicals and bleaches. "Nobody's health is good in a laundry," one woman worker told investigators. "Inhaling the steam keeps your throat dry and standing all day keeps your feet swollen. Some women get so weak they lose their grip in their hands and arms." Workers suffered serious injuries operating the laundry mangles, and tuberculosis germs bred easily in the warm dampness.[98]

After twelve years of unsuccessful attempts to get the AFL laundry union to recognize women laundry workers, Schneiderman tried another tack. Using her authority as an NRA official, she announced that the first minimum-wage code to be applied in New York State would be in the laundry industry. Frieda Miller, then head of the Bureau of Women in Industry and the minimum-wage division of the state's Labor Department, appointed Pauline Newman to negotiate that wage. Arguing that the $.31-per-hour minimum wage mandated by the NRA was too low for New York, Newman was able to convince employers to approve a higher state minimum.[99]

The response of women laundry workers was exactly what Schneiderman and Newman had predicted: certain that the government was behind them, they flooded the regional Labor Board with complaints about minimum-wage violations. In December 1933, citing blatant wage and safety violations, women in nine New York laundries struck. And as Schneiderman had promised, they flocked into a union. After a decade of organizing, the NYWTUL-sponsored Brooklyn Laundry Workers Union had boasted only nine members. By the spring of 1934, more than eight hundred women had paid their dues.[100]

Still, it was as hard to get the press to cover a strike centered in African American ghetto neighborhoods as it had been a quarter century earlier to win sympathetic coverage of a strike by Jewish and Italian immigrants. The NYWTUL used the same strategy it had then: it called in the "mink brigades." Newspapers marveled at the sight of wealthy white women emerging from limousines in the heart of the nation's second-largest black ghetto, Brooklyn's Bedford-Stuyvesant. One limo bore the license plate P-1, for the governor of Pennsylvania. It had brought Mrs. Cornelia Bryce Pinchot, the Pennsylvania governor's wife, to picket at the Sunshine and Colonial laundries. Pinchot told reporters that she had come to protest "outrageous and un-American" wage and safety standards. The following day, Mrs. R. S. Childs of Childs' Luncheonettes walked with the African American women strikers. She announced a movement among some of New York's wealthiest women to get the city's large hotels to revoke contracts with laundry owners who refused to negotiate with striking workers.[101]

But during this strike the NYWTUL also did something it could not have done twenty-five years earlier: it used government connections to prosecute laundry owners for violating the law. Strike organizer Eleanor Mishnun, finding that many of the laundries were dramatically in arrears on their city water taxes, passed that information on to regional Labor Board director Eleanor Herrick, a close friend of both Pauline Newman and New York mayor Fiorello La Guardia. The mayor promptly announced that the city would begin seeking back taxes from two hundred laundries that were paying less than the NRA-mandated minimum wage. Simultaneously, state Women's Bureau director Frieda Miller began issuing summonses for violation of New York state's NRA code. The results were immediate and dramatic—significantly shorter work weeks *and* 100 percent pay increases for many of the city's laundry workers.[102]

Although historians have seen the League's organizing heyday as the period from 1909 to 1914, NYWTUL leaders involved in both eras viewed the laundry campaign, and concurrent campaigns to organize hotel chambermaids and beauty parlor workers, as successes on a par with their garment union organizing two decades earlier. In both cases they were reaching out to unionize and protect unskilled women workers whom no male-led union had seriously tried to organize. And in both eras they had utilized a cross-class coalition of women to enhance the clout of an extraordinarily poor and exploited group of women workers.

But there were also key differences between these later drives and the earlier ones. First, they were attempting for the first time to organize large numbers of Latina, Caribbean, and African American women workers. Schneiderman would say that she was simply following the changing demographics of New York's industrial workforce. During the 1920s and 1930s, an increasingly large percentage of New York's women workers were Puerto Ricans, Caribbeans, and African Americans who were concentrated in service rather than manufacturing industries.

Second, League organizers now had some powerful friends in government. The NYWTUL's chief organizer, Eleanor Mishnun, worked tirelessly with laundresses, waitresses, and hotel maids, taking jobs in each of those trades to win the trust of the workers. But unlike earlier organizers, she could turn for help to League members who held appointments in the state Department of Labor—an agency that hadn't even existed in 1909.

Not only had the NYWTUL been one of the driving forces in creating such an agency; by the late 1930s the New York WTUL had for all intents and purposes *become* the New York State Department of Labor. In March 1937, Governor Herbert Lehman appointed Rose Schneiderman secretary of labor for the State of New York. In 1938 he made Frieda Miller the state's industrial commissioner; besides Perkins, she was the only woman in the country to occupy such a post. Nell Swartz was head of the state's Compensation Board, and Pauline Newman doubled as the state's minimum-wage expert and chief NYWTUL lobbyist.

While in earlier years they had offered others advice on state labor policy, now they were making and enforcing labor policy themselves. They had influence in the legislature as well, working together in a tightly linked network of officials and lobbyists to push for laws researched and framed by the New York WTUL. By day the women haunted the corridors of the state capitol, writing, speaking, twisting arms. Working as a team, they achieved several of their major goals. For the first time, New York extended legal protections to domestic and farm workers and ended the use of children as agricultural laborers.[103]

By night they met at Nell Swartz's Albany house for dinners. They cooked for each other and strategized together, and on occasion they played penny-a-point poker. Through depression and prosperity, through the war and into the peace that followed, Schneiderman, Newman, Miller, and Swartz played poker into the night, sometimes joined by Elisabeth Christman, Mary Dreier, Frances Perkins, and others. In some ways their overlapping friendship and politics mirrored the old boys' networks that had long reigned supreme in Albany and Washington, D.C. But it also reflected back on the goals of industrial feminism. Even in their playing of such a ritualized male politician's game as poker, they celebrated the longevity of their unique personal/professional network, their success as a team, not their competition as individuals.[104]

Still, there was a bittersweet tinge to the network's success, particularly for Rose Schneiderman. Her 1937 appointment as secretary of labor followed the death of Maud Swartz, her partner of twenty-five years. Swartz's health had been deteriorating for some time, but she and her friends had ignored the signs, blaming her deepening exhaustion on too much work. In mid-January, Swartz and Schneiderman attended FDR's second inauguration dinner. A few days later, Swartz, whose dangerously high blood pressure had ceased to respond to medication, suffered a heart attack.

"I am sorry to tell you," Schneiderman wrote Eleanor Roosevelt on January 29, "that Maud . . . was taken to the New York Hospital yesterday morning and cannot see anybody. It is her heart. . . . I am just terrified at the idea of what may happen." Swartz died two weeks later. Roosevelt traveled to New York to comfort Schneiderman at the funeral.[105]

Schneiderman was appointed to succeed Swartz as New York's secretary of labor. Just a few days after her partner's death, Schneiderman sat at Swartz's old desk at the Department of Labor. Telegrams of congratulations from colleagues in labor, women's, and Jewish organizations poured in while a dazed Schneiderman mourned her longtime friend. "I shall miss Maud terribly," she wrote Roosevelt, even in grief unwilling to reveal anything about their relationship. "We had been pals for twenty-three years. . . . Her loss is an irreparable one."[106]

It was a time of transition in Schneiderman's life. Her mother Deborah died in that same period. The mother and daughter had been unusually close, sharing an apartment throughout Schneiderman's adulthood. Rose reeled under the impact of the two losses. She went into seclusion for a few weeks at the West Redding, Connecticut retreat that Newman and Miller had built for themselves some years earlier. Then she began to rebuild. She emptied out the apartment in the Bronx where she had lived with her mother for many years. Then, at age fifty-six, Schneiderman rented the first apartment she had ever lived in alone.[107]

Schneiderman's pain and sense of loss was intensified by news of growing Nazi violence against European Jews. Writing Eleanor Roosevelt that she was "sick with anguish" over cousins still in Poland, she asked if there was anything Roosevelt could do. Frances Perkins helped Schneiderman to bring one elderly relative to this country. It is not clear what happened to the rest.

Wanting to rescue more than a handful of individuals, Schneiderman joined Max Zaritsky of the capmaker's union and Fannia Cohn and Mary Goff of the ILGWU in a labor consortium to get Jewish refugees out of Germany, Austria, and Poland. Her efforts brought her to the attention of Albert Einstein. During the summer of 1939, a few weeks before the beginning of World War II, he wrote her, "We have no other means of self-defense than our solidarity. . . . It must be a source of deep gratification to you to be making so important a contribution toward rescuing our persecuted fellow Jews from their calamitous peril and leading them toward a better future."[108] Her involvement in the refugee crisis exemplified Schneiderman's strategy for healing herself in the aftermath of emotional trauma—she threw herself passionately into work.

Her transition to the Labor Department, she wrote Eleanor Roosevelt, was easy "because of my close relationship with the Department all these years and also because the work of the Department . . . is so closely related with the work of the League." As New York's secretary of labor, she worked tirelessly to ensure enactment of the remaining pieces of the WTUL legislative agenda. At the top of her priority list was, after decades of struggle, to frame a state minimum-wage law for women that would finally stand up in court. Schneiderman and Newman had been working on this goal for twenty-five years. Just one year earlier, the U.S. Supreme Court had overturned yet another New York minimum-wage law. Now, in a surprise 1937 decision, the Court upheld a Washington State law similar to the one they had been trying to pass in New York. Within a short time, New York State had a minimum wage. Fittingly, Pauline Newman, one of the very first advocates of such a law, was appointed to negotiate codes in the industries where women predominated. A year later, Congress enacted the Fair Labor Standards Act, guaranteeing a minimum wage for all industrial workers.[109]

With these laws in place, Schneiderman was finally able to achieve victory in what she called "our own Thirty Years' War," the NYWTUL campaign to unionize New York's laundry workers. The successful 1934 strikes that followed the enactment of the NRA laundry code had brought enough laundry workers into unions that, in Schneiderman's words, "at last there was a basis for an organization in the laundry industry." Building on those successes and on the rapport she had established with Sidney Hillman of the CIO-affiliated Amalgamated Clothing Workers during their days at the NRA, in 1938 Schneiderman convinced the ACW to admit laundry workers. Dramatic changes followed quickly. Within a year, New York boasted a union of twenty-seven thousand laundry workers under contracts that guaranteed decent wages, reduced hours, sick leave with pay, and paid vacations.[110]

Similar use of the machinery of government enabled the League to pressure New York hotel owners to settle with striking hotel workers, including the much-overworked and -underpaid cleaning staff. The 1938 hotel settlement brought to successful conclusion another of the League's longest campaigns— to increase wages, shorten hours, and win a six-day week for New York's mostly black and Puerto Rican hotel maids.[111]

Finally, during that period the New York WTUL won some victories for the group of women workers who had proven most difficult for them to organize or to legislate protections for: domestic laborers in private homes. In 1939 the NYWTUL called a citywide conference on household employment. A central theme of the conference was what to do about "slave markets"—the depression-era phenomenon that brought desperate black women workers to selected street corners around New York City, where white housewives came to offer daily work to the lowest bidder.

The NYWTUL, the Communist Party, and the Negro Labor Committee (of which Rose Schneiderman and Fannia Cohn had been founding members) had all tried to unionize domestic workers during the 1930s. But organization, always slow, was nearly impossible among women who worked alone in private homes. And organizing black domestic workers raised a delicate problem: a majority of the organizers and many of the offending employers were Jewish. A great irony of the "slave markets" was that more than a few of the women who came to bargain on corners were the wives of trade unionists. For Jewish trade unionists to win the trust of African American domestic workers under those circumstances was not easy.[112]

The League decided to use its only real weapon, the state Department of Labor. Frieda Miller, now New York's industrial commissioner, convened a Street-Corner Committee composed of state and city officials, trade unionists, and welfare workers to try and eliminate the city's "slave markets." Chaired by NYWTUL secretary Cara Cook, the committee decided that the best short-term solution to the problem was to establish makeshift state employment bureaus on the street corners where the women gathered. Women workers would need little encouragement, they reasoned, to come in off the streets to offices where minimum-wage standards and working conditions could be regulated.

The bureaus worked beautifully. The first two, opened in the Bronx, reported more than six hundred successful employee-employer negotiations per day, for a total of nineteen thousand during their ten months of operation. But before the model program could be further developed, it was eliminated when the U.S. entry into World War II forced the government to shift funds from domestic programs to the war effort. The NYWTUL network did win one important improvement in the lives of domestic workers: it finally got New York to extend Social Security and workers' compensation to domestic workers. Ultimately, it was World War II, not the League, that brought an end to most of the slave markets by opening up employment opportunities for black women in defense-related work and other types of manufacturing.[113]

With the coming of war and the mobilization of millions of American women into defense work, the WTUL faced a whole new set of challenges. Schneiderman was anxious to return to her job at the League to help plan strategy for the war and the peace that would eventually follow. Though newly elected Republican governor Thomas E. Dewey asked her to stay on in her post, Schneiderman submitted her resignation as state secretary of labor shortly after the election of 1942. Early in 1943 she returned to her past office as president of the New York and national Leagues, where she set about working on wartime goals. As much as the war opened up opportunities for women workers, it also created new problems. The WTUL fought to preserve and enforce prewar regulations on wages, hours, and conditions, which came under attack by conservative legislators as soon as the war began. They planned and negotiated to try to preserve some of the heavy manufacturing jobs that the war had made available to women workers, and they pushed the federal government to establish a precedent by mandating equal pay for women workers under government contract.[114]

In 1942, President Roosevelt, who had been lobbied heavily by Rose Schneiderman and by his wife, issued an executive order mandating equal pay for women in plants doing wartime production. Frieda Miller appointed Pauline Newman to do the groundwork for enforcing that order in New York State. Newman found that 150 New York factories with government defense contracts admitted paying women workers less than men for the same work. The only way to really enforce the executive order and to extend equal pay benefits to all industrial workers, Newman argued, was to pass an "equal pay for equal work" bill. As in World War I, opponents warned that the bill would be expensive and unpatriotic and would promote greater expansion of government. Newman replied that there was only one real issue here: "the main and simple issue of paying women the same amount as men would be paid when they are doing the same job."[115]

In 1944, New York's Republican governor, Thomas Dewey, signed the Todd-Falk Bill, which outlawed pay discrimination in New York State on the basis of sex. Pauline Newman and NYWTUL secretary Blanch Freedman were hired as consultants to advise the state on how to put this law into practice. They found that antidiscrimination laws were virtually unenforceable, since manufacturers could always claim that the work women employees did was in some way less valuable than the work of men. Frustrated but unbowed, the NYWTUL began its last great legislative battle—for comparable worth laws.[116]

In 1945, Rose Schneiderman outlined her criteria for comparable worth. It should, she argued, apply "wherever the work involved is of the same general type, requires comparable skill, results in approximately equal productivity and is substantially of like quality." Looking back ten years later on a struggle the WTUL had not yet won, Schneiderman noted that laws prohibiting sex discrimination were meaningless without an enforceable comparable worth bill. That remains as true today as it was then.[117]

The WTUL never did succeed in passing either a state or federal comparable worth bill. But they raised an issue that would be taken up by later feminist activists both in union and legislative struggles. And though the intense political reaction of the postwar years would insure that New York's equal pay bill was one of the last legislative victories for the League network, conservative politicians would not be able to undo the changes that the WTUL had wrought over the preceding three decades. During the years between the two World Wars, a revamped cross-class women's alliance had helped to transform state and federal labor policy in the United States. Rose Schneiderman, Pauline Newman, Maud Swartz, Frieda Miller, and their two most powerful friends, Frances Perkins and Eleanor Roosevelt, were key to that transformation.

The minimum-wage and maximum-hours standards for which they had argued since the 1910s were now written into federal laws that covered millions of American workers. The structures they created to insure that women workers benefited from workers' compensation strengthened social insurance for all workers. Their success at extending Social Security and workers' compensation to domestic workers brought government protection to one of the most exploited sectors of the American working class. Last, their pioneering of equal pay laws and of criteria for comparable worth set the terms for future feminist struggles.

EMOTION

STRAINED

THROUGH A

THINKING

MIND:

FANNIA COHN,

THE ILGWU,

AND THE

STRUGGLE FOR

WORKERS'

EDUCATION,

1915–1945

Your ways of expressing the aims of labor's culture are a combination of genuine emotion strained through a thinking mind.—Historian Selig Perlman in a 1952 letter to Fannia Cohn

In 1916, Fannia Mary Cohn, then thirty-one years old, became the first woman to be elected vice president of a major U.S. union. After more than ten years of shop-floor organizing, Cohn, a small, swarthy woman with penetrating eyes and short-cropped graying hair, seemed poised to exert real influence over the garment union she had helped to build. Conscious of the historic moment, Cohn solemnly took upon herself the task of representing the women of the ILGWU. Of all the aspirations she had heard working women voice on picket lines, at meetings, and in late-night study groups, she believed one to be at the heart of their interest in trade unionism: the desire for personal development through education.

Education was central to the industrial feminist vision that had animated the women's strikes of 1909 through 1917. Before that era, young women workers had educated themselves any way they could—in night schools, in study groups, in collectives that pooled money to buy books. Now that their strikes had galvanized strong national garment unions, they expected workers' education to become a priority.[1]

In the years between the two World Wars, Cohn, Newman, Schneiderman, and Lemlich all heeded that call. Each worked to create educational programs for working-class women. Schneiderman cofounded and guided the New York WTUL School for Women Workers, which educated thousands of working women between 1923 and 1955. In 1923, Newman was appointed health educator for the ILGWU's Union Health Center, where for sixty years she developed programs to educate union members about nutrition, hygiene, mental health, and medicine. Lemlich led women's study groups and promoted newsletters written and edited by working-class housewives in the 1920s and 1930s.[2]

But none would so completely identify with the cause of workers' education as Fannia Cohn. With evangelical fervor, she argued that workers' education could transform the labor movement. Unions could succeed only if women participated fully, she believed. But female unionists had been crippled both by male prejudices and by their own lack of confidence. Workers' education, Cohn declared, held the potential to "change masculine attitudes toward women" and to "help to develop in working women a consciousness of their own importance."[3]

Cohn assured labor movement leaders that workers' education would inspire greater union loyalty among women, but she was far more concerned with consciousness-raising than with creating obedient foot soldiers. Educating women, Cohn wrote, "cannot but make them understand how small a return they are getting for their labor, and may make them wonder why, though they play so essential a part in our economic life, they are accorded a place so unimportant in administrative, political and social affairs."[4]

Some union officers may have anticipated that education would make union women question the justice of an all-male leadership. Others simply worried that she was trying to educate workers out of their class. They were more than a little ambivalent about Cohn's educational initiatives. But they recognized that these programs were an enormous publicity coup for the union, making it appear well ahead of its time. So, against a constant background of grumbling, they provided her with funds. In 1916 she persuaded ILGWU officers to create the first unionwide Education Department in the nation. She then kept it afloat, often single-handedly, for more than four decades.

Cohn's pioneering workers' education programs planted the seeds for the growth of workers' schools nationwide, including the NYWTUL School for Women Workers, Brookwood Labor College, the Bryn Mawr Summer School for Women Workers, the Southern Summer Schools for Women Workers, and the Hudson Shore Labor School. By 1932, there were three hundred workers' schools across the United States. As the summer schools expanded and became coeducational during the 1930s, they adapted and changed Cohn's model; some fell back on a more conservative pedagogy than she supported. And in the years after World War II, many of the schools adopted an industrial relations model that had far less to do with worker empowerment than with easing class tensions. Still, the idea of schools for workers endured. That workers' education grew and flourished was in large part due to Cohn's tireless, almost fanatical labors on behalf of the cause. By the time she retired in 1962, workers' education programs had taught hundreds of thousands of men and women and had left an indelible mark on adult education. And the name of Fannia Cohn had become synonymous with the very idea of educating workers.[5]

An outgrowth of the industrial feminist vision, Cohn's brand of workers' education aimed to empower students, not socialize them. Cohn detested the sex-stereotyped classes then being taught in city-sponsored night schools. Instead, with assistance from some of the leading educators of the day, Cohn generated pedagogically innovative classes that combined the experiential philosophies of progressive educator John Dewey with the peer education techniques pioneered in shop-floor study groups.

Although union classes were open to workers of both sexes, it was women who flocked to them. In 1918, Cohn excitedly hailed the emergence of a fresh force in the labor movement. "The phenomenal success of the American Worker's Education Movement," she wrote, "is greatly due to women. Women in the rank and file of unions, especially Jewish women, have been among the most ardent supporters of worker's education."[6]

Much of their enthusiasm stemmed from the hope that education could give them greater control over the direction of their union. Fannia Cohn encouraged that hope. In classrooms, on field trips, and on retreats, Cohn urged women workers not to settle for small changes but to seek empowerment in the broadest sense—an improved quality of life, economic advancement, and intellectual stimulation. They did. Emboldened by courses in history, economics, and current events, militant women workers in the late 1910s began to articulate their own vision of what the ILGWU could be—an egalitarian and socially transformative community of workers. "It has always been our conviction," Cohn wrote in support of that ideal, "that the Labor Movement stands, consciously or unconsciously, for the reconstruction of society."[7]

But to an immigrant male leadership seeking political power through the elite inner circles of the American Federation of Labor, such sweeping calls for social transformation were anathema. Male leaders' fear of women's insurgency stemmed partly from what union vice president Benjamin Stolberg called "the weight of oligarchical continuity. They were there first."

Their fear was also rooted in competing gender-based visions of unionism. In stark contrast to women workers' ideal of a unionism with "soul," the ILGWU's officers clung to what they thought of as a more practical and useful vision: a labor movement built on the solidarity of skilled male workers. ILGWU officials wanted the numbers that women workers could provide; in an industry where women predominated, they had to organize women. But they were unwilling to share power with them.[8]

The internecine union struggles of the 1920s have usually been attributed to growing divisions between Socialist and Communist organizers. But it was women shop-floor workers educated in union-sponsored classes who shot the first volley. Beginning in 1919, they made a play for power in the ILGWU. Their movement for union reform spread to many of the union's most militant men, and by 1920 the new Communist Party had tapped into the growing discontent. The ensuing battle raged through the early 1920s and nearly destroyed the union.

Justifying draconian measures as protection against a Communist takeover, the ILGWU officers crushed the reform movement and purged its leaders. That purge, and an accompanying economic depression, created a mass exodus of women workers from the union. The loss of tens of thousands of militant women between 1920 and 1924 marked a decisive turning point in the history of the ILGWU. As the union narrowed its aims and its leaders grew increasingly remote from members, any pretext that the ILGWU would struggle simultaneously for class and gender equality disappeared.

Fannia Cohn was faced with a difficult choice. Unlike many of the militants trained in her programs, she chose to remain with the ILGWU. But the union's officers never forgave her for refusing to condemn the rebellion she'd helped to spark. And Cohn's unshakeable loyalty to the ILGWU hurt her credibility among many militant women activists, who felt that she had capitulated to a grasping and corrupt union leadership.

Tracing Fannia Cohn's career sheds light on the thorny path faced by a single woman determined against all odds to promote the ideals of industrial feminism from inside a male-dominated labor movement. Cohn never married or cultivated a lasting romantic relationship; instead she chose to devote her life entirely to workers' education. By cultivating younger workers and an array of enthusiastic educators and intellectuals, she won affection and wide acclaim. But by choosing the masculinist arena of organized labor as the center of her personal and professional life, Cohn inevitably cut herself off from those who would have been her most natural allies. In a poisonous atmosphere of mutual dislike and distrust, Cohn struggled with the ILGWU's male leaders nearly ceaselessly for over forty years.

By nature a brittle and overly sensitive woman, Cohn's battles on behalf of the ILGWU Education Department drove her to the brink of breakdown several times during the 1920s and 1930s and to actual physical collapse twice. "It was not the work that broke me down," she wrote to a friend, "but rather the atmosphere that surrounded me." She felt isolated and marginalized in a union run by men who dismissed what they called her "old-fashioned feminist" ideas and who deeply resented her tenacity. Unable to force her out, the

ILGWU officers came to see her, in David Dubinsky's words, as their "cross to bear."[9]

Given all this, it is not surprising that many of Cohn's union colleagues depicted her as a sad and lonely figure who toiled without recognition and continued to haunt the halls of ILGWU headquarters long after she should have retired. Yet contemporaries outside the union held a strikingly different view. Many leading intellectuals in the United States and abroad knew of the ILGWU largely through Cohn's work and considered her an educational pioneer. As early as 1919, progressive historian Charles Beard, who would become a lifelong friend, wrote to Cohn, "I am constantly grateful to you for your splendid efforts in the field of labor education. No one in America is doing more than you are. . . . You hearten workers throughout the country."[10]

Cohn's supporters within the ILGWU understood how much her work had contributed to the union's growing reputation. In a furious letter to union president David Dubinsky, vice president Rose Pesotta, who'd first found her voice in union-sponsored classes, railed, "Fannia Cohn's service to our organization is only recognized by those on the outside who can dispassionately evaluate such unselfish efforts on the part of one person for the cause of worker's education. . . . She remains a tragic figure amidst her own fellow workers, whom she helped to gain prestige with the outside educational world. Were she a man it would have been entirely different."[11] For just that reason, the stormy career of Fannia M. Cohn provides important insights into the truncated growth of industrial unionism in the United States.

THE BEGINNINGS OF WORKERS' EDUCATION
FOR WOMEN, 1907–1917

Though a strong supporter of women's suffrage, Fannia Cohn never threw herself into the movement with the same energy that many other union women had. The vote, she argued, was tangential to women's deeper social, economic, and political disfranchisement. "Women's desire for political equality," she wrote in 1917, "only touches the fringe of the entire woman question, or, as it is sometimes called, 'Feminism.' . . . Change in . . . their status in society must be brought about by the women themselves. . . . Woman must not be content to assume an innocent mien or remain . . . passive. . . . She must stand at the forefront of affairs and not merely as an onlooker."[12]

A year into her term as the first woman on the ILGWU General Executive Board, Cohn was optimistic about the possibilities for union men and women to link arms and shatter old shibboleths about sex roles. Once union men were exposed to energetic, competent women activists, she argued, they would shed their "foolish prejudice" and realize that they could now share deeper, more meaningful relationships with women—as colleagues as well as wives, mothers, sisters, and daughters. Conversely, seeing "an intelligent, capable woman organizer" would encourage young women to become more active in their unions. Arguing for greater cooperation between men and women in the labor movement, she wrote, "Competition between men and women must be abolished once and for all, not because it is immoral, yes, inhuman, but because it is impractical. It does not pay. Working men must become alive to the fact that in a world where an unnatural difference is made between the sexes . . . men and women cannot really be happy." She believed that union-sponsored workers' education programs could train women for leadership while teaching the working man "facts about the character and psychology of women which he will have to admit he did not know before."[13]

The first schools for women workers were a far cry from Cohn's ideal, although they were an improvement on the rigidly sexist English-language classes that many immigrant women had taken in city-sponsored night schools. Knowing that many working women were as frustrated as she had been by the childish and coercive curriculum offered by the night schools, Rose Schneiderman had persuaded the New York WTUL as early as 1907 to sponsor discussion groups and English classes for women workers. The early League classes were relevant, affordable, and engaging—and they stressed unionism in every lesson, no matter what the subject.

The first lesson in the NYWTUL English primer focused on Yetta, a newly arrived Jewish immigrant. Yetta's boss had hired her for $5 per week to undercut the wages of American-born women in the same shop, who were making $9 per week. Yetta was confused by the hostility of her co-workers until another immigrant woman, even newer to the United States, was hired for $4 per week and Yetta was told to accept a pay cut or lose her job. Yetta had learned her lesson; never again would she allow herself to undercut the wages of her fellow workers. English phrases to be memorized at the end of Lesson 1 included "I must have as much pay as the American girls."[14]

As Schneiderman had predicted, the classes drew new recruits to the League, for young women were grateful to the organization that gave them the opportunity to educate themselves. In the winter of 1911, the Chicago WTUL emulated the NYWTUL's example. They offered classes in six different working-class neighborhoods, often holding lessons in the kitchens of Italian garment workers, knitters, shoemakers, and candy workers. Many of the students who had formerly been reticent about unions joined the League upon graduation.[15]

The political potential demonstrated by the local New York and Chicago programs convinced WTUL president Margaret Dreier Robins to found a national School for Women Organizers. After years of hearing AFL leaders argue that they couldn't appoint women organizers because there were no women qualified for such a job, Robins decided that the WTUL should train promising young women unionists. At the 1913 WTUL convention, delegates voted to create the country's first residential school for workers. Its year-long program at the University of Chicago would include history, economics, labor law, parliamentary procedure, English, organizing techniques, and union administration.

The first class consisted of three students who were chosen and sponsored by their unions and local WTUL branches: Louisa Mittlestadt, a Kansas City brewery worker; Myrtle Whitehead, president of the Crown, Cork and Seal Operatives' Union in Baltimore; and Cohn, president of Local 41 of the ILGWU, which had just pulled off a successful general strike of white goods workers that year. Cohn accepted the offer, saying she needed rest and wanted to learn English. But she found on her arrival that the program was not yet in place; the three mostly sat in on regular university classes.

Cohn would later describe the program as boring and insulting for someone with considerable organizing experience. Workers, she believed, needed courses taught in ways that recognized and validated their life experiences. She left the school before the year was out. But she came away with a clearer sense of her own priorities as an educator: she was determined to develop an educational program geared to the needs and desires of the women workers she knew.[16]

She was pleased when the 1914 ILGWU convention resolved that the union needed to begin offering more "systematic education" to its members. Following the convention, union president Benjamin Schlesinger signed an agreement with the Rand School to provide courses in trade unionism, methods of organizing, and English. But the convention had specifically called for something "more solid" than the "superficial forms of agitation and propaganda which have been the main features of our educational work in the past."[17]

The first full-scale union educational program in the country was developed in 1915 by Cohn, Schneiderman, Newman, Barnard history instructor Juliet Poyntz, and the members of ILGWU Local 25. The purpose of their program, which was directed by Poyntz, was twofold. It was intended to promote self-confidence among the young immigrant women who comprised the vast majority of its membership. It was also designed to promote a feeling of community and sisterhood among the workers, much like the atmosphere within the informal study groups that Newman, Schneiderman, Lemlich, and Cohn had created in their youth.[18]

New programs like this one, Cohn argued in the labor press, were essential to any campaign to unionize women, because they appealed to women workers' idealism. In organizing any group of workers, she argued, "we must keep in mind the character of the group—its racial and social background . . . its conception of proper modes of feminine conduct. . . . In the organization of workingwomen . . . other facts must also be taken into consideration . . . their ideals, what inspires them, what appeals to their emotions and imaginations." The union, she insisted, must offer women "something more than the economic question." Pauline Newman made similar arguments in her articles: a union serious about organizing women, she wrote, had to cater to their "human desire for recreation and sociability." The Local 25 program attempted to address these needs.[19]

On a purely statistical level, the new program was a resounding success. Dress and waistmakers enthusiastically attended discussion groups on trade union principles and classes in history, literature, art, political theory, and parliamentary procedure. By 1919, just four years after its founding, Local 25's Education Department reported that ten thousand students, mostly young immigrant women, were enrolled in classes. Union-sponsored lectures, concerts and plays attracted another seven thousand. Assisted by Cohn and Newman, dressmakers' locals in Philadelphia and Chicago developed similar programs.[20]

The greatest significance of these programs lay not in the numbers of women they drew but in the fierce trade union partisanship they engendered. Like the study groups of the early 1900s, the new ILGWU Education Department classes sparked a spirit of resistance among a new generation of young women workers. Because the classes stressed leadership training, they attracted talented shop-floor radicals anxious to rise up in the labor movement and interested in making their unions more sensitive to women's needs. Rose Pesotta, a future ILGWU vice president and one of its finest organizers, wrote that by studying "subjects of social significance . . . we gain knowledge and poise and confidence." Mollie Friedman, the woman who would later unseat Cohn as vice president, told delegates at the 1918 AFL convention that the Local 25 program had changed her from a reluctant member into a union stalwart:

I am a product of that education. Working at the machine or sticking pins in dresses does not do much for the education of the members, but . . . I was offered an opportunity by my organization to study. . . . Our International found out that teaching girls how to picket a shop was not enough and they taught us how to read books. . . . In 1913 I came to America. I knew nothing about the trade union movement of America or any other trade unionism in the world. When I was asked to join the union, I felt I had to join it, but now I feel that I would give my life for an organization that will educate its members.[21]

More than anything else in the women's labor movement, the education program of Local 25 embodied the spirit of bread and roses, the idea that working women's organizations should improve not only a woman's life in the shop but also her life's overall quality. In that spirit, Local 25 decided to create a vacation center for its members. They rented a house in the Catskill Mountain town of Pine Hill, New York, and called it Unity House. Other locals in the women's trades soon followed suit. Philadelphia dressmakers bought a retreat in Forest Park, Pennsylvania, that was formerly "a summer resort for millionaires," and Italian dressmakers established Villa Anita Garibaldi in Staten Island. These cooperatively run workers' resorts became havens where young women in the union tried to live out romantic ideals of working-class sisterhood.[22]

Pauline Newman offered this nostalgic reminiscence after the summer of 1917:

> All those who were at Unity House last summer have wished and hoped that something more of the Unity Spirit might spread in our union. . . . A trade union is something more than an organization to fight for our rights, to increase our wages in the shop. It is also a great cooperative group which should spend together as well as earn together, which should enjoy together as well as suffer together, which should learn together as well as fight together. . . . We learned at Unity House that there is a mysterious bond between working sisters just as there is between sisters in a family. And we only wished that that devotion and that sisterhood would have more opportunity to lift its head in our shops.[23]

A STRUGGLE FOR POWER IN THE ILGWU, 1917–1923

For a brief time during and after World War I, it seemed that Cohn, Newman, and Poyntz might succeed at injecting the ILGWU leadership with the "Unity Spirit." Buoyed by the success of the Local 25 program, in 1916 Fannia Cohn was able to convince the ILGWU's executive board to create a unionwide Education Committee. But the board rebuffed Cohn by appointing Juliet Poyntz the ILGWU's first educational director. Cohn had to settle for second place: a clerical position as "organizing secretary" of the Education Committee.[24]

Though they shared the same educational philosophy and "social unionist" vision, Cohn disliked Poyntz and was not pleased about having to work for her. It is possible that Cohn resented the young Nebraska-born college professor for taking the position she felt should have been given to her. She may have begrudged Poyntz the adulation she received from the young women of Local 25. Or maybe it was just a personality clash. Cohn would later spitefully call Poyntz a manipulator who "had surrounded herself with a group of well-meaning young girls. . . . It was her intention to use these same girls to support her in every suspicious plan of hers."[25]

Cohn and Poyntz did not work well together, but they produced results. In 1917 the ILGWU opened the nation's first Unity Center, offering "semi-entertainment with a cultural slant." There workers could not only attend classes and lectures but also hold union meetings, drink coffee, work out at a gymnasium, swim, dance, watch movies, and listen to live music. Well ahead of its time, the Unity Center provided child care so that young mothers could participate fully. Four more Unity Centers were opened during the next two years, based in public schools within easy walking distance of densely populated working-class neighborhoods. The union hired teachers of literature, economics, applied psychology, American history, trade union principles, and music appreciation. The New York City Board of Education provided teachers in spoken English, reading, writing, and physical education.[26]

Like Unity House in the Catskills, the Unity Centers were designed to provide a relaxing, prounion atmosphere where workers could study and get to know each other. To make the still predominantly Jewish ILGWU membership feel comfortable, some of the courses and lectures at the New York Unity Centers were offered in Yiddish. But here the educational aims of the city and of the ILGWU Education Department came into conflict. The New York City Board of Education, which had agreed to make the public schools available in order to speed the Americanization of immigrant workers, threatened to close all Unity Centers where business was conducted in languages other than English. The union had little choice but to accept the rule.

When workers protested, Cohn put the best face on it. In fact, she saw some good in the decision: like virtually every member of the ILGWU's executive board, Cohn spoke heavily accented English liberally spiced with Yiddish, and she recognized that the next generation of union leaders would have to speak English. Classes at the Unity Centers would enable union members to practice their adopted language, which they could not do on the shop floor, because much of the business of New York City garment shops was still conducted in Yiddish.[27]

Building on the success of the Unity Centers, Cohn and Poyntz decided to offer more advanced courses for workers seeking college-level instruction. On January 4, 1918, the ILGWU opened its first Workers' University at Washington Irving High School in Manhattan. Cohn was able to convince professors from New York area colleges to teach courses in labor problems, industrial economics, American social and political history, accounting, and modern literature.

Gus Tyler observed Cohn's faculty recruitment methods with some amusement: "There was a determination and a sincerity about her and no sense of humility. She had a quiet, matronly air of *chutzpah* [nerve]. She would go to the head of the history department of Columbia University and say, 'My name is Fannia Cohn. I come from the garment workers, the girls. They want to know about history. I want you should come and give me a lecture.' They all came. She got the top faculty at Columbia to come and give lectures."

She won converts in this process, none more devoted than former Columbia professor Charles Beard, who agreed to teach the workers U.S. economic history. Beard had been one of the founders of the Ruskin College, the workers' university in England, and he favored establishment of a similar institution in the United States. That shared goal formed the basis of his friendship with Cohn.[28]

ILGWU colleague Leon Stein believed Beard was drawn to the breadth of Cohn's vision: "She was the epitome of that type of trade unionism that came out of the East Side, that valued education and character as much as wages and hours. Beard apparently recognized in this emphasis on quality of life something that he had perceived at the Ruskin College in England, where he got his background. He came back to America with that idea in his head and he latched onto Fannia."[29]

Many other scholars quickly joined Beard in expressing enthusiasm for Cohn's ideas. The comments of Professor B. J. R. Stolper of Teacher's College, Columbia University, are typical of letters sent to Cohn after 1918 by leading educators. Praising her "wise, strong, sisterly method" of dealing with adult students, Stolper effused, "I have never before met a woman with quite your amount of unselfish idealism . . . uncommon 'common sense' and ability for real constructive planning." Even Gus Tyler, no champion of Cohn, marveled at her teaching style: "She could go in front of a group after professorial discussions and say things that were utterly down to earth and she would walk away with an evening."[30]

Despite the great success of the program, the General Executive Board was ambivalent. They were disturbed by the fact that union classes were attended mostly by women. And they disapproved of the number of courses devoted to literature and art. They had felt all along that workers' education was somehow suspect, a womanish distraction from more "serious" union business.

Benjamin Stolberg noted rather jealously that classes in English poetry, taught by an instructor with "matinee-idol" good looks, "packed them in by the hundreds" while his course in trade unionism attracted only "a dozen earnest souls, more willing than comprehending." He believed that Cohn had misread the motivations of her woman students: "It was soon discovered that the motives which made the average working girl enroll in the Workers' University had rather little to do with a thirst for knowledge. More often than not these students were moved by some different urge—a desire to make new friends, especially young men; interest in a sentimentally rather than academically fascinating instructor; or the plain wish to escape loneliness or a narrow and dreary family circle." Stolberg, like many male union leaders, believed that the female rank and file lacked the intellect and discipline for serious academic work. "All democratic theories to the contrary notwithstanding," he wrote, "most dressmakers cannot very well follow a discussion of the wage structure of the United States."[31]

Underlying union officers' condescension was a legitimate fear. There was a paradox inherent in the type of workers' education Cohn was promoting. She wanted to offer as many courses in humanities and social sciences as in labor history, trade union negotiating techniques, and economics. Union leaders worried that she was encouraging middle-class fantasies that would distract workers from the day-to-day grind of fighting for greater union power. They believed, in short, that her approach would educate workers out of their class and out of the labor movement.

This argument, though, was not entirely sincere. Cohn never downplayed the importance of brass-tacks courses in union fundamentals. Indeed, throughout her career she sought out promising women to take officer-training courses. That rankled many male officers at least as much as her attempts to teach women poetry. "One can train leaders of Boy Scouts or baseball teams," Stolberg snorted in his memoirs, "but one cannot train leaders of social movements. . . . Courses in leadership are given by people who have no understanding of leadership or they would not attempt to teach it; and they are attended by people who have no instinct for it or they would play the game of power instead of studying it." The strong implication here is that it was as absurd to train women to be leaders as to train them to be economists.[32]

At the 1918 convention in Boston, Fannia Cohn fought against these sentiments, pleading with the executive board to increase appropriations for workers' education. A more knowledgeable membership, she insisted, could only strengthen the union. Over some grumbled objections, the board assented, actually doubling the budget of the Education Department. Hinting at Cohn's arm-twisting skills, one friend commented, "There are very few that could evade the persuasiveness of Fannia Cohn." It is equally likely that her fellow vice presidents understood that the union's education work had begun to bring it influential friends.[33]

But the decision to continue funding the Education Department did not reflect a willingness to let its women founders run it as they pleased. Shortly after the 1918 ILGWU convention, Juliet Poyntz resigned under pressure from the General Executive Board—the first of many women leaders associated with the Local 25 education program to be forced out by insinuations of disloyalty. Within a few years, Poyntz would become an organizer for the Communist Party.

Unwilling to give the job to another woman—especially Cohn, who had been battling the other vice presidents since her election—the board appointed the first in a series of male education directors. Cohn was angry, telling a friend that she had thrown herself "heart and soul into the development of Worker's Education." She would relive the same sense of disappointment many times over the next three decades, as one man after another was appointed director of the program she had initiated.[34]

Cohn's designation as secretary was clearly intended to relegate her to an administrative position. By putting a pragmatic, credentialed man in control, they hoped to blunt all the talk about "social reconstruction" and give their education program a more practical spin. However, the first two men to follow Poyntz at the Education Department—Louis Friedland and Alexander Fichandler—shared Cohn's vision and were personally committed to her. Fichandler urged the union to cut back his hours and give part of his salary to Cohn. "The Labor movement and the International are to be congratulated to have a worker of such character as she," Fichandler wrote. "Her enthusiasm, zeal, devotion, sincerity and ability are sources of inspiration, not only to me but to all who have at heart the welfare of labor." Together Cohn, Friedland, and Fichandler greatly expanded the union's educational offerings, establishing education programs in Cleveland, Boston, and Philadelphia.[35]

But the future of the program was again called into question when women students began a shop-floor rebellion that confirmed ILGWU leaders' suspicion about Cohn and Poyntz's approach to workers' education. Like many of the union's most militant initiatives, the movement for union democracy began in the waistmakers' union, Local 25, which accounted for one-quarter of the union's total membership. In 1917, students formed a permanent Current Events Committee that began to publicly criticize leaders of the local and international union. As the union's official historian, Louis Levine, described it, "The desire of this group of 'girls' to impart a 'soul' to their union . . . gave rise to an organized and persistent effort to 'rejuvenate' the local by getting rid of 'old' leaders and officers who were regarded as 'too practical' and 'conservative.' "[36]

What Levine neglected to say is that all of those "old," "practical" leaders were male in a local that was more than 75 percent female. Drawing on the confidence they had gained in their classes and discussion groups, "the girls" had begun to question why their local had not a single woman officer. A demand for union democracy now swelled the ranks of those who wanted to give it a "soul"; by early 1919, reform groups had formed in other locals in New York, Chicago, Philadelphia and Boston.

Emulating insurgents in the English trade union movement, in 1919 Local 25 formed a Shop Delegates' League, which called for sweeping reform in union governance. The rebels argued that only established national leaders had the name recognition to win unionwide office under the existing system. The Shop Delegates' League instead proposed that each shop elect two delegates to a unionwide assembly, which would select the executive board and standing committees. Since just about every shop chair in Local 25 and many of the other union locals was female, this switch would have dramatically increased women's power in the union. Conversely, it would have dramatically decreased the power of the established union bureaucrats.[37]

In a time of economic instability in the garment industry and of political backlash nationwide, union leaders felt deeply threatened. Worried that the shop-floor movement would spread to other locals, ILGWU president Schlesinger tried to brand the insurgents as dangerous malcontents whose aim was the union's destruction. The waistmakers, he said, had "radical traditions" that they were now attempting to foist off on the more mild-mannered dressmakers. To thwart what he called a "Bolshevik" threat, he dismembered Local 25.[38]

Splitting Local 25 into three locals and placing it under the administration of the male cloakmakers' union did not end the insurgency, which by this time had spread to other locals. But what had begun as a campaign by militant women workers for greater voice in their union was quickly taken over by a group of insurgent male organizers. Women's issues were soon overshadowed by a battle between "lefts and rights." Communist Party organizers in the ILGWU, working for William Z. Foster's Trade Union Educational League (TUEL), were able to attract discontented unionists of both sexes to the TUEL.[39]

Fannia Cohn was caught in the middle. Though she distrusted the motives of Communist Party organizers, Juliet Poyntz among them, she had encouraged the young women insurgents, and she supported many of their goals. Pauline Newman, who was caught in the same quandary, warned ILGWU leaders to pay attention to the genuine concerns of union members or lose their loyalty. "The rank and file," she wrote, "look upon the union not as a vehicle for the realization of their self-interest but as something remote, run by paid officers chiefly with their own interest [in mind]."[40]

Cohn, too, placed much of the blame on union leaders, challenging them publicly in ways they would never forgive: "The deep seated conservatism of some of the higher leaders of the labor movement, their fear for the new and untried was fatal, since it obsessed their minds to confuse destructive opposition with creative criticism . . . and to confuse the intentions of friend and of foe."[41]

That fatal vision moved union leaders to declare war. Accusing TUEL members of dual unionism—organizing for two competing unions simultaneously —in 1923 the ILGWU's executive board ordered all of its members to resign from TUEL. Those who refused were hauled before union tribunals in New York, Chicago, and Boston. These trials resulted in the expulsion of many of the union's most militant shop-floor leaders, many of them trained not in Communist Party cells but by the ILGWU Education Department. The association of the department with the rebellion did not strengthen its fortunes with the executive board.[42]

The political infighting and a severe economic downturn during the early 1920s weakened the union dramatically. Between 1920 and 1924, the union lost over 17,000 members—a 16.3 percent drop. A far more telling statistic is the drop in both the number and percentage of women belonging to the union. Women went from 75 percent of the total membership to only 38.7 percent. In 1920 there were 79,050 women in the ILGWU; on January 1, 1924, there were 34,125. While 20,000 men joined the ILGWU, 45,000 women left.[43]

Tellingly, union leaders showed little interest in recouping those losses. When Fannia Cohn urged her colleagues at the 1924 convention to press the AFL to help organize women, they turned her down flatly. "It can be stated without contradiction," they declared in a committee statement, "that as yet no successful methods of organizing women have been found." Cohn and Pauline Newman must have been astonished to hear that assessment after their organizing drives had brought tens of thousands of women into the ILGWU. Roughly 40 percent of all unionized women in 1920 belonged to garment unions; 80 percent of these had joined during the women's strikes of 1909–19.[44]

Cohn and Newman surely recognized that the departure of more than half of those women would hobble their efforts to shape an industrial feminist union. But as union stalwarts, they were caught in the middle when the battle for greater rank-and-file control exploded. When women's bid for power in the ILGWU was thoroughly defeated and the shop-floor militants were forced out, Newman and Cohn did not go with them.[45]

There are many possible reasons why. Cohn and Newman were deeply attached to the union; the ILGWU was central to their identities as Jews, as radicals, and as workers. Approaching middle age after devoting their youths to organizing, neither woman could bear the prospect of leaving the Jewish labor movement. That would have been tantamount to self-imposed exile. Nor could they imagine trying to build a competing union—as the Communists proposed to do—after all the years they'd devoted to the ILGWU. So they insisted, not entirely convincingly, that with all its problems the ILGWU was still the best hope for improving the daily lives of women workers.

Their decision cost them dearly. Newman and Cohn lost credibility among the most militant women who felt they had been forced out of the union. But because they also refused to parrot the leadership's denunciations of the shop-floor radicals, the two lost what influence they might have had with the men who paid their salaries. Newman managed to hang on by keeping only one foot in the union while firmly planting the other in the Women's Trade Union League.

Fannia Cohn, too, saw the handwriting on the wall. Though she bore a good deal of animosity toward Communist Party organizers, whom she felt were bent on tearing apart the union, she nevertheless refused to bar Communist Party members from Education Department activities. This decision left union leaders furious. Given their anger and the fact that her base of support within the union had been severely eroded by the exodus of women workers, she knew that she would have to establish an independent footing for workers' education if it was to survive. As early as 1920, she moved to formalize alliances with influential people outside the union who shared her belief in workers' education.

Together with Charles and Mary Beard, Alexander Fichandler, labor journalist Arthur Gleason, and a group of other movement activists and educators, Cohn created the Workers Education Bureau (WEB)—a national "clearinghouse for worker's education enterprises." The bureau developed correspondence courses for workers, sent a traveling library to unions around the country, and held conferences to distribute information on techniques and programs. It was the nerve center for labor education, independent of any union or labor federation.[46]

The following year, Cohn, pacifist minister A. J. Muste, Rose Schneiderman, and several others founded Brookwood Labor College in Katonah, New

York. Brookwood, which offered one- and two-year programs, was the country's first full-scale residential school for union organizers, far larger in scope than the national WTUL school in Chicago. Brookwood was also unique in that it allowed its adult students a large measure of control over course content as well as school governance.[47]

The flip side of the independence enjoyed by Brookwood and the Workers Education Bureau, however, was that neither organization had solid, reliable funding. As vice president of the bureau and a trustee of Brookwood, Cohn swallowed her pride and took a step she'd been unwilling to take for her own education: she asked her family for money. Her brother, sister, and brother-in-law—with whom she had remained very close—had amassed a comfortable sum of money through their ownership of a successful pharmacists' supply company. They responded generously to their sister's requests for donations, and over the years they would continue to provide vital support for Cohn's workers' education projects. But Cohn told no one of their largesse for more than thirty years.[48]

One can only speculate as to why Cohn felt it important to keep that a secret. Perhaps she thought it would further erode already tense relations with skeptical male leaders in the ILGWU and the AFL. It is also possible that Cohn was uneasy about her family's wealth. Given her oft-stated disapproval of "do-gooders," she may have felt that she would look foolish to her fellow trade unionists if it became known that she came from more than comfortable stock. Also, she may have rightly feared that the union would further cut her already meager salary, figuring her family could support her.

Ironically, even as Cohn was reaching out to her affluent family, she was reluctant to join a new cross-class women's alliance promoting workers' education for women. In 1921 U.S. Women's Bureau chief Mary Anderson and NYWTUL president Rose Schneiderman invited Cohn to join with them and Bryn Mawr College alumnae and faculty to create a special summer school for women workers at Bryn Mawr. The purpose, Anderson wrote, was to create a residential program for working women aged eighteen to thirty-five. The women would study history, English, literature, science, and art in a setting removed from the workaday world. The focus, Anderson assured Cohn, would be to make them more effective organizers and union members.[49]

Cohn initially refused to be involved in the Bryn Mawr experiment. She told Anderson that she distrusted cross-class collaborations and feared that the summer school would be dominated by middle-class ideas and values. Cohn still remembered her experience at the WTUL School for Women Organizers in 1914. She insisted that true workers' education had to be geared to and controlled by workers, not university professors. However, though workers held only partial control of the Bryn Mawr program, Cohn allowed herself to be drawn in. It is not clear why. Perhaps she couldn't stand the thought of a school for women workers that she had no part of. Soon she was visiting the school every year and consulting regularly with staff and students.[50]

Allies in the Workers Education Bureau, at Bryn Mawr, and at Brookwood became essential sources of comfort to Cohn. From the early 1920s on, her Education Department was under nearly constant attack by the union's executive board. The vice presidents complained of low attendance at classes and suggested that the department was a luxury the union could no longer afford.[51]

In 1921, Cohn was still the only woman vice president, and hers was often the only voice raised in defense of the workers' education movement. Give it time, she pleaded. After only four years in existence, the ILGWU Education Department boasted seven Unity Centers, along with two Workers' Universities in New York City and one each in several other major cities. In a furious, increasingly desperate outpouring of energy, Cohn gave talks, wrote letters to unionists across the country, and contributed a stream of articles to the ILGWU publication, *Justice*.

According to colleague Mary Goff, Cohn was willing to do almost anything to increase attendance numbers. She demanded attendance lists for every lecture, bus tour, and cultural event, and she could be overbearing about getting them. Unable to take attendance on a bus trip because of a broken arm, Mary Goff asked her husband to come along as scribe. There would have been hell to pay, Goff hinted later, if she had returned empty-handed.[52]

Cohn exhausted herself physically and emotionally trying to keep the educational program afloat. In a deepening economic depression, the other ILGWU-vice presidents had become increasingly resistant. In December 1923 she wrote to a friend, "To formulate a policy for this movement that will assure its success and will serve the interest of organized labor is more than one person can do, because it means constantly being on the lookout and continuous dispute with many persons with whom I would prefer to be rather on friendly and pleasant terms; it means being aggressive and misunderstood." Once again, Cohn returned to the family well. "When the ILGWU was torn by strife, financially helpless," she wrote later, "I then accepted money from my family to help finance the Education Department." Charles Beard was the only person who knew, Cohn said, as he and her brother shared a mutual friend.[53]

Union leaders suspected that Cohn's family was keeping her from the brink of destitution; they must also have assumed that Cohn was getting outside funds to support union work, since they were not providing her with any. But they were so taken up with the union's other troubles that they paid little attention to the Education Department unless Cohn forced them to. The

ILGWU was so broke during the mid-1920s that it paid its officers only a pittance. At one point, officers were forced to shut down the elevator at the union's six-story headquarters because they couldn't pay the electric bill.[54]

Cohn lived on next to nothing, devoting most of her family's contributions to educational work. She ate little, wore her few dresses till they were threadbare, and owned no furniture. Colleagues describe Cohn's cavernous apartment as "so empty that you could hear your voice echo." Her only indulgence was hiring a young woman to whom she dictated her articles on workers' education. Since she wrote only for labor publications, she received no remuneration for her articles. But she said, characteristically, "In this way I make my contribution to the subject and movement which is close to my heart and this is my compensation."[55]

Along with her siblings and the Beards, a few close friends provided crucial intimacy and support for Cohn during the roller-coaster years of the early 1920s. Labor journalist Arthur Gleason, a co-founder of the Workers Education Bureau, was a sensitive spirit whose emotional openness and poetic style seemed to mesh well with Cohn's own. Gleason shared Cohn's faith in the labor movement as a force for social reconstruction and, like her, tried to steer clear of destructive sectarian battles.

He considered Cohn a revitalizing force in a labor movement that had gone stale. Gleason "[paid] tribute to the powerful, patient, lonely furrow you have ploughed" and to "that long-enduring and unquenchable quality in you." After a summer visit in 1921, he told her, "You give vitality and hope to what is as yet a new growth in labor—a timid and anemic thing it is, and needs the strength of faith." Hailing her earthiness and fierce belief in democracy and the human spirit, he wrote, "You are a true follower of Whitman."[56]

Gleason's sudden death in 1923 robbed Cohn of a steadfast friend and political ally. But two women on the fringes of the movement became her most loving and enduring friends: wealthy reformer Evelyn Preston and economist Theresa Wolfson. She would rely heavily on both of them in the years to come.

During the winter of 1922, Cohn was approached by New York socialite Evelyn Preston, who had heard of Cohn's work and wanted to help. Preston was young, very wealthy, and more than a little starry-eyed about the working-class struggle. The two quickly developed a deep rapport. Despite Cohn's skepticism about cross-class bonds between women, her relationship with Preston was typical of the kinds of women's friendships that grew at the intersections of the suffrage, Progressive reform, and labor movements during the first quarter of the twentieth century. Like Schneiderman's friendship with Eleanor Roosevelt, Leonora O'Reilly's with Mary Dreier, and Newman's with Frieda Miller, Cohn's friendship with Preston was part of a pattern of women's bonding across class lines that made possible much of what industrial feminists were able to accomplish through World War II.

Age as well as class separated the two; Cohn was thirty-seven when they met, Preston was twenty-three. Thus, as in many of Cohn's attachments, the older woman played motherly mentor as well as friend. Under Cohn's influence, Preston became deeply committed to workers' education. She taught at the Bryn Mawr Summer School for Women Workers and studied for a master's degree in labor history and economics at the University of Wisconsin. But Preston was not simply a protégé; she was one of Cohn's most generous financial backers. Without her, many of Cohn's pet projects would have dried up for lack of funds. Indeed, it was largely due to Preston's benevolence that Brookwood survived for the next fifteen years.[57]

The lines were somewhat blurred in their emotional dealings as well. For Preston was clearly enthralled—if only for a while—with Cohn, who had already acquired near-celebrity status in the labor movement and radical New York literary circles. She sent Cohn flowers "and my love" and begged her to "teach me to see life wholly . . . and to have the patience that comes with vision." Cohn's responses, while not as breathless, reflect her hunger for love and pleasure at Preston's attentions. "I shall willingly and gratefully accept . . . your youthful and inspiring friendship, your love and your devotion," she wrote Preston.

The moody and solitary Cohn noted that "in my minutes of depression I read your hearty, artistically written letters and think of you and this gives me much pleasure." What little leisure time Cohn seems to have allowed herself, she spent with Preston, dining out, attending the theater, even going swimming at Coney Island. They planned to share an apartment in Manhattan, but Preston's postgraduate ambitions intervened, and she left for the University of Wisconsin to study the labor movement. Still, they stayed in close contact across the miles.[58]

In 1922, Cohn's health began to decline from overwork and poor nutrition. Preston begged her to accept money to pay for dental and medical bills. Hoping to sidestep Cohn's stubborn pride, Preston made her offer "in common love of the labor movement. . . . You are one of its leaders, one of those we all need most and you should therefore do all you can to keep your health and vigor." Though sick and exhausted, Cohn refused. "I never had," she wrote Preston, "a desire to spend more on my livelihood than what the movement could pay me; and as little as it does pay, I'm still getting more than what our members are getting."[59]

But Cohn soaked up Preston's love and respect. She sorely needed it in the midst of her bruising struggles with the other ILGWU vice presidents. "What a delight it was," Cohn wrote, "after a two days' strenuous session of our General Executive Board with its excitements, and in addition fourteen men in the same room smoking constantly, to read your lovely, poetical letter. It is so full of beauty, color and life." Preston responded in kind. "I wonder if you realize," she wrote Cohn, "that your coming into my life this winter has been the happiest thing that has happened to me in a long, long while."[60]

When Cohn lost her mother during the winter of 1923, Preston wrote to comfort her. But Cohn had found her own means of assuaging grief: she threw herself into work with an even greater fury. Preston again began to worry about her. "Please do find some time off for a rest," she wrote. "We all need you too much to risk you."[61]

The summer after her mother's death, Cohn's friends and doctor convinced her to take a real vacation in Bermuda. Not surprisingly, she devoted much of her time probing local working conditions, race relations, and the political status of the island's women. When she learned from a cab driver that Bermudan women did not have the vote, she joked that she would return with a delegation of black and white U.S. women to stir things up. She returned to find the power struggle between the Communists and the Socialists raging, though, and quickly forgot her brief idyll.[62]

Over the next few years, Cohn's friendship with Preston lost its intensity as the young woman matured, read D. H. Lawrence, and found out "why sex is the most important thing in the world." Cohn seemed to understand that this was inevitable, explaining to Preston at one point that she believed her to be in a "transition period between childhood and womanhood." Still, the friendship had come at an important time for Cohn, providing a rejuvenating draught of innocent affection that enabled her to continue her work amid a battle that was tearing her union apart.

"It is very difficult for a woman of my make-up to hold an executive position in the labor movement in these trying days," Cohn wrote Preston. "At such a time of intolerance and mutual distrust, one is in danger of getting hardened and embittered. That I would never survive. It is you and a few other dear friends of mine that keep my spirit at a high and keep the fire burning in me." The two women remained in touch, though much less frequently, into the 1940s. And though Cohn came to look to others for daily intimacy and emotional sustenance, Preston continued to finance some of Cohn's most cherished workers' education projects.[63]

Of her close friends in that era, none was more important than Theresa Wolfson, or "Tania," as she signed her letters to Cohn. When the two women met in 1921, Wolfson was a graduate student in economics and was earning her keep as an inspector for the ILGWU Joint Board of Sanitary Control. Cohn was juggling responsibilities at the union, the Workers Education Bureau, and Brookwood. Theirs was a closeness of equals, of grown women moved and challenged by one another. It was animated by the tension peculiar to unusually close friendships.[64]

Wolfson was never shy about grappling with Cohn's precipitous mood swings. When the two were sharing a room at the 1922 ILGWU convention in Cleveland, Wolfson came upon a letter Cohn was writing. "My attention was riveted to one word—'lonely.'" Writing to Cohn to apologize for reading her letter, Wolfson said, "I understand you too well to misunderstand your legitimate emotions and I am sorry that you of all people must have them. But it has ever been the history of the man who climbs high, who aspires much—to walk the 'tight-rope' alone—and that unfortunately is your fate."

But Wolfson accused Cohn of hiding behind her work and warned her that few people would be willing to undertake the Herculean task required to get to know her: "You have never sufficiently detached yourself from your work to become really human in your relations with others. It is only when one knocks, and knocks and knocks that one can perceive the real 'you' and how many people are there ready to knock when souls can be had for the asking?"

Cohn's replies illustrate the complexities of her character. Describing herself as a woman with "the sensitive heart and tender emotions of the artist and the poet," she told Wolfson that "it is not the married life or the 'cut loose from oneself' that will make me happier. Not at all!" Cohn understood herself well enough to know that she was a difficult person for whom happiness was elusive: "To satisfy my own inner self, I must be surrounded by true friends, who possess beautiful souls, loveable hearts and tender feelings. Such friends never for a moment doubt my motives and always understand me thoroughly." But Cohn did not end on that note of chastisement. Instead she reached out to Wolfson, assuring her that "I enjoyed and am enjoying my life as much as any of my friends. . . . What more can I say than that in you I feel a true friend who tries to understand me and whose nearness is always a great pleasure to me."[65]

The two women's intellects clicked well together. Wolfson consulted regularly with Cohn while working on her dissertation, "The Woman Worker and the Trade Unions," which was published in 1926 and became an influential text. Watching Cohn's struggles in the ILGWU deepened Wolfson's understanding of sexual tensions in the union movement. "Never have I realized with such poignancy of feeling what it means to be a woman among men in a fighting organization," Wolfson wrote Cohn in 1923, "as last Monday when I heard your outcry and realized the stress under which you are working." Sharing her research with Cohn, she was able to affirm what they both already knew—that the animosity of Cohn's colleagues was not just personal. As she told Cohn in a letter, it was part of a historic pattern of union sexism: "The early struggles of women to enter trade unions, the peculiar sex-antagonism which they have had to fight everywhere has quite overwhelmed me. There certainly is less class consciousness than I dared hope for—for everywhere all through the annals of the history of the Labor Movement I find the strong, invidious fight between male and female."[66]

Social and economic forces exacerbated gender tensions in the labor movement during the 1920s. Political reaction, economic depression, and several disastrous strikes nearly gutted the garment unions. In her study, Wolfson estimated that nearly four million industrial workers lost their jobs in the depression of 1920–21, which hit the garment, textile, and shoe industries particularly hard. Given the predominance of women in these industries and their concentration at the bottom of the skill ladder, it is reasonable to assume that a disproportionate number of those laid off were women. A rise in seasonal unemployment in these trades also hit unskilled women workers harder than other groups. These forces contributed mightily to weakening women's power base within the unions.[67]

In December 1925, that erosion of support hit home. At forty-one, after nearly ten years as union vice president, Cohn was defeated in her bid for reelection by Mollie Friedman, a talented organizer whom Cohn had trained in the Local 25 education program. Colleagues attributed the loss to a variety of factors. Some said Cohn had come to focus so narrowly on education that she had lost touch with workers on the shop floor. Friedman had the support of ILGWU president Morris Sigman, who resented Cohn for refusing to bar Communists from the Education Department. Others touted Friedman's youth and vigor, but in fact she was only two years younger than Cohn, whose Old World manner and frumpy attire made her seem older than she was.

Mary Goff noted that women in the union were torn between Cohn and Friedman and frustrated by the unwritten rule limiting women to one seat on the board. Cohn would always believe that had she been willing to make some back-room deals, she might have preserved her position. But she deemed the prospect of "attending caucuses or making deals with clicks [sic] . . . repugnant." Making deals to defeat Friedman would not have benefited anyone but her. A more interesting question than why Cohn lost is why the women members couldn't manage to elect both Friedman and Cohn.[68]

Ten years later, with this defeat clearly in mind, Cohn wrote, "Working women who aspire to leadership find . . . that hardly one place out of thousands in the labor movement is available to them. Some, therefore, consider every other woman who aspires to leadership as a personal opponent, if not an enemy. Frequently they are forced to act as a herd of hungry animals to whom one piece of food is held up."[69]

But at the time Cohn had no such emotional distance. She was devastated by the loss. It "had such an effect on me," she wrote her lifelong friend Florence Thorne of the AFL, "that I had a mental and physical breakdown and I could not see clearly." Colleague Sadie Reisch recalled that Cohn said she had nothing to live for and threatened to jump from a window in the ILGWU headquarters. Reisch, believing that Cohn was just engaging in histrionics, told her to go ahead.[70]

Instead, Cohn retreated, sinking into a depression that lasted six months. When she emerged, she was determined to close the door on the past. "What makes me happier than anything else," she wrote Thorne that June, "is the fact that I had a moral victory over myself. No bitterness, no bad feeling finds a place in my heart or soul. I am glad that I was saved from the thing that frightened me most." To overcome her feelings of rejection, she redoubled her attentions to the cause that kept her going. "I am now more certain than ever," she wrote, "that in my position as head of the Education Department, I should not be involved in politics." Given what was then going on in her union, it was nothing short of willful oblivion to think that she could keep the Education Department free of political infighting.[71]

She was more honest in a 1927 letter to British labor activist Marion Phillips. "It is awfully difficult now, for one who follows a progressive policy to function in the labor movement," she wrote. "Each side wants you to hate for the sake of love, to fight . . . for the sake of unity and solidarity. But for all of this there is a group of us which is making an effort to develop a progressive labor policy and to influence younger people in the labor movement."[72]

Much of this effort had to take place outside the union. Because A. J. Muste, Brookwood's director, was far more interested in organizing women than either the AFL or the ILGWU was, Cohn frequently used the independent labor school as a forum. She and Rose Schneiderman organized a series of conferences to address two major concerns for trade union women: how to bring the younger, so-called apolitical "flapper" generation into the labor movement, and how to organize the wives and mothers of workers through women's auxiliaries. In 1926, Cohn began designing education programs specifically for wives and mothers.[73]

Such activities were deeply political, whatever Cohn wanted to call them, and angered the male leaders of the AFL and ILGWU. Brookwood came to be seen as squarely in the left wing of the labor movement, and Cohn was tarred for her association with it. When Muste criticized the AFL in 1928 for its failure to reach out to unskilled workers, women, and blacks, the AFL's executive council charged the college with teaching "anti-religious and pro-Soviet doctrines." It launched a commission to rethink the AFL's workers' education policy and directed member unions to suspend their funding of Brookwood. (A number of unions, including the ILGWU, ignored the directive.) Fannia Cohn stood shoulder to shoulder with Muste in protesting the decision. But then, against Cohn's advice, Muste formed the Conference for Progressive Labor Action to organize workers who had been excluded from the AFL. The Federation cried dual unionism and, in 1929, urged the Workers Education Bureau to expel Brookwood.[74]

Once again Cohn was caught in the cross fire. In exchange for AFL funding, the WEB had gradually curbed its politics until it was little more than an affiliate of the conservative labor federation. By 1929, completely dependent on the AFL, it had little choice but to follow orders. After a heated discussion during which Cohn argued passionately for Brookwood, the bureau's members voted to expel the labor school and to remove Muste from the WEB executive board.

Cohn announced that she would give up her seat on the WEB board to protest Muste's expulsion. It is possible that she was just grandstanding, for she accepted renomination and reelection at the next convention—and was roundly condemned for doing so. But as the lone woman on the all-male board, and the lone progressive voice in what had become a conservative, AFL-dominated bureau, Cohn determined to tough it out, to "fight for my idea of workers' education" within the organization she had founded.[75]

THE NRA, DAVID DUBINSKY, AND WORKERS' EDUCATION
IN THE AGE OF INDUSTRIAL UNIONISM, 1930–1945

Between the Crash of 1929 and the election of Franklin D. Roosevelt in 1932, the ILGWU slid toward dissolution as membership and financing withered away. Racketeering was rampant in the garment trades, and sweatshops once again began to replace the larger shops. Manufacturers fled New York, heading to the South and the Midwest in search of nonunion workers. At such a time, Cohn's insistence on keeping the union's "soul" alive seemed more frivolous than ever to Benjamin Schlesinger, who was once again president of the ILGWU. With the union desperate for funds, he suspended Cohn's salary. Brookwood hovered on the brink of bankruptcy, and the union was considering selling Cohn's beloved Unity House, the workers' country retreat. Her situation was dire, she told a friend on the University of Chicago faculty: "Circumstances cornered and trapped me and it is very difficult for me to escape their deadly effect. I remember how complimentary you were about my office. It is no longer as it used to be. I have no permanent assistance. Nothing is being filed and it looks like a storage room. You would not recognize it."[76]

The stress seems to have strained her closest friendship as well. She lashed out at Theresa Wolfson, accusing her of not being supportive. Perhaps, too, there was a crisis about the nature of their relationship. Wolfson snapped back: "I . . . thought that I am building a lasting friendship but it seems that I failed in this. . . . You intimate that I have no intention of seeing you. I can come and see you but will you be satisfied with a conventional visit? I am waiting to hear from you." A *nudge* but not a fool, Cohn recovered her equilibrium. She mended fences with Wolfson and hustled funds to save Unity House, and with Preston's help, Brookwood hung on a while longer.[77]

At this low ebb in the union's history, the forty-eight-year-old Cohn returned to street-level organizing for the first time in fourteen years. Together with WTUL organizer Sadie Reisch, Cohn mobilized the young women of Local 38 in a twenty-two-week strike that called attention to conditions as bleak as those she remembered from twenty years earlier. "I threw myself into this with my former vigor, energy and devotion. . . . Every morning at 7 o'clock I was already on the picket line, never had my meals on time and never did go to bed before one o'clock." The strike ultimately failed, but it sparked a series of organizing drives that breathed new life into the ILGWU. Cohn felt that she had demonstrated her loyalty and willingness to do whatever it took to rebuild the union.[78]

When David Dubinsky became president of the ILGWU in 1932, Cohn hoped that her troubles with the union leadership had come to an end. She wrote him a long letter recalling her quarter century of service to the union and detailing a series of misunderstandings she believed were to blame for her troubled relationship with his predecessor. But despite Dubinsky's assurances that he supported her work, Cohn's position within the union continued to deteriorate.[79]

Leon Stein, editor of *Justice* and one of Cohn's few friends among the new generation of union officials, believed that Cohn's problems with Dubinsky stemmed not only from the same clash of political visions that had alienated her from the earlier leaders—"Fannia was a humanist in the trade union movement"—but also from shifting demographics: "When Dubinsky came in in the thirties the union was no longer anchored to the East Side, to the Jewish intellectuals. You know, they had a very rich conceptual life with arguments. Oh how they could argue! . . . Dubinsky had his roots in it and indeed most of our members had their roots in it when the union was chiefly Jewish and Italian. . . . But with the New Deal the ethnic character changed. The emphasis now became more on Pennsylvania than New York. . . . Fannia couldn't handle it."[80]

Personal animosities were briefly put on hold in the euphoric months following Franklin D. Roosevelt's inauguration in 1933. Prospects seemed brighter for the labor movement as a whole. And for a whirlwind season, Cohn was ushered back into the limelight. At the invitation of John Dewey, Cohn attended a conference of political activists interested in creating a labor party. She was the only woman invited to represent labor at a Continental Congress for Economic Reconstruction in Washington, D.C., joining Sidney Hillman of the Amalgamated Clothing Workers, Max Zaritsky of the United Cloth Hat and Cap Makers, A. Philip Randolph of the Brotherhood of Sleeping Car Porters, and Dubinsky of the ILGWU. That summer, Rose Schneiderman invited her to offer expert advice at the NRA code hearings for the dress industry.[81]

Earlier that summer, Cohn, Rose Pesotta, and a group of young women militants had led a successful general strike of dressmakers, called by Dubinsky to set the stage for the code hearings. Dubbing the strike "the Uprising of the Sixty Thousand," Cohn proudly declared these dressmakers "heirs" to the radical tradition of the 1909 waistmakers. Her hyperbole evoked the emotions and imagery of the 1909 shirtwaist strike: "It was an outburst of long suppressed resentment . . . a protest against conditions brought about by four years of depression which had robbed the dressmakers of those standards of wages and decency for which countless numbers of them had struggled for over twenty-five years and for which many had even given their lives. . . . Once again the dressmakers convinced the skeptics that women and even young girls can be organized."[82]

In numerous articles she wrote for labor and nonlabor publications in the early 1930s, Cohn self-consciously compared the newly revived union spirit and that of the 1909 vintage. Teaching workers labor history spurs greater militancy, she argued, and she stressed the importance of informing "newcomers" about "the heroic struggles conducted by our ILGWU beginning with the Uprising of the Twenty Thousand." Cohn went so far as to write a play about the event which was produced and staged.[83]

One young woman who helped to organize the 1933 strike remembers that it was important to her to come to understand the union's past. Maida Springer, a Panamanian woman who had joined the ILGWU in 1932, began taking classes immediately after the strike. "I took the position that I can't work at this without knowing what I'm doing and what I'm talking about . . . this was part of the social revolution." She became a devoted advocate of workers' education. She soon became chair of her local's education committee and, eventually, the union's first black business agent.[84]

But David Dubinsky had no interest in looking backward. Building on the momentum gained from Section 7a of the National Industrial Recovery Act, which guaranteed workers the right to organize, Dubinsky had sent organizers throughout the United States to try to unionize "runaway shops" from Kentucky and Pennsylvania to Los Angeles. He had little sympathy for Cohn's desire to offer educational programs that appealed to young people's "militancy and . . . joy of life." He wanted, instead, a department that would train "true and loyal union men and women."[85]

In 1935, Dubinsky removed Cohn from effective control of the ILGWU Education Department. Arguing that Cohn could not appeal to the native-born "NRA babies" the union now sought to organize, he stripped her of her executive secretary title and brought in former Brookwood instructor Mark Starr as the union's new education director. Cohn was devastated. She wrote to Dubinsky, "It seems as if a conscious attempt has been made to eliminate my name from the labor movement and to bury me alive. Who is responsible for this?" When she got no response, Cohn did what she had always done: she cut her losses and continued designing workers' education programs that reflected her vision. Though she bitterly resented Mark Starr and felt that the younger man patronized and misunderstood her, she told a friend in April 1935, "Please do not bear bad feelings toward Mark Starr. I never treated the union as my personal property. . . . There are so many problems to be solved in the Educational Department . . . [it] can best be done by two persons."[86]

Indeed, the job of unionwide Education Director had grown quite complicated by 1935. As membership grew and diversified both regionally and ethnically, education directors in each local claimed a familiarity with the new rank and file that the overall education director could not possibly attain. "They knew their people," Leon Stein said. "And they felt that somebody sitting in the general office on Broadway doesn't know *my people* as well as I do." As a result, the unionwide education director could choose one of two roles: administrator or visionary. Starr, according to Stein, managed "the central stockroom, intellectually." Cohn claimed the mantle of guiding light.[87]

Working without budget or power, Cohn continued to speak as an ILGWU official, refusing to be forced out, almost daring them to fire her. Leon Stein recalls, "There was a situation between her and Mark Starr. . . . These two people were so different. She had the Jewish motherly feel about her. . . . And he was so non-Jewish. He looked like a minister's son. Very nice guy. Nothing wrong with him and nothing wrong with her but they couldn't get along. And their offices were adjacent so that each could see what the other was doing. I look back and laugh now but it was not funny at the time."[88]

Dubinsky's appointment of Mark Starr—who was indeed a British minister's son—as head of the Education Department was part of a larger plan for reshaping the union. Dubinsky had left the Socialist Party for the Democratic Party of Franklin D. Roosevelt, having concluded that trade unionism needed capitalism. He sought to distance his union from Cohn's social reconstructionist vision, dismissively summed up by Vice President Benjamin Stolberg as a fusion of "old fashioned feminism" with "the romantic concept of the Worker as the Redeemer of Society." Instead, the new Education Department under Mark Starr promised to mold "a well disciplined body of men and women" who understood that "what is good for the union is good for the members."[89]

Starr and Cohn were contemptuous of one another and conducted a prolonged cold war. By 1940 they were barely speaking. Starr's animosity was deepened by Cohn's habit of opening his mail. "She had taken my mail because anything addressed to the Education Department *must* be for her," he said. "Only uninformed people put my name on it." Starr urged Dubinsky to force Cohn to retire. Shrugging off the request with feigned resignation about having to work with women in positions of influence, Dubinsky sighed, "FDR has got Fannia Perkins and I've got Fannia Cohn. We've both got our cross to bear."[90]

Starr had more than just a personal problem with Cohn. He strongly objected to her style of workers' education. In a 1940 pamphlet that was a clear slap at Cohn, he wrote, "There is in worker's education the possibility of creating the perpetual student—the member who knows more and more but does less and less. . . . Then too workers' education has sometimes produced members who felt that they personally were so advanced in their views . . . that they could sit down and wait for the rest of the world to catch up to them . . . but who had little interest and no advice to offer concerning an immediate program of action." Rose Pesotta was outraged at such pronouncements. In a letter to Dubinsky, she questioned how much credit an education director deserved "who has entered the field after the thorns were weeded out, the marshes dried and all other obstacles removed."[91]

Professional denunciations were not the worst of what Cohn had to endure from her colleagues. They teased her mercilessly about her physical appearance, suggesting, among other things, that she looked like a man. Cracks about her having a mustache were common. And behind her back, the boys at headquarters remarked smirkingly that you could tell what Fannia had eaten for lunch that day from the crumbs on her bosom.[92]

But Cohn was resilient and, now and then, even capable of a wry comment about her predicament. "I am not as downhearted as I seem from a distance," she wrote a friend in 1937. "I suspect there is a limit to the endurance of my nerves, but somehow . . . they . . . serve me well in an hour of need."[93]

Although Cohn's official responsibilities were now reduced to ordering texts for union-sponsored courses, she oversaw the development of educational programs in women's labor auxiliaries around the country and corresponded with leading figures in labor and adult education around the world. In her work Cohn consciously crossed generational and racial lines, challenging Dubinsky's depiction of her as a relic of the union's Jewish heyday who couldn't communicate with the younger and ethnically diverse workers then entering the garment trades.[94]

One "NRA baby" to whom Cohn reached out during the 1930s was dressmaker Miriam Speishandler, who recalls that Cohn was at first a little difficult for a young American-born worker to understand. "Fannia had a very thick Jewish accent and every other word a Jewish word crept in," she says. "So sometimes I had difficulty following her. But she was very good natured and she took a liking to me." Leon Stein remembered that no matter how bad things got between Cohn and the male leadership, "she loved the young people and the young people loved her." She paid them special attention, he said; she took them out to dinner, tutored them, and talked with them, and they responded.[95]

For many years a committed member of the NAACP and the Urban League, Cohn also focused her attention on the concerns of black workers in trade unions. Along with Rose Schneiderman and Frank Crosswaith, an African American ILGWU organizer, Cohn helped establish the Negro Labor Committee, which organized black workers in a wide variety of trades from 1933 to 1945. Her outspoken advocacy on behalf of black workers won praise from numerous black leaders. A. Philip Randolph, founder of the Brotherhood of Sleeping Car Porters, wrote, "You have given encouragement, support and cooperation during the years and dark days of my struggle to organize the Negro workers. . . . There is no comment on my humble efforts that I prize more highly than yours."[96]

Young workers of varied races and nationalities flocked to one of Cohn's favorite 1930s programs—the Student Fellowship. So did leading intellectuals. Union leaders watched in disbelief as figures of the caliber of economist John Kenneth Galbraith, literary critic Van Wyck Brooks and an array of historians including Charles Beard of New York and Merle Curti of the University of Wisconsin came to teach for the Student Fellowship. These intellectuals were stimulated by the chance to teach and interact with adult workers. Jack Barbash, a University of Wisconsin economist, spoke of "the great debt of so many people, particularly intellectuals like me whom you introduced to the labor movement with an excitement and stimulation that has left a lasting imprint. . . . For many people the fine reputation of the ILGWU was represented through Fannia Cohn."[97]

Happy to take the credit, "the union leaders bragged about the things she did," Leon Stein recalled, "but never about her." Like many of the men who worked with Cohn in the ILGWU, Stein was intrigued by the allegiance and affection of intellectuals. The "great men," Stein said, seemed to get a kick out of the way she mothered them. "She would use my office to feed the speakers before the forum. And you should see the way Galbraith could put away a big pastrami sandwich that Fannia ordered from the Stage Delicatessen. . . . 'Es nokh a sandwich Kenneth,' she would say to him. Eat another sandwich. And he did. She was a real Jewish mother without a family."

The fellowship gave Cohn an opportunity to deepen her relationship with an aging Charles Beard, who, despite his failing health, enthusiastically volunteered to teach. They wrote each other frequently during this period, discussing courses and Beard's final collaborative book with his wife Mary and reminiscing about their quarter century of friendship. "A letter from you always cheers up the day," Beard wrote Cohn. In 1945, alluding to the Nazis' twisted use of technology and education, Beard assured Cohn that her ideas about education were more timely than ever. "Learning without fellowship may be sterile, may even serve evil causes. But combined with fellowship it is needed more than ever now that our world has become so complicated for us."[98] Beard would remain involved in Cohn's programs until he literally could no longer do so. In 1947, he wrote her sadly to say that his health had deteriorated to the point that he could no longer teach classes for her. "My strength for pulling oars is, alas, diminishing," he wrote. "Sorry to fail you."[99]

By the early 1940s, Cohn had passed the half-century mark, and she too began to think of posterity. She saw the Student Fellowship as a way to bequeath a legacy to younger women. Through the fellowship she identified young women whom she thought had the talent and gumption to change the union. Maida Springer was one of these. So was Miriam Speishandler, now Miriam Stein, who says she received her education in gender politics from Cohn. At the time, Stein says, she thought Cohn seemed a bit obsessed with men's slights against women. But over the years, she says, she came to believe that Cohn was right on target. "After the meetings she would take me out to dinner. And she'd tell me about her work for the union. . . . This was a woman who gave her all to the union and the labor movement. And she felt that she was dealt a very poor hand, that she wasn't appreciated enough. She said she thought it was because she was a woman, because men are running the union. Looking back upon it now, I can see that she was right. There was really something to what she was saying."

At a certain point in their evenings, Miriam Stein recalls, Cohn would shift from her own story to the role she believed could now be played by younger women.

She would say to me, "Someday they'll have younger women who'll be coming in and they are going to go right up the ladder to the executive board." I asked, "Is there one now?" And she said, "Yes." Rose Pesotta was on the board at that time. So I said, "How many members do we have in the union who are women?" And she said, "80 percent at least." So I said, "That's not adequate representation." She said, "I agree with you. Something is wrong. From the Student Fellowship we have here, I am hoping that the young people will be willing to go into their respective locals and be rash enough and aggressive enough to become officers. And then you move up. *And don't let them keep you down!*"[100]

Fired up by her dinners with Cohn, the young Speishandler decided to ask some of the higher officials in the union why there had never been more than one woman on the executive board at any given time.

I went to Max Danish, who was the editor of *Justice*. And I asked him, "Why do they only have one woman on the executive board?" And he said, "Because women get married and they have children and they interrupt their working years in the union. So where can they get?" I said, "I don't think that's a good reason. Because when you have a baby you can come back and get the same position you had before." He said, "Miriam, don't be a proselytizer for the women. We're doing pretty well. We have somebody." I said, "Just one. Rose Pesotta. I'm sure there are more. Like Jenny Silverman. And Vin Lurie. She was a real bombshell in Pennsylvania. They could be vice presidents." He said, "They're officers in their locals." I said, "So why can't they move up? It's one union." He said, "You want to become that?" I said, "Maybe someday I do."

Encouraged by the friendship and support of Cohn and Local 22 education director Louis Corey, Speishandler, Springer and several other young women from Local 22 visited different shops to speak to unorganized women workers. In 1940, Speishandler was nominated as a delegate to the national convention of the ILGWU. There she attended a luncheon in honor of Rose Pesotta and, taking Cohn's words to heart, made her stand.

Fannia Cohn wanted me to present flowers to her. I was scared to death. And I went there while she was sitting on the dais. And I handed the flowers to her and I said how much we admired her in the student union and how we wished that we could have more women like her on the executive board, not just one token. Well, she burst out laughing. Dubinsky got hysterical. He said, "Hey, who are you?" I said, "I am Miriam Speishandler." He said, "Where are you from?" I said, "Local 22." He said, "Yeah, I heard you had a good group there." That was it. Nothing happened.[101]

Instead, four years later, Rose Pesotta, who had risen to the executive board from Local 25 and was a graduate of the local's education program, resigned her position after a decade as vice president. She argued that no one woman on the executive board could adequately represent a union whose membership was 85 percent female. It was time, she said, to erase the unwritten rule limiting women's representation on the board to one seat.[102]

Of Cohn's core from Local 22, several went on to greater success within the union, but none were elected to the board. Some simply stopped trying. Miriam Speishandler married ILGWU organizer Leon Stein and decided to drop out of union politics to raise her children. Others followed suit. Those who stayed in the union faced overwhelming odds. The longer Dubinsky ran the union, the more difficult it became for opposition candidates to campaign for high union office. Layer upon layer of new rules and regulations were added, making it virtually impossible for anyone but a small group of insiders to attain unionwide office.[103] Dubinsky and other members of the executive board never openly objected to having more women and blacks on the board, Pauline Newman later recalled. They simply argued that there were none qualified.[104]

Newman and Cohn believed that by staying in the union and nurturing younger women, they could ultimately break down that barrier. Maida Springer was the most successful of their protégés. First an organizer, then education director of Local 22, Springer was appointed business agent of Local 22 in 1947. Springer's appointment was made in part to quiet growing criticism of Dubinsky's regime by civil rights groups. Leon Stein believes Springer would eventually have become the first African American ILGWU vice president, if only because "then they would have had a woman and a black at once, eliminating the need to have another woman or another black person." But Springer didn't wait around for that to happen. She left the ILGWU in 1961 to become African affairs representative for the AFL-CIO.[105]

Springer's testimony suggests that Cohn and Newman's work with younger women had real impact. Springer frequently cited them among those who had the greatest influence on her:

Fannia Cohn, that name in ILG history. . . . Even when she was old and walking around with a tattered notebook, for me she made sense, and I respected and revered her no matter how many times she told me the same thing over and over again. . . .

Fannia Cohn, Pauline Newman, and a host of others were among the rambunctious tenacious women who made themselves heard. Talk about the Uprising of the Twenty Thousand, and when the men in the unions wanted to settle for less, these women were prepared to go on and be hungry and to march into the winter.

These women, Springer said, made it possible for her to envision herself as something more than a shop-floor worker. They led her to believe that this was her union too and that she could serve it better as a leader than as an obedient follower.[106]

It is worth noting here that Newman and Cohn presented two distinct leadership models. Their differences affected the way younger workers and male colleagues responded to them. In describing Cohn, Gus Tyler cryptically noted that "you can fight with honey or you can fight with acid." He says Cohn chose the latter, claiming the moral high ground in every clash with her colleagues. Newman, they felt, had a sweeter style. She quietly ran her own programs out of the Union Health Center—away from the ILGWU headquarters, where Cohn and the union officers worked—and rarely created confrontations. She was as fierce an advocate for women workers as Cohn, but she channeled much of her feminist energy through the Women's Trade Union League rather than the ILGWU. And her WTUL work brought the ILGWU closer to key government officials who could help the union out in various ways. This increased her value in their eyes.

Newman also had a personal life outside of the union. Says Leon Stein, "she had Elisabeth. She had Frieda. She had a life, unlike Fannia." However odd Newman's lifestyle choices may have seemed to the men in the ILGWU, they were still more comprehensible than Cohn's slavish devotion to the union. Cohn's insistence on making the union her one home and passion annoyed her colleagues to the point of outright hostility.[107]

But Cohn liked living at a pitch of great intensity, and she did not feel entirely unrewarded for her work. "It is not easy for a woman to be in a leading position, especially in the labor movement," she wrote to one of her longtime friends, historian Selig Perlman. "But I think I live a full, interesting and satisfying life. The appreciation my efforts get from the membership and the local leadership is my reward." She also told him, with palpable glee, that some "outstanding literary men" had approached her to write magazine articles about her life. But true to form, she turned them down—for fear, she said, that her critics would claim she was trying to use the Education Department as "a vehicle for personal publicity."[108]

Fannia Cohn was stubborn, idealistic, and melodramatic. But she was not as politically unsophisticated as her union colleagues seemed to think, or as she sometimes chose to portray herself. Her absolute unwillingness to be pushed out of the ILGWU made her the butt of cruel jokes by men in the union hierarchy. But their hostility derived in part from their understanding that they were stuck with her. By 1945, Fannia Cohn had become a labor movement institution. Because of her extensive contacts in American higher education and in the left wing of the labor movement, Fannia Cohn was the most famous member of the ILGWU after Dubinsky. In some circles she was better known than Dubinsky, and certainly better respected.

She took advantage of her reputation to force the ILGWU, against the will of its national leadership, to reckon with its roots. In her long fight against those who tried to declare her irrelevant, she repeatedly invoked the image of the militant young women on whom the garment unions had built their success. And she reached out to young women—Jews, Italians and, later, Blacks and Puerto Ricans—to stir in them the industrial feminist spirit. She insisted that "flappers and NRA babies," who had been deemed unreachable by many in the labor movement, were indeed organizable. Her principled stands on racial equality challenged the union's monochrome leadership, while her plays and articles taught a new generation of workers about women's historic role in the labor movement. Cohn's influence was limited by the profound sexism and the increasingly antidemocratic tendencies of the ILGWU leadership. But as much as one woman could, Fannia Cohn kept alive the spirit of industrial feminism in the ILGWU long after most others had declared it dead and buried.

The young mother Clara Lemlich with her first child, Irving, in Brownsville, Brooklyn, ca. 1915 (Courtesy of Evelyn Velson)

Between 1909 and 1913, Pauline Newman traveled the Northeast and the Midwest organizing for the ILGWU, the WTUL, and the Socialist Party. (Courtesy of Elisabeth Burger)

The New York Women's Trade Union League circle, at the Bryn Mawr Summer School for Women Workers, 1925. From left: Pauline Newman, Agnes Nestor, Frieda Miller, Maud Swartz, Marion Dickerman, Rose Schneiderman (Rose Schneiderman Collection, Tamiment Institute Library, New York University)

Unity House Symposium on Women in the Labor Movement, 1925, organized by Fannia Cohn and Rose Schneiderman. Cohn is seated on the speaker's platform. The speaker is probably labor economist Theresa Malkiel, Cohn's closest friend. (Fannia Cohn Papers, Rare Books and Manuscripts Division, New York Public Library)

Rose Schneiderman and FDR at Hyde Park in 1929, on the twenty-fifth anniversary of the New York WTUL (Rose Schneiderman Collection, Tamiment Institute Library, New York University)

Fannia M. Cohn, secretary of the ILGWU Educational Department, late 1920s (Fannia Cohn Papers, Rare Books and Manuscripts Division, New York Public Library)

Clara Lemlich Shavelson and Joe Shavelson, Brooklyn, 1920s (Courtesy of Martha Schaffer)

Clara Shavelson and her two daughters, Martha (left) and Rita (right), in Brooklyn, late 1920s (Courtesy of Martha Schaffer and Evelyn Velson)

The Shavelson family, Brighton Beach, 1930s. From left: standing, *Irving, Joe;* seated, *Rita, Clara, and Martha (Courtesy of Martha Schaffer and Evelyn Velson)*

Pauline Newman (left photo) and Frieda Miller (right photo) with their daughter, Elisabeth Burger, at their home in West Redding, Connecticut, 1932 (Courtesy of Elisabeth Burger)

Fannia Cohn at Unity House with a young student, late 1930s (Fannia Cohn Papers, Rare Books and Manuscripts Division, New York Public Library)

Rose Schneiderman, the lone woman on the National Recovery Administration Labor Advisory Board, Washington, D.C., 1933 (Rose Schneiderman Collection, Tamiment Institute Library, New York University)

Left: Pauline Newman in the mid-1930s. She was then educational director of the ILGWU's Union Health Center and vice president of the New York WTUL. (Courtesy of Elisabeth Burger)

Below: Pauline Newman and Maud Swartz, gardening together at Newman's country home during the summer of 1936. Swartz died of a heart attack in February 1937. In a poem written the following summer, Newman remembered their last day of gardening together. She wrote, "I have need of you now, Maud, and always shall." (Courtesy of Elisabeth Burger)

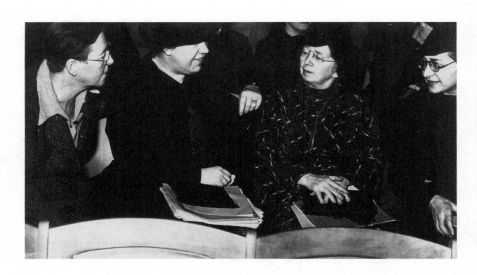

The NYWTUL *women strategizing in Albany, late 1930s.* From left: *Pauline Newman,* WTUL *secretary Elisabeth Christman, Rose Schneiderman, and unidentified woman (Rose Schneiderman Collection, Tamiment Library, New York University)*

6

SPARK PLUGS

IN EVERY

NEIGHBORHOOD:

CLARA LEMLICH

SHAVELSON AND

THE EMERGENCE

OF A MILITANT

WORKING-CLASS

HOUSEWIVES'

MOVEMENT,

1913—1945

There had to be one or two or three spark plugs in every neighborhood who could really talk and get the women excited. Clara Shavelson was one of these spark plugs.
—Rose Nelson Raynes

By 1913, four years after she sparked the shirtwaist makers' uprising, Clara Lemlich had established herself as a maverick on all fronts: on the shop floor, in the union, and in the suffrage movement. Blacklisted by New York shirtwaist manufacturers for organizing their shops, she had been working in garment factories under assumed names. For a while she worked for the union as a factory inspector. But many of the ILGWU leaders saw her as a troublemaker, a loose cannon. At a time when they were trying to smooth and formalize relations with big employers, Lemlich made them nervous, because she could not be controlled. "They were afraid for the bosses," she recalled, amused. "Such a radical . . . She'll turn things upside down!" Courted by Mary Beard, she switched for a time to suffrage organizing, but she clashed with Beard as well. So at age twenty-six, Lemlich found herself out of work.[1]

That same year she married Joseph Shavelson—a printer, union man, and devoted revolutionary. The two first met around the time of the 1909 strike, at a Socialist evening school. "We began to like each other," Lemlich explained, "but we were afraid of one another." Slowly, as they worked on political projects together, the two overcame their shyness. In 1913, Joe proposed and Clara accepted.[2]

For Lemlich, whose siblings and parents did not approve of her politics, Joe Shavelson's family provided a welcome sense of political community. Part of the wave of activist Jews who emigrated to the United States after the failed Russian revolution of 1905, Joe and his two sisters had all been involved in the underground political activities in Russia. One sister had even lost the use of her fingers during an abortive armed uprising. Clara would become swept up in their stories of revolution, sometimes almost wishing she could go back to Russia.[3]

That wish faded when she and Joe moved to Brownsville, Brooklyn, in the years just before World War I, and Clara finally found herself in a community bonded by militancy. A longtime Jewish immigrant ghetto, Brownsville had been an activist hotbed for at least fifteen years before the Shavelsons got there. Jewish immigrant families had begun moving to the neighborhood of two- and three-family homes around the turn of the century to escape the overcrowded Lower East Side. And they had brought their politics with them. In 1913, the neighborhood had a strong union presence and many competing radical cultural and political organizations. Brownsville housewives had organized several consumer boycotts in the preceding five years. At home in the atmosphere of political ferment, the young couple decided to settle down. They had three children there: Irving, Martha, and Rita.[4]

Unlike the other three women chronicled in this book, Clara Lemlich Shavelson chose a socially sanctioned path: to marry, quit working, and raise a family. But marriage did not diminish her militancy or her commitment to activism. On the contrary: an active member of the Communist Party and a tireless community organizer throughout the 1920s, 1930s, and 1940s, Shavelson remained unrepentantly radical. Her life highlights both the subversive possibilities and emotional difficulties of trying to balance radical politics with conventional personal choices, for Clara Shavelson could no more have given up organizing for marriage and motherhood than she could have given up breathing. "When you don't work," she said later, "and you don't work in the movement, you're nothing."[5]

For a brief time after her marriage Shavelson harbored the hope of finishing high school so that she could fulfill her longtime dream of becoming a doctor. But then she started having children. By 1917, thirty-year-old Shavelson had a three-year-old son and infant daughter. There was no time for school. She worked part-time in a neighborhood tie shop to supplement her husband's wages and took care of her children. But because Clara Shavelson always viewed her surroundings through a highly politicized lens, she began thinking about the possibilities for organizing in her community. No longer on the shop floor, she turned her attentions to a group that had been utterly ignored by trade unions, Socialists, and Communists alike: working-class wives and mothers. For the next thirty-eight years, they would be her constituency.[6]

By the mid-1930s, Shavelson's appeal to poor wives and mothers would resonate throughout the United States. Building on the early-twentieth-century Jewish housewives' consumer protests, Shavelson and other working-class women organizers would forge a nationwide depression-era housewives' movement to combat the rising cost of living. Though her place in most histories of the twentieth-century United States has been restricted to a cameo appearance as the "girl" who ignited the 1909 shirtwaist strike, her role in creating a very different kind of uprising during the Great Depression deserves recording. For the 1930s housewives' movement was as astonishing to observers of politics as the young women's strikes of the 1910s. And its impact was in many ways as lasting and as widespread.

Shavelson's friend and neighbor Rae Appel recalls that Clara reached out to women with children when few other activists did. She pushed them "to become conscious of ... their role not only as mothers and wives, because that they knew, but as part of the overall picture ... helping to create a better world for their children. And in creating a better world for their children, helping to create a better world for all children." With her powerful lungs and theatrical style, Shavelson became a street-corner favorite during the 1920s and 1930s in Jewish working-class neighborhoods throughout New York City. Says Appel: "Her voice was so eloquent and so clear and her reasoning so good that people would stop and listen whether they agreed or not."[7]

Clara Shavelson, says Rae Appel, told housewives that "they shouldn't feel they just have to stay in the kitchen and cook, that they can play a major role in organizing and combating hard times ... that picketing for the staff of life is just as important" as "picket lines in the needle trades." In an era of economic convulsions and expanding government, poor wives and mothers responded to that message. Through sit-ins, consumer boycotts, demonstrations, and political lobbying, they consciously campaigned to change the system they blamed for the ravages of the Great Depression.[8]

In part, these angry housewives were moved to action by a rapid decline during the 1920s in the working-class standard of living. In the years after World War I, union men like Joe Shavelson could provide a decent living for their families. But inflation steadily eroded the quality of life for American workers. By the end of the 1920s, even the wives of employed union workers were having trouble making ends meet. These women—former shop workers, wives, sisters, and mothers of union men—began to adapt union strategies like strikes and boycotts to the problems facing them as consumers. Initially these housewives' actions were nothing more than unlinked local protests. But through the efforts of a small group of seasoned women organizers, these disparate protests were forged into a national movement.

By the mid-1920s, veteran women activists were feeling discouraged about the possibilities for addressing women's concerns through either trade unions or the Communist Party. Fannia Cohn, Pauline Newman, and Rose Schneiderman had long argued the importance of reaching beyond the shop floor to involve the wives and mothers of union workers in the working-class movement. These arguments, like most of their suggestions about how to reach women, had been largely ignored by male union officers. Communist Party women, Shavelson among them, were finding national CP leaders similarly indifferent to women's issues.[9]

Frustration moved them to begin acting on their own. By the onset of the depression, trade union women, including Fannia Cohn and Rose Schneiderman, had been working for several years to politicize women's union auxiliaries; and Communist Party women had laid foundations for a network of neighborhood-based housewives' councils in New York, Chicago, Los Angeles, and Detroit. Both campaigns were attempts to create sturdy political organizations through which working-class wives and mothers could make themselves heard. Fannia Cohn explained, "I am extremely interested that wives of trade unionists should have an organization through which they can function just as well as middle-class women, business and professional women function through their organizations. Women of the middle class have excellent organizations in the United States and they are such a power in our social life that no political party or leader can afford to ignore them."[10]

It was this desire to maximize working-class women's political influence that moved organizers to build the housewives' movement around consumer issues. As workers, women were segregated into the lowest-paid, least-skilled sectors of the labor force. But as consumers, U.S. working-class women spent billions of dollars annually. Organized as consumers, even poor women could wield real economic and political power.[11]

Campaigns to organize working-class housewives did not sit well with either trade union leaders or Communist Party officials, whose notions of class struggle excluded such seemingly irrelevant actors as housewives. Though they paid lip service to housewives' organizations, they were unwilling to accept the home as a center of production or the housewife as a productive laborer. Scoffing at the notion that production and consumption were linked, they downplayed the importance of housewives to the working-class movement.

But poor housewives implicitly understood the relationship between production and consumption. They had no doubt that their work in the home was linked to the labor of their husbands in fields and factories, to the national economy, and to rapidly expanding government agencies. As one farmer's wife and Farmer-Labor Party activist explained, "A woman's place may be in the home but the home is no longer the isolated complete unit it once was. To serve her home best, the woman of today must understand the political and economic foundation on which that homes rests—and then do something about it."[12]

What they did during the 1930s, as the depression dragged on, was to organize and protest on an unprecedented scale. From New York City to Seattle, from Richmond, Virginia, to Los Angeles, and in hundreds of small towns and farm villages in between, poor wives and mothers staged food boycotts and antieviction demonstrations, created large-scale barter networks, and marched on Washington. Understanding their power as a voting bloc, housewives lobbied for food and rent price controls and ran for political office in numerous locales across the country. They demanded a better quality of life for themselves and their children, asserting that housing and food, like wages and hours, could be regulated by organizing and applying economic pressure.

Echoing the language of trade unionism, the housewives' movement of the 1930s broadened the terms of the working-class struggle and stretched the limits of U.S. women's organizing. Through more than a decade of activism, working-class housewives brought consumer and tenant concerns to the center of U.S. politics. They also politicized marriage and motherhood in important and innovative ways, challenging deep-seated notions of how "good" wives and mothers behave. This created tensions inside many working-class homes—including that of Clara Shavelson, perhaps the country's best-known housewife-activist. Her life during the 1920s and 1930s reflects the complexities of politicizing the emotionally charged roles of wife and mother.

Clara Shavelson's family life was wracked by conflicts during those years. Her husband and children complained that her political commitments left her too little time for her own home and family. Clara strongly disagreed, for her vision of radical motherhood recognized no boundaries between private and public spheres, or between her family and other families. Rae Appel recalls that faced with the choice between "things in the house" and "speaking in a way that [would] benefit her own children *and* other people around her, Clara felt she had to make the choice of going out to speak." Her certainty made her a compelling political leader, but it left her husband and children feeling emotionally abandoned sometimes. She always seemed to be telling them that something else—the movement—was more important.[13]

Clara Shavelson's life between 1913 and 1945 provides insight into the tricky balancing act required of a woman who refused to choose between political activism and family. Shavelson's brothers, religious Jews who did not approve of her radicalism, ostracized her for years. Her husband and children were proud of her and shared her politics. Still, they bitterly resented the time her activism took from more traditional motherly responsibilities. But Clara Shavelson would not back down. She stubbornly insisted that it was possible to be both a good wife and mother and a committed organizer. Refusing to leave her politics at the front door, she fought as hard in her own home as she did in the streets. Long before 1960s feminists began stirring up conflict in kitchens across the United States by declaring the personal political, Clara Shavelson was testing the limits of her family's tolerance for that vision.

The roots of the 1930s housewife movement can be traced to the Brooklyn communities of East New York and Brownsville, where Clara and Joe Shavelson lived during the 1910s. Clara Shavelson quickly found her niche in East New York, where she and Joe moved immediately after their wedding. As soon as her children were old enough to walk, she took them to Socialist meetings, joined a Socialist women's group and, through it, organized a strike to protest rent increases. Her role in that strike got the Shavelsons evicted. Their search for a new home brought them to Brownsville, where they found young families who were equally consumed by politics.

Sophie Melvin Gerson, who grew up in Brownsville and was a close friend of the Shavelsons' eldest child, Irving, recalls the political atmosphere of that community: "Come Saturdays there would be open-air meetings on every corner there. The Socialist Party, the Communist Party, the Democratic Party, and what there was of a Republican Party. The participants were by and large community people. . . . You came with your little ladder or platform or a chair and some literature. And you spoke. And before long there was a big crowd. And they stayed and listened. Because they wanted to talk. . . . They wanted to air their views."[14]

By the early 1920s, Clara Shavelson had become a well-known "soapboxer," even in a neighborhood with speakers on every corner. Dragging her soapbox from corner to corner, Clara Shavelson sought supporters for her unusual cause: housewives' unions. She argued that organizations of housewives, built around consumer, housing, and educational issues, could become as important to the working-class struggle as labor unions.

Sophie Gerson recalls Shavelson's effect on crowds: "There were no loudspeakers. You had to have pretty strong lungs. But it was the passion and conviction with which she spoke that got people's attention. . . . She had a simple motto in her approach to meetings. You speak the truth, she said, and people will listen. . . . I rarely remember there being hecklers . . . or interruptions."[15]

In Brownsville, where everyday discourse was saturated with the language of Socialism and trade unionism, Shavelson was able to galvanize wives and mothers. Wartime food and rent increases became fodder for her talks. In 1917, Brownsville housewives joined Jewish women across New York City in a series of food riots followed by boycotts of kosher meat to protest wartime price increases. The following year, Brownsville women led the way for what would become an intense, months-long battle between tenants and landlords in several Jewish neighborhoods.[16]

These battles clearly echoed Jewish housewives' uprisings about food and housing between 1902 and 1908. But in contrast to earlier actions, this rent strike resulted in the formation of a permanent advocacy group made up primarily of housewives. This new level of organizing had been made possible in part by U.S. War Department agents, who during World War I mobilized millions of housewives into Community Councils for National Defense. On the foundations of these councils and traditional Jewish women's charitable associations—carried over from Eastern Europe, where women volunteered to visit the sick as well as to gather food and clothing for orphans, the blind, and the indigent—neighborhood organizers like Clara Lemlich Shavelson began to build tenant and consumer groups.[17]

Out of the 1918 rent strike, Brownsville women formed the Brooklyn Tenants' Union, one of the first tenant advocacy groups in the United States. Modeled on the principle of trade unionism, its members had union cards, walked picket lines, and spoke the language of class conflict. Pledging to fight both rising rents and evictions, the Brooklyn Tenants' Union won support in a community composed largely of union families.

Brownsville tenants responded eagerly to Brooklyn Tenants' Union organizers, because they had few other options. A virtual moratorium on building during the war years had left the entire city in the grip of a severe housing shortage. Families who could not pay rent increases had virtually no chance of finding other living quarters. By May of 1919, the tenants' union boasted four thousand members who pledged not to pay their rents until increases were rolled back.[18]

Shavelson's neighbors, the wives and mothers of unionized workers, were the core of the antieviction movement. They patrolled the streets of their neighborhood wearing banners advertising their rent strike in Yiddish and English. They negotiated fiercely with landlords, demanding rent rollbacks and year-long leases. Shavelson led her building on a rent strike while she kept up the strike spirit throughout the neighborhood. In every speech she hammered away at a simple theme. Drawing parallels between the condition of renters and wage laborers, she told listeners that the bottom line for the working class was that they were denied control over their lives. In the neighborhoods where they lived, as in the shops where they worked, the point of forming unions was to gain a measure of control.

The 1919 tenants' movement spread through New York's Jewish neighborhoods, and the city faced a crisis: the courts were jammed with tenant/land-lord hearings, and thousands of evictions seemed imminent. One judge ac-cused strike leaders of seeking to form "a tenant's soviet." Even New York's tough, blustery Tammany mayor, "Red Mike" Hylan, infamous for his anti-progressive stands, was fearful of further unrest. He formed a Committee on Rent Profiteering and urged judges to be lenient in eviction hearings. He also appealed for federal aid, convincing the U.S. Army and Navy to provide cots and tents for those who were evicted. Methodist and Episcopal churches announced that they would open their doors to the thousands of families facing evictions.[19]

The women rent strikers, however, had no intention of being evicted quietly. In Brownsville, housewives attacked two landlords who were trying to evict their tenants. They poured boiling water from teakettles on those who arrived to carry out evictions. And in an incident that made the front page of the *New York Times*, women tenant activists successfully blocked the eviction of 450 families by showing the movers their tenants' union cards and appealing to their solidarity as union men not to break the rent strike. Housing court judge Leopold Prince called for municipal, even federal action to quell the tenant rebellion. "Bolshevism," he declared, "appears to be running riot over the city."[20]

The judge's language was a bit overblown, but news of the Russian revolu-tion had certainly electrified Jewish immigrant radicals. And many, like the Shavelsons, drew comparisons between their struggle and that of the Bolshe-viks. With the founding of the Communist Party USA in 1919, many trade union militants and neighborhood activists felt that they finally had an institu-tional base. There is some confusion about when exactly Clara Shavelson joined the Party. Some accounts describe her as a founding member. The most accurate information seems to be that she joined in 1926, at the age of forty, when, she says, "I began to understand what Communism is, real Commu-nism, not just the name, but the really interesting ideas, the people who . . . sacrifice to make things better."[21]

Shavelson's decision to join the Party did not mean that she had ceased to believe in trade unionism. But by the mid-1920s, the ILGWU had certainly lost its luster for her. There could be few illusions left about its being a vehicle for revolutionary dreams, industrial feminist or otherwise. Unions, she had come to believe, were brass-tacks organizations whose leaders focused on short-term concrete gains. But the new Communist Party had an allure that the unions had lost. It shone with fervent commitment; it spun visions of fulfill-ment like those which had sparked the mass women's strikes of a decade earlier. "The great majority of workers merely believe you have to get a little more pay," Shavelson later explained. "A Communist wants more than that. . . . You joined for a higher life."[22]

It was a decision that would alienate her from many old friends, including Pauline Newman, who had known her since the 1909 shirtwaist strike. Blaming the Communist Party for some of the troubles plaguing her beloved ILGWU during the 1920s, Newman ended her friendship with Shavelson. Years later she explained, in her usual terse fashion, "Clara joined the ranks of the Communists and I lost track of her. Her politics were not my cup of tea." But Shavelson made no apologies to anyone for her devotion to the Party. And within the Party she resolutely followed her own path.[23]

In 1926, she and Kate Gitlow, who was married to Party leader Ben Gitlow, founded the United Council of Working Class Housewives (UCWCH). Their goal was to broaden the class struggle by organizing wives and mothers. Far more than just a battle by male workers over shop-floor conditions, the working-class movement had to become, they believed, a communitywide activity. That vision of fully politicized community life was shaped by the neighborhood where they lived—Brownsville, where parents raised their children to be radicals.

In the culture of radical Jews in Brownsville, Sophie Gerson would later say, politics suffused all aspects of family life. She remembered a circle of families affiliated with the Communist Party in which parents and children were bound by ideological as well as emotional ties. "That was a time," Gerson says, "when we were all committed to what we called the movement. And the movement was a very all-inclusive word for . . . us. . . . Almost always there was picketing to do," she says. Not only in support of striking workers but also in support of Third World revolutions or in protest against U.S. military engagements. Gerson recalls attending a 1928 rally for Augusto Sandino, the Nicaraguan rebel leader, during which she stood between the women she knew as "Mother Gitlow" and "Mother Shavelson." The Shavelsons' oldest son Irving—or "Shavey," as he was called by his friends—was there too. He went to every demonstration.[24]

Gerson, who grew up as part of a group of deeply militant Brownsville youngsters, felt that there was "no generation gap in those days" because children and parents were working together for the same goals. Parents like the Shavelsons "at all times made their stand and their commitment to their class, and that's what they wanted for their children." At an age when other children were joining the Y and the Scouts, the children of Brownsville parents became active "in the left-wing movement" through the Pioneers and the Young Communist League, according to one friend of Irving and Martha Shavelson. And the children approached this work with as much passion as their parents did.[25]

Just like his mother, Irving Shavelson began organizing before he was out of his teens and quickly became a leader among the radical youth of his generation. Clara had trained him from childhood on. Dora Smorodin remembers Irving accompanying Clara when the United Council of Working Class Housewives made its first attempt at large-scale organizing, during the Passaic textile strike of 1925–26. While the women of the UCWCH raised $20,000 for the strike fund, collected food from sympathetic shopkeepers, and opened soup kitchens in worker neighborhoods, Smorodin says, thirteen-year-old "Shavey" mobilized the children of workers to picket. Sophie Gerson, who was then sixteen, remembers that they also ran a "Victory Playground for children so their parents could conduct the strike. Fifteen hundred children came every day."[26]

Raising her children into "the movement," Clara Shavelson melded the concepts of duty to family and loyalty to class. Gerson recalls Clara beaming "when . . . Shavey became the soapboxer and represented the family. There was a sort of *nakhes* [pride and joy] she had. But it was more than that. The kids were following the footsteps of the parents because there was an understanding and a dedication that they had instilled in these children and now they saw in fruition." This was, of course, a big part of what the movement to organize housewives was about, their role in politicizing the next generation. Clara Shavelson took that responsibility very seriously.[27]

Still, though, Shavelson—ever the iconoclast—envisioned more for the UCWCH than simply teaching mothers to mold their children into good Communists. After twenty years of searching for an appropriate venue for organizing working-class women, Shavelson was ready to break free of the male-dominated movements she'd been involved in. She and other Communist Party women were growing frustrated that food, clothing, education, and housing issues "are overlooked by our comrades who are trying to organize the workers in the factories." They wanted to move beyond strike support activities to organize housewives around issues related to their own work: housing, education, and the cost of living. They found many working-class housewives throughout New York who were excited by this idea.[28]

These housewives did not necessarily have any interest in the Communist Party. The CP had only a handful of members in those years; few were drawn to its message of Soviet-style revolution in the United States. For that reason, Shavelson and Gitlow did not ask or expect the housewives they organized to join the Communist Party. They focused their appeal on the issue of "quality of life." This tapped a deep vein of housewife discontent over their families' steadily deteriorating standard of living.

Since the end of the war, prices had been rising steadily, and inflation was eroding the buying power of working-class families. In 1927, Kate Gitlow noted that the rising cost of living was forcing many working-class wives back into the paid labor force and prompting many others to become politically active in the hope of stemming the rise in food and housing costs. The result, Gitlow concluded, was that "it is much easier to organize them than it was before the war."[29]

Desire to learn, to understand what was going on in the wider world, was another key factor in sparking housewives to action, just as it had been for them as young workers in the shops. Account after account of the housewives' councils alludes to this motivation. This comment was written by Tillie Litinsky, a Communist Party activist, after she attended a 1927 conference of the Housewives' Councils of Greater New York, New Jersey and Connecticut: "To see some two hundred women . . . erstwhile kitchen drudges, sitting through a seven hour session and pondering vital, very vital problems, was truly inspirational." Like the shop-floor uprisings of the 1910s, the housewives' actions of the 1920s, 1930s, and 1940s had their roots in more than economic hardship. They were based as well in married women's desire to move beyond the narrow roles to which their sex, as well as their class, had consigned them.[30]

Though unable to convince Party leaders of the importance of organizing around cost-of-living issues, Communist Party women were able to win approval for the creation of a CP Women's Commission in 1929. From the beginning, the commission was a neglected stepchild, and its members were considered mavericks within the Party, but it did receive some minimal staff support and funding. Taking advantage of these resources, Clara Shavelson attempted to revamp and expand the housewives' councils.[31]

On June 22, 1929, Shavelson gathered a group of activist Communist housewives to lay plans for a network of neighborhood women's councils throughout New York City. They created a new umbrella organization they called the United Council of Working Class Women (UCWW). It would become a model for housewives' activism nationally. The UCWW grew out of Shavelson and Gitlow's United Council of Working Class Housewives. Most of its founders were women in their late thirties and forties, but members expressed their desire to reach out to a younger generation. That hope of bridging generations was reflected in their choice of leaders. One was Shavelson, then forty-three years old and a mother of three; the second was ILGWU activist Rose Nelson, twenty-nine, who was appointed the movement's full-time organizer.[32]

The irony of choosing Nelson—who would become a leading personality in the Party, largely because of her success at organizing housewives—was that her unmarried state made it possible for her to devote herself to the cause full-time. No husband or children made demands on her time. (Nelson did eventually marry a man named Alex Raynes, but not until much later.) Shavelson devoted herself to the movement as fully as she could, but her loyalties were divided; she had family responsibilities she could not ignore. The conflicts that a mother/organizer like Shavelson faced clarify the limits of the 1930s housewife movement, but they also suggest its truly subversive potential.

By breaking through poor women's isolation in the home, by encouraging them (as Rose Nelson and Clara Shavelson did) to learn about and become active in changing the world they lived in, the housewives' movement promised to empower and to liberate wives and mothers, for when mothers became activists they also became individuals, no longer simply relational beings existing only in reference to husbands and children. That required of children and husbands an acknowledgement of the mother's personhood—a difficult thing for many family members to grant. Despite her resentments then, Martha Schaffer can see it now. "My mother was just trying to say, 'I am a person in my own right.' "[33]

Rose Nelson remembers the longing felt by so many women she knew during the 1930s:

> There was a need on the part of the mother, the woman in the house. She wanted to get out. There were so many things taking place that she wanted to learn more about. So women came to our organization where they got culture, lectures. Some developed to a point where they could really get up and make a speech that would meet any politician's speech today. It came from the need, from the heart. We felt we wanted to express ourselves, to learn to speak and act and the only way was through a women's council.[34]

Through the housewives' movement, Shavelson and Nelson hoped to give working-class mothers a sense of their individuality at the same time as they awakened them politically. According to Rae Appel, Clara Shavelson "wanted women should become alert and become conscious." She sought to spark in housewives a sense that the working-class movement "doesn't only belong to the workers in the shop, but also to us." That spirit was embodied in the founding document of the ucww, which asserted "that only through the common struggle of men and women in the shops, factories and at home, can the interests of the working class be protected."[35]

Shavelson, Appel believes, was unusually radical in both her class and gender politics. She was frustrated when other women could not see the importance of melding Marxism and feminism. Some women her age, who had participated in the strikes of the 1910s and in the suffrage movement, could appreciate her gender analysis; but many of them rejected her Communism. Some of the women of her children's generation, raised in the Communist youth movement, could understand and share her class analysis; but her fiercely held feminism was harder for these younger women to grasp.

"She liked to teach us young women," Smorodin recalls. "I remember us all sitting in her kitchen. *Her kitchen*. Clara was definitely the dominant personality in that house. She would stand at the stove and cook but she was listening to every word of our discussions. Suddenly, she would get angry. 'You young ones don't understand,' she would say. 'Women have to fight for what they want. You can't wait for the men to give it to you.' "[36]

But neither the Communist Party nor many of the women Shavelson hoped to organize shared her impassioned feminist analysis. So the literature of CP housewives' councils appealed to wives and mothers using language and arguments that reinforced their traditional roles. UCWW leaflets played to a high emotional pitch, emphasizing mothers' willingness to sacrifice for their children. Rather than a delight and escape from drudgery, political activism was portrayed as a painful but necessary path. This 1929 leaflet was typical: "The working class mother finds it impossible to provide her children with proper food and clothing, to which our children have a full right. The unsanitary conditions in the tenements, the poor clothing in wintertime, the lack of playgrounds and healthy recreation, lack of proper food is the reason for many diseases among the children of the working class. Many . . . women cannot withstand all this misery." The UCWW promised to help mothers fight for "lower rents, for lower prices of food, for adequate relief . . . , better and more schools, free food and clothing for children of unemployed workers, safe playgrounds, protection for mothers."[37]

Though many UCWW organizers were, like Shavelson, seasoned and committed political activists, they presented themselves as mothers driven to act by concern for their children. That made them less threatening—not only to apolitical women who feared association with Communists but also to those who thought it improper for mothers of young children to be parading the streets with picket signs. Clara represented herself in her campaign literature not as the rabble-rouser who sparked the 1909 strike but as a "real . . . mother fighting to maintain an American standard of living for her own family as well as for other families."[38]

As if some might doubt this, Shavelson often pointed out her children when they passed her speaker's platform on the way home from school. Her daughters hated it. Martha Schaffer recalls one afternoon when both she and her sister were spotted: "I would kind of slink by and my friends would say: 'Oh look, there's your mother.' And I would say, 'Come on, hurry up!' . . . Here she was pointing at you: 'And we have before you my child! My little girl! My Ritala.

Ritala, stand up! Raise your hand. This is my little girl Ritala. And over there . . .' By that time I had disappeared."[39]

Though Shavelson's displays of maternal pride were undoubtedly genuine, they also made for good street-corner agitating. This strategy was applied wherever UCWW leaders organized. After meeting women organizers in the park with their babies, in food markets, and then at street-corner meetings, formerly timid housewives began to feel more comfortable with the idea of joining a housewives' council to deal with their problems. Sophia Ocher, member of a mother and child unit of organizers, wrote about one Bronx community that "work among these women was not difficult for there was the baby, the greatest of all issues, and there were the women, all working class mothers who would fight for their very lives to obtain a better life for their babies."[40]

Shavelson and her colleagues had no idea just how successful this organizing strategy would become. During the early years of the Great Depression, massive unemployment combined with drastic wage cuts to impoverish the poor and working-class districts of New York. The high prices of the late 1920s held fairly steady, and crisis conditions developed quickly. By the end of 1931, the UCWW boasted forty-eight branches in New York City alone. By 1935, similar housewives' groups would be formed in Philadelphia, several New Jersey cities, Seattle, Chicago, Los Angeles, San Francisco and Detroit.[41]

In New York, where the movement began, this phenomenon was an outgrowth of the tradition of Jewish housewives' activism on subsistence issues that dated back to the first years of the century. Clara Shavelson, among others, provided a living link between the 1930s protests and the earlier Jewish women's actions. Arrest reports show a predominance of women between thirty and sixty; thus it is not surprising that the organizing techniques they used during the 1930s echoed those used in the protests of 1902–8 and of 1917–19, or that the depression-era housewives' movement got its start in the same neighborhoods where the earlier protests had taken place.

In 1931 as in 1908, housewives organized on a neighborhood basis. Women strode the main shopping strips of each community and went door to door to promote their strikes. Picket lines were set up in front of butcher shops or bakeries to make sure that no one broke the boycott. Local women spoke at daily open-air mass meetings to keep up the vitality and solidarity of the community.

And in 1931 as in 1908, the housewives' uprisings were centered in Jewish neighborhoods—older areas like Brooklyn's Williamsburg and Brownsville, and newer neighborhoods on the outskirts of the city, like Brighton Beach and Coney Island in Brooklyn and the Grand Concourse in the Bronx. Having "a solid Jewish working-class community" was a basis for organizing, Rose Nelson Raynes says. But "there had to be one or two or three spark plugs in every neighborhood who could really talk and get the women excited. . . . Clara Shavelson was one of these spark plugs."[42]

Shared ethnicity helped women activists galvanize their neighborhood-based movement. Organizers like Clara Shavelson understood the customs and gender norms of the communities they were trying to organize. As Shavelson had done in Brownsville during the 1910s and 1920s, depression-era organizers built housewives' councils on the foundations of traditional Jewish women's charitable and religious organizations. They also addressed street-corner crowds in both Yiddish and English. As the example of Bronx Communist activist Sonya Sanders suggests, knowledge of Jewish customs was often as important in getting neighborhood councils going as organizing skill. After Sanders cleaned one ailing Jewish mother's house, bathed her children, and prepared an impeccably kosher dinner for her family, the woman invited friends to come and listen to Sanders discuss ways to fight evictions and high prices. Before long a new neighborhood council had been born.[43]

Such bridges were less easily built in communities where organizers and housewives did not share the same ethnic background. In the years to come, women of different races, religions, and ethnicities would join the movement, but only after exhortations by women from their own racial or ethnic groups. In New York, the movement would remain largely Jewish until the mid-1930s.

"We never intended to be exclusively a Jewish organization," Rose Nelson Raynes insists, "but we built in areas where we had strength. Maybe it was because of the background of so many Jewish women in the needle trades, maybe it was because of the concentration of immigrants from the other side, I don't know. But there was a feeling in the Jewish working class that we had to express ourselves in protest of the rising prices."[44] Nowhere was that feeling stronger than in the densely populated Brooklyn neighborhood of Brighton Beach, where the Shavelsons moved in 1924.

ONE MILITANT HOUSEWIFE'S JOURNEY, 1924–1938

In 1924, after Clara Shavelson had her third child, the family began to look for more comfortable quarters. Just then the sleepy bungalow colony community of Brighton Beach, Brooklyn, was experiencing a furious building boom. In the grip of the 1920s real estate frenzy, developers erected dozens of airy "art-deco" apartment buildings along a narrow strip of land on Brooklyn's Atlantic shore. Since the early years of the century, Jewish immigrants had been coming to the area in summer to be close to the sea. With rooftop solariums and saltwater taps in the bathtubs, these new apartments lured young New Yorkers with the promise of "a year-round resort lifestyle."

Because of its history as a Jewish summer haven, Brighton appealed particularly to more comfortable members of the Jewish working class. By the late 1920s, thousands of Jewish immigrant families had relocated to Brighton, leaving behind aging inner-city neighborhoods like Brownsville, Williamsburg, and the Lower East Side. Most of them—like the Shavelsons—were union families, ready to enjoy a bit of the better life that World War I union wage scales had brought within their reach.[45]

In Brighton Beach the Shavelsons found an atmosphere that suited them well. By 1928, it was as highly politicized as any community in the United States. The fifteen-block-long neighborhood had its own branches of the Socialist, Communist, Labor Zionist, Democratic, and Republican clubs as well as neighborhood associations for members of the Amalgamated Clothing Workers, the ILGWU, and the Shoe Workers Union. Street rallies occurred almost daily. Radical political groups opened after-school programs to train the next generation. A proliferation of youth groups added to the rich ideological brew.

The Communist Party was particularly visible, recalls longtime Brighton Beach resident Walter Edberg: "It seemed like every Communist in New York City descended on Brighton at that time. Every day there would be people by the subway selling the *Daily Worker*. . . . I remember the speeches. This was a genuine hotbed of Communism. People would go into the polls and vote Communist and tell everyone about it. No one was scared."[46]

To refugees from the overcrowded inner city, life in Brighton Beach had a particular zest that distinguished it from other political centers. Residents summed it up in a Yiddish phrase: "It had *tam* [flavor]." On summer evenings, all Brighton gathered on the boardwalk, a wooden walkway that stretched the length of the neighborhood. The strains of mandolins and violins mingled with the sea breeze and the sounds of heated arguments over whether capitalism had reached its apex. Union organizer Sidney Jonas remembers, "It was a time when you heard only Communist songs on the boardwalk, in English, in Yiddish, and in Russian. We really believed that revolution was coming."[47]

In contrast to older immigrant neighborhoods, Brighton offered a radical milieu highlighted by pleasure and healthy living rather than poverty and overcrowding. Convinced that the ocean air promoted good health, Clara Shavelson began leading neighbors in daily exercises on the sand, and she swam in the ocean well into autumn. "She became a polar bear," says daughter-in-law Evelyn Velson. "She became a health nut," says her daughter Martha

Schaffer, explaining that Shavelson developed a complex dietary system based on achieving a balance between vegetables and proteins.[48]

Even political community was enhanced by the joys of living close to the sea. Rae Appel recalls gatherings with the Shavelsons and a small group of friends in the movement. "We got together on the beach . . . and we'd go swimming and sunning and discussing. Someone would bring out a thermos of coffee. Someone else would bring sandwiches. . . . It was delicious . . . since all of us were very much involved in the same work . . . to sit together and talk."[49]

The Crash of 1929 changed the tenor of Brighton life, as it did that of every community in the United States. Desperate and afraid, thousands more people came pouring into the neighborhood looking for rooms to rent or share with friends or relatives. Three and four generations crowded in together, pooling their money to pay the rent, hoping to stave off eviction. But Brighton was less grim than many other devastated corners of the country in 1930. The ocean was still there and still free. Clara Shavelson and her friends still exercised and swam, although, Appel remarked, "there were times we felt like we were committing a sin, bathing when there were so many things to be done." But such pleasures provided necessary release from the pressures of overcrowding and economic hardship and replenished their will to fight against the ravages of the depression.[50]

Everyone they knew shared their obsession with political work. Like the Shavelsons, a sizable percentage of the neighborhood's residents were veterans of the trade union battles of the 1910s who now committed themselves to fighting the Great Depression. Former CP activist Jack Friedman, then in his twenties, felt awe and respect for the older generation: "We had leaders here who were raised in the sweatshops, and they knew how to organize. They had come from Russia in a time of revolutions and they did not take crisis sitting down. These people viewed the depression not as a crisis you threw your hands up about. It was a crisis that required organizing, sticking together." One of the loudest voices drawing the various factions together, Friedman says, was that of "a figure out of history": Clara Lemlich Shavelson.[51]

By the early 1930s, Shavelson had become as familiar a sight on Brighton street corners as she had been in Brownsville and the Lower East Side. "Those years," says Rae Appel, "many struggles were carried on in Brighton Beach, with the leading figure Clara Shavelson. Bread strikes, rent strikes, any struggles that were carried on, she was always there to help the downtrodden people that needed her most." Shavelson played key roles in Brighton's branch of the United Council of Working Class Women, its Unemployed Council, and a tenants' group called the Emma Lazarus Council. Whether she held official positions in all these organizations is not clear. But "it wouldn't have mattered," says Rae Appel. "She was not a very shrinking violet."[52]

The women of Brighton attached significance to their decision to name their organization after Emma Lazarus, the poet whose words are inscribed on the base of the Statue of Liberty. To Shavelson and Rose Nelson, Lazarus seemed to embody the braided elements of their own political identities. Lazarus was a feminist and a strongly identified secular Jew and was sympathetic to Socialism. As immigrants and Communists, Shavelson and Nelson were also drawn to Lazarus's image of America as a haven for the politically persecuted and shelter for the homeless.

In 1931, the Emma Lazarus Council made a bold declaration: no one will be evicted in Brighton for inability to pay. Jack Friedman recalls that "Many people here couldn't pay their rent . . . so the women organized themselves. . . . Every time the landlords would put the furniture out onto the street, the women from the Emma Lazarus Council would come and move the furniture back into the apartment. There were many evictions then all over America. But not here, because we didn't allow it to happen."[53]

During the summer of 1931, Clara Shavelson and Rose Nelson led rent strikes not only in Brighton and Coney Island but across the city. Antieviction actions, Rose Nelson believed, galvanized the women for later consumer struggles, because housing was an even more pressing and immediate concern than the price of food. A family could live with dignity for a short time without bread or meat, but there was no dignity once a family was on the street. The anger and humiliation that accompanied evictions made it easy for organizers to convince women to join neighborhood councils.[54]

Brighton resident Shirley Kupferstein joined both the CP and the Emma Lazarus Council in 1930, though she says she had little real interest in politics. For her there seemed few other options. "We were starving. There was no food stamps then. My mother and father were dying. We didn't have the money to buy them painkillers. Sure we went to Communist rallies. . . . You couldn't help being a Communist if you were starving." Shavelson was able to tap into that anger to mobilize thousands of men and women who would never have joined the Communist Party but who enthusiastically joined CP-sponsored tenant, consumer, and unemployed councils. In the early years of the depression, the indefatigable Shavelson seemed to be everywhere at once.[55]

She organized Brighton's first Unemployed Council and led members on marches to city hall to demand municipal unemployment compensation. (The city eventually appropriated $1 million for relief.) In 1931 and 1932, she led four hundred women to Washington, D.C., to join thousands of self-proclaimed "hunger marchers" from across the United States, who had come to demand federal unemployment insurance. The UCWW women brought truckloads of food for the marchers, but they were unable to deliver it: most of the protesters were herded onto a side street, where they were held for three days by armed police and firemen, and National Guardsmen used tear gas to scatter the rest.[56]

But Shavelson returned home unbowed. She spoke at street demonstrations in support of workers trying to organize the Brighton Hand Laundry and a local candy factory. These were bitterly contested battles, and Shavelson was beaten after one speech. But she continued to organize protests against high-priced bread, milk, and meat through the 1930s. And all her crusades bore her unique, colorful stamp, right down to what hat she wore. Rae Appel recalls that when Shavelson spoke publicly "she always wore pretty hats. . . . They had to be just so. It had to say Clara Shavelson, the hat. . . . She never walked out without putting lipstick on, tucking her hair in. Sometimes she would wear a little veil. Just so. But she always looked elegant. Always made every effort to look elegant."[57]

Shavelson's theatrical style was showcased in a housewives' bread boycott during the winter of 1931–32. To get a sense of her activist life in those days, says Appel, imagine the same scenario for "every other struggle that took place in Brighton" during the depression: "She would walk from one end of the street to the other and stop at every bakery and use her voice, which was very eloquent and very appealing, to convince passersby not to buy bread. And when the owners of the stores would come out to chastise her or threaten her with physical harm, the people were always there to protect her, because they recognized her as a leader and as a person who was working for the welfare of all the people in the neighborhood."[58]

Clara Shavelson's leadership activities always began but never ended with public speaking. During the frequent bread and meat strikes of the early 1930s, the Brighton Beach housewives' council held daily open-air meetings, at which Shavelson spoke from atop a stepladder. But she also organized a circulating library for housewives' councils throughout New York, led discussions about how the bread and meat strikes related to other issues in the news, and created a community bulletin board on which members could post their own writings. In her own neighborhood, she convened a housewives' political theory study group. Many women in the community, Appel recalls, found Communist Party publications difficult to understand. Shavelson, says Appel, had a talent for translating Marxist jargon into plain English.[59]

Shavelson's daughter Martha says that her mother was deeply committed to the idea of self-education for working-class women as both a political principle and a personal goal: "She never really kowtowed to people who insisted that they were smarter. She did a lot of self-education. I can remember sitting in the living room while I was growing up and she would bombard me with questions. 'What does this mean? What does this mean?' . . . She used to have a little steno pad along with her. She used to write down words that were not familiar to her and then she would practice them." She eventually developed her writing skills sufficiently that she could contribute to both local and national CP publications.[60]

Her children and their friends remember Clara as an obsessive reader who loved to grill young people on books. Sophie Gerson recalls that the first question Clara always asked her when she entered the Shavelson home was, " 'Did you read this book? Did you read this article?' She kept tabs on all the things that were happening." In the years after Franklin Roosevelt's election, Shavelson would have the opportunity to project many of the ideas sparked by her studies onto a larger political stage.[61]

1933 through 1938 were unusually busy years for Clara Shavelson. Unlike Schneiderman and Newman, she was not directly involved in the changes emanating from the New Deal. Still, with the emergence of a more responsive government, she became increasingly interested in electoral politics. Like other politically minded Americans, Shavelson saw possibilities in the expanding welfare state. She came to believe that housewives, like other groups, could win gains through a strategy of carefully applied economic pressure, demonstrations, and lobbying.

In 1933 she made her first run for elected office, as a Communist Party candidate for a seat on the New York Board of Aldermen. Shavelson never expected to win, says Sophie Gerson, so friends were surprised when she invested in a new white ruffled dress for the campaign. It was not the sort of indulgence she allowed herself during those years and was thus a measure of how seriously she took the race. "She regarded this as another opportunity to be in contact with people," says Gerson, "to teach people who needed to be reached." And that was something Clara Shavelson always took seriously.[62]

The following year, Shavelson attempted to broaden her political base and, more important, to expand the influence of the housewives' movement. Well before the Communist Party issued its Popular Front policy, which urged members to work with "progressive" non-Communist groups, the UCWW had begun reaching out to non-Communist New York women's organizations, offering to make common cause around issues of food and housing. The overture was greeted enthusiastically despite long-standing hostilities between the Communist Party and other working-class organizations. This marked an important turning point in the housewives' movement. Although the UCWW had always claimed to be an independent organization, its officers were all Party members and its initial operating budget had come from Party coffers. This had led most trade union women to keep their distance.

Now, asserting their shared interests, UCWW representatives hashed out differences with women's union auxiliaries, neighborhood mothers' clubs, church groups, and black women's groups. The delegates agreed to gather and pool information on living conditions in various regions, on food prices and school overcrowding. These information networks would provide data for housewives' lobbying efforts in Washington over the coming decade. In early 1935 the women decided to create a national network. In February and March 1935, housewives' council leaders convened two regional conferences at which women from across the United States, both city dwellers and farm women, met to plan a full-scale nationwide assault on the high cost of living. Out of these conferences grew the most ambitious action yet mounted by the UCWW—a meat boycott that began in New York City and spread throughout the nation.[63]

Shavelson and Nelson launched the strike on their home turf. On May 22, 1935, they formed picket lines in Brighton and Coney Island, blocking access to every butcher shop in those communities. Within a week, housewives' picket lines appeared in Jewish and black neighborhoods throughout New York. Harlem, with its strong Communist Party base, quickly became one of the strike strongholds. Led by West Indian immigrant and civil rights activist Bonita Williams, self-proclaimed "flying squadrons" of between three hundred and one thousand Harlem women swept from butcher shop to butcher shop urging the owners to cut their prices. Hundreds of butchers throughout the city agreed to close their shops to honor the strike. It was a difficult choice; meat wholesalers pressured butchers, warning that anyone who stopped ordering during the strike would be cut off permanently.[64]

Through the first three weeks of June, Clara Shavelson and Rose Nelson made several speeches daily. Pictures of housewives picketing Manhattan's meat-packing plants appeared regularly on the front pages of the city's newspapers. By the time it was over, more than 4,500 butcher shops had been shut down. Scores of men and women around the city had been arrested. The New York State Retail Meat Dealers Association had threatened to hold Mayor LaGuardia responsible for damage to their businesses as a result of the strike, and Mayor LaGuardia had asked federal officials to study the possibilities for reducing retail meat prices.[65]

By mid-June, leaders of the UCWW had begun to receive threats of physical violence if they did not call off the strike. Rose Nelson Raynes remembers that "the strike was successful to a point where we got a warning that the gangsters were going to get us. I don't know who it was and I never questioned. But we had a meeting and we said we better call this thing off." First, however, they planned to stage one final public protest.

On June 22, 1935, carrying signs that depicted the storming of the Bastille during the French Revolution, hundreds of women from striking neighborhoods around the city boarded the subways and headed for midtown Manhattan. Says Raynes, "We organized a mass picket line in front of the wholesale meat distributors. At that time they were located on First Avenue and Forty-fourth Street. About three, four hundred women came out on the picket line. It was supposed to be a final action. But . . . instead of being the wind-up it became a beginning."[66] Unwilling to give in to "the gangsters," New York strike leaders met with housewife organizers from other cities to lay plans for a nationwide meat boycott.

Clara Shavelson was triumphant. Writing for the Communist Party Women's Commission magazine, *Working Woman*, she exulted, "The splendid fight carried on by the New York housewives against the meat trusts . . . came to a close on June 22, after more than a thousand shops reduced meat prices. Four weeks of picketing, demonstrating before wholesale meatpackers, battling police and gangsters convinced the meat trusts that the housewives of New York meant business." This was not, she said, a vendetta against local butchers but a coordinated protest against the large corporations controlling meat prices in the United States.[67]

What happened next demonstrated the evolution of housewife-activists' political sophistication in the twenty years since Shavelson had led her first rent strike. In negotiations during the New York meat boycott, municipal officials had told housewife leaders that their action was ineffective. The increase in meat prices was a nationwide phenomenon, they explained, and had been caused not by meatpackers' greed but by Department of Agriculture policies. Although UCWW leaders only partially believed the explanation, they decided to go to Washington and find out for themselves.

Just a few years earlier, the federal government might have seemed unapproachable. Even when housewife-activists traveled to the capital, as in the 1930 and 1932 hunger marches, it was to demonstrate rather than to lobby. But by the summer of 1935, working-class housewives' groups had been established across the United States. Housewives' groups in Chicago, Los Angeles, and Detroit were poised to stage major meat boycotts of their own. Understanding that they represented one of the largest interest groups in the country, housewife-activists saw no reason why they should not personally question

Secretary of Agriculture Henry Wallace about the impact of federal policy on meat prices.[68]

In July 1935, Clara Shavelson led a delegation of housewives from New York and Chicago to meet with Wallace at his Washington office. They insisted that he order wholesalers to stop withholding meat from the market in order to keep prices up. To allow such a practice in a time of hunger, they said, was outrageous. They also demanded that he rescind new meat-processing taxes that were driving prices up further.

Wallace nervously sidestepped the issue of federal responsibility. An extended drought, he claimed, was responsible for that summer's high meat prices. Surely, he told the housewives, you are not suggesting that meatpackers be penalized for circumstances beyond their control. American housewives don't believe that explanation, the women replied, because they had seen mountains of meat rotting in meatpackers' warehouses. If the hoarding of meat continued, they warned, housewives would do whatever it took to bring prices down.[69]

Following the meeting Shavelson made a plea to "housewives, farm women . . . regardless of nationality or political belief" to "start the ball rolling for a movement that will sweep the country like wildfire." Writing in *Working Woman*, she slammed the Department of Agriculture for protecting the meatpackers: "The meat packers and the Department of Agriculture in Washington tried to make the strikers' delegation from New York and Chicago believe that the farmer and the drought are to blame for the high price of food. But the delegation would not fall for this. They knew the truth—that while prices remain sky-high—there are millions of tons of meat stored in the Chicago warehouses, that the meat packers are the only ones profiting from the high prices."[70]

Class-conscious housewives, she concluded, "have the job of lining up the consumers, trade unions, farmers and small butchers into a united struggle against the meat trusts." Less than a month later, housewives stormed Chicago meatpacking plants. To dramatize their contention that high prices were not the result of shortages, they doused thousands of pounds of meat with kerosene and set it on fire, filling the streets of Chicago with the smell of burning meat.[71]

Joining the housewives of Chicago and New York, women across the country rose to Shavelson's challenge. By summer's end, housewives had boycotted meat in Detroit, St. Louis, Chicago, Kansas City, Philadelphia, Boston, San Francisco, Los Angeles, Indianapolis, Denver, and Miami. Although in New York the movement had included only Jewish and black women, outside of that ethnically balkanized city the boycott was embraced by housewives from a wide range of backgrounds: farm and city women, black and white women, native-born Protestants, and immigrant Jews, Poles, and Scandinavians.

These new housewives' coalitions succeeded in bringing prices down in hundreds of urban neighborhoods across the United States. Using similar tactics to those pioneered in the meat boycott, they staged successful protests during the late 1930s at relief bureaus, local boards of education, and city housing offices. To preserve and expand on the gains they made through direct action tactics, strike leaders convened a National Consumer's Congress in Washington that winter, kicking off an annual campaign of lobbying by housewife leaders.[72]

Far more sophisticated than their early-twentieth-century counterparts, housewife-activists in the 1930s used radio and newsletters to spread their message. They lobbied city, state, and federal politicians and developed complex political programs. They also ran for political office. Clara Shavelson lost, but others did not. In Washington State and in Michigan, housewife-activists were elected in 1934 and 1936 on platforms that called for government regulation of food prices and housing and utility costs. And in Minnesota, farm wives were key players in the creation of a national Farmer-Labor Party in 1936.[73]

The range of their political program reflects the degree to which housewives by the mid-1930s had come to accept the idea of a benevolent activist state. Like farmers and factory workers, housewives had begun to see themselves as a political interest group that by organizing and lobbying could force the New Deal state to respond to its needs. While earlier housewife-activists had no program beyond immediate reduction of prices, depression-era housewife leaders called for government regulation of the meat and milk industries; construction of more low-cost public housing and public schools; reform of prostitution laws; unemployment insurance; job security for working mothers; an end to discrimination against married and older women workers; and free access to birth control devices. Through savvy political campaigning and use of the media, they forced politicians to address these issues.

A less tangible but perhaps equally important legacy of the 1930s housewives' movement was the sense of personal liberation that many participants felt. "It was an education for the women," UCWW activist Dorothy Moser recalls, "that they could not have gotten any other way." Immigrant women, poor native white women, and black women all learned to write and speak, to lobby in state capitals and in Washington, D.C., to challenge men in positions of power, and sometimes to challenge their own husbands.[74]

Though most of the housewives who joined women's union auxiliaries and neighborhood councils during the depression were initially moved to action by need rather than political conviction, they were inevitably radicalized during the course of a decade of struggle. Since political organizing was seen as out of character for wives and mothers, they were often called upon to justify their actions. In defending their right to engage in politics, many working-class housewives came to believe that their needs and their abilities were as important as those of their husbands.

Clara Shavelson's dream of mobilizing poor housewives into an effective political force had been realized in dramatic style. Tillie Litinsky's "erstwhile kitchen drones" now felt competent to address their elected representatives, demanding that supporters of a balanced federal budget attempt to balance the household budget of the average working-class housewife. Faced with the wrath of angry housewives, elected officials began to develop what *The Nation* dubbed "a consumer consciousness." Housewives' militancy had injected a new element into U.S politics. "Never has there been such a wave of enthusiasm to do something for the consumer," the magazine noted in 1937.[75]

If this was so, it was because working-class housewives had demonstrated a keen understanding of their importance to both local and national economic stability. A few years of militant activism had forever shattered the notion that wives who consume are inherently more passive than their wage-earning husbands. In 1936, the *New Republic* remarked that the housewives' activism of the past few years had stretched the ideology of the labor movement, forcing male union leaders to admit reluctantly that "the roles of producer and consumer are intimately related."[76]

The 1930s housewives' movement propelled the American housewife and consumer into the center of U.S. political discourse. But even at its height, the movement's potential to force a rethinking of gender relations within the family was blunted by a strong visceral resistance to the idea that housewives could assert political leadership. That response came from government officials, from the Communist Party, and from the labor unions. And in more painful ways, it came from within the home.

A 1934 essay contest sponsored by the magazine *Working Woman* provides a window onto such conflicts. Contestants were asked to offer advice to a woman whose husband would not let her join her local housewives' council. A Bronx housewife insisted that political "struggle" keeps a woman "young physically and mentally" and called on husbands and wives to share child care as "they share their bread. Perhaps two evenings a week father should go, and two evenings, mother." A Pennsylvania miner's wife claimed to have told her husband that "there can't be a revolution without women. . . . No one could convince me to drop out. Rather than leave the Party I would leave him." And a Texas farm woman warned, "If we allow men to tell us what we can and cannot do we will never get our freedom."[77]

During the 1930s and 1940s the Shavelson home was rife with tensions intrinsic to a movement that sought to politicize marriage and motherhood. Conflicts between Clara and her family members were both mitigated and deepened by the fact that she was no mere recruit to the movement but its leader. The passion that drove her politically lit their home, making it a lively, warm, and exciting place. Family friends recall feeling a special charge when they visited. But that same quality in Clara sparked frequent brush fires. According to Rae Appel, "The fights were really on in those years" as Clara battled with family members caught in the maelstrom of her conflicting identities: feminist, Communist, housewife, mother, and nonstop community organizer.

CLARA SHAVELSON AND THE AMBIVALENCE OF
RADICAL MOTHERHOOD, 1935—1945

Clara Shavelson was as busy after the 1935 meat strike as before. In the years that followed the strike she was deeply involved in Communist Party efforts to cement ties with non-Communist working-class organizations. In 1936 she presided over the transformation of the ucww into the Progressive Women's Councils—a Popular Front league embracing both Communist-affiliated organizations and non-Communist women's groups. She also traveled annually to Washington as part of a consortium of urban housewives' groups to lobby for food and rent price controls. And during the 1938 elections, she both ran for state assembly on the Communist Party ticket and campaigned tirelessly for the new American Labor Party (ALP).

The ALP had been created during the summer of 1936 by garment unionists, including Rose Schneiderman and Fannia Cohn, to enable Socialists to vote for Franklin Roosevelt without registering with the Democratic Party. Despite this very specific aim, many unionists—Schneiderman and Cohn among them—hoped to make the ALP a strong independent voice for labor. In 1937 the Communist Party decided to cooperate with the ALP in hopes of generating a viable third-party coalition in New York. Anxious to support a labor-based electoral coalition, Communist Party members contributed their skills as neighborhood organizers. That was how Clara Shavelson became a stump speaker for the ALP.[78]

Shavelson was attracted to the ALP in part by her admiration for Socialist congressman Vito Marcantonio, who had inherited Fiorello LaGuardia's district in 1934. During Marcantonio's victorious 1938 campaign on the ALP ticket, Shavelson shared speakers' platforms with him in working-class districts across New York. The two were a powerful draw wherever they spoke, says Rae Appel, because they exuded warmth and down-to-earth appeal. Instead of filling their speeches with campaign promises, says Appel, they tried "to explain to the people how important it is for them to become politically conscious." People responded to them, she says, because they were less interested in winning than in building a movement.[79]

In her own district, Shavelson explicitly played on her reputation as a consumer activist, using those credentials to soften people's resistance to the idea of voting Communist. One campaign leaflet began, "Bread, Meat, Milk. If these items play a part in your life, this story is for you." Clara Shavelson, the leaflet assured voters, was "a real American mother . . . a typical member of the Communist Party . . . typical of the slogan which life itself is proving— Communism is Twentieth Century Americanism."[80]

But even as Communist Party leaders were trumpeting Shavelson's broad appeal, they had decided to withdraw support from the housewives' councils. With tacit approval from national leaders, local CP officials diverted funds raised by council organizers into other work not related to women. In 1937 the Party discontinued publication of *Woman Today* (formerly *Working Woman*), the magazine in which Shavelson, Nelson, and other housewife leaders had reported on the housewives' movement. And after the 1938 election, housewife organizers still receiving CP salaries were transferred to other work.[81]

A battle royale soon raged within the Communist Party over the issue of organizing housewives independent of their husbands. Mary Inman, a leading CP theorist, was regularly savaged in the Party press during the late 1930s for publishing a book which argued that wives and mothers were as vital to the working-class struggle as shop-floor workers. In a pamphlet called "Marxism and the Woman Question," Party leader Avram Landy warned that to believe Inman was "to glorify and exaggerate the social role of the housewife." He ridiculed Inman's assertion that motherhood was a socially constructed institution subject to change through political organizing. "Motherhood," he wrote, "is a phenomenon of nature and not of society." Women, Landy insisted, will never achieve power by organizing as wives and mothers. The only route to equality between the sexes, he concluded, is for women to become workers and join trade unions.[82]

Inman retorted that it was impossible for the majority of American women to join trade unions. "Women wage workers are eligible to join trade unions, and should do so. But three fourths of the women of the working class in the United States work only at home, raising children . . . and performing necessary work in the renewal of the labor energy of existing workers." Neither trade unions nor union auxiliaries address the particular concerns that they face as workers in their own homes. Wives and mothers, she insisted, should be seen as "labor power production workers." Like all workers, they require "an independent organization designed primarily to improve the working conditions of its members." Destroying the housewives' councils, Inman concluded angrily, was inimical to the interests of the class struggle. Her views were not welcomed by CP leaders. Inman was forced out of the Party, and her books disappeared from CP bookstores.[83]

Despite the dismantling of the housewives' councils, Clara Shavelson did not leave the Party, then or ever. She did not, like many Party wives, subsume her political career in that of her husband, but she was unlike the handful of women who achieved positions of leadership in the Party—Ella Reeve "Mother" Bloor and Elizabeth Gurley Flynn, for example. These women had neither husbands nor young children to exert conflicting pulls. Though she worked briefly during the early years of the depression, selling oil burners to keep her family fed, Clara Shavelson genuinely represented that most controversial of social figures: a class-conscious housewife-activist. Never a paid organizer for the Party, she was able to retain a measure of independence throughout her career. But that was a tricky task. As Peggy Dennis, wife of CP leader Eugene Dennis, noted, "The dilemma was . . . [how] to be both wife-mother and Communist activist. The Communist Party organizational milieu provided little possibility for both, especially in the upper levels of leadership."[84]

But Shavelson, like most women who organized or joined housewives' councils, did not deal directly with "the upper levels of leadership." The major resistance most housewife-activists encountered was from their husbands. The refusal of women like Clara Shavelson to make what Peggy Dennis called "either-or choices" meant that their husbands were sometimes left with child-care or housekeeping responsibilities. Even politically radical husbands—men like Joe Shavelson, who claimed to believe in equality between the sexes—rebelled at that.

In her 1936 "Open Letter to Progressive Husbands," Rose Nelson tried to quiet the rebellion by suggesting that politically educated wives made better companions.

A few words to the Progressive husband. You married her to be your companion and partner in life and still you go out to educational meetings . . . without giving your wife a chance. . . . Women's councils . . . hold educational meetings on literary, economic, political and health subjects.

What a school this is for the wife who is unable to achieve such education in any other manner! Yes, Mr. Husband she will be a more interesting companion. . . . This will be the reward for even a little effort in sharing the care of babies when your wife must attend the meeting of her Council, Mother's Club or other neighborhood organization. Worth considering, isn't it?[85]

Martha Schaffer says that her father, Joe Shavelson, would have had no quarrel with that logic. "My mother didn't have to fight to be a liberated woman," she says, "because my father expected that everyone would pull their own weight." Activism was a way of life in the Shavelson family, for the children as well as the parents. All that activity made their home crackle with excitement. But it took a toll on family intimacy. "The fact that my mother was active in one place and he was active in another and we were all active somewhere else was just an accepted fact of life," says Schaffer. "The thing that finally upset my father was . . . he was tired of not ever seeing us. We'd never be home." So Joe Shavelson made a rule that everyone had to be home for dinner together at least one night a week.[86]

There were some very happy times when the family was together. Rae Appel recalls that the family's three-room apartment "was always filled when they were all together, either with talking, arguing, or singing." Schaffer remembers her mother having both a great voice and a great love for singing. Clara would sing and dance while she worked in the kitchen. Appel remembers Joe as "a very alert man, full of life, full of mischief, telling all kinds of jokes in a very loud voice."

There were trips to Niagara Falls and the Catskills and the 1939 World's Fair. These were even more adventurous when Clara, who learned to drive only in her fifties, was behind the wheel. "On the way back we always sang," says Martha. "The car was always jammed with people and we sang folk songs." The Shavelson family was not lacking in love and affection. Family and friends recall Joe's sweetness and Clara's warmth. The house was constantly filled with the Shavelson children's friends, says Irving's second wife, Evelyn Velson. There was music and good food and an aura of openness. But this unusual family's highly politicized lifestyle also generated tensions.[87]

Interestingly, none of the children felt ambivalent about their politically active father, maybe because fathers were then, and are now, expected to have their attention divided between public and private spheres. Or perhaps it was a question of personality. "There was something so sweet about that man," says Evelyn Velson. "It stays with me to this day." On the other hand, says Appel, Clara was always sure that "her way is the right way." All the warmth in the world doesn't make that attitude easy to take.[88] The major source of conflict seems to have been over how much time Clara spent away from the house. Velson remembers Irving saying "that the children might have felt differently toward Clara had she been around more." A particularly heated battle ensued over Clara's decision to attend the 1934 International Women's Congress against War and Fascism in Paris.[89]

The trip was vitally important to Clara because it enabled her to return to Russia, the country of her birth, for the first time since 1903. She was overcome by emotion at seeing her homeland again. "We went by train to Moscow and there was a bus there to meet us. But I wouldn't get on it. . . . This was the country where they wouldn't even let me go to school—where if I walked into a city they would have made me wear a prostitute's badge. And now—I wanted to stand there for a long time with my feet on the soil of a worker's country." Clara's joy at being in Socialist Russia does not seem to have been dimmed by the harsh realities of Stalin's rule. But when she returned home, she had to face the anger of her ten- and seventeen-year-old daughters, who were upset that she had left the family for so long.[90]

It wasn't that Joe and the children didn't think Clara's work was worthwhile; it didn't mean they weren't proud of her. But her admirable commitment to politics had ramifications at home—like who was going to do the cooking and cleaning. There was a good deal of resentment about the fact that Clara expected her husband and children to help with the housework. Says Rae Appel, "Martha would lament and cry that her mother didn't iron her blouse, that she had to do it herself. . . . Clara often explained to her, it isn't that she didn't want to do it, but she felt that the work she was doing was very important. Not that the blouse that Martha needed was not important but . . . she had to make a choice."[91]

Often her family felt that she had made the wrong choice. Joe would say, according to Appel, "that it was important for a man to attend union meetings. But not for his wife to be on the streets talking." Martha Schaffer remembers that she had mixed feelings when other young people in the neighborhood would tell her how much they admired her mother. She was proud of her mother but she still would have preferred for Clara to be "in the house giving me cold milk and warm cookies."[92]

Children are rarely happy about having to share their mothers; that normal childhood craving for a mother's attention was intensified for the Shavelsons by the fact that their mother was not only a driven woman but also a celebrity. "To you, your mother is an ordinary person," says Schaffer. "To other people she's a public person. You say to yourself, that's not my real mother." Clara's children sometimes felt that having a famous mother destroyed the family's privacy, putting them in the public eye when they didn't want to be. Schaffer recalls flinching when strangers asked them if they planned to follow in their mother's footsteps. She recalls wistfully, "Living up to a living idol. It's not easy."[93]

Clara took mothering responsibilities seriously, but she gave them a decidedly political cast. To Clara, class-conscious motherhood entailed more than nurturing one's own children; an activist woman had a responsibility to reach out to and train the next generation of radicals. That notion fit well into a tradition of U.S. women's political activism, from coal-mining organizer "Mother Jones" to the women elders of the Communist Party—"Mother Bloor," "Mother Gitlow," and "Mother Shavelson"—who were held up as examples to young Party members. In that sense, Clara was a very good mother. All of her children became activists.

Her eldest son, Irving—who changed his name to Charlie Velson to make organizing easier among non-Jewish workers—became a revolutionary union leader. In his late teens he joined the National Guard to learn about military tactics in preparation for the coming revolution. At age nineteen he married a childhood sweetheart, Ruth Yugelson, who—as Ruth Young—would become one of the most important women labor leaders of her generation. Charlie and, later, his sister Martha worked for the International Longshore Workers' Union, the militant alternative to the corrupt AFL dockworkers' union. Charlie became a leading figure in West Coast longshore organizing, a close friend and colleague of controversial labor leader Harry Bridges. Martha became active in the civil rights movement and the California farmworkers' union. Rita's political work was less clearly ideological, but she too became an activist in New York Jewish organizations. According to Martha Schaffer, Clara also "had a great influence" on her nieces and nephews. "Some of them say they are radicals because of what they learned at my mother's knee."[94]

Clara Shavelson's nurturing of young political activists spread well beyond her family. A Brighton neighbor would later tell Martha Schaffer that he saw Clara as his political mother. "You know, I used to love coming home from school," he told her, "and standing on the street corner and listening to your mother, because I felt I was listening to my mother. . . . My mother didn't go in for that sort of thing. My mother was very conservative."[95]

Some young people came to Clara through her leadership of a long campaign to get New York City to build more public schools in Brighton, a bitter battle that culminated in a boycott by five thousand schoolchildren. Others were inspired by her pacifist work for the League against War and Fascism. During the early 1930s she spoke frequently in support of peace campaigns. Her daughter Martha was active in one of these, urging high school students to sign the Oxford Pledge, a statement refusing military service.[96]

In the early 1980s, a gray-haired man approached Martha Schaffer on a street in San Diego. Half a century back, as high school students, they had worked together for the Oxford Pledge. The principal of their high school had called him in and threatened him with expulsion if he did not bring his mother to school the next day. Because his mother would not have approved of his actions, he decided to ask Clara Shavelson, whom he had watched for years on Brighton street corners, if she would be willing to speak to the principal. She did, Schaffer recalls. "And my mother said, 'If you don't treat my son right, I will take him out of your school.' And she told him all about the rights that students have. And that people can demonstrate against fascism and . . . that, if the principal had a conscience, he would be on that picket line with them."[97]

If Clara Shavelson was a master at what, in late-twentieth-century street parlance, is called "speaking truth to power," she was less comfortable in power struggles with her own children. One of her sons-in-law believed that this was because "she was a public woman." Clara Shavelson, he said, "sometimes didn't speak well. She talked to you and she didn't always make sense. . . . But when she had to make a speech, she would organize it and make a beautiful speech." She had, he decided, "two personalities, a political personality and a family personality. And it was two different people. . . . You couldn't imagine it was the same person."[98]

This duality was vividly dramatized when one of the Shavelson children began dating a married African American. Clara and Joe would not even speak to the suitor. And when talk turned to marriage, they threatened to disown their child. Rae Appel, who strongly disapproved of their response, notes that they had taught their children "to recognize the need for equality for black people. . . . They were very much with Negro people in the Communist organization. That was why this was such a contradiction."[99]

At the very same time, says Martha Schaffer, Clara was deeply involved in organizing women to fight "the hideousness of people selling themselves on the streets. On this corner, people used to stand there, black women used to stand there and wait for the rich Jewish ladies to come and pick them. She felt that it was a terrible thing, and I agreed with her." Clara was so horrified by this depression-era practice known as the "slave markets" that she refused to hire anyone to clean her own house. "She felt that it was a terrible thing to ask people to do," Schaffer says. Instead, she insisted that her daughters, who were now working full-time, help her with the housework. This sparked regular and bitter fights.[100]

Tensions between Clara and Joe's political and personal desires can also be seen in their determination to put their children through college. Despite much fighting and cajoling, the Shavelsons could not convince their son Irving to forestall union work long enough to finish school. Raised in a revolutionary household according to a credo Schaffer describes as "workers have to stick together; even if others forget that, you should always live that way," Irving was anxious to join the worker's struggle. His parents, on the other hand, wanted him to "better himself" by going to college. Overruling them, Irving moved out on his own, went to work in the Brooklyn Navy Yard, and got married, all before he was twenty. Interestingly, given his problems with his mother's activism, he chose to marry childhood friend Ruth Yugelson (who changed her last name to Young, also to facilitate organizing among non-Jews). Young was as active in the labor movement as he was, and she had no intention of giving up union work when she had children.[101]

But even Young, a fierce advocate for women's rights in the United Electrical Workers, had an uneasy relationship with Clara. The two women could not seem to get close to one another. Evelyn Velson believes that Young's work outside the home created some tensions in her marriage to Irving. Perhaps the source of these troubles was, in Martha Schaffer's words, that "they both put their work first." Whatever the case, despite Clara's fierce insistence on her right to do political work outside the home, she adopted the most traditional of motherly stances: that her son should have a wife who would dote on him. Politics and love are a complicated mix. It seems ironic, but perhaps it is not, that Clara's easiest relations may have been with her least politically involved child, Rita.

In part, conflicts between Clara and her radical children were sparked by her absolutist personality. She was always sure she knew what was right, Rae Appel says. And she gave everything a political cast—*everything*. Appel remembers that Clara turned even her obsession with nice clothing into a matter of political strategy. "She used to be very critical of people, women especially, who came shabbily dressed for a demonstration. . . . Very critical. She would say, 'You stand out like a sore thumb. The police will recognize you right away. Many of you come shabbily dressed because you don't know any better. . . . And the police, thinking you're politically oriented, you're the first ones they'll beat.'" Some younger women like Appel accepted Clara Shavelson's leadership and were not put off by her controlling side—because, Appel says, Clara was so loving. "Everyone who came to her felt an intimacy and a warmth and an understanding that they couldn't find in any other person. And because of that . . . she was always looked up to. So you see that Clara Shavelson was not only a leader but a human being, a warm friend."[102]

But not everyone felt that way. Sometimes, says Martha Schaffer, her mother's need to take charge could have a chilling effect on younger women's desire to participate in political work with her. "Mother was concerned that they weren't attracting more young women. But I don't know if she understood that when they came in, there wasn't much room for them to act." Clara Shavelson, like all the women in this study, was caught in the paradox of the activist personality. From the beginning of her life she had a political compulsion that drove her to speak out against injustice, to put her body on the line for what she believed in, to put in the long, hard hours that organizing takes. Her passion enabled her to accomplish a great deal but also made it hard for her to let go and let others take the lead. And it took a toll on her relations with those she loved most.[103]

Still, her certainty about "the right thing to do" was what gave her the courage to return time and again to picket lines during the first years of the century, despite "a hail of blows that fell like rain." It gave her the energy to lead a political movement while raising three children. In 1944, when Joe's heart was weakening and he could no longer work full-time, it gave her the strength to go back to the garment shops as a rank-and-file worker. And it would enable her in her sixties, after working long hours as a hand-finisher on cloaks, to once again attend union meetings, to fight "with both boss and foremen" and to attend protests against U.S. interventions overseas and loyalty investigations at home. Her colleague Rose Nelson Raynes described her as a spark plug, but she seems to have been more—an inexhaustible power source.[104]

The Progressive Women's Councils, which Shavelson led from the 1930s through their demise in the early 1950s, remained active throughout the Second World War, although militant consumer activities gave way to knitting circles and war bond drives between 1941 and 1945. By war's end, the Progressive Women's Councils had merged with the Women's Division of the International Worker's Order (IWO), a CP-sponsored society offering medical insurance, death benefits, cultural and educational activities, and summer camps. Clara Shavelson became secretary of the New York City branch of the IWO Women's Division, a position that would leave her vulnerable in the Red-hunting days to come.[105]

Anti-Communist hysteria would soon undermine the housewives' movement in New York and across the country as state and federal legislative bodies launched investigations of CP influence on consumer activism. But before those investigations began, Shavelson and other housewife leaders would spark two more nationwide meat strikes. In 1948 and again in 1951, consumer militance would sweep the country as housewives organized boycotts that were even broader in their influence and their participation than the famous "meatless summer" of 1935.

In the thirty-one years between Clara Shavelson's departure from the garment shop floor in 1913 and her return in 1944, she had guided, inspired, and helped organize one of the most unusual social movements of the 1920s and 1930s. The national housewives' coalition alleviated the worst effects of the Great Depression in many working-class communities: bringing down food prices, rent, and utility costs; preventing evictions; and spurring the construction of more public housing, schools, and parks. By the end of the Second World War it had forced the federal government to regulate food and housing costs and to investigate profiteering on staple goods. A decade of intense antieviction struggles and years of lobbying for public housing helped convince New York City and other localities to pass rent control laws. It also increased support in Congress for federally funded public housing.[106]

Finally, Clara Lemlich Shavelson and other housewife-activists brought gender politics into the working-class home, shining a bright light on the hidden power relations between husbands and wives, parents and children. The result was often uncomfortable. The tensions between Shavelson and her children say a great deal about the complexities of mixing motherhood and politics. In the end, the movement did not much alter the traditional sexual division of labor, even in the homes of working-class activists; nor did it empower wives and mothers in all the ways Shavelson hoped it would. But it issued a loud challenge to sexual power relations in the home, well before the so-called "second wave" of twentieth-century feminism.

PART FOUR.

THE ACTIVISTS

IN OLD AGE:

THE TWILIGHT

OF A MOVEMENT,

1945–1986

WITNESSING

THE END OF

AN ERA:

THE POSTWAR

YEARS AND

THE DECLINE

OF INDUSTRIAL

FEMINISM

The feeling we had was of witnessing the end of an era, the end of more than fifty years of activity in organizing, educating, legislating for the working woman. . . . We were proud of our share but very sad to see it dissolve.
—Pauline Newman, on the dissolution of the WTUL

By the end of World War II, Rose Schneiderman, Pauline Newman, Fannia Cohn, and Clara Shavelson found themselves operating in a new and quite hopeful political climate. Much of what they had so long been working for suddenly seemed realizable. Women constituted 36 percent of the U.S. labor force, more than ever before. Nearly three million women workers were unionized, and half a million more would enter unions as a result of strikes immediately following the war. All national unions in both the American Federation of Labor and the Congress of Industrial Organizations now admitted women members. The National Labor Relations Act of 1935 ensured labor leaders a permanent voice in government. And the Fair Employment Standards Act of 1938 extended federal minimum-wage and maximum-hours standards to workers of both sexes.[1]

The irony in all this for longtime activists was that World War II had, almost overnight, created changes that they had been unable to bring about through decades of lobbying and organizing. The number of women belonging to unions had more than quadrupled between 1939 and 1945. By war's end, women's average weekly wages in some regions had nearly doubled. The war had precipitated at least a temporary breakdown of sex segregation in the labor force; women now filled skilled positions in the heavy manufacturing sector, which had long been closed to them. A 1942 complaint by women of the United Electrical Workers (UE) and the United Auto Workers (UAW) had moved the National War Labor Board to endorse the principle of equal pay for men and women—the first time the federal government had done so. And a consortium of women's organizations, including the rarely allied WTUL and National Woman's Party, had pushed through equal pay laws in several states.[2]

Though women trade unionists were encouraged by these wartime gains, they were aware that many of them were temporary, incomplete, and easily reversible. The bulk of newly organized women had joined unions only because their wartime jobs required them to; the upsurge in unionization did not reflect the emergence of a politicized female workforce. A wartime Women's Bureau study showed that few women occupied high offices in national unions. The bureau also found that sex-based wage differentials had persisted through the war. Women's wages were much higher in 1944 than in 1941, but the gap between women's and men's salaries remained.[3]

In unions like the UAW and the UE, whose huge female memberships included large numbers of outspoken women, equal pay provisions had become a standard part of most contracts. And a few employers in key defense industries paid by the job, not the worker. But in most industries and unions, the Women's Bureau noted in 1944, wages remained "inadequate for women." Hard-won equal pay legislation did little to improve the situation. Pauline Newman, who collected data on sex-based wage differentials for New York's 1944 Equal Pay Bill, understood that the bill had great symbolic importance but that it was essentially unenforceable. Continuing sex-segregation in the labor force made it virtually impossible to evaluate the relative worth of men's and women's work.[4]

Reckoning with these realities, the WTUL worked out a new set of legislative priorities for the postwar period. Given the inadequacy of state equal pay bills, the officers decided to focus attention on state comparable worth laws. Rose Schneiderman, fresh from six years as New York's secretary of labor, volunteered to develop criteria for assessing comparable worth. The League also began thinking about how it might frame antidiscrimination laws to prevent the wholesale firing of millions of women from the high-paying positions they now occupied in heavy manufacturing industries. Finally, recognizing a crucial demographic change—more than half of women workers were now over thirty-five and married—the League made publicly funded day care centers a major priority.[5]

League leaders were encouraged in 1944 when Secretary of Labor Frances Perkins chose Frieda Miller to replace Mary Anderson as head of the Women's Bureau. Anderson was retiring after twenty-five years of service, and WTUL officers had been concerned that they might lose their decades-long tie to the bureau. Instead, as one of her first major decisions, Miller created a permanent Labor Advisory Board, with representatives from fifteen unions. The board included many women she had known through twenty-seven years in the WTUL—most notably her partner, Pauline Newman. It is perhaps ironic that women trade unionists were not integrated into the policy-making apparatus of the Women's Bureau until Miller, the mill owner's granddaughter, replaced Anderson, the bootmaker and union organizer.

Not surprisingly, one of the first products of the Labor Advisory Board was a "Reconversion Blueprint for Women," which echoed the goals of the WTUL. It called for antidiscrimination procedures to guide postwar layoffs, retraining programs for laid-off workers, and higher wages in traditionally female trades, particularly service industries like laundry and domestic labor. An aura of hopefulness surrounded the document's release in the spring of 1945.[6]

The housewives' movement, too, was buoyed by a flush of postwar optimism as activists regrouped quickly after war's end to demand an extension of wartime price controls. In February 1946, several organizations that had cooperated during the mid-1930s consumer actions joined together to create an umbrella group called the Congress of American Women (CAW). The CAW promised to promote a full women's agenda that linked consumer and tenant issues with such concerns as equal pay and day care. Both the WTUL and the Progressive Women's Councils, led by Clara Shavelson, joined the CAW. Within a year, nineteen women's organizations had affiliated with the group.[7]

The years immediately following the war were busy and productive ones for industrial feminists. They fought with great energy both to preserve the wartime gains made by women workers and to lay a firm foundation for working-class women's activism in the second half of the twentieth century. But several intertwining forces would soon snuff out the hope that industrial feminism could survive into the 1950s.

The first was age. After more than four decades of struggle on behalf of working-class women, activists of the 1909 vintage were growing tired. By the war's end, Rose Schneiderman was sixty-three, Fannia Cohn was sixty, Clara Shavelson was fifty-nine, and Pauline Newman was in her mid-fifties. As pragmatic as they were idealistic, the four women had tried to adapt their analyses and strategies to the changing world they lived and worked in. Still, by 1945, there could be little question that their effectiveness as leaders was diminished: theirs was the worldview of an earlier era. If working-class women hoped to effectively tackle the myriad problems of the postwar years, these aging warriors would have to relinquish the mantle of leadership to younger women.

There were many likely candidates. CIO organizing drives during the depression and the war had brought a new generation of women organizers into the limelight. These women came from a variety of racial and ethnic backgrounds —Jewish and Catholic, white and African American—and many had proven to be militant advocates for women in the labor movement: Eleanor Nelson had just been elected president of the United Federal Workers, only the second woman ever elected to lead a national union in the United States. (The first had been glovemaker and WTUL officer Agnes Nestor, forty years earlier.) Ruth Young, Clara Shavelson's daughter-in-law, was on the executive board of the United Electrical Workers by war's end. Maida Springer of the ILGWU was one of two women chosen by the AFL in 1945 to represent American labor on a postwar tour of Great Britain. Other women as well had emerged as leaders in their unions, including Ann Berenholz of the United Office and Professional Workers; Miranda Smith of the United Cannery and Packinghouse Workers Allied Union; and Dolly Robinson and Charlotte Adelman of the laundry workers.[8]

Some of these women labor leaders had been nurtured by Newman, Schneiderman, Shavelson, and Cohn. But despite their emphasis on education and their long-standing interest in training younger women for union leadership, the four were not quite ready to step aside and let a new generation take over. In some ways, they were caught in the vortex their own activism had created. These were driven women, with a level of stamina and endurance rare even among their labor movement colleagues. Tenacity and assuredness had taken them all far. But after decades of bruising struggle, during which they constantly had to defend themselves politically as well as personally, the four had grown more rather than less certain that theirs was the only right way. This quality of certitude made it hard for them to solicit the counsel of younger women or to admit that they were on the backward-looking side of a generation gap. By the 1940s these women were, in many ways, out of step with the times.

In the years after the war, Rose Schneiderman and Pauline Newman cost the WTUL allies by hewing to a dated political perspective. They alienated younger men and women in the labor movement who felt that the time had passed for protective legislation for women and that labor should endorse the Equal Rights Amendment. Even more damaging, the two women remained loyal to the craft-based, conservative AFL in an era when the majority of unionized women belonged to the rival CIO.

Committed to organizing workers on an industrywide basis regardless of craft or skill level, the CIO was far more interested in recruiting women than the more hidebound AFL. Large CIO unions like the UAW and the UE organized hundreds of thousands of women workers during the 1930s and early 1940s. New to unionism and excited by the ideological ferment of the CIO, these women initially flocked to the Women's Trade Union League. They represented new blood for the League, the possibility of a future. But threatened AFL officials began attacking local WTUL branches for welcoming CIO women.

AFL leaders warned that they would withhold financial support if the WTUL did not sever ties with CIO unions. Schneiderman and Newman did not know how to handle this situation; so they did nothing while AFL leaders bullied the WTUL's local groups, and the League began to wither.

But the decline of working-class women's activism after World War II cannot be blamed simply on the weariness or shortsightedness of a group of aging women organizers. Few progressive organizations survived the postwar years of inquisition and innuendo, government investigations, and congressional backlash against the labor movement. That pervasive political and cultural reaction was the most important factor in the final dissolution of the WTUL, the housewives' councils, and the militant women's union auxiliaries. Workers' education programs did survive this time, but in a very different form than that originally conceived by women of the 1909 vintage—a form that reinforced union hierarchies rather than challenging them.

There was no simple causal relationship between the chilled political climate of the postwar years and the decline of industrial feminism. Few industrial feminists were actually investigated. Of the four women profiled in this book, only Clara Shavelson was subpoenaed to testify, restricted in her travel, and visited by the FBI. The anti-Communism of Rose Schneiderman and Pauline Newman was never challenged. And Fannia Cohn was considered trustworthy enough that she could serve as a character witness for friends who came under government scrutiny.

Still, the cold fear that gripped the nation made all kinds of Americans wary of association with any group tainted by radicalism. Middle-class financial and political support for working-class causes evaporated. Both AFL and CIO unions began to purge their most militant members. The small number of women who had risen to leadership positions during the 1930s and early 1940s were isolated and put on the defensive. Some, like Ruth Young, would repudiate their militant pasts and recast themselves as strong anti-Communists. Others censored themselves politically, anxious to avoid the dread label "Communist." In those years there was little negotiating room for feminists or working-class militants.[9]

Rose Schneiderman chose to end her public career a few years after the war. But Newman, Shavelson, and Cohn did not. Though the scope of their activism diminished as they aged, all three continued working, speaking up for what they believed in, and nurturing younger protégés. The story of their ongoing activism through times of harsh repression highlights a key element in the long, slow process of creating political and social change: the stamina and will of tenacious individuals.

Once World War II ended, the wages and status of women workers deterio-rated rapidly. Between July 1945 and May 1946, more than four million women left the paid labor force. One million women were laid off at the nation's aircraft plants, shipyards, ammunition factories, and other defense industries. The wartime production crunch was over. Soldiers were returning from over-seas and needed civilian jobs. As a result, the same government agencies that had sold the idea of heavy manufacturing work to millions of women from 1941 to 1945 now strongly urged women to give up their jobs and return to hearth and home.

The problem was that though the wartime manufacturing jobs may have been temporary, many of the women who'd filled them were not temporary workers. They were working-class women—former garment, domestic, laun-dry, and textile workers who had improved their salaries and working condi-tions dramatically during the war. These women had to work, and they were not happy about returning to the lower-paid "women's trades." As late as the spring of 1945, the WTUL and the Women's Bureau had hoped that women could hold onto at least a portion of the unionized, high-paying jobs that the war emergency had opened up to them. By May 1946, Women's Bureau director Frieda Miller and her League allies had clearly given up that hope.[10]

"Rosie the Riveter and her industrial co-workers . . . upgraded themselves during the war," Miller wrote in the *New York Times* in 1946. It is only natural that "they would like to retain some, if not all, of the gains." However, women workers were pragmatists, said Miller. They accepted that the sexual integra-tion of the labor force brought about by war was not likely to survive the peace. Thus, Miller announced, women workers were now switching strat-egies. They wanted to see wages and working conditions in "the kind of jobs women had always performed" elevated to the much higher standard prevail-ing in the traditionally male-dominated industries.

A great deal remains to be done, Miller warned, "before Rosie the Riveter, Winnie the Welder, and other women of the war sorority of industrial workers will be content to return to the woman-employing fields that are characterized by substandard wages and unreasonably long hours." In the name of justice and the general welfare of the nation, Miller concluded, women workers must be assured of "wages that permit them to maintain the standards of living they already have achieved, hours of work that are conducive to health, and de-cency standards and working environments that are a far cry from those of some pre-war establishments." Miller and the WTUL would spend the next four years trying to do just that.[11]

Miller and the League were particularly interested in extending the minimum wage to domestic workers, who were uncovered by existing labor laws and had suffered precipitous pay cuts when postwar factory layoffs forced them back into domestic labor. But expanding labor legislation was an uphill battle in those years. The war had threatened many of the labor laws already on the books; indeed, many states had completely suspended hours and safety standards in the interest of promoting wartime production. Now that the nation was again at peace, WTUL activists were left to repair and update the protective legal structure they had been slowly building since the 1910s.[12]

One of their few successes at expanding that structure was the passage in 1945 of the Domestic Workers' Compensation Law in New York State. It was a limited gain at best, covering only workers who lived in cities with populations of over forty thousand and worked for one employer for forty-eight hours each week. Still, WTUL leaders hoped that this legislation would be the first step in bringing wage and hour protections to all domestic workers. The League also won a victory in Wisconsin, which raised its minimum wage "closer to the actual cost of living" and included domestic workers among those covered by the law.

Because the League had been working since the 1920s to extend government protection to domestic workers, NYWTUL secretary Blanch Freedman described the new legislation as "historic." The importance of such laws, Freedman argued, lay not in their exact content but in the assumptions that underlay them. They changed the way domestic workers were perceived by the state and by their employers. Sooner than later, Freedman predicted, the domestic worker would be treated "like any other wage earner."[13]

But those who grasped these small victories as harbingers of new life for the Women's Trade Union League were quickly brought back to reality. By the spring of 1946, it was clear that the League was losing steam fast. Rose Schneiderman, Pauline Newman, Mary Dreier, Helen Blanchard, Mabel Leslie, and Blanch Freedman called a meeting of all twenty-three branches of the League to "develop a program of action that would meet the immediate needs of wage-earning women." WTUL leaders traveled to New York from as far west as Seattle and as far south as Birmingham, Alabama, to plan the future of the working woman's movement. The delegates had no shortage of ideas. But without funding, the League would be unable to translate these plans into action. Though 1946 was a year of massive labor unrest, described by the Bureau of Labor Statistics as "the most concentrated period of strikes in the country's history," the WTUL did not bounce back. Hundreds of thousands of women textile and auto workers, teachers, and municipal workers walked picket lines that year, yet the WTUL won few new members. "To put it bluntly," longtime WTUL secretary Elisabeth Christman wrote Schneiderman, "our League needs a shot in the arm."[14]

Christman, who had single-handedly run the national WTUL offices for more than two decades, joined Schneiderman in a last-ditch campaign to get affiliated unions to contribute money. But the campaign fell flat. Most local union officials expressed no interest. Some responded angrily, asserting that there was simply no need for separate women's organizations. Even the New York WTUL, always the strongest and best funded of the local branches, was finding it extremely difficult to attract new members or to get money from old ones. As resources dwindled, so did the organization's political effectiveness.[15]

League leaders were at least partly responsible for the decline of their own organization. One key contributing factor was Rose Schneiderman's long-standing refusal to take a stand on the battle between the AFL and the CIO. From 1935, when proponents of industrial unionism left the craft-based AFL to form the CIO, Schneiderman had tried unsuccessfully to keep herself and the League on the fence. She and Newman had long advocated the principle of industrial unionism—organizing all workers in an industry into one large union, rather than dividing them into different unions by craft. Still, they feared that "our strength, our influence, our power . . . our very usefulness depends upon our contacts with the unions of the AFL." While "not defending the form of our organization," Newman said, "I think it a little late to make drastic changes." Schneiderman tried to appease both sides. "We will organize women where it is necessary," Schneiderman said in 1940. "We will work with the AFL, we will work with the CIO."[16]

It was a nice idea, but Schneiderman knew very well that such a position would be impossible to sustain. AFL officials had reacted with fury in 1935 when John L. Lewis of the United Mine Workers led a convention-floor revolt and formed the Committee for Industrial Organization, comprising eight of the Federation's largest unions. Relations deteriorated rapidly, and the following year the AFL expelled the CIO unions. In New York City, Rose Schneiderman had been the only delegate on the Central Trades and Labor Council—a consortium of city unions—to vote against expelling CIO affiliates. However, fearing the consequences for the League if she gave up her seat on the council, she did not resign when the expulsion was carried out.

After that, Schneiderman grew even more cautious. In 1938, despite vehement objections by several women on the NYWTUL's executive board, Schneiderman refused the New York CIO's request to send a League delegate to its first annual state convention. Even more damning was her response when the United Electrical, Radio and Machine Workers—which had one of the largest and most militant female memberships of any U.S. union—requested League aid in a 1937 strike. Schneiderman declined, pleading poverty. Her unwillingness to aid a striking union badly damaged her reputation as a leader of working women.[17]

Perhaps more importantly, such responses crippled the NYWTUL, driving it further into poverty. Schneiderman's failure to speak out when the AFL bullied local League branches into expelling CIO members permanently alienated the CIO unions. They began cutting off donations to the WTUL and publicly questioning its effectiveness. NYWTUL secretary Cara Cook warned that organizing women workers would be "practically impossible until we take an unequivocal position." Schneiderman refused to be pushed. The two clashed over the issue, and eventually Cook resigned.[18]

Resignations were draining WTUL branches in other cities as well. During the 1930s, women from CIO unions flocked into the Rhode Island, Boston, and Seattle groups, providing an infusion of fresh blood and youthful enthusiasm. Angry AFL officials, taking advantage of the postwar political climate, branded the new members Communists and warned League leaders that the AFL would withdraw its members from any local League branch that did not expel CIO-affiliated women. By the beginning of the war, the Rhode Island WTUL had lost its most active members. Rose Norwood, president of the Boston WTUL, resigned in exasperation to work for the CIO and took most of her fellow officers with her. And a year after the war, Carrie McDowell, president of the Seattle branch, was forced to resign when the AFL ordered all women AFL members to leave the League in retaliation for McDowell's refusal to expel CIO members. By 1947, the three local League branches that had held the most promise for the future were dead or moribund.[19]

New battles over the eternally thorny issue of protective legislation also drained energy from the League. Worried that laws prohibiting night work for women were adding to the forced displacement of women workers from their wartime jobs, Rose Schneiderman and Elisabeth Christman decided to abandon their long-held support of such laws. Pauline Newman, however, refused to budge. Schneiderman was furious with her old friend. "Pauline becomes more conservative day after day and once she has made up her mind on anything she is a bad loser," Schneiderman wrote Christman. "It makes me tired to be so niggardly as to keep thousands of women out of jobs. . . . It's enough to drive a fellow into the ranks of the Woman's Party."[20]

But Schneiderman was as rigid as ever when it came to her decades-old bogey: the Equal Rights Amendment. Her continued opposition to the ERA led some in the labor movement to brand Schneiderman as reactionary and out-of-date. When she publicly rebuked Herbert Merrill, secretary of the Schenectady Federation of Labor, for sponsoring a pro-ERA resolution at a 1946 convention, he made no official reply. But privately he wrote Schneiderman this letter: "My personal view is that the time for being parochial is past. The Atomic Age has brought in a new world and regardless of New York State and its police power laws under which women are made a protected sex, the world trend is for absolute equality of women with men, economically and socially as well as politically."[21]

Schneiderman was hurt. She and Newman certainly did not see themselves as reactionary. They genuinely believed that the idea of "absolute equality" with men was a meaningless abstraction in a world where working women continued to suffer real discrimination because of their gender, race, and class. Yes, things had improved, but the majority of women workers remained in 1946—as they had been in 1916—segregated into low-skill, low-paying, and often physically dangerous jobs. Without protective laws, Schneiderman and Newman maintained, the most disfranchised of women workers would have absolutely no recourse to improve their conditions.

But Schneiderman could see the writing on the wall, and she moved to find a compromise. The League began working on an alternate constitutional amendment that would ensure legal equality between the sexes, like the proposed ERA, but would also preserve existing women's labor legislation. During 1946 and 1947, the League campaigned for their alternative. The ERA did not pass Congress, nor did the League's amendment.[22]

By the late 1940s, advocates of labor legislation had little hope of passing any new labor-friendly laws. Conservative politicians had ridden to victory in the 1946 midterm elections on a burst of antilabor sentiment fueled in part by resentment at the unprecedented labor unrest that had swept the nation soon after the war. Between 1946 and 1948, the WTUL was forced to devote most of its energy and resources to fighting repeal or erosion of existing laws. The 1948 election only made matters worse. "All through the year," Schneiderman wrote in her annual report, "but especially after the November election, anti-labor hysteria has been whipped into intensity. The League has . . . faced a very changed and very deteriorated situation."[23]

The organization's weakness was reflected in the size and mood of the last national WTUL convention, which was held in Kansas City, Missouri, in 1947. Local groups could afford to send only sixty people to the meeting. Schneiderman tried in her presidential address to give the League its badly needed "shot in the arm," but it was hardly an upbeat speech. The major theme of her talk was the 1947 Taft-Hartley Act. The most antilabor Congress since the early

1920s had just outlawed "closed" (union-only) shops, secondary boycotts through which nonstriking unions could aid a union on strike, and the use of union dues to support lobbying efforts or political candidates. Taft-Hartley also forced unions to require all elected officers to swear an oath disavowing the Communist Party. This last provision had created a climate of fear that reinforced the antidemocratic tendencies of some union leaders, enhancing their power to crush dissent among the shop-floor membership.[24]

The second half of Schneiderman's speech that day was devoted to sketching the declining status of women workers since the war. That did little to cheer the convention attendees. The wartime integration of the manufacturing workforce had already been reversed. The majority of women workers in the United States, Schneiderman reported, were once again laboring in traditionally female trades. And only a minority of these women were unionized. As for women who worked as domestic and farm laborers, hospital workers, and white-collar employees, most of them were still excluded from Social Security, workmen's compensation, minimum-wage, and maximum-hour laws.[25]

As the tone of her speech reflected, Schneiderman, sixty-five, was feeling tired and frustrated. She saw little hope for improvement in either the financial or the political situation in the near future. Though she did not want the 1947 convention to be the League's last, she simply did not have the energy for further organizing or fund-raising. The introduction to the 1948 annual report of the NYWTUL evokes her sense of desperation: "We find ourselves on a consolidated island of all our past gains which is constantly being hacked away by . . . lawmaking bodies. Not only has it been impossible to secure the fulfillment of labor's present needs . . . but new vigilance has had to be mobilized to forestall the shattering of the much needed gains which were attained after so much working and waiting."[26]

Schneiderman participated in her last successful organizing drive during the summer of 1947, when she helped New York's registered nurses to unionize city hospitals. At strike's end she knew that she had done her last turn as a union organizer. Forty-three years after her first major strike—the capmaker's walkout that had catapulted the red-headed twenty-two-year-old to the forefront of the labor movement—Rose Schneiderman began fantasizing about retirement. "I have gotten terribly stale," she wrote Elisabeth Christman, "and I feel that young blood will do the League a lot of good."[27]

Christman was terrified at the prospect of giving up what had been their life's work together. "I get weak in the pit of my stomach when I think of your leaving the League. . . . It is just too much at one time. Well—we have heard a lot about letting younger women take over—maybe they can work wonders. Who knows?"[28]

The only problem with this idea was that the local WTUL branches were not attracting younger women. The AFL, always capricious about its donations, was giving the League next to nothing by this point. Neither the local nor the national organizations were receiving financial support from the major CIO unions. Even the wealthy New York women who had given so generously for so many years seemed to have found other charities. By 1948, there were few allies left.

This was at least in part a result of the postwar Red Scare. In 1947, the House Un-American Activities Committee (HUAC) launched hearings on Communist Party influence in Hollywood that brought a parade of famous and infamous faces before a fascinated American public. The 1948 investigation and subsequent perjury conviction of State Department official Alger Hiss confirmed many Americans' fears that Communists had infiltrated the highest levels of government. With his confessional style and litany of wild charges, Hiss's accuser, Whittaker Chambers, set the tone for the wave of state and federal investigations that followed. The spectacle of accusations and counter-accusations fed a rising tide of antiradicalism, anti-Semitism, xenophobia, and homophobia. In this climate, people did not respond enthusiastically to requests for money to fund an organization devoted to unionizing women workers.[29]

Even though its leadership was devoutly anti-Communist, the Women's Trade Union League felt the sting of the late 1940s Red-hunts. Many friends of the WTUL—including industrial reformer Mary Van Kleeck and Schneiderman's lawyer, ACLU board member Dorothy Kenyon—were summoned to appear before both HUAC and Senator Joseph McCarthy's Subcommittee on Internal Security. Largely because of her affection for Schneiderman, Eleanor Roosevelt continued to defend and financially support the League. But most other former supporters either had lost interest or feared association. Feeling weary and frightened by the political climate, Schneiderman decided to retire.[30]

On April 6, 1949, Rose Schneiderman called reporters to the parlor of the League's Manhattan headquarters to announce that she was stepping down after thirty-one years as president of the New York Women's Trade Union League. In forty-five years in the labor movement, she mused, she had seen "progress beyond our wildest dreams." But the League's hard-won gains were now threatened, Schneiderman told them, and she did not have the energy to guide the League through these rough seas. At age sixty-seven, Schneiderman was worn out by years of walking the tightrope between class and gender politics, the AFL and CIO, militancy and respectability. She had no greater plans, she told reporters, than to write her memoirs, read books, and attend plays.[31]

The day after her announcement, Schneiderman was the focus of a *New York Times* editorial that reflected glowingly on her long career. As fear of subversion held the country in a white-knuckle grip, the most venerable of U.S. journalistic institutions hailed Rose Schneiderman as a symbol of moderation. "If trade unionism has become respectable," the editors enthused, "wise and statesmanlike leadership like hers has contributed to that end. . . . She has earned a rest." The editorial affirmed the choice she had made a quarter century earlier to abandon the fires of Socialism for the warm embrace of Democratic Party politics. Perhaps the angry "Red Rose" of 1911 would have rejected such a laurel, but the white-haired Rose of 1949 was pleased.[32]

As word of her retirement spread, friends and colleagues expressed shock and sadness in a deluge of telegrams and letters. On April 25, 1949, the day of her retirement, Schneiderman's closest friends at the New York League—Pauline Newman, Blanch Freedman, Mary Dreier, Mabel Leslie, Bessie Engelman, and the incoming president Gerel Rubien—presented her with thirty-one roses to symbolize her thirty-one years as president. A few weeks later, three hundred guests attended a luncheon in her honor, hosted by Eleanor Roosevelt. Rose Schneiderman stepped out of the public eye amid accolades from government and labor.[33]

Schneiderman held onto her position as president of the national WTUL, though it was largely a symbolic post by that time. Loyal as always to her friend, Newman followed suit by retaining her vice presidency of the national League. The two were as reluctant as Christman to end the working relationship between the women who had run the League for so long. By June 14, 1950, they felt they had no choice. Christman, who had been executive secretary of the national League for twenty-eight years, was designated to announce its death. She was proud of the League's major accomplishments, but she could not stop herself from reflecting wistfully on what the League might have done if the money had not run out.[34]

Agricultural, migratory, domestic, and white-collar workers, she noted, desperately needed help organizing. They also needed advocates who would fight to guarantee them minimum-wage, hour, and safety standards. The federal government had yet to pass an equal pay law. And despite all the League's efforts, there were still only a handful of women occupying top positions in their unions. Though trade union leaders argued that the League was no longer needed to advocate for working women, Elisabeth Christman clearly did not believe anyone would do it once the League was gone.[35]

A quarter century later, Pauline Newman recalled the last board meeting of the WTUL.

The feeling we had [was] of witnessing the end of an era, the end of more than fifty years of activity in organizing, educating, legislating for the working woman. . . . We were proud of our share but very sad to see it dissolve, because we had the feeling that we could still do quite a bit of work with the unions, for the unions and simply for the women workers. . . . Elisabeth Christman was on the verge of tears. Rose Schneiderman was practical. She said, "Well, we can't go on without money so what's the use?" Mary Dreier said, "I wish I had money to have it go on." And so, we didn't feel happy about dissolving, but there was nothing else to do.[36]

For the women who gathered at the International Machinists' Union building in Washington, D.C., that summer day in 1950, the dissolution of the national WTUL was far more than a political or professional decision. It was a judgment on their whole lives. Rose Schneiderman had been a member for forty-five years, Newman and Christman for forty-one. Mary Dreier had been there almost from the very beginning, for forty-seven years. Shared struggle had cemented their bonds and deepened their affection. What had been most satisfying about their work was what made that afternoon so frightening.

Their energy and passion had yielded extraordinary results, illustrating what even a small group of activists can accomplish if they are dedicated enough. Still, the women of the WTUL felt their failures keenly on that day. The dream that the WTUL represented had come to an end not with a bang but with a very quiet whimper.

The New York WTUL hung on for another five years, and despite her much-heralded retirement, Rose Schneiderman could not seem to stay away from League meetings or refrain from voicing her opinions. After 1949, she possessed only an honorary position in the NYWTUL. But if the role she played in the decision to dissolve the organization is any indication, she remained its most powerful member until the end. When the New York group fell on hard financial times in 1955, Schneiderman urged the executive board to disband. There was contention about this. Some younger members fervently wished to keep the League going, but Schneiderman was adamant.

It is not clear why. Perhaps she did not want to take on the task of training the younger members in fund-raising and administration. Perhaps, given the climate of the 1950s, she did not believe that anyone could summon enough support for the organization to keep it afloat. (Indeed, a group of young Milwaukee workers, who revived their local WTUL in 1948, were unable to sustain it for more than a decade.) But it seems equally possible that Schneiderman was just too possessive of the League, that it had become so thoroughly identified in her mind with her and her friends that she couldn't imagine it carrying on without them. Maybe she believed that a new organization would have to be founded to meet the needs of young working women in the second half of the twentieth century. Whatever her reasoning, she prevailed. The New York Women's Trade Union League passed out of existence in 1955, fifty-two years after it was founded.

In a speech that year on WEVD Radio, Schneiderman summed up the work of the WTUL and its locals and laid out some challenges for the future. Trade union women, she asserted, still had their work cut out for them. "There are three million or more women enrolled in the AFL and CIO, intelligent, able and energetic women," she noted. "Despite this there is not a single woman on the executive councils of either the AFL or the CIO. Nor are there more than one or two women vice presidents or members of general executive boards of the large international unions, even those whose membership is made up predominantly of women." Although discrimination was partly responsible for this, Schneiderman concluded, she also blamed women trade unionists for not being aggressive enough in pursuing positions of leadership in the trade union movement. She called on younger women to carry on the work begun by the WTUL.[37]

But as far as Rose Schneiderman was concerned, her work was done. After 1955, she retreated to a quiet daily routine in her East Village apartment. She spent her days reading the *New York Times* and twentieth-century U.S. history books, walking and listening to the radio. She saw her old WTUL friends regularly and remained in almost daily contact with Mary Dreier, Pauline Newman, and Mabel Leslie. And she kept up a correspondence with Eleanor Roosevelt, whom she saw on occasion. She worked on her memoirs and scoured histories of reform politics and the labor movement, challenging historians who she believed gave the WTUL short shrift. But while she sustained a deep interest in contemporary politics—she adored John Kennedy and abhorred Richard Nixon—by 1960 the seventy-eight-year-old Schneiderman was spending most of her time looking backward.[38]

THE HOUSEWIVES' LAST HURRAH, 1948–1951

Like the WTUL, the housewives' movement would die out within a few years of the war, but not before a couple of spectacular last gasps. Cost of living—of food, housing, education, and health insurance—was nearly as vital an issue for working-class women after the war as it had been during the Great Depression. In an attempt to coordinate activism around these issues, the Congress of American Women was formed in 1946. One of the most active participants was Clara Shavelson, now one of the women leaders of the International

Worker's Order. A cultural and benevolent society with strong ties to the Communist Party, the IWO boasted nearly 200,000 members from a wide variety of racial and ethnic backgrounds. One of the strongest wings of the IWO was the Jewish People's Fraternal Order, to which Clara and Joe Shavelson both belonged. Through this group, Clara Shavelson, Rose Nelson Raynes, and June Croll Gordon reorganized the Progressive Women's Councils into the Emma Lazarus Division of the IWO.[39]

In December 1947, the Emma Lazarus clubs joined nineteen women's organizations in a CAW-sponsored day of lobbying in Washington to demand that Congress establish peacetime price ceilings on food and housing. Six hundred twenty-nine housewives from New York, Chicago, Cleveland, Boston, Baltimore, Philadelphia, and Trenton poured into the offices of their congressmen and senators. Insisting that the average housewife understood more about the difficulties of balancing a budget than any politician did, the women handed their representatives copies of a proposed national rent control bill, urged them to vote for a pending public housing bill, and demanded that Congress enact price controls on meat, milk, and bread. They were not easily dismissed. Mrs. Lee Maran, who represented the Brooklyn Council on Rent and Housing, was asked by her Democratic congressman to understand that a minority party could only do so much. She told the *New York Times* that she replied, "You need not be a minority party if you will come out with a clear-cut position on the needs of the people."[40]

Disgusted with the inaction of Congress, the housewives increased the pressure on their elected representatives by returning to their cities and taking to the streets once more. During the summer of 1948, they launched a nationwide meat boycott that dwarfed even the huge depression-era actions. The 1948 meat boycott began in Texas when Mrs. R. D. Vaughan, a seventy-year-old grandmother, called her friends and urged them not to buy meat from their local grocer until prices dropped. Word traveled fast, and within two days there were "Don't buy meat" movements in seventeen Texas towns and cities. A day later the *New York Times* reported that support for the meat boycott had spread to Georgia and Florida. The boycott soon hit Ohio, Michigan, New York, and New Jersey as well.[41]

The reason for this rapid spread was simple: by 1948 even most poor families had telephones. In earlier meat strikes, the only way to organize had been by going door to door. Now housewife committees could organize large numbers of women with relative ease. One Cincinnati housewife explained to reporters that "we have assigned fifty-eight women ten pages each of the telephone directory." The same technique was applied in cities across the country. In New York, where Clara Shavelson was a key organizer, 150,000 housewives boycotted meat. The Progressive Women's Councils staged rallies and mother/baby picket lines. During one week in August, they staged two hundred such demonstrations.[42]

When cattlemen announced a reduction in prices at the end of that summer, they insisted that it was not in any way a result of the boycott. An unusually hot summer had forced them to send the cattle to early slaughter, they claimed, thus lowering prices. Few accepted this explanation. The strike seemed to herald an era of consumer activism on an unprecedented scale.[43]

In fact, there would be only one more flourish before the end—a series of meat boycotts that rocked the country during the winter of 1951. Rapidly organized, again by telephone, these boycotts forced meat wholesalers in New York, Chicago, and Philadelphia to lower prices. In the New York metropolitan area alone, it was estimated that one million pounds of meat went begging during the last week of February.

The militancy of Brooklyn housewives, led by Clara Shavelson, forced retailers to cut meat prices so dramatically that housewives from other parts of the city began flocking to Brooklyn to buy their meat. In response, grocers in Manhattan, Queens, and the Bronx began to cut prices. When 10 percent cuts offered by the wholesalers did little to boost sales, unionized butchers joined the housewives in calling on the federal government to enforce lower meat prices. If sales did not resume, the union warned, thousands of butchers would be driven out of business. By the end of February, even New York–area wholesalers were calling for federal price controls on livestock, warning that they would have to shut down if something was not done immediately.

Finally the U.S. Office of Price Stabilization ordered a 10 percent cut in livestock prices and more rollbacks in the months to come. When reporters questioned why meat prices across the United States were dropping, everyone gave the same answer. As this front-page *New York Times* article put it on February 26, 1951, "Experts at the crossroads of the country's livestock and meat industry explained that the housewife . . . had taken the problem of cutting meat costs into her own capable hands."[44]

When cattle producers tried to drive prices back up by withholding cattle from the market, the housewives' response in New York, Chicago, Philadelphia, and Boston was sufficiently strong that the low prices held. The New York Council of Meat Dealers reported that an estimated 60 percent of New York housewives stopped buying meat that winter. Meanwhile, poultry, cheese, and fish dealers were reporting a phenomenal increase in sales. That June, a worried Congress announced price controls.[45]

But even as these actions made front-page news across the country, the housewives' alliance was breaking apart over the issue of Communist involvement. As early as 1939, Hearst newspapers had charged that the consumer movement was little more than a Communist plot to sow seeds of discord in the American home. The Dies Committee of the U.S. Congress took these charges seriously and began an investigation that was halted only by the bombing of Pearl Harbor. Consumer protest had quieted during the war, thanks to government-enforced rationing and price controls. But protests resumed as soon as price controls ended, and so did the investigations. During the nationwide 1948 boycott, some newspapers charged housewife leaders with being too friendly to Progressive Party presidential candidate Henry Wallace. In 1949, the House Committee on Un-American Activities announced it was looking into the backgrounds of the women who'd organized the 1947 consumer march on Washington.[46]

A few months later, HUAC announced its conclusions: the Congress of American Women was a major link between U.S. and Eastern European Communists "composed primarily of a hard core of Communist Party members and a circle of close sympathizers." According to HUAC, this consumer's group was actually a "specialized arm of Soviet political warfare. . . . Rarely does it happen that Communist front organizations are formed with such unconcealed Communist leadership." On January 6, 1950, officers of the CAW were ordered to register with the Justice Department as foreign agents. Muriel Draper, CAW president, protested. But the attorney general refused to back down. With its membership under government surveillance, the CAW soon quietly collapsed.[47]

A similar fate befell the International Worker's Order (IWO). In 1950, the New York State Insurance Department began investigating the IWO Benefits Division. Agents were ordered by Governor Thomas Dewey to dig up as much information as they could on the group's officers, Clara Shavelson among them. In June 1952 the state ordered the group's dissolution. IWO lawyers tried to appeal the decision. They got as far as the Supreme Court, but the justices refused to hear the case. Thus, in 1952 the IWO was dissolved and its insurance funds were dispersed. Members tried different tactics to hold the organization together.[48]

The Emma Lazarus Division molted its political skin in 1951 and became the Emma Lazarus Federation of Jewish Women's Clubs (ELF). In some ways, the "Emmas," as members called themselves, appeared to be a traditional Jewish women's charitable organization, much like the neighborhood groups the United Council of Working Class Women had first politicized twenty years earlier. The ELF raised funds for the Red Mogen David (the Jewish Red Cross) in Israel, for the Emma Lazarus Day Care Center for working mothers in Tel

Aviv, and for concerts and cultural events celebrating the history of Jewish women.

But the Emma Lazarus Federation was clearly different from other Jewish women's groups. Throughout the 1950s they took unpopular stands, protesting state and federal hearings on subversion, the development of nuclear weapons, and the Korean War. The ELF worked actively with black women's organizations in the civil rights struggle, forging a particularly close relationship with a New York group called the Sojourners for Truth. In the late 1950s, the ELF sent truckloads of supplies to Mississippi civil rights workers; in the early 1960s, they supported the Freedom Riders and participated in the 1963 March on Washington. Through the 1960s, the ELF lobbied for the United States to ratify the UN's Genocide Convention of 1948. (It finally did so in 1986.) And members marched in opposition to the Vietnam War. Against a political context of fear and repression, the Emmas embraced a tradition of Jewish women's resistance from the Old Testament to Emma Lazarus and positioned themselves as *ayshes chayil*—staunch women of valor.[49]

THE ACTIVISTS IN OLD AGE, 1946–1978

By 1950, Clara Shavelson could no longer devote all her energies to the Emma Lazarus Division, for she was once again a full-time garment worker. Six years earlier, her husband Joe had suffered a heart attack and was forced to restrict his working hours. Then fifty-eight, Clara returned to the shop-floor she had left thirty-one years earlier. A waistmaker in her youth, Clara Shavelson now became a skilled "feller hand," sewing the linings into cloaks. Though she learned a new craft, her personal and political style remained the same. Throughout her sixties, Shavelson spoke out forcefully at union meetings, and she told one interviewer that she "fought with both boss and foreman."[50]

Then, in 1951, her life changed radically. Driving home from work on the day he had announced his complete retirement, Joe Shavelson died suddenly of a heart attack. It took the police hours to locate family members because no one was home. Clara and all three of her children were at work. Martha Schaffer recalls that the police found her brother and sister before they could reach Clara. When Irving arrived at the station house, his father's body was lying uncovered "on the cold police station floor in the bathroom. . . . My mother asked later, 'So where did you find him?' And I remember my brother saying, 'Oh. He was on a cot. They have a cot there for policemen to sleep on and they had him on the cot and he was covered up. They were very kind.' "[51]

Widowed, and with her children grown and married, Clara Shavelson found herself alone for the first time in thirty-eight years. She set about healing herself in the one way she knew: she threw herself back into political work. Shortly after Joe's death, she joined the American Committee to Survey Trade Union Conditions in Europe, a consortium of left-wing trade unionists led by her son. In 1951, the committee visited the Soviet Union. Clara had not been there for seventeen years. Sobered by the Stalin-Hitler pact and revelations of Stalin's concentration camps, Shavelson was determined to resolve concerns raised by friends who had long since left the Communist Party. She was particularly troubled by charges of Soviet anti-Semitism. Perhaps hoping to lay to rest troubling questions in her own mind, Shavelson prepared a carefully numbered questionnaire to take with her to the USSR:

1. Is there an iron curtain around the USSR?
2. Does the USSR have slave labor camps?
3. Is there religious freedom in the USSR?
4. Are the Soviet people starving?

A fluent Russian speaker, Shavelson interviewed workers, religious leaders, artists, and health care providers. Convinced that her linguistic skills would conquer all barriers, she seems to have been untroubled by doubts about whether the average Soviet citizen in 1951 would have felt safe enough to offer honest responses. Shavelson gave the USSR a glowing review. She raved about the high quality of Soviet health care, education, and housing, the abundance of food, the wide dissemination of culture, and the sanctity of religious freedom.

"Coming into Moscow," Shavelson wrote, "you immediately get the feeling that a new world is being built. The streets are broad and wide. The squares are immense and spotlessly clean . . . [C]rowds of well-dressed men and women go in and out of stores which are full of all kinds of food stuffs, shoes, clothes. . . . Laughter and gaiety attract the attention of every foreigner."[52]

Shavelson, in all other respects a thorny iconoclast, clung dearly to an icon that, for most U.S. Communists, had long since shattered. It is difficult to tell from her descriptions whether the American trade union committee was shown only the brightest face of Soviet Russia at the end of the Stalin era or whether Shavelson saw everything through rose-colored Communist Party lenses. Only years later, says her daughter-in-law Evelyn Velson, did Shavelson admit guiltily that she had been willfully blind to evidence of anti-Semitism in the Soviet Union.[53]

She never changed her mind, however, about the truth of one deep impression the trip had made on her: that the Soviet people in 1951 did not want war with the United States. Deeply moved, she wrote about what she saw in a country "where the ruins are still standing, and like accusing witnesses, remind the world of the bestialities . . . committed by the Nazi hordes." She returned home convinced that for a people living every day among such grim reminders, the thought of another war was unbearable. She told an interviewer for *Jewish Life*, a left-wing Jewish magazine, "We were convinced that our job was to go back and tell American workers that if they too would struggle for peace, there could be no war."[54] Shavelson returned from Europe determined to do just that.

During the early 1950s, Shavelson engaged in a whirlwind campaign to protest the arms race. She collected signatures for the Stockholm Peace Petition and for a five-power peace pact. She spoke at women's clubs, political clubs, and civic and religious organizations, warning of the danger of nuclear weapons buildup and the crying need for better international relations. She had been a peace activist before, as a member of the American League against War and Fascism during the 1930s. But it was a very different matter to campaign against the military in the 1950s, at the height of the Cold War. By the second half of the decade, it was becoming increasingly difficult for her to find audiences.[55]

Shavelson's campaign for peace with the Soviet Union was given sharp poignancy by the death sentence of Julius and Ethel Rosenberg, Communist Party activists convicted of delivering the secret of the atom bomb to the Soviet Union. Shavelson organized, spoke, and picketed on their behalf in New York and Washington. By serving on their defense committee for two years, Shavelson broke with the CP leadership, which was keeping its distance from the case.[56]

Martha Schaffer remembers "that when I talked to her then, it was the most important part of her life." Though Shavelson did not know the Rosenbergs personally, Schaffer says, she felt their impending execution deeply. "I think it was, for any activist woman with children, a horrifying thing. It could have just as easily been my mother and her husband as Ethel Rosenberg and her husband."[57]

Clara Shavelson's activities did not go unnoticed by federal and state investigating committees. Her work with the CAW, the IWO, and the American Committee to Survey Trade Union Conditions had already brought her to the attention of congressional Red-hunters. In 1951, her passport was revoked. (The same fate befell all the other American trade unionists on her recent trip to the Soviet Union.) Soon she was summoned to Washington to testify. Newly widowed, Shavelson felt alone and under siege. And, as her husband had feared it might if she were ever called to testify, her natural loquaciousness got her into trouble.[58]

"It was a real Star Chamber proceeding," says Martha Schaffer, "with no lawyers permitted. This was after Papa died, and one of the things he had told her . . . is just answer the questions that are asked of you. . . . In the course of their asking her the first basic question, which was 'Where do you live and how many children do you have?,' she had to tell them everything. She didn't even realize she was volunteering. . . . She told them about her son and her son-in-law. Everything."[59]

Clara was not the only member of her family to be subpoenaed during the 1950s. Both HUAC and Senator James O. Eastland's Internal Security Subcommittee launched full-scale investigations of Clara's son, Charles Velson, that lasted through most of the decade. Two former Communist labor organizers testified that Velson had led a group of young radicals in a plot to infiltrate and subvert the armed forces during the 1930s. Witnesses cast both his World War II Navy service and his union work in a suspicious light. One testified that his organizing work for the International Longshore Workers' Union was just a cover for his real job: to report to his Soviet superiors the vital statistics about New York's docks and harbors.[60]

Velson's controversial past made Clara Shavelson and her children frequent targets of FBI surveillance and questioning. Agents visited both the Shavelson parents' and children's homes with some frequency during the 1950s and 1960s. Schaffer recalls, "It was very difficult getting them out of the house. I kept saying 'No. No. You really have to leave.' And they wouldn't. They just stood there in the hall and they kept asking. 'Do you know so and so? And do you know so and so? And what do you know about . . . ?' I said, 'You get out of here or I'm going to call the police.' I didn't even know what the hell I was saying. Who was I gonna call? God?"[61] Julia Velson, the daughter of Clara's son Charlie, recalls a particularly cruel trick the FBI liked to play on her family. Well into the 1960s they would call her mother—Velson's second wife, Evelyn—to say that Charlie was lying when he told her he was at union meetings. The truth, they insisted, was that he was visiting another woman.[62]

Despite the fear that gripped her family and friends, the sixty-eight-year-old Shavelson continued to speak out. In 1954 she publicly denounced U.S. government attempts to destabilize the democratically elected government of Guatemala's president, Jacobo Arbenz. Her interest in U.S. policy toward Central America dated back to the late 1920s, when she had raised money for Nicaraguan rebel Augusto Sandino and demonstrated against the use of U.S. Marines to track him down. "Look who tries to talk for Latin America!" she raged to a *Jewish Life* reporter when Secretary of State John Foster Dulles pushed a strong anti-Communist resolution through the Tenth Conference of the Organization of American States. When a U.S.-sponsored coup overthrew Arbenz later that year, Shavelson marched in protest.[63]

But even so tireless a firebrand as Shavelson began to feel the ravages of time. In 1954, she decided to retire from her cloakmaking job and shortly thereafter applied for a pension. This did not seem like a terribly radical thing for a sixty-eight-year-old working woman to do. But Clara Lemlich Shavelson was no ordinary retiree; so her pension application turned into a pitched battle with the union leaders who had for so long been ambivalent about the woman who sparked the 1909 uprising. The benefits office rejected Shavelson's application, informing her that only members with fifteen consecutive years of service qualified. When she protested that she had organized one of the union's first locals, forty-eight years earlier, she received only a terse response. The rules could not be bent for anyone, the letter said. Shavelson did not let the matter drop.

She reminded ILGWU officials that only recently they had paid tribute to her as one of the union's founders. In preparation for the ILGWU's fiftieth anniversary celebration, the editors of *Justice* had launched a search for some of the union's pioneer organizers. The magazine had published the following query: "Does anyone know where Clara Lemlich is?" Schaffer recalls what happened next: "She went to the union and she knocked on the door. And she said, 'I understand you're looking for Clara Lemlich.' And they said, 'Yes, do you know where she is?' And she said, 'Yes.' They said, 'Where is she?' She said, 'Where is she? Here she is. She's standing right in front of you.' Everybody fell all over themselves." In the weeks that followed, union journalists interviewed her extensively, and when the ILGWU's fiftieth anniversary commemorative book came out, it included a lengthy and emotional description of Lemlich's role in the 1909 shirtwaist strike. It was only after the book's publication, her daughter believes, that union leaders learned of her activities in the years since 1909. They realized that Clara Lemlich was in fact Clara Shavelson, a Communist diehard and the insistent elderly woman cloakmaker who had been making trouble in her local for the past decade. Then, says Schaffer, "they didn't want to touch her with a ten-foot pole."[64]

Still, the pension dispute was embarrassing for the union, so in August 1954, ILGWU president David Dubinsky intervened. Clara Lemlich Shavelson was granted an honorary lifetime membership, with the pension benefits that accrued to any lifetime member. Shavelson, who had been a bit hard-pressed since Joe's death, wrote to thank Dubinsky:

Little did I dream way back in the sweatshop days of 1906 when, with a few pioneers, we organized Waistmakers' Local 25 of the ILGWU, that almost half a century later this organization would provide me with a pension in my later years. The early battles that we carried on in 1908 and 1909 helped lay the foundation for the strong and powerful union that we have today. I feel that the pension I received from the union is in some measure a tribute to the early band that struggled and fought to eliminate the sweatshop system and bring the benefits of unionism to thousands of workers.

But five years later, Shavelson's $40-per-month allotment was suddenly suspended. She received a letter from ILGWU Welfare and Health Benefits director Adolph Held informing her that what she had been voted in 1954 had not been a lifetime pension but a $3,000 special sum to be paid out quarterly. By 1959 it had run out. Shavelson, now seventy-three, had no income apart from her paltry Social Security check.[65]

Shavelson was deeply upset by what she saw as a capricious turnabout by the union. She wrote back,

> The reasons given me as to why I could not be entitled to the regular pension were the merest technicalities. I am sure you will . . . recall my work in organizing and building our great union, beginning as far back as 1906, and that, as organizer of Local 25, I am the proud possessor of one of the first membership books in this local. . . .
>
> You will also recall that our Union, itself, recognized the valuable work I had done by honoring me in the magazine published commemorating our Fiftieth Anniversary with a glowing description and history of my activities. . . .
>
> It seems strange and incredible to me that a Union so powerful as ours, and as proud in its consideration of the welfare of its members, cannot provide for one of its veteran organizers and members.

In June 1960, Shavelson was voted another $2,000 special sum to be paid out in installments of $125 every three months. When it ran out in June of 1964, no more money was forthcoming. The seventy-eight-year-old Shavelson was unceremoniously cut off by the union that would continue to celebrate her name on every major anniversary of its founding.[66]

Fannia Cohn's last decade and a half with the ILGWU was not much better. In 1946, at the age of sixty-one, Cohn suffered her second nervous collapse, when, as her doctor explained, her mind wore out her body. Her first full breakdown had come at the nadir of her struggles with the union leadership in the early 1930s. She believed that the cause was not "overwork, but rather . . .

not having something definite to do in the office. A man at my age is considered as being in the prime of life. I have the same feeling about myself and this wears me out." During the 1930s Cohn had worked overtime to compensate for the lack of official responsibility. She ran her strength down writing, lecturing, and teaching classes at a feverish pace. Her second breakdown, over a decade later, seems also to have been the result of overwork and lack of recognition.[67]

Friends and colleagues wrote to wish her a speedy recovery. "Such is our life," wrote Mary Goff, Cohn's old colleague from the white goods workers' union. "In harness when we are well, we don't stop to think of ourselves." Charles Beard sent comforting and loving words, as always. Even conservative AFL vice president Matthew Woll wrote a kind letter. But though she languished in the hospital for nearly a month, Cohn heard nothing from David Dubinsky. Not the kind of woman to let things pass, she apparently sent him a letter saying that she was hurt. "I planned to visit you at the first opportunity, or at least telephone," he wrote back testily. "However, your letter makes that impossible for me as I never do anything under duress. Am asking others how you are doing." Perhaps to annoy Dubinsky, she returned to work soon after, claiming to be fit and hardy.[68]

Kudos from outside her union suggest that she remained busy and vital well into the 1950s. In 1949, she published a new booklet, *Worker's Education in a Troubled World*, which received high praise from many quarters, particularly from historians. Arthur Schlesinger, Jr., reviewed it glowingly. University of Wisconsin historian Merle Curti wrote to congratulate her. The writing, he said, has "all your old youth, vigor, freshness and punch. It is grand to know the years and the times can't get you down." The following year, the Organization of American States wrote to tell her that three of her pamphlets had been translated into Spanish for use in Latin America. Newly elected New York governor Herbert Lehman wrote to thank her for her work on his campaign. And Ed Lewis of the Urban League, in which Cohn had long been active, thanked her for her "splendid work" and called himself a "keen admirer."[69]

Cohn's influential political contacts put her in a good position to aid old friends caught in the anti-Communist fury. When Spencer Miller, whom she had known for thirty years through the Worker Education Bureau, was investigated for disloyalty in 1951, Cohn assembled a group of character witnesses to speak for him. "I cannot think of anyone in labor whom I would rather have them come to than you," he wrote when she told him she would speak to the FBI. "We have been friends and collaborators so long that they can get the truth from you about my devotion to the ideals of America."[70]

Miller was cleared of the charges and became one of an impressive group of scholars who participated in Cohn's ongoing Student Fellowship programs and invited her to speak at various universities. Through the first half of the 1950s, Cohn lectured frequently at New York–area colleges and universities. She also visited the University of Wisconsin, where her longtime friends Selig Perlman and Merle Curti taught.

As Cohn neared what they assumed would be her retirement age, her scholar-friends urged her to take the time to reflect on the meaning of her life's work. Columbia University historian Harry J. Carman, among others, tried to convince Cohn to write an autobiography. New York State labor mediator Julius Manson also urged her to write, insisting that "the credit for the kind of teaching I do should go to you." And Alvin Johnson of the New School wrote, "I have watched your work with admiration through many years. I have been vividly aware of the difficulties you have had to surmount in your educational pioneering. . . . You have never received full credit for what you have achieved, but as I know you, you have never cared much for credit."[71]

By the late 1950s, many people were letting her know what an important contribution they felt she had made. Letters poured in from a wide array of admirers: union members, teachers, scholars, retiring New York governor Herbert Lehman, and incoming Supreme Court Justice Felix Frankfurter. Lehman reminisced about their old days together "fighting sweatshops." Frankfurter thanked her for a letter which, he said, had brought him "happy memories and what is more important fortifies my faith in what high ideals, when pursued with courage, wisdom and pertinacity can accomplish." He went on to praise her for her work building the ILGWU Education Department, which he described as the union's "most important activity." Cohn carefully saved these letters alongside less friendly communications from Dubinsky and Education Department director Mark Starr. But she did not retire, nor did she begin work on her memoirs.[72]

Through the 1950s she worked for the Book Division at the union's national headquarters in Manhattan. Without any friends in the central hierarchy besides Leon Stein, Cohn continued to produce research papers on labor education, to sponsor panel discussions and, in whatever way she could, to mentor younger women she thought might be interested in becoming officers. Stein remembered her working late every night, seven days a week. "If you'd go up to the office eight o'clock at night, she was there," he remembered. "She would go out and eat something someplace. I could see her from my window. She'd take a little walk. Then she'd go back in."

In 1962, when Cohn was seventy-seven years old, the union leadership decided to retire her. "They had to," Stein insisted. "She just wouldn't retire."

The officers of the ILGWU informed Cohn that they were planning to give a luncheon in honor of her retirement, to be held on August 27, 1962. Although female friends and family members also attended the luncheon, the official photograph of the occasion shows Cohn seated on the dais, the lone woman among the union's male officers, as she so often was in her ILGWU career.[73]

Grandiloquent speeches were made. David Dubinsky praised Cohn as "an apostle of trade unionism on this continent" and expressed the union's "deep recognition and appreciation for what she has symbolized and for the service she has rendered." First Vice President Luigi Antonini paid her a compliment that reflected both the grudging admiration and discomfort that the union leadership felt around Cohn. Other women, he noted, had found it difficult to be both wives and mothers and labor movement activists. "She stuck to the union," he concluded, "making it her family while others left to raise their families in a more traditional manner."[74]

The reality underlying this public homage was that for fifty-three years the male ILGWU leadership had been unable, despite their dislike for her, to pry her loose from the union. Dedicated to the point of obsession both to educating workers and to increasing the numbers of women leaders in the labor movement, Fannia Cohn had outlasted most of her male colleagues and detractors. As a result, many outside the ILGWU saw her name as synonymous with the union's history.

When her retirement was announced, Dick Deverall of the AFL-CIO Education Department wrote to assure Cohn that she would never be forgotten. "Fannia," he insisted, "the ILGWU without you will be as naked as a manniken in a Fifth Avenue window without the dress. You are not the ILGWU but, in a very big way, the ILGWU is you." And Lewis Lorwin, an early ILGWU historian, noted, "The story in *Justice* is good but doesn't do justice to your contributions. . . . I hope that another historian . . . will record in the near future your distinctive and distinguished acts . . . and pay you the full appreciative tribute . . . you so richly deserve."[75]

Interestingly, Dubinsky and the other ILGWU officers treated Pauline Newman very differently than they had Shavelson or Cohn. Like Cohn, Newman chose to work until the end of her life, feeling no need or reason to retire. But the union leadership never even thought of pushing her out. Leon Stein, who was as close to Newman as he was to Cohn, had this theory as to why: "Maybe part of it was that they respected her. She had a life outside the union. She had Frieda and Elizabeth. The union wasn't her family. She could go home at the end of the day. But it was also that Pauline was one of the boys in many ways. She could smoke a cigar with the best of them." While Newman's emotional independence may have been part of the reason for the treatment accorded to her by ILGWU officials, her willingness to accept a marginal position and make the best of it had something to do with it as well. Stein commented,

> Pauline recognized her fate it seems to me almost immediately. It was to work in the labor movement, no matter how. To be of service. . . . Can you imagine that she sat in the office of the Educational Department of the Union Health Center for more than half a century? That's not an inspiring life.
>
> What was her real contribution? People would come with trouble on their hearts. The human psyche is a frail thing and it gets damaged and you need help and Pauline was skillful at that. She sat there year after year handling cases like that. That was in addition to the other work she did. She did lectures. She went to conferences and congresses. She was a very busy organizational woman.[76]

As a young organizer, Newman had struggled bitterly against the sexism of male union leaders. She had fought to realize the industrial feminist vision of how the union should be run and what it should become. Deeply torn by her dual loyalties to the WTUL and the ILGWU, she had left one and then the other. But ultimately she had decided that she could not leave either. And she found a peace in that decision that Fannia Cohn never did, perhaps because the WTUL gave her a support network and a channel through which to express her commitment to women workers.

This isn't to say that Newman did not challenge the leadership of the labor movement to include more women in the top ranks. She did. But Newman never rocked the ILGWU boat in quite the same way that Cohn did. As Miriam Stein recalls, "Fannia Cohn would tell everyone who would listen that women were being discriminated against in the ILG. Newman never talked about that. She did her job." Leon Stein believed that many of the male leaders of the union were very attached to Newman. "She was to us like some kind of a long lost *tante* [aunt]," he said. Indeed, in the late 1950s and 1960s, union friends became Newman's solace as her personal life began to fall apart.[77]

The years immediately following the war had been good times for Newman and Frieda Miller. During the autumn of 1949, after resigning from the NYWTUL, the two had traveled together at the behest of the State, Army, and Labor Departments to investigate working conditions for women in Germany. A shocked Newman wrote to Schneiderman describing "miles and miles of ruins. . . . No one who has not seen it can even imagine." Newman spoke with women living in grim refugee shelters and noted, with a fierce anti-

Communism her Washington sponsors no doubt appreciated, that women they spoke to "welcome this rather than endure . . . life in the Russian zone."[78]

After her return, Newman was appointed to several international commissions. With Dorothy Kenyon, she served on the United Nations Subcommittee on the Status of Women. She worked with Miller and Schneiderman as legislative experts for the United Nations' International Labor Organization, engineering the relaxation of night-work laws worldwide for women and children. In 1950, she was called to Geneva to work on the ILO's Subcommittee on the Status and Conditions of Domestic Workers. And in 1951 she attended the Mid-Century White House Conference on the Child as an expert on the history of child labor during the twentieth century. For the remainder of the Truman years she worked as a consultant for the U.S. Public Health Service, studying industrial hygiene.[79]

None of these were taxing or terribly time-consuming assignments, which suited her fine. She was hoping for some time to slow down and relax with Frieda and her family. It didn't turn out that way. Since 1944, when Miller began directing the U.S. Women's Bureau, she and Newman had maintained two households, one in New York and one in Washington. The understanding seems to have been that when Miller stepped down, they would both retire. But Miller changed her mind. She wrote Newman, "Paul Darling, I'd be very glad to quit if I had the wherewithal for living in retirement. It's . . . the spur of necessity that drives me on now." Both women decided to continue working.[80]

Money was something of a problem for Miller and Newman, but it was clearly something more than "the spur of necessity" that drove Miller in the years after 1953, when incoming president Dwight Eisenhower asked the Democratic appointee to resign from the Women's Bureau. Miller was then nearing sixty-five, and no one would have found it surprising had she chosen to retire to New York, or to the Pennsylvania country house she and Newman both loved. But restlessness overtook her. In 1954 she accepted an assignment from the ILO to assess Third World women's labor conditions. From 1955 through 1957 she traveled through Burma, Ceylon, India, Indonesia, Japan, Pakistan, the Philippines, and Thailand. Between 1960 and 1964 she returned to India and also traveled to Turkey, Iraq, Rangoon, Hong Kong, and Switzerland. Through all these years she wrote Newman regularly, but an unmistakable distance crept into her letters as the decade wore on.[81]

What happened between Newman and Miller? Why did Miller choose to spend the last years of her active life on the road? Clearly she loved and was excited by travel. Also, no doubt, she had enjoyed the celebrity she earned as the director of a federal agency, and her work for the ILO enabled her to continue living in the limelight. Many newspapers, from the *New York Times* and the *Times* of London to the *Nippon Times* and the *Pakistan Times*, covered her visits to various Asian and Middle Eastern cities. The headlines were often quite flattering. One typical headline (from the Sunday *Times* of London) hailed Miller as a "World Famed Woman Labor Expert." Still, love of fanfare was not all that kept her on the road.[82]

Miller's nearly constant traveling from the mid-1950s to the mid-1960s reflected a growing brittleness in her feelings for Newman. It is not clear exactly what the roots of this tension were, but despite all their years together, the two were still plagued by their class and ethnic differences. Miller had had a great deal more formal education than Newman. She came from the owning rather than the working class. And her German Protestant family had trained her to be refined and quiet in her interactions with others. That was certainly never Newman's way.

It would seem as though such distinctions should have faded over time, especially since Newman had completely lost touch with her own family. But somehow they didn't. "It was an odd relationship in ways," recalls Elisabeth Burger, "in that the differences didn't disappear. . . . Much later on I think my mother found the relationship a bit of a drag. And little jokes that used to be sort of funny about Pauline's pigheadedness and that sort of thing were a little less kindly said." Perhaps at the beginning, the two women's differences had been what drew them together. But as the novelty wore off, over many years together, what had once seemed intriguing and exotic became just irritating.[83]

Here it is hard to separate tensions over class and ethnicity from questions of personal style. Though she was well loved for her big-heartedness, says Elisabeth Burger, Newman had a gruff exterior. She was, says grandson Michael Owen, a "give-them-hell kind of person." It is not clear whether this carried over into their home life, but Miller's public image was quite the opposite. During her tenure as New York's industrial commissioner, the *New York Evening Star* dubbed her "'mother' to 4,500,000 workers," noting appreciatively that "She Seldom Needs 'Big Stick' to Settle Labor Problems." The *Christian Science Monitor* described "Mother Miller" as a woman who held "simple, old fashioned notions," was "guiltless of cosmetics," and liked to embroider during interviews and meetings. When she was made chief of the Women's Bureau, the *New York Herald* called her a "practical, lovable champion of feminine rights," and the *New York Post* decided that "sensible . . . is the word for her."[84]

That homespun image notwithstanding, Miller clearly had a taste for adventure. She chose to spend her retirement years wandering Asia and the Middle East, while Newman went to work each day at the ILGWU's Union Health

Center and spent weekends with Elisabeth; her husband, David Owen; and their two sons, Hugh and Michael. Sometime during this period, Miller met a man in India with whom she had what seems to have been a brief but intense affair. Newman responded with a bitter fury. Miller refused to engage it and instead withdrew. Between 1958 and 1964 the two women hardly saw each other. When both were in the United States, one stayed in their Coffeetown, Pa., house, the other in their New York apartment.[85]

Here, for the last time, Miller's longstanding ambivalence about being romantically involved with another woman emerged. Burger says that her mother once insisted to her that the relationship with Newman was not fully sexual. We will never know whether this was the truth or Miller's own uncertainty and embarrassment speaking. Burger believed her mother when Miller said that she and Newman were not "lesbians in the conventional sense." But as even Burger admits, Miller was quite reticent about personal matters and deeply concerned with propriety. It is worth restating here that concern about appearances had moved Miller to keep secret from Elisabeth for seventeen years the fact that she was her biological mother. For forty years, Newman and Miller had shared a home, a bedroom, a deeply intimate correspondence, and such affectionate salutations as are generally reserved for lovers. And certainly Newman's response to Miller's affair and their subsequent rift can only be described as heartbreak.[86]

During their late sixties, Newman and Miller were estranged from one another for almost six years. Newman's journal entries from this period reveal the depth of her pain and confusion over the split. One autumn evening in 1958, Newman waxed rhapsodic in her journal about watching a Hudson River sunset through the window of the West Village apartment she and Frieda had shared. In the midst of this description, she lapsed into lovelorn misery: "But oh how much more this beauty would mean if shared with one who at one time was there to do that—those days are gone, never to return.... F. left on Thursday knowing that I was ill and in bed, she never called to find out how I am—it has come to that! . . . I try not to think of the present relationship with F. It hurts too much. . . . It is hard to bear it alone, yet there is no one I care to talk about it [with]—no one."[87]

In a journal entry three years later, Newman battled suicidal thoughts. "It may not be right," she wrote, "to 'hang on' to life when life becomes difficult." But suicide was not an acceptable way out for an old fighter like herself. She fought the impulse, comforting herself with work and with memories. Like many elderly people, the seventy-one-year-old Newman began to immerse herself in memory as a way of coping with grief and loss. She summoned up vivid sensations to cut through the numbness of depression:

Just remember walking through the woods with your best friend [the term she always used to describe Miller] looking for and finding . . . a field of wild irises, or the hilltop of daffodils at Coffeetown . . . or remembering the voices of Caruso and other great artists . . . or with my mind's eye to once again watch Elisabeth playing "house" . . . and later to watch her children Hugh and Michael building castles in the sand. . . . All those memories pull you back from the inevitable end if only for a little longer.[88]

Newman claimed in her journal that she talked to no one about her private sorrows. But she continued her active social life. She went to work daily at the ILGWU, frequently meeting Rose Schneiderman and other WTUL friends for coffee and dinners. Like many older women, they shared favorite books, particularly historical treatments of the Roosevelts and the New Deal. Newman devoted many of her days and nights to caring for Hugh and Michael, while Elisabeth and David Owen traveled for the UN. And finally, she exchanged letters with scores of old and new women friends from the movement. Esther Peterson and Vera Peterson Joseph both wrote often. Esther Peterson was a legislative representative for the AFL-CIO, later appointed by John F. Kennedy to head the U.S. Women's Bureau. Vera Peterson was an African American physician who had grown close to Newman when both worked at the Union Health Center. These friends and family assuaged Newman's craving for love and companionship. And sometime around 1965 or 1966, Miller and Newman reconciled. It is not clear that the problems disappeared. But there was too much history between the two septuagenarians for them to simply walk away from their relationship. During the mid-1960s the two resumed their life together in the apartment on West Twelfth Street.[89]

Michael Owen recalls their coming for large family dinners every Sunday afternoon during that period. After lunch, "my father would conk out for his thirty winks . . . my grandmother would start making soup out of any leftovers in the refrigerator . . . and Pauline would sit there with a magnifying glass and read. . . . She would always ask for any socks or clothing items that needed mending. That would be her contribution in the bloated snoozing time of the afternoon." It was a warm and fairly typical family scene—except that the house, Owen remembers, was filled with "all these pictures of Pauline and my grandmother. There was this 'Pauline Newman for Sheriff of New York' poster on one of the walls as a Socialist Party candidate," he says. "Pictures of my grandmother with Harry Truman. Pictures of the United Nations declaration with her name on it." Still, there was no sense that Newman, Miller, or their relationship was unusual, say Owen. They were simply "my affective grandmothers."[90]

This happy period was cut short in the late 1960s by Miller's descent into an illness that weakened and clouded her mind. Friends wrote to acknowledge Newman's suffering as she watched her life companion deteriorate. In 1969, unable to care for her, Newman and her daughter were forced to move Miller into the Walsh Home for the Aged in Manhattan. Newman visited her as much as she could. "When my mother was ill at the end of her life," Burger recalls, "it was Pauline she asked for all the time. And Pauline was there."

When Miller died in 1973, letters poured in to comfort Newman. Many were from other women in the movement who had been nurtured by the two. "She and you have always been among my heroines," Esther Peterson wrote, "my models—as they say now. These last years have been difficult for you I'm sure. I'm also sure that your great strength and spirit will stand you in good stead now." Newman found her strength again working for the union.[91]

By this period, Newman had become the union's unofficial link with its own history, and she spent much of her time making rousing speeches about the tough early years. Michael Owen remembers that whenever anyone wanted to know about the ILGWU, the leaders "rolled out Pauline Newman, expert. She was there. She could give them the eyewitness account." One of Leon Stein's favorite anecdotes, about the 1965 ILGWU convention, beautifully illustrates the way Newman played that role:

> We were beginning to ring the curtain down. I went up and I whispered in Dubinsky's ear, "Pauline hasn't talked yet." Well, he loved her. He was always talking about her. He honored Rose Schneiderman. He loved Pauline for who she was. Fannia Cohn he couldn't stand. . . . He said, "Get Pauline up here." And it was one of the most dramatic sessions we ever had. She reviewed the union history. My generation, how we built and fought. Then she asked, "Are you keeping the faith?" After she finished, a woman raises her hand in the audience. And she wants to say something. We had a strike at that time in South Carolina. She was one of the strikers. And guess what she says? "We're keeping the faith!" Ohhhh. And then she couldn't talk. And she began to cry right into the mike. "We're keeping the faith."[92]

Clara Shavelson kept the faith, too, until the end of her life. Through the Red Scare of the 1950s, the radical shift of the 1960s, and the retrenchment of the 1970s, Clara Shavelson never repudiated her beliefs. Martha Schaffer believes that this unshakeable firmness was characteristic of the women activists of her mother's generation and was both a positive and a negative trait. "What they said the first time they said the twenty-fifth. I don't think they memorized it. I think it was written in blood."[93]

As if sheer will could stave off the encroachments of age, Clara Shavelson kept to the strict regimen of exercises she had been doing for more than three decades. The results were impressive, according to her daughter-in-law, Evelyn Velson. Clara could do a full split at sixty-five. Nevertheless, by the late 1960s the eighty-year-old had begun to slow down. The loss of her second husband, Abe Goldman, accelerated her decline. Goldman, an old friend from the labor movement, had been in love with Clara for decades. "He treated her like a queen" during their happy eight-year marriage, says Martha Schaffer. His death in 1967 left Shavelson bereft. Lonely and frightened, she asked her children if she could live with them. For a while she came to live with Martha and her family in San Francisco.[94]

Schaffer recalls attending meetings of the Emma Lazarus Federation in San Francisco with her mother in 1968:

> When she came in there were a lot of people who recognized her that she didn't know and I didn't know either. I would look at these people and think, "They can't possibly know Mama." But they did. "Oh, Shavelson is here. Come sit by me." "No, sit by me." "No, sit by me."
>
> I can picture her now. She was a little bit under five feet. She was really a very slight woman. And she would shake her head and pull back her shoulders and take it as her due. She sparkled. She was the belle of the ball. That's how I remember her best.
>
> What do they say? Rank has its privileges. That's just about the way she treated them. She worked the room. "Yes Ma'am. Where are you from? Oh is that so?" She never was afraid to say "No, I don't remember who you are. Tell me your name." It used to bother me at first but later I recognized it was the greatest gambit in the world. "So tell me about yourself." She was a politician.[95]

In her early eighties, Shavelson divided her time between the Schaffer family in San Francisco and her son Charlie Velson's family in southern California. She took a great deal of pleasure walking in the warm sunshine. But her mind was beginning to betray her, and she couldn't always find her way back. It was a sad time in some ways, but, says Schaffer, even in her weakened state, Clara had a charisma that drew people to her:

> We lived behind the Presidio Park and I would go up and there's my mother sitting on a bench with a book or a newspaper and always some man next to her. "I can't understand it," she'd say. "The men here are so forward. The minute you sit down, just because you have a book, right away they want to talk." . . . It wasn't made up, this idea that people were always wanting to talk to her. She had a wonderful knack for talking to people and making them

talk to her, encouraging them to do whatever it was she felt was right for them to do. She really was an extremely understanding person.[96]

In 1968, confusion, cataracts, and deafness forced Shavelson to move into the Jewish Home for the Aged in Los Angeles. The home was located in Boyle Heights, the old Jewish and Mexican immigrant quarter of Los Angeles. It was a good location for Shavelson, who continued to visit old friends and colleagues at the Emma Lazarus Federation in Los Angeles. Though not completely happy about being there, Shavelson remained active and engaged. Schaffer recalls that her mother "maintained her interests. She read the *Freiheit* [the Yiddish Communist daily]. She read the *Times.*" And amazingly, she continued to organize.[97]

In 1969, Clara Shavelson convinced the management of the Jewish Home to honor the United Farm Workers' boycott of grapes and iceberg lettuce. " 'It's a shame,' " her daughter recalls Shavelson telling them, " 'that a Jewish Home should allow grapes to be eaten, should buy grapes in such huge quantities.' She went on and on and on. And eventually they pulled the grapes."[98]

Shortly thereafter, the eighty-three-year-old rabble-rouser helped the nurses and orderlies at the home to unionize. "You'd be crazy not to join a union," she chastised uncertain staffers. "How much worse could these conditions get?" Her daughter Martha remembers that "she told them and she told them and she told them. And the ones she knew voted for a union. But not enough people did. So they came back to her and they were crying. 'They didn't hear what you said.' And she said to them, 'So what? Are you giving up already? You're only at the beginning of your life.' And eventually they did become unionized. The nurses and the LVNs. It was fantastic." After that, Schaffer says, the staff sang Clara's praises. Many of them were unwilling to accept the tips offered by Clara's children. "No," they told her. "We couldn't. Clara's a friend."[99]

Unfortunately for Clara Shavelson, the Jewish Home for the Aged closed this Los Angeles branch during the early 1970s, and she was transferred to another home in the San Fernando Valley, far from the activist Jewish community of Boyle Heights. Though her children and grandchildren visited her as often as they could, Shavelson was no longer part of the radical community that had sustained her throughout her life. The death of her roommate, an old friend from Brownsville, started her on a long, slow decline.

Almost a decade after she entered the home, Shavelson was visited by a colleague from forty years earlier: Rose Nelson Raynes, of the United Council of Working Class Women. Raynes found the ninety-two-year-old Shavelson in good spirits, bored but still proud. "We got there and nobody could find her. She wasn't in her room and she wasn't in the sitting room they had. So they looked all over the home and finally they found her and she came out with a big smile. Do you know where she was? She was in the arts and crafts room working. She said, 'You see, I'm still busy.'"[100]

Martha Schaffer summed up her mother's life in the following way: "Over the years, she became more, not less, energetic about doing what she thought was the right thing." That applies as well to Newman and Cohn. And it is a remarkable coda for any activist career.

In the aftermath of World War II, delegations of housewives staged frequent demonstrations at municipal offices, in state capitals, and in Washington to demand housing reform, rent control, and construction of public housing. This tenants' demonstration took place in front of New York City Hall during the summer of 1948. (Photo by Julius Lazarus)

During the summer of 1948, a housewives' meat boycott swept the nation, dwarfing the housewives' meat protests of the summer of 1935. From August 9 to 16, two hundred demonstrations took place in New York City alone. Many of them, like this one in front of the Second Avenue public market, involved both mothers and their children. (Photo by Julius Lazarus)

Fannia Cohn and one of her ILGWU-sponsored classes, 1948, New York City (Fannia Cohn Papers, Rare Books and Manuscripts Division, New York Public Library)

Clara and Joe Shavelson, shortly before his death, 1954 (Courtesy of Evelyn Velson)

Left: Pauline Newman and
Frieda Miller in Miami
Beach, 1951 (Courtesy of
Elisabeth Burger)

Below: Fannia Cohn, January
27, 1951, at Cooper Union
with what she called her
"worker-students" and several
of the intellectuals who loved
her. Facing Cohn are Prof.
Ralph Ross and Dean Paul
Mcghee of the New York
University School of General
Education. (Fannia Cohn
Papers, Rare Books and
Manuscripts Division, New
York Public Library)

Fannia Cohn and George Meany, president of the AFL-CIO, at a Labor Independent Democrats luncheon in 1954 (Fannia Cohn Papers, Rare Books and Manuscripts Division, New York Public Library)

The fiftieth anniversary of the Triangle Shirtwaist Factory fire, March 25, 1961. Left to right, between policemen: *Pauline Newman; former secretary of labor Frances Perkins; Rose Schneiderman; and ILGWU president David Dubinsky (Rose Schneiderman Collection, Tamiment Institute Library, New York University)*

Rose Schneiderman and Eleanor Roosevelt, 1961. Schneiderman was being honored by the YWCA and the National Council of Jewish Women; Eleanor Roosevelt presented the award. (Rose Schneiderman Collection, Tamiment Institute Library, New York University)

Fannia Cohn's retirement dinner, September 27, 1962. She is seated, as she so often was throughout her career, among the all-male executive officers of the ILGWU. Seated to the right of Cohn is Gus Tyler of the ILGWU Educational Department; to the left is the union's president, David Dubinsky. (Fannia Cohn Papers, Rare Books and Manuscripts Division, New York Public Library)

As one of the last survivors of New York's sweatshop days and of the early union battles, Pauline Newman was approached frequently for interviews during the 1970s and early 1980s. Here she is on March 25, 1980, on the site of the Triangle Shirtwaist Factory fire. (Courtesy of Elisabeth Burger)

EPILOGUE.

REFLECTIONS

ON WOMEN

AND ACTIVISM

———————————————

I did my share, that's all.
—Pauline Newman, on
the significance of her
long career

In September 1962, *Justice* ran a two-part profile of
Fannia Cohn. The ILGWU journal paid tribute to the
elderly woman warrior as an organizer and as the
driving force behind the international workers' education movement. "Throughout the world," Leon
Stein wrote, "those concerned with worker's education know her well. . . . Her name, many years ago,
came to stand for pioneering efforts to increase the
educational opportunities for men and women in
the shops."[1]

With those articles and her testimonial lunch, the
ILGWU officers felt that they had given Cohn an
honorable send-off. But those who were close to her
knew how hard it would be for Fannia Cohn to leave
the union to which she had devoted her life. In what
he called a "deeply felt love letter," protégé Jack
Sessions, then working in the AFL-CIO Education
Department, tried to reassure and comfort her,
knowing how frightened she was of retirement:
"Your life is dignified because you have helped so
many others to walk in dignity. Your life is beautiful
because you have helped so many others find
beauty. I know that because of the life you have lived
retirement will demand greater courage of you than
it does from most people, Fannia. But I know too
that you will find the courage because you have
taught so many others to be courageous."[2]

But Cohn was unable to tear herself away from
the union, even to work on her memoirs. She just
could not let go. She continued to come to the
ILGWU headquarters daily and put in long hours at
her desk, furiously writing ideas for new programs
that the union would never fund. Perhaps this attempt at forced retirement seemed to her just one
more assault by her detractors in the union. Somehow, she may have told herself, she would outwit the
naysayers and convince the disbelievers.[3]

Exasperated, Dubinsky ordered her desk and papers removed to prepare the office for its next occu-
pant. Still Cohn refused to give in. Every day for the

next four months, the short, stubby seventy-seven-year-old came to "work." Day after day she sat silently in a small chair in the waiting room outside what had been her office. Sometimes she did not even remove her coat and hat. In the final battle of wills between Fannia Cohn and the ILGWU leadership, she lost only because her body gave out. On December 23, 1962, Fannia Cohn's chair sat empty for the first time in years. Her body was discovered in her apartment the following day. The tiny, unswerving activist had died of a stroke.[4]

The speeches at Cohn's funeral, held on December 27, 1962, reflect the ambivalence with which she was regarded throughout her career. In death as in life, she was caught between male labor leaders who grudgingly recognized but did not like her, male academics who adored her, and female protégés who both liked and respected her but could not breach her isolation. Cohn was first eulogized by David Dubinsky. Without irony, Dubinsky called Cohn "a shining light to young immigrant girls working in sweatshops and thirsting for knowledge." Rose Pesotta, the former ILGWU vice president for whom Cohn had been a mentor, spoke next. Pesotta, who had resigned eighteen years earlier to protest the union's failure to recognize the talents of women, had fought with Dubinsky behind the scenes in defense of Cohn. In her eulogy, Pesotta praised Cohn as a "zealot" who had served the union "diligently, devotedly and unselfishly."[5]

Pesotta's choice of the word *zealot* is telling. Dictionary definitions of the word draw a thin line between "fervent partisanship for a cause or an ideal" and "fanatical devotion." Even Cohn's admirers—Rose Pesotta, Miriam Stein, and Maida Springer among them—were overwhelmed by the fierceness of the older woman's commitment to the labor movement. None of these union women thought Cohn crazy. Stein would later believe that even Cohn's bitterest perceptions of union sexism were more than a little true. Springer said of Cohn that "to me she made sense . . . no matter how many times she told me the same thing over and over again." Those who loved and respected Cohn recognized her contributions. But they also understood that Cohn's drivenness had taken a toll on her.[6]

Nearly sixty years earlier, Cohn had chosen the working-class struggle as her life's work. She turned her back on middle-class comforts, eschewed the prestige of a college degree, and went to work in a Brooklyn sweatshop. Though she left the shop floor forever ten years later, Cohn never turned her back on the ILGWU or lived a more extravagant life than her scant union salary made possible. During this century, many members of the middle and upper classes have allied themselves with the working class. A smaller number have enjoyed the novelty of briefly living a worker's life. But very few have been willing to shed their class privileges for good. Fannia Cohn never looked back.

With tenacity and talent she championed the cause of workers' education, developing programs and schools that practiced a respectful, innovative, and worker-friendly pedagogy. Her vision, dedication, and warmth won her the respect of leading scholars and educators. Her sympathy for the underdog and passion for justice also won her the affection of younger workers, both male and female, and of important African American labor and civil rights activists. Fannia Cohn left a vital legacy as a pioneering educator and as a torchbearer for industrial feminism in a bureaucratized and hierarchical labor movement.[7]

Despite all this acclaim, Cohn often found herself an object of derision in her own union. Partly this was because her commitment to a gender-integrated labor movement challenged ILGWU leaders' vision of a worker-brotherhood to which women, by definition, could not belong. And partly it was because her single-minded devotion to education for its own sake seemed irrelevant to men who wanted, in ILGWU vice president Benjamin Stolberg's words, to "play the game of power instead of studying it." Rather than grapple seriously with her ideas, they caricatured her as an overwrought feminist and derided her political commitment as the rechanneled frustrations of an unmarried woman.[8]

Had a man chosen activism over marriage, he might have been lauded as a dedicated leader. But most men did not need to make such a choice. A man could commit himself to the movement without giving up the support of a relationship and family. For women activists, the choices were more complicated and the risks of social condemnation much greater. Women who chose not to marry were chided about it by male union organizers. Fannia Cohn was repeatedly described by ILGWU officials as being "married to the union," in ways that were only partly admiring. Rose Schneiderman's "marriage" to the WTUL was treated more respectfully, but the clear undertone was that there was something wrong. The attitude of many of the men who worked with Schneiderman and Cohn was epitomized by ILGWU organizer Abraham Bisno, who wrote in his memoirs that the single women he knew in the labor movement were odd creatures who did not have "a personal life in relation to men" and "did not succeed in establishing themselves in homes." Such views left women in the public sector little space to choose their own path.[9]

Cohn chose to remain with the ILGWU in order to try changing it from within. She did so with a total commitment that precluded either the kind of marriage and home life Shavelson made for herself or participation in the kind of cross-class women's community to which Schneiderman and Newman belonged. Cohn's failure to transform the ILGWU to fit her vision of community did not detract from her accomplishments as an educational pioneer. But it meant that she was constantly fighting colleagues in her own movement. Endless struggling exhausted and isolated her. Her loneliness amid renown and great achievement suggest just how conflicted life could be for an activist working-class woman of her era.

To remain active in politics over a lifetime requires great dedication of anyone. For a woman activist there is the added stress of living outside the protective walls of feminine respectability. As the years went on, Schneiderman, Newman, Cohn, and Shavelson began to show the signs of strain. They all grew more ideologically rigid. They reacted emotionally to the social pressures they felt as women, displayed insecurity because they lacked education and polish, and grew frustrated at continually having to ask for financial support from more affluent allies. All of these feelings colored the women's final reflections about the meaning of their lives and long careers.

After the demise of the New York WTUL in 1955, Rose Schneiderman began working on her memoirs. It was a torturous process, during which she ran through a succession of young assistants. Her nephew, Ralph Taylor, was the first to tackle the project. He quit, claiming emotional problems. Schneiderman fired her next aide for asking questions about her sexual history. There is no record of this woman's name or of what she said that provoked Schneiderman. She may have pushed a little bit too hard for answers to the questions that are raised by any examination of Schneiderman's life: by Pauline Newman's early letters to her; by Schneiderman's grief when Rose Rishon moved away in 1911; and by her quarter-century-long relationship with Maud Swartz.[10]

Was Schneiderman a lesbian? Few women in public life would feel safe answering that question even now, in the relatively tolerant 1990s. In the fearful atmosphere of the late 1950s, when homosexuality was equated with subversion as well as perversion, it would not be surprising if Schneiderman reacted badly to such a question. She would not have been wrong to worry that revelations of "deviance" might move historians to dismiss her political career. Schneiderman's late seventies were strained by internal conflict, as her desire to leave some record of her work competed with fear of how she would be viewed if historians gained access to her private correspondence.[11]

In 1961, Schneiderman sent a rough draft of her memoirs, written without help, to Eleanor Roosevelt. To her surprise and pleasure, Roosevelt wrote that she "found it readable." Still, Schneiderman worried that she would be unable to complete the book before her strength ran out. "I am at my wit's end," she wrote Roosevelt, "trying to find someone who could help me with my book. A person who would go over the material, set it up and edit it when I have done."

As she had done so many times, Roosevelt came to Schneiderman's aid. She gave her the name of a literary agent who introduced Schneiderman to experienced freelance journalist Lucy Goldthwaite. Relieved, Schneiderman sent Roosevelt "everlasting thanks." It was one of their final communications. Roosevelt died soon thereafter, as did another of Schneiderman's oldest friends, WTUL pioneer Mary Dreier. Their deaths shook the eighty-year-old activist, heightening her fear that she would be unable to finish her memoirs.[12]

But working with Goldthwaite did not ease Schneiderman's anxiety, for the journalist was determined to create a multifaceted portrait that reflected the complexities of the activist's long career. Schneiderman had a different idea about the image she wanted to leave to history. She had decided to discuss her personal life only in passing, to downplay her Socialist youth, and to emphasize the political moderation for which the *New York Times* had praised her in 1949. She wanted to highlight what she felt to be the high points—particularly her work with Franklin and Eleanor Roosevelt—and to skate lightly over the battles she'd fought with others in the labor movement.[13]

Nervous and uncomfortable about the whole process of completing her memoirs, Schneiderman would not show the manuscript to anyone. Pauline Newman told an interviewer that even she was not allowed to see the book, though while writing it, Schneiderman had called her daily to check the accuracy of her memories. And when seventy-seven-year-old Clara Shavelson interviewed the eighty-one-year-old Schneiderman for a 1963 article about the WTUL for an Emma Lazarus publication, she found her former ally reluctant to answer even basic questions.

Ironically, Shavelson's frustrating afternoon with Schneiderman foreshadowed later unsuccessful attempts by historians to interview *her*. More than four decades after the end of the suffrage movement—the last time the two had worked together—both women were in the process of rethinking their lives, mulling over the history they'd helped to create. There were many things the two elderly activists might have talked about that afternoon. Instead, they simply skimmed the surface, carefully avoiding sensitive subjects, offering few insights into the different choices each had made. Shavelson summed up the visit in an admiring but faintly caustic profile:

Rose lives alone. She occupies a two room apartment on the fourteenth floor. The rooms are neatly furnished. An entire wall is covered with all kinds of books which I admired. "I read a lot," she said, "but not enough. I must save my eyes." When I put a number of personal questions, she said, "about myself I will not speak. I am now writing my memoirs and if I talk to you it is not advisable." Maybe she thought I would steal her thunder. She is now eighty years old and does her own shopping and cooking. She was dressed very neatly. She told me, "I don't go to the Beauty Parlor." She does wear lipstick and her lovely smile is still with her. Her white hair looks like a silver crown on her head. We will look forward to reading her memoirs. I am sure she will have lots of interesting things to tell.[14]

In fact, when it was finally published in 1967, Rose Schneiderman's memoirs did not have many interesting things to say about her long and varied career. Schneiderman was unhappy with the final version of *All for One*, which she thought was of poor quality. Lucy Goldthwaite vehemently disassociated herself from the book. She blamed Schneiderman for having a "mania for respectability which suffocated the story and robbed it of all drama or controversy."[15]

How can we make sense of Schneiderman's "mania"? In part, it must have been a reaction to the national witch-hunting hysteria of the 1950s and early 1960s. Schneiderman worried about being tarred with the brush of radicalism. But her determination to appear mild and moderate dated back to well before the 1950s and stemmed from something deeper than a concern over her political reputation. It grew out of a personal reticence that had caused her to camouflage and curtail her emotional life, to keep her feelings hidden even when she was in pain.[16]

As early as 1917, Schneiderman had admitted to Newman that she was accustomed to repressing her desire for a lover. Whether this was because her romantic feelings were for other women we will never know. Sometime during the course of writing her memoirs, Schneiderman destroyed almost every piece of evidence about her personal life. But the fragments that remain suggest that from a fairly young age, she had found it painful to open herself to others. She was thirty-five when she wrote, "I know just how alone one can feel . . . eurning, eurning [*sic*] all the time for warmth and tenderness from a loved one, only to be worn out and settled down to the commonplace everyday grind. . . . [Still,] whatever I have done, could not be done any other way because of the kind of personality that I am. . . . If the craving for the utmost fulfillment of love would have been stronger . . . [it] would have been fulfilled. . . . I am used to going without the things most wanted."

What is most interesting about this letter is that at the time it was written, Schneiderman had already known Maud Swartz for five years. Their relationship may well have become more intimate in succeeding years. We'll never know. But Schneiderman certainly did not grow any easier about revealing its more personal dimensions. Only a few days after Swartz's death, Schneiderman adopted a plucky, distanced tone in writing to Eleanor Roosevelt, who surely knew the nature of the two women's relationship. "I shall miss Maud terribly. We had been pals for twenty-three years and, while we differed on a good many questions, we never allowed our differences to affect our friendship."[17]

Some of this reticence was just Schneiderman's way. But her obsession with appearing mild and respectable must be seen in light of the scars she carried from a lifetime in the public eye. Naturally, Schneiderman hated being a target for anyone who felt inclined to speculate about what she did and did not do in her private life; she also chafed at having to constantly ask others for financial support. In a 1960 letter to Eleanor Roosevelt, Schneiderman explained, "For close to fifty years, I begged for money—for my own union, for strikers . . . the shirtwaist makers, laundry workers, candy workers etc. When I became president of the League I had to raise the budget. The unions were poor and so I had to seek help from the outside. You may not believe it but I am a very shy person and I quaked inside before approaching my victims."[18]

"I have never asked for anything for myself," she concluded proudly. But clearly she felt a sense of shame, as if she had. She had hoped that retirement would free her. However, Rose Schneiderman had to go begging one last time to get her memoirs published. It was a painful process. When she first sent chapters to publishers in the late 1950s, a sympathetic editor told her sadly that Americans just would not buy a book about the life of a woman labor organizer. Even after she had spent years revising, the only house willing to publish the book insisted that Schneiderman guarantee sale of the first printing. She turned for help to David Dubinsky, who, in his last year as ILGWU president, agreed to buy five thousand copies for local union libraries.[19]

Dubinsky's act of kindness is worth noting here for two reasons. It suggests the extent to which Schneiderman remained, to the end of her life, dependent on the intercession of more powerful allies. And it highlights some important differences between her relations with male union leaders and those of the other three activists. Clara Lemlich Shavelson had been a maverick from the start; they saw her as a troublemaker. Fannia Cohn was too pushy and, in their eyes, strange. Newman, though she was well liked, was treated more like a formidable maiden aunt than a political player of significance. Schneiderman, however, had enjoyed the friendship and admiration of several union presidents. They liked her personally and respected the fact that she had been close to power.

Dubinsky's loyalty stemmed from a sense of indebtedness, because at crucial times Schneiderman had been able to help him out. First, in her position on the NRA Labor Advisory Board, she had engineered a dramatic rescue of the bankrupt ILGWU by pushing through NRA codes beneficial to the union. Then, as New York's secretary of labor, she had performed smaller favors for Dubinsky and his union. Because he was a man who prided himself on paying back debts, he came to the aid of Schneiderman and the NYWTUL several times during their most threadbare years. His final gesture of respect came two days after Schneiderman's death.

Rose Schneiderman died on August 11, 1972, at the age of ninety. Pauline Newman was shaken by the sparse turnout at her best friend's funeral. She was among fewer than a dozen people who attended, mostly members of Schneiderman's family. "I went to the services and I thought I'd find a lot of people who knew her and for whom she worked all her life. . . . I could not believe it, you know? . . . Not that it mattered to her but it was very sad." Newman wondered if perhaps there was no one left who cared about the women of the League or remembered the work they'd done. According to Leon Stein, Dubinsky felt badly about how few people had shown up to honor Schneiderman, so he called a friend of his at the *New York Times*.[20]

The following day, August 14, 1972, the editorial page carried this glowing tribute:

A tiny red-haired bundle of social dynamite, Rose Schneiderman did more to upgrade the dignity and living standards of working women than any other American. . . .

She pioneered in the mission of emancipation that reached flower . . . in the campaign for women's suffrage and the current movement for women's liberation. Franklin D. Roosevelt and his wife, Eleanor, both learned most of what they knew about unions from her—lessons that eventuated in the Wagner Act, the National Industrial Recovery Act and other New Deal landmarks.

The editorial praised Schneiderman as a forerunner of the new "women's liberation movement." There was an irony in this, the editors noted, for modern feminists sought an Equal Rights Amendment that would overturn the labor laws that were Schneiderman's legacy. But this, the *Times* concluded, was appropriate. "The upward march that Rose Schneiderman did so much to start had now progressed to a point where women felt able to stand on their own feet, with walls of special protection as unwelcome as walls of prejudice. That progress is her monument."[21]

Within a year of Schneiderman's death, the AFL-CIO voted to endorse the ERA. Four years after that, Pauline Newman watched trade union delegations gather for a pro-ERA march on Washington. "Equal Rights is the Union Way," their banners said. That slogan suggests how much trade union feminists had changed their views since Newman's day. With most federal labor protections now extended both to male and female workers, union women had begun to feel that they too would benefit from such an amendment.

Still, their support of the ERA did not signal a break with earlier trade union women who had fought the amendment. They understood their pro-ERA position as the culmination of long years of struggle by women who had come before them; for if the 1970s women's movement highlighted the differences between generations of women trade unionists, it also sparked a renewal of interest in the historic traditions of women's labor militancy in the United States. Young women trade unionists and women's historians began to rediscover the activists of Newman's generation. In 1973, Vera Peterson Joseph, a physician at the Union Health Center, wrote Newman, "You know how tremendously I admire you and Frieda—and the women of your time—who went out and moved mountains. Your accomplishments are for all times. . . . I wish some of our Women Libbers would do some homework and read history!" One of the first groups to do so was the Coalition of Labor Union Women (CLUW).[22]

Founded in 1974, CLUW was in many ways a direct descendant of the Women's Trade Union League. And though CLUW championed new goals, including the ERA and reproductive rights, it paid tribute to the WTUL and the 1909 vintage in a platform that incorporated all the major goals of older women labor activists: more women in trade union leadership; job training for women; equal treatment of women workers in pension and seniority benefits; union and government support for day care and maternity leave; and labor legislation to insure healthy conditions and a livable minimum wage. Like the WTUL, CLUW committed its resources to organizing U.S. woman workers. And CLUW established an education program for women workers that was modeled on the schools created by Fannia Cohn and the WTUL.[23]

In 1978, CLUW gave Pauline Newman its Lifetime Achievement Award "for her distinguished service in furthering the participation of women in unions." Newman was nearing ninety by then and felt too weak to attend the conference in Washington, D.C. For the past few years, CLUW member and historian Barbara Wertheimer had been recording Newman's oral history, and in the process she had won the trust of the prickly old activist. Now Newman asked Wertheimer to read her speech to the CLUW members.[24]

Accepting CLUW's honor, Newman acknowledged that her generation had accomplished a great deal. But she insisted that "much still remains to be done." She challenged younger women workers to continue fighting for empowerment and improved conditions, and she urged them to exert whatever pressure they could to get women elected to the top offices of the labor movement. She reminisced, "When I talked to union women, I'd hold up a picture of the Executive Board of the AFL, or the AFL-CIO later, and ask them what was wrong with the picture. They would think and think and then I'd say: 'You can see. . . . They are all men.'" That was as true in 1978, Newman noted, as it had been fifty years earlier. She reminded her audience that it had been nearly seventy years since she was appointed the first woman general organizer of a national trade union. Despite all the talented organizers who had come after her, there had never been a woman on the AFL-CIO's executive board. Newman lived to see the first woman elected to that ruling body: Joyce Miller, vice president of the Amalgamated Clothing and Textile Workers and president of CLUW. But this goal was not achieved until 1980—seventy-three years after Newman, Shavelson, and Cohn began organizing garment workers, and seventy-six years after Rose Schneiderman led her first strike.[25]

Newman enjoyed such opportunities to speak to younger workers and students of labor history. By the mid-1970s, she was doing so fairly frequently. After years in relative obscurity, Newman began to receive requests for interviews and speaking engagements, not only from labor unions but also from historians and reporters. Elisabeth Burger recalls that "Pauline got a kick out of the fact that here she was—a woman with no formal education—and in her old age all of these professors and Ph.D. students were coming to her." Pleased as she was by the recognition, she felt a nagging uncertainty about those who now called on her to speak for her generation of women trade unionists. Unsure about their motives, she answered their questions cautiously, worried about how she and her friends would be seen by future generations.[26]

Leon Stein says that she feared that their fascination with personal matters would lead them to write about her life in ways she would not recognize or approve of. When one interviewer came right out and asked whether she and Schneiderman had been lovers when they were young, Newman became convinced that her history would be distorted and sensationalized if she cooperated with the young historians who came to call on her.[27]

There was another conflict as well, says Burger. All the acclaim and attention made Newman feel guilty. There were other women whom she believed had done as much for the movement but had received no recognition. Often, Burger recalls, Newman would respond to historians' questions about her youth by telling the story of a Philadelphia waistmaker who had contracted pneumonia and died after distributing leaflets in the freezing rain during the 1910 strike. Knowing the sacrifices others had made, Newman resisted assertions that she had done more than her share.[28]

But if Newman sought to downplay her personal contributions, it wasn't because she saw no historical significance in the movement she'd helped build. On the contrary, since her youth she'd taken upon herself the task of chronicling women workers' struggles. And during the last twenty years of her life, the act of remembrance became her special contribution. As one by one the members of her WTUL circle retired, sickened, and died, it was Newman, with her keen sense for details and vivid writing style, who took it upon herself to commemorate them.

Her work as a memorialist had begun in 1937 with the death of Maud Swartz. Newman wrote poems and speeches that are far more evocative of the shock Swartz's friends felt at her sudden death than anything Schneiderman has left us. Newman conscientiously characterized Swartz as "logical, often brilliant and always convincing." But she also let her own pain show. One year after the last day they spent gardening together, Newman wrote, "I have need of you now, Maud, and always shall." In the decades to come, Newman wrote profiles of the rest of her WTUL circle: Agnes Nestor, Elisabeth Christman, Mary Dreier, Mary Anderson and, finally, Rose Schneiderman. Not all of these women had been personally close to Newman, but for half a century they had all shared a life in the League. Newman felt it incumbent upon her to try to distill and record each woman's contributions.[29]

By the mid-1970s, Newman was the only League veteran still living. She was also one of the last survivors of New York's sweatshop past. Throughout her eighties she was trotted out regularly as a living symbol, her craggy face and gravelly voice conveying as powerfully as words the course her life had taken. Barbara Wertheimer began to bring Newman in regularly to tell her story to labor history classes. The New York Fire Department escorted her each year to speak at their annual March 25 commemoration of the Triangle Shirtwaist Factory Fire. On Labor Days and anniversaries of the fire, throughout the 1970s and early 1980s, newspaper reporters came to hear her stories, which she had told so many times they had become almost like litanies. Newman sometimes grew annoyed at interviewers, but she continued to play her role. She saw it as the last political work she could do—passing on her memories of the struggle to the next generation.[30]

When I interviewed her in 1984, the ninety-five-year-old Newman, frail but sharp as glass, deftly sidestepped questions about her own life. "About myself, I will not speak," she said firmly. But she softened immediately when asked about her friends. Her voice warmed and swelled with affection; she became impassioned and expansive. Her memory was crystal clear even when she was recalling details about friends as long dead as Maud Swartz and Leonora O'Reilly. Describing O'Reilly's speech-making style, a reminiscence from seventy years prior, Newman's voice cracked and tears filled her eyes. When she talked of Frieda Miller, the tiny old woman's shoulders literally lifted with pride, though her tone was wistful. "No one knew her better than I did," she said.

Her guardedness began to return, however, when I asked questions about Rose Schneiderman. She reminded me of her friend's "bad experiences" with interviewers. "Why should I talk to *you*?" she asked suddenly. "Don't you want historians to write your story?," I questioned. "I'll write my own story," she said, nodding her head strongly, affirming her own decision. "No one else would get it right." It would, she acknowledged, be a taxing task at ninety-five, but she had simply been too busy until now to get to it. When I pressed her for some summary statement about her long career, she flashed me the sort of look one might turn on a maddening mosquito: "I did my share," she said finally, "that's all."[31]

Clara Shavelson was no less thorny around the reporters and historians who began to seek her out around the time of the sixty-fifth anniversary of the 1909 strike. When one historian visited Shavelson at the Jewish Home in Los Angeles, interviewer and subject both ended up frustrated, says Shavelson's daughter Martha Schaffer. Shavelson, whose confinement to an institution had not stopped her from organizing the orderlies, expressed impatience when asked about her radical youth. "Why are you here interviewing me about what *I* did?" she grumbled. "If you want to do something, do something."[32]

Shavelson thought the reasons for activism were obvious. She couldn't figure out why interviewers felt the need to probe for her motivations. Even when her grandson Joel interviewed her as part of an oral history project he was doing on her life, initially she was not cooperative. Schaffer recalls that her mother bristled when asked why she became involved in the union. "What do you mean, why did I do it?," she said peevishly. "Why shouldn't I do it? I don't understand."[33]

Eventually she softened and acknowledged that her life might have some historic interest. She spoke about her past with pride but also with a sense of resignation. Her rabble-rousing days were behind her, and she seemed unsure what the point was of talking about them now: "I admit that I have led some very good strikes. I was very known and popular and effective. I have done some good work in my life. Now I am an old woman. I learned from other people, people who thought they knew more than me. I learned from people who thought they knew it all. And then I would show them that I knew as much." Eighty-eight years old and living in a nursing home, Clara Shavelson was still battling those, probably long dead, who she felt had not taken her seriously enough.[34]

Never willing to rest on her laurels, Clara Shavelson had worked hard during her old age to pass on her political views and historical interpretations. Martha Schaffer remembers that Clara took special pains to explain the 1950s to her grandchildren because she didn't want fear of persecution to stop them from becoming politically active. Her mother was angry, Schaffer says, at former radicals who "backed off after the 1950s, who burned books from their own shelves." "You can't blame everything on McCarthy," she'd say. "The fact is, if they [the U.S. government] had their way they'd always do what they did then and the only thing that keeps them from doing it is when we organize."[35]

Shavelson, however, did not always know how to react when younger family members did pick up the torch of radicalism. Clara's relations with her most militant child, her son Irving, were filled with pride but also strained by ambivalence. Her dealings with his first wife, UE leader Ruth Young, were no easier. And when a grandson announced that he was going to follow in Clara's footsteps, Schaffer remembers her mother being nonplussed: " 'I'm going to be a radical,' he said. 'That's nice,' Clara answered, 'a radical what?' 'I'm going to be a radical like you, Grandma.' 'You can't just be a radical. You have to have a trade.' "[36]

Shavelson knew from long experience the difficulties that such a choice created. In a 1974 interview, she said, "Not all people who are called radicals are really radicals. Some are just socially. Some are real ones. You either are a radical with your full heart or you're just an imitator." Clara Shavelson had been a radical with her full heart, and for a wife and mother, that was not always a happy or an easy path; for although Clara felt most at home on a political soapbox, she found herself more often at the kitchen stove. In her household she shouldered primary responsibility for cooking, child care, and contraception, among other wifely duties. "You know I often wonder now," Martha Schaffer muses, "with all the meetings she ran to, how could she ever get dinner ready with all the parts ready at the same time."[37]

Shavelson accepted these responsibilities, but not without some anger. In particular, Schaffer says, her mother was "furious" that contraception was considered a woman's problem, though it was far easier before World War II for men to obtain condoms than for women to get diaphragms. Schaffer remembers that on the eve of her wedding, her mother confided that she had had numerous illegal abortions. As the two traveled home in a crowded subway car, Clara raged "about the indignities women suffered at the hands of men because they weren't powerful."[38]

But Clara wasn't always on the receiving end of domestic indignities. Daughter-in-law Evelyn Velson still remembers vividly a tension that reveals an essential contradiction of Clara Shavelson's character. Fiercely independent, even to the point of hurting family members' feelings, Shavelson displayed at the same time a stunning loyalty to the Communist Party. Velson says that there was a period when she and Clara's son Charlie had so little money that they could rarely afford both to hire a babysitter and pay for an evening out. Despite this, Clara refused to babysit unless she was paid. When Charlie and Evelyn protested, Clara explained that she wanted to give the money to the Party.[39]

It may be that no one could sustain a lifetime commitment to activism without the kind of certainty that resists soul-searching examinations. But a guided human missile is not easy to live with. "I know I have my faults," Clara Shavelson told her daughter, grandson, and son-in-law in 1974. "I know I have a lot of minuses when it comes to my family." Her reflections had an air of both apology and self-justification. "We are not," she concluded, "to make up our minds that we are smart on everything. It's not good to make up your mind, I know it all."[40]

Martha Schaffer compares her feelings about being raised by such a dominant personality as Clara to those of the Woody Allen character in the film *New York Stories*. Allen depicted his mother as a woman who appeared regularly as a giant specter over the skies of New York to ask her son embarrassing questions in front of millions of people. "For me what was hard," says Schaffer, "were the expectations that were laid on you. You have such a wonderful mother. . . . What are *you* going to do? . . . I got tired of hearing it." Only with the perspective of years, and after she had personally experienced the difficulties of combining mothering and her own political work, did Schaffer come to see Clara in a more sympathetic light. "When I look back now I think sometimes she was just trying to tell us 'I am a person in my own right.'" There may be no better epigraph for Clara Lemlich Shavelson's life. Shavelson died in Reseda, California, at the Jewish Home for the Aged on July 12, 1982. She was ninety-six.[41]

At a memorial for Shavelson held in New York that autumn, Sophie Gerson held her up as an empowering symbol to women workers of the late twentieth century. Noting that garment sweatshops again dotted New York, Gerson reflected, "If Clara would know that, she would be turning in her grave." But the story of Clara Lemlich Shavelson, she concluded, reaches across the generations, allowing the immigrant workers of 1909 to touch women workers of the 1980s. "What saddens me is that we've let history sleep so long. I'm sure that today there are Puerto Rican women, black, Chinese, and other women who should know about Clara. I'm sure that there are new Claras among them who need the . . . example of Clara. I hope that today will be a beginning to make Clara Lemlich Shavelson a vibrant, dynamic name and an inspiration to women workers of today."[42]

Four years later, Clara's name was invoked as an inspiring icon in a very different context—Broadway theater. In Herb Gardner's 1986 hit play *I'm Not Rappaport*, an elderly Jewish grandfather repeatedly invoked Clara Lemlich's 1909 Cooper Union speech as an emblem of a time when young people still cared about combating injustice. He had named his daughter Clara in the hope that she would be inspired by her name to fight for a better world.

Like every history text in which Clara Lemlich makes a cameo appearance as the symbol of early-twentieth-century working women's militancy, the play gave little sense of the flesh-and-blood woman. When Martha Schaffer was introduced to the Los Angeles cast of *I'm Not Rappaport*, they were shocked to realize that Clara Lemlich had actually existed: that she had married, borne children, doted on her grandchildren, baked cookies, shouted, and danced in her kitchen. The story of how Clara Lemlich sparked the 1909 uprising is—as many activists, historians, and the author of *I'm Not Rappaport* have realized—a powerful call to action. But to turn Clara Lemlich into an icon is to obscure the significance of her life. To understand what it meant for a poor immigrant woman to choose a lifetime of political activism, it is necessary to examine the full life of Clara Lemlich Shavelson in all its human messiness and complexity.[43]

Pauline Newman, the last survivor of the four, understood that on some level. Despite her reticence around historians, she decided during the late 1970s to deposit her papers at the Schlesinger Library at Radcliffe, the nation's premier women's history archive. Nothing could have indicated more clearly her desire to have feminist scholars study her life and work. She felt that she had a unique historical perspective to offer. "My papers," she wrote Schlesinger Library director Patricia King, "differ from those of my friends, Miss Frances Perkins, Mary Dreier . . . and others in that I can tell of those sweat shop years not from observation but from bitter experience. . . . Today I am, I think perhaps the oldest person . . . who can still remember what it was like just to exist in those days."[44]

But Newman included far more in her collection of papers than remembrances of sweatshop days. Unlike Schneiderman, she did not destroy evidence of her personal life. On the contrary, she included extremely revealing writings in the materials she gave the archive: love letters from young coworkers, poems, thirty years' worth of correspondence with Miller, journal entries describing her ups and downs with Miller. Perhaps her sensibility as a writer made her feel that private thoughts and feelings are as important as public pronouncements. Maybe her decision to donate personal documents reflected a recognition that the choice she'd made to live with and raise a child with another woman was a political act, and thus historically significant. We can never be sure what her motivation was. But by mixing together writings about her most intimate experiences and documents from her public career, Newman left behind a historical record that vividly illustrates the interactions between personal and political in one woman activist's life.

The papers she selected to donate to archives, like the speeches she made and the interviews she gave, reflected Newman's concern that future generations understand what her generation had done for them. "She felt that too many younger people take things for granted," says Elisabeth Burger. Michael Owen recalls that Newman sometimes wondered if all that women of the 1909 vintage had accomplished was to give late-twentieth-century workers "more time to watch the *Hollywood Squares*." She decried a lack of seriousness among the young. She supported the civil rights, antiwar, and women's movements, but they also put her off. The grunginess and irreverence of many young protesters made her wonder if there was not more style than substance in their activism. Says Owen, "If she saw someone . . . with long hair, dirty, unkempt, in blue jeans, she would find that unpleasant, whatever it stood for. Her idea of radicals would be the people who went down South to ride buses because they were clean-cut and neat and yet in some ways what they were doing was far more against the grain . . . than the people who were dressing like hippies."[45]

Of course, Newman had flouted cultural norms in many of the same ways that hippies did in the 1960s. She had lived as she wanted, spoken out about the things that mattered to her, and loved whom she pleased—and she had certainly eschewed conventionally feminine dress, favoring suits and short, slicked-back hair. Leon Stein recalls that visitors to the Union Health Center would sometimes comment on the imposing woman who strode the halls authoritatively, dressed and coiffed like a man. But androgynous dress and aggressive behavior in women evoked different responses in the 1920s and 1930s than in the era of gay liberation.[46]

Newman became more cautious in her last years, in part because she was not sure she wanted to be hailed by a generation whose values she did not always understand or approve of. In her eighties, she began to dress more softly. And even though no one used the word, she reacted furiously when historians hinted that she and Miller were lesbians. After an article was published that briefly discussed the two women's relationship, Newman threatened to sue and restricted access to her personal papers. A lifetime in the public eye had accustomed her to shielding her private life. She did not enjoy seeing her pleasures and sorrows become grist for public consumption, her painful personal struggles turned into revealing historical insights. Who would? And yet it is just that kind of examination that reveals the interpersonal dynamics that bubble under the surface of historical changes.[47]

For if Newman's fifty-six-year partnership with Frieda Miller illuminates the key role that women's cross-class friendships played in enacting industrial reform in this country, it also suggests the difficulty of sustaining love across lines of class and ethnicity. Newman walked an identity tightrope. By day she had to mold herself to the gruff, emotional Jewish workingman's world of the ILGWU. At night she had to blend into the more polished upper-class feminine style that defined the character of her home with Frieda and Elisabeth.

Newman's sisters and brother might have provided a separate support system for her, but she seems to have lost all contact with them after her mother died in the 1920s. Was this rift caused by Newman's relationship with Miller, or by her politics, or was it simply the result of geographic distance? Newman has left us no indication. All we know is that by the mid-1920s, Frieda and Elisabeth were the only family she had. And even in that little haven, there were ways in which Pauline did not always fit in.

Newman could be "vehement and uncompromising in her approach," Burger remembers. "That was definitely not my mother's style. She didn't enjoy it and she wasn't good at it. . . . Everyone recognized that giving them hell was Pauline's specialty. . . . [But] children don't like behavior that they think is sort of odd, that sticks out. And so, though I realized that she had a special talent, it slightly embarrassed me." Burger recalls one time when Newman lodged a complaint with a restaurant manager: "I remember feeling like crawling under the table with my dog."[48]

It is possible that such memories plagued Pauline as she thought back over her life. On the other hand, what family is free of tensions? By all indications, Newman and Miller created a loving, if unconventional, family in which Newman was deeply engaged. The records that the two women have left of their private life illuminate an important and hidden dimension in the history of the U.S. family. Long before the 1960s sexual revolution, and well beyond the privileged upper-class worlds of Gertrude Stein or Natalie Barney, there were women in this country creating alternative families—with children, and even grandchildren. "Just as Pauline was a pioneer in her role as an organizer of women in sweatshops and factories," Burger says, "the home that I grew up in was in some respects a harbinger of things to come—a female-headed household made up of two employed women and a child."[49]

And gruff, give-'em-hell Pauline was very much a family woman. During years when Miller was on the road and Elisabeth was traveling with her husband David, it was Newman who cared for the Owens' sons, Hugh and Michael. She considered the two boys her grandsons, and it is to them that the only notes she ever made toward an autobiography were dedicated. Burger recalls, "When my children were very little my mother was living in Washington for a time where she was working and so she wasn't always in New York. But Pauline was always in New York and she would come over most Sundays. . . . She adored my sons and would play with them. . . . She was just totally generous with her time. . . . I hate to think how many hours Pauline put in babysitting."

That care was reciprocated in Newman's final years. When Newman slipped and injured herself in 1983, Burger took her in. Upset at the loss of dignity that Frieda Miller had experienced in her years at the Walsh Home, Burger did not want to put Pauline into a home. Newman had continued to live in her Greenwich Village apartment and to work at the Union Health Center for as long as she could. Finally, though, she could no longer work or live alone. Says Burger, "You can't take without giving. . . . Since Pauline lived so long, I mean it was a question of helping her or just not caring, not paying attention and I didn't feel like doing that. She lived with us about two and a half years." Pauline died at the Burger home in April 1986. She was approximately ninety-six years old.[50]

On June 23, 1986, the ILGWU held a memorial gathering to "bid farewell to Pauline" and to honor her seventy-five years of service to the union. More than one hundred people—many union members, a handful of journalists, and a few stray historians—packed the Katie Murphy Amphitheater at the Fashion Institute of Technology in the heart of Manhattan's garment district. First, ILGWU president Jay Mazur eulogized Newman. Then there were remembrances by union people who had worked with her. Elisabeth Burger, who spoke last, captured the sentiment of the day.

She told the audience that Newman felt the ILGWU had saved her life by pulling her out of the Triangle Shirtwaist Factory. Had she not been hired at age eighteen as the union's first woman general organizer, Newman believed that she would have died in the 1911 fire that claimed so many of her friends and acquaintances. Newman had put it this way, Burger recalled: "I owe my life to the ILG and I worked for it all my life." Burger concluded, "I would suggest that the ILG and others who knew Pauline owe much to her for the courage, honesty and sense of mission that she always imparted."[51]

Pauline Newman's death seemed to evoke a deep sense of loss in all quarters of the ILGWU. Indeed, the outpouring of love that followed her passing obscured any memories of the long-standing conflicts that had strained her relationship with the union. But it also conveyed a truth about Pauline Newman's life and work. Somehow she had made her balancing act work and had found peace in a bitterly divided union. She used that inner calm to help others find refuge. As Leon Stein put it, she healed people "with trouble on their hearts." Shortly after Newman's death, the Union Health Center published a memorial booklet with a laudatory text and pictures that spanned her eighty years of union activism. "Treasures never die," the booklet comforted. "Pauline Newman was an ILGWU treasure. Her memory belongs to garment workers, just as her life was dedicated to workers everywhere."[52]

In writing the histories of Fannia Cohn, Rose Schneiderman, Clara Lemlich Shavelson, and Pauline Newman, I have tried to sketch them as fully as possible—not to iconize them but to portray them in their flawed and complex humanness. That has not always been easy. I have had to grapple with a tangled web of motivations and resistances: not only my own impulse to lionize these women but also their deep ambivalence about being historical subjects. All four women fought throughout their lives to be recognized as people "in their own right." They tried to build a movement that would recognize ties between working-class women's work and their private lives. Still, they resented it when historians began to probe the intimate details of their lives in the interest of revealing links between their personal and political decisions.

It is not hard to understand their reticence. Few people would feel comfortable having strangers read about their private conflicts and pleasures. Yet it is through those very intimate details that the four activists are transformed from political symbols to flesh-and-blood women. The conflicts they faced and the choices they made shed light on the sticky human realities that underlay public campaigns for social and political change.

Perhaps because of the difficulties an activist life entails, few women of the 1909 vintage remained politically active for as long as Cohn, Schneiderman, Shavelson, and Newman. In 1949, *Jewish Currents* contacted women who had been leaders of the 1909 shirtwaist strike. Many echoed the sentiments of Shavelson's shop-floor friend Fannie Zinsher, who clearly was not transformed either by the 1909 strike or the Triangle fire: "I was very young at the time and it was my first and last experience in the industrial field. It is true that some of the organizers and some of the members of the Women's Trade Union League had great aspirations for me as a future organizer but, being of a peaceful nature, violence and disorder had no appeal for me. . . . All I remember is that it was a very trying experience and now it seems like a nightmare of long ago."[53]

What distinguished Cohn, Schneiderman, Shavelson, and Newman from Zinsher and others who participated in the 1909 strike was that their political vision extended far beyond demonstrations and picket lines. Their imaginations were captured by the idea of large-scale social transformation, and they understood that the only way to achieve that was by educating themselves and others. Protest was exciting, but it was only a beginning. Perhaps because they loved learning and study so much—Clara Shavelson used to save a book for "dessert"—they all wanted to be teachers. The laws they helped to pass, the unions they galvanized, are important elements in the legacy they've left us. But just as valuable, though less tangible, is the part they played in training younger generations of women organizers.

Even in their declining years, the four reached across generational, racial, and ethnic divides, inspiring younger women of many different backgrounds to become leaders. Among these was Panamanian-born Maida Springer, who became the first black business agent in the ILGWU and one of the first women of color to achieve a high-level position in the AFL-CIO. When she was asked in the late 1980s who her teachers were, she replied that "the Rose Schneidermans and the Fannia Cohns and the Pauline Newmans" had taught her to lobby and introduced her to both black and white women trade unionists in New York.

> I think part of . . . my own constant passion about the labor movement with all of its bumps and warts is because I came up at a time when there were so many role models. . . . Pauline Newman . . . was one of the giants, determined, articulate, volatile about workers' dignity, and the pursuit of excellence. . . . And so Pauline Newman was one of my mentors. [Also,] Rose Schneiderman who headed the Women's Trade Union League and focused attention on women workers and brought the women of wealth and prominence to understand the concerns, the problems of working women.

Knowing these women, she said, and studying with them "gave you greater strength and gave you support as an activist in your own union."[54]

Women like Springer highlight a vital though invisible contribution of Schneiderman, Cohn, Shavelson, and Newman. They were role models, teachers, and mentors. Through Clara Shavelson's mothering of young activists in Brighton Beach; the "comradeship beyond the classroom" at the New York WTUL School for Women Organizers and Fannia Cohn's Student Fellowship; Pauline Newman's nurturing of women in her union; and in many other ways, the four forged human links between generations of working-class women activists. And the women they nurtured carried their work forward. Esther Peterson, who rose through the AFL-CIO to direct the U.S. Women's Bureau under John F. Kennedy and the Consumer Affairs Office under Jimmy Carter, wrote this in 1978 to the eighty-seven-year-old Newman: "I think of you so often and especially of all the help that you and Frieda gave me. . . . I am trying to carry on in the same tradition and help other women as they come along."[55]

Ninety years after these women first took the political stage, much of what they struggled for continues to seem radical. Long before the most recent wave of feminist activism began, they attacked sexual segregation in the workplace; they attempted to unionize not only industrial women but also white-collar and domestic workers; they lobbied for state regulation not only of factory and office working conditions but also of working conditions in the home. They fought for comparable worth laws, government-funded child care, and maternity insurance. And they mobilized housewives to fight for fair rents and food prices, better housing and public education.

Finally, they urged women to demand not just economic independence but also the right to personal fulfillment. That ideal, as much as the government protections most American workers now take for granted, is the legacy of Fannia Cohn, Rose Schneiderman, Clara Lemlich Shavelson, and Pauline Newman. Their lives and work are a reminder that social and political movements must not be measured only by concrete achievements but also by the meaning that participants find in the struggle. For they did not simply ask for roses. They gave roses to themselves.

INTRODUCTION

1. Benjamin Stolberg, *Tailor's Progress: The Story of A Famous Union and the Men Who Made It* (New York: Doubleday, 1944).

2. Alice Kessler-Harris, Meredith Tax, Barbara Wertheimer, and Sarah Eisenstein pioneered with studies that demonstrated the extent to which American working women did attempt to unionize. More recently, Kathy Peiss, Ardis Cameron, Elizabeth Ewen, and others have published studies illustrating that American working-class women had their own work and neighborhood cultures. Jacquelyn Dowd Hall, Elizabeth Faue, Joanne Meyerowitz, Vicki Ruiz, and others have broken out of the Progressive Era and begun to look at women workers in the 1930s and 1940s. These studies have made excellent use of oral histories, government statistics, and the literature created by feminist social reformers.

See Alice Kessler-Harris, *Out to Work: A History of Wage-Earning Women in America* (New York: Oxford University Press, 1982); Meredith Tax, *The Rising of the Women: Feminist Solidarity and Class Conflict, 1880–1917* (New York: Monthly Review Press, 1980); Barbara Mayer Wertheimer, *We Were There: The Story of Working Women in America* (New York: Pantheon, 1977); Sara Eisenstein, *Give Us Bread But Give Us Roses: Working Women's Consciousness in the United States, 1890 to the First World War* (London: Routledge and Kegan Paul, 1983); Kathy Peiss, *Cheap Amusements: Working Women and Leisure in Turn-of-the-Century New York* (Philadelphia: Temple University Press, 1986); Ardis Cameron, "Bread and Roses Revisited: Women's Culture and Working-Class Activism in the Lawrence Strike of 1912," in *Women, Work, and Protest: A Century of U.S. Women's Labor History*, ed. Ruth Milkman (London: Routledge and Kegan Paul, 1985), 42–62; Elizabeth Ewen, *Immigrant Women in the Land of Dollars: Life and Culture on the Lower East Side, 1890–1925* (New York: Monthly Review Press, 1985); Vicki Ruiz, *Cannery Women, Cannery Lives: Mexican Women, Unionization, and the California Food Processing Industry, 1930–1950* (Albuquerque: University of New Mexico Press, 1987); Jacquelyn Dowd Hall, "Disorderly Women: Gender and Labor Militancy in the Appalachian South," *Journal of American History* 73, no. 2 (September 1986): 354–82.

3. Leon Stein, interview by author, Cranbury, N.J., October 19, 1988; Pauline Newman, interview by author, New York, N.Y., February 9, 1984.

4. Schneiderman and Newman frequently referred to their goals as "just common sense." They used "common sense" as a slogan in their 1911–12 campaign to draw working women into the suffrage movement. *Senators vs. Working Women* (1912 suffrage pamphlet), Papers of the Wage Earners' League for Woman Suffrage, a subset of the Leonora O'Reilly Papers, Tamiment Institute Library, New York University (hereafter cited as O'Reilly Papers).

5. Rose Schneiderman, *All for One* (New York: Paul S. Eriksson, 1967), 129; Paula Scheier, "Clara Lemlich Shavelson: Fifty Years in Labor's Front Line," *Jewish Life*, November 1954.

6. Mildred Moore, "A History of the Women's Trade Union League of Chicago" (M.A. thesis, University of Chicago, 1915), cited in Diane Kirkby, "The Wage-Earning

Woman and the State: The National Women's Trade Union League and Protective Labor Legislation, 1903–1923," *Labor History* 28, no. 1 (Winter 1987): 54–74.

7. Newman, interview by author.

8. In the last fifteen years, feminist scholars have undertaken a thorough analysis of the relations between women and the American welfare state. For a summary of this scholarship see Linda Gordon, "The New Feminist Scholarship on the Welfare State," in *Women, the State, and Welfare*, ed. Linda Gordon (Madison: University of Wisconsin Press, 1990), 9–36.

9. For an excellent summary of the new scholarship on theories of women and social protest, see Guida West and Rhoda Lois Blumberg, "Reconstructing Social Protest from a Feminist Perspective," in *Women and Social Protest*, ed. Guida West and Rhoda Lois Blumberg (New York: Oxford University Press, 1990).

PROLOGUE

1. Pauline Newman, "Letters to Hugh and Michael" (1951–69), Box 1, Folder 3, Pauline M. Newman Papers, Schlesinger Library, Radcliffe College, Cambridge, Mass. (hereafter cited as Newman Papers).

2. Ibid.

3. Ibid.; *New York Times*, November 2, 25, December 3, 26, 1907.

4. Newman, "Letters to Hugh and Michael."

5. "The Testimony of Miss Pauline M. Newman," in *Hearings of the New York State Factory Investigating Commission* (Albany: J. B. Lyons Printers, 1915), 2868–71.

6. My estimate of Newman's age is based on evidence suggesting that she was around eighteen years old at the time of the 1909 shirtwaist strike. Newman, like many Jews of her generation, never knew for sure how old she was. Her birthdate was recorded only on the flyleaf of the family Bible. After the Bible was lost in transit, she could only guess at her age.

7. For analyses of the position of Jews in Russian society at the turn of the century, see S. Ettinger, "The Jews at the Outbreak of the Revolution," in *The Jews in Soviet Russia since 1917*, ed. Lionel Kochan, 3d ed. (Oxford: Oxford University Press, 1978), 15–30; see also Salo Baron, *The Russian Jew under Tsars and Soviets* (New York: Macmillan, 1976).

8. Solomon Schwartz, *Jews in the Soviet Union* (Syracuse, N.Y.: Syracuse University Press, 1951), 72.

9. According to the 1897 census, the largest number of Russian Jews engaged in artisanal work or factory production were tailors and seamstresses. The next most popular trade was shoemaking (Ettinger, "Jews at the Outbreak of the Revolution," 21 [n. 2]). Of those engaged in "trade or business," most were either peddlers or innkeepers. Jewish peddlers lived in symbiotic relationship with non-Jewish peasants, trading manufactured goods for foodstuffs in the weekly market. Innkeeping was one of the few jobs open to Jews, and in the late nineteenth century, when the government took away their licenses to make liquor, many Jews lost their livelihood.

10. See Ettinger, "Jews at the Outbreak of the Revolution," and Irving Howe, *World of Our Fathers* (New York: Harcourt Brace Jovanovich, 1976), 2–26.

11. Sidney Jonas, interview by author, Brooklyn, N.Y., August 10, 1980; Newman, "Letters to Hugh and Michael"; Paula Scheier, "Clara Lemlich Shavelson: Fifty Years

in Labor's Front Line," *Jewish Life*, November 1954; Ricki Carole Myers Cohen, "Fannia Cohn and the International Ladies' Garment Workers' Union" (Ph.D. diss., University of Southern California, 1976), 5.

12. Newman, "Letters to Hugh and Michael"; Cohen, "Fannia Cohn," chap. 1; Scheier, "Clara Lemlich Shavelson"; Fannia M. Cohn to "Dear Emma," May 15, 1953, Fannia M. Cohn Papers, Astor, Lenox, and Tilden Foundations, Rare Books and Manuscripts Division, New York Public Library (hereafter cited as Cohn Papers).

In March 1903, gangs organized by Russian police rampaged through the Ukrainian town of Kishinev, killing 51 Jewish men, women, and children, and wounding at least 495 others. The pogrom shocked the world and sent a wave of fear through Russian Jewry. For the most recent scholarly source, see Edward H. Judge, *Eastern Kishinev: Anatomy of a Pogrom* (New York: New York University Press, 1992).

13. Newman, "Letters to Hugh and Michael"; Pauline Newman, interview by author, New York, N.Y., February 9, 1984.

14. See Charlotte Baum, Paula Hyman, and Sonya Michel, *The Jewish Woman in America* (New York: New American Library, 1977), 55–91; Elizabeth Ewen, *Immigrant Women in the Land of Dollars: Life and Culture on the Lower East Side, 1890–1925* (New York: Monthly Review Press, 1985), 37–49; Jack Kugelmass and Jonathan Boyarin, eds., *From a Ruined Garden* (New York: Schocken, 1983), 42–44; Annelise Orleck, "Reminiscences—The First Wave," in *Brighton Beach: A World Apart*, unpublished manuscript.

15. Scheier, "Clara Lemlich Shavelson"; Newman, "Letters to Hugh and Michael"; Rose Schneiderman, *All for One* (New York: Paul S. Eriksson, 1967), 11–15.

16. See Baum, Hyman, and Michel, *Jewish Woman in America*, 55–91; Mark Zborowski and Elizabeth Herzog, *Life Is with People* (New York: Schocken, 1962); Kugelmass and Boyarin, *From a Ruined Garden*; Orleck, *Brighton Beach*.

17. These sentiments can be found not only in the reminiscences of Schneiderman, Cohn, Newman, and Lemlich but in a wide range of interviews done by the author with a slightly younger group of East European Jewish immigrant women. See Orleck, *Brighton Beach*, and Baum, Hyman, and Michel, *Jewish Woman in America*, 71–89.

18. Newman, "Letters to Hugh and Michael"; Cohen, "Fannia Cohn"; Scheier, "Clara Lemlich Shavelson."

19. Schneiderman, *All for One*, 10–22.

20. Newman, "Letters to Hugh and Michael."

21. Ibid.

22. Ibid.; Newman, "Notes toward an Autobiography," October 11, 1958, Box 1, Newman Papers.

23. Scheier, "Clara Lemlich Shavelson."

24. Ibid.; Martha Schaffer, telephone interview by author, March 11, 1989. The Kishinev pogrom of March 1903 motivated thousands of Jewish families, including Clara Lemlich's, to emigrate. Judge, *Eastern Kishinev*.

25. In her entry on Fannia Cohn, Susan Stone Wong notes that Cohn's parents, "although prosperous, . . . espoused radical political views." Wong, "Cohn, Fannia Mary," in *Notable American Women: The Modern Period*, ed. Barbara Sicherman and Carol Hurd Green (Cambridge: Belknap Press of Harvard University Press, 1980), 154–55.

26. FMC to Selig Perlman, December 26, 1951, Box 5, Cohn Papers.

27. FMC to "Dear Emma," May 15, 1953, Box 5, Cohn Papers. See also Cohen, "Fannia Cohn," chap. 1.

28. FMC to Perlman, December 26, 1951; FMC to "Dear Emma," May 15, 1953, Box 5, Cohn Papers.

29. The Lower East Side continued to receive Jewish immigrants from Eastern Europe into the 1920s. Russia's defeats between 1914 and 1917 made matters worse for Eastern European Jews; the government expelled hundreds of thousands of them from their homes on twenty-four to forty-eight hours' notice. Between 1917 and 1920, Jews in the Ukraine and in eastern Poland were the victims of terrible pogroms at the hands of Polish and Ukrainian armies. During that period another 750,000 Jews fled Russia and Poland to settle in the United States. Like their predecessors, most of them came through New York Harbor, and most of those settled down at least for a while in New York City. These newcomers, fresh from the drama of Revolutionary Russia, intensified the radical character of New York's Jewish immigrant communities and of the garment shops where so many of them worked. See Ettinger, "Jews at the Outbreak of the Revolution," 19–22; Celia Heller, *On the Edge of Destruction* (New York: Schocken, 1980), 45–55; and Howe, *World of Our Fathers*, xix.

30. Newman, "Letters to Hugh and Michael."

31. Louise Bolard More, *Wage Earners' Budgets: A Study of Standards and Costs of Living in New York City* (New York:H. Holt and Co., 1907), cited in Ewen, *Immigrant Women*, 102. The importance of women peddlers to the Jewish family economy has been noted above. In *World of Our Fathers*, Irving Howe comments on the importance of Jewish women peddlers to the Jewish immigrant family economy (p. 174).

For evidence of the entrepreneurial activity among immigrant women of other ethnicities, see Elizabeth Pleck, "A Mother's Wages: Income Earning among Married Black and Italian Women, 1896–1911," in *A Heritage of Her Own*, ed. Nancy Cott and Elizabeth Pleck (New York: Simon and Schuster, 1979), 367–92; Thomas Kessner and Betty Boyd Caroli, "New Immigrant Women at Work: Italians and Jews in New York City, 1880–1905," *Journal of Ethnic Studies* 5, no. 4 (Winter 1978); Michael Weber, "Eastern Europeans in Steel Towns: A Comparative Analysis," *Journal of Urban History* 11, no. 3 (May 1985): 280–313. See also Judith E. Smith, *Family Connections: A History of Italian and Jewish Immigrant Lives in Providence, Rhode Island, 1900–1940* (Albany: State University of New York Press, 1985). And an invaluable early source is Margaret Byington, *Homestead: The Households of a Mill Town* (New York: Charities Press, 1910).

32. Schneiderman, *All for One*, 29.

33. Ibid., 30–31. Linda Gordon points out that between 1880 and 1930, single mothers lost their children to institutions more frequently than did two-parent families or single fathers. These mothers were caught in a double bind. If they worked outside the home, their children might be removed for truancy or lack of supervision. If they worked only at home, they could lose their children because of poverty, which produced other signs of child neglect: for example, malnutrition, improper clothing, and chronic disease. See Gordon, *Heroes of Their Own Lives: The Politics and History of Family Violence* (New York: Viking Penguin, 1988), 82–115.

34. Newman, "Letters to Hugh and Michael."

35. Clara Lemlich, "The Inside of a Shirtwaist Factory: An Appeal to Women Who Wear Choice and Beautiful Clothing," *Good Housekeeping* 54, no. 3 (March 1912): 367–69; Scheier, "Clara Lemlich Shavelson"; Kessner and Caroli, "New Immigrant Women"; Louise Odencrantz, *Italian Women in Industry: A Study of Conditions in New York City* (New York: Russell Sage Foundation, 1919), 18.

36. More, *Wage Earners' Budgets*, cited in Ewen, *Immigrant Women*, 102.

37. One interesting analysis of the role of the Socialist newspapers in the acculturation of Jewish immigrant women is Maxine Seller, "Defining Socialist Womanhood: The Woman's Page of the Jewish Daily Forward," in *American Jewish History* 76, no. 4 (June 1987): 416–38. See also Newman, "Letters to Hugh and Michael."

38. See Norma Fain Pratt, "Culture and Radical Politics: Yiddish Women Writers, 1890–1940," *American Jewish History* 70, no. 1 (September 1980): 68–90; Seller, "Defining Socialist Womanhood"; Newman, "Letters to Hugh and Michael."

39. Newman, "Letters to Hugh and Michael."

40. Jonas, interview by author; Book of Isaiah, 1955 translation, Jewish Publication Society of America.

41. Paula Hyman makes this point in her essay "Immigrant Women and Consumer Protest: The New York City Kosher Meat Boycott of 1902," *American Jewish History* 70, no. 1 (September 1980): 91–105. See also *New York Times*, May 13, 16, 17, 18, 23, 25, 1902; July 13–September 2, 1904; November 30–December 9, 1906; December 26, 1907–January 27, 1908. These sources also indicate that many of the women involved were the wives and mothers of garment workers.

42. *New York Times*, June 24, 25, 1908.

43. Information on meat protests in early Hasidism from a lecture by Prof. Yaffa Eliach, Brooklyn College, February 24, 1980.

44. *New York Times*, June 1, 1908.

45. Hyman, "Immigrant Women"; *New York Times*, May 13, 16, 17, 18, 20, 23, 24, 25, 1902.

46. Hyman, "Immigrant Women."

47. Ibid., 92.

48. Schneiderman, *All for One*, 29–30.

49. In "The Rent Strike in New York City, 1904–1980: The Evolution of a Social Movement," *Journal of Urban History* 10, no. 3 (May 1984): 235–58, Ronald Lawson estimates that seventeen thousand East Side residents lost their homes as a result of the construction of the Manhattan and Williamsburg bridges. See also Jenna Weissman Joselit, "The Landlord as Czar: Pre–World War I Tenant Activity," in *The Tenant Movement in New York City, 1904–1984*, ed. Ronald Lawson and Mark Naison (New Brunswick: Rutgers University Press, 1986), 39–50.

50. Newman, "Letters to Hugh and Michael"; *New York Times*, November 2, 25, December 3, 26, 1907.

51. *New York Times*, December 27, 1907.

52. *The Worker*, January 11, 1908.

53. *New York Times*, December 26, 27, 28, 29, 30, 1907; January 1, 2, 3, 6, 7, 9, 1908. See also *The Worker*, January 4, 11, 18, 1908.

CHAPTER I

1. Pauline Newman, "Letters to Hugh and Michael" (1951–69), Box 1, Newman Papers.

2. Pauline Newman, "Historic Notes on the Work of the New York Women's Trade Union League," n.d., Box 1, Newman Papers.

3. In *Daughters of the Shtetl: Work and Unionism in the Immigrant Generation* (Ithaca:

Cornell University Press, 1990), 122–31, Susan A. Glenn argues that the garment trades attracted ambitious young women because they provided opportunities to rise to relatively highly paid positions, unlike textiles or canning, the other trades that hired mostly women workers. She sees a link between that ambition and the high degree of unionization among women garment workers.

4. Clara Lemlich Shavelson to Morris Schappes, March 15, 1965, published in *Jewish Currents* 36, no. 10 (November 1982): 9–11.

5. Nancy Schrom Dye, *As Equals and as Sisters: Feminism, Unionism, and the Women's Trade Union League of New York* (Columbia: University of Missouri Press, 1980), 23.

6. Annie Marion MacLean, *Wage-Earning Women* (New York: Macmillan, 1910), 36, 61. See pp. 31–73 for analysis of the conditions among New York and Chicago garment workers during the summer and fall of 1907.

7. Clara Lemlich, *New York Call*, March 28, 1911; Clara Lemlich, "The Inside of a Shirtwaist Factory: An Appeal to Women Who Wear Choice and Beautiful Clothing," *Good Housekeeping* 54, no. 3 (March 1912): 367–69.

8. Clara Lemlich, "Remembering the Waistmakers' General Strike, 1909," *Jewish Currents*, November 1982; Newman, "Letters to Hugh and Michael."

9. Much has been written about the importance of women's colleges to the various social reform movements of the Progressive Era. Stephen Norwood makes a similar argument for high schools. In his study of the Boston telephone workers, Norwood notes that between 1900 and 1920, a girls' peer culture began to develop in high schools, in part because high school girls outnumbered boys by almost two to one. See Norwood, *Labor's Flaming Youth: Telephone Workers and Labor Militancy, 1878–1923* (Urbana: University of Illinois Press, 1990).

10. J. A. H. Dahme to PMN, July 13, 1906, Box 9, Newman Papers.

11. Newman, "Letters to Hugh and Michael"; Pauline Newman, interview by Barbara Wertheimer, New York, N.Y., November 1976; Pauline Newman résumé, n.d., Newman Papers.

12. Pauline Newman, interview by author, New York, N.Y., February 9, 1984; Newman, interview by Wertheimer.

13. Joan Morrison and Charlotte Fox Zabusky, eds., *American Mosaic* (New York: E. P. Dutton, 1980).

14. See Rose Schneiderman, *All for One* (New York: Paul S. Eriksson, 1967), 35–42, and Susan Porter Benson, "The Customers Ain't God: The Work Culture of Department Store Saleswomen, 1890–1940," in *Working-Class America*, ed. Michael Frisch and Daniel J. Walkowitz (Urbana: University of Illinois Press, 1983), 185–212.

15. Paula Scheier, "Clara Lemlich Shavelson: Fifty Years in Labor's Front Line," *Jewish Life*, November 1954. See also Glenn, *Daughters of the Shtetl*, 122–31.

16. Schneiderman, *All for One*, 48.

17. Ibid., 48–50.

18. Ibid.

19. Ibid.

20. Ricki Carole Myers Cohen, "Fannia Cohn and the International Ladies' Garment Workers' Union" (Ph.D. diss., University of Southern California, 1976), 11–21.

21. FMC to Selig Perlman, December 26, 1951, Box 5, Cohn Papers.

22. Information on the problems of organizing the white goods trade is located in Minutes of the Executive Board of the NYWTUL, February 28, August 22, and Novem-

ber 26, 27, 1907, Reel 1, Papers of the New York Women's Trade Union League, Tamiment Institute Library, New York University (hereafter cited as NYWTUL Papers); information on Cohn comes from Cohen, "Fannia Cohn," 11–21.

23. Schneiderman, *All for One*, 39–40.

24. Scheier, "Clara Lemlich Shavelson."

25. Mary Van Kleeck, *Working Girls in Evening Schools* (New York: Russell Sage Foundation, 1914), cited in Charlotte Baum, Paula Hyman, and Sonya Michel, *The Jewish Woman in America* (New York: New American Library, 1977), 129; Anzia Yezierska, *Hungry Hearts and Other Stories* (New York: Persea, 1985); MacLean, *Wage-Earning Women*, 52. There is little scholarship on working-class women's education during the early twentieth century. One excellent article is Maxine Seller, "The Education of Immigrant Women, 1900–1935," *Journal of Urban History* 4, no. 3 (May 1978): 307–30.

26. Pauline Newman, "The White Goods Workers' Strike," *Ladies' Garment Worker* 4, no. 3 (March 1913): 1–4.

27. Scheier, "Clara Lemlich Shavelson"; Pauline Newman, Fragments 1958–61, Box 1, Newman Papers.

28. Newman, interview by Wertheimer; Newman, interview in Morrison and Zabusky, *American Mosaic*.

29. Scheier, "Clara Lemlich Shavelson."

30. Louis Levine [Lewis Lorwin], *The Women's Garment Workers: A History of the International Ladies' Garment Workers' Union* (New York: B. W. Huebsch, 1924), 148–49.

31. This information is pieced together from Scheier, "Clara Lemlich Shavelson"; Dora Smorodin, interview by author, Maplewood, N.J., March 12, 1991; and Levine, *Women's Garment Workers*, 148–49.

32. Newman, interview by Wertheimer; Newman, "Letters to Hugh and Michael."

33. Ibid.

34. Schneiderman, *All for One*, 58–60.

35. Ibid., 73–77; Minutes of the NYWTUL Executive Board, February 24, March 24, 1905, Reel 1, NYWTUL Papers.

36. Dye, *As Equals and as Sisters*, 110–22.

37. Ibid.; Minutes of the NYWTUL Executive Board, January 25, 1906, Reel 1, NYWTUL Papers.

38. Newman, interview by Wertheimer.

39. Newman, interview by author. See also letters between the three women in Box 1, Newman Papers, and in Reel 4, O'Reilly Papers, and Reel 1 and File 18A, Rose Schneiderman Papers, both in Tamiment Institute Library, New York University.

40. Schneiderman, *All for One*, 83; Scheier, "Clara Lemlich Shavelson"; James Field to Fannia Cohn, July 13, 1914, Box 1, Cohn Papers.

41. Minutes of the NYWTUL Executive Board, February 24, March 24, May 5, August 25, September 24, October 26, 1905; January 25, February 29, March 29, April 26, June 28, August 1, September 12, November 22, December 20, 1906; February 28, April 24, June 27, July 25, August 22, September 26, November 26, 1907; January 28, 1908, NYWTUL Papers; Schneiderman, *All for One*, 83.

42. *New York Evening Journal*, July 15, 1907.

43. Ibid. See also Alice Kessler-Harris, "Rose Schneiderman," in *American Labor Leaders*, ed. Warren Van Tine and Melvyn Dubofsky (Urbana: University of Illinois Press, 1987), 160–84.

44. Minutes of the NYWTUL Executive Board, February 24, 1905–February 1, 1909, Reel 1, NYWTUL Papers.

45. Schneiderman, *All for One*, 84.

46. Ibid., 84–86.

47. Ibid.; Minutes of the NYWTUL Executive Board, November 26, 1907, Reel 1, NYWTUL Papers; Dye, *As Equals and as Sisters*, 71.

48. Schneiderman, *All for One*, 86; East Side Organizer's Report, Minutes of the NYWTUL Executive Board, August 25, October 27, 1908, Reel 1, NYWTUL Papers.

49. Minutes of the NYWTUL Executive Board, February 28, August 22, November 26, 27, 1907, Reel 1, NYWTUL Papers; Levine, *Women's Garment Workers*, 220.

50. Minutes of the NYWTUL Executive Committee, November 26, 27, 1907, Reel 1, NYWTUL Papers.

51. Levine, *Women's Garment Workers*, 220; Cohen, "Fannia Cohn," 36–43.

52. Scheier, "Clara Lemlich Shavelson."

53. Martha Schaffer, telephone interview by author, March 11, 1989; Joel Schaffer, Evelyn Velson, and Julia Velson, interview by author, Oakland, Calif., September 9, 1992.

54. Scheier, "Clara Lemlich Shavelson."

55. Clara Lemlich Shavelson, interview by Martha and Joel Schaffer, Los Angeles, Calif., February 2, 1974.

CHAPTER 2

1. Mary Brown Sumner, "The Spirit of the Strikers," *The Survey*, January 22, 1910. The strike has been called variously the "uprising" of 20,000, 30,000, or 40,000 women. See Louis Levine [Lewis Lorwin], *The Women's Garment Workers* (New York: B. W. Huebsch, 1924), chapter titled "The Uprising of the Twenty Thousand"; Meredith Tax, *The Rising of the Women: Feminist Solidarity and Class Conflict, 1880–1917* (New York: Monthly Review Press, 1980), chapter titled "Uprising of the Thirty Thousand"; and *New York Call*, November 27, 1909, story under the headline "Strike of 40,000."

2. For information on the many women's strikes of the period, read the WTUL publication *Life and Labor*, which covered them all in some detail; Tamiment Institute Library, New York University, or Schlesinger Library, Radcliffe College. The magazine *The Survey* (1909–14) also has good coverage of most of the strikes. The 1913 Brooklyn strike is covered by the *Ladies' Garment Worker*. See Pauline Newman, "The White Goods Workers' Strike," *Ladies' Garment Worker* 4, no. 3 (March 1913): 1–4. On the Chicago strike see also Mari Jo Buhle, *Women and American Socialism, 1870–1920* (Urbana: University of Illinois Press, 1981), 194–98. On the Kalamazoo strike see Karen M. Mason, "Feeling the Pinch: The Kalamazoo Corset Makers' Strike of 1912," in *To Toil the Livelong Day: America's Women at Work, 1780–1980*, ed. Carol Groneman and Mary Beth Norton (Ithaca: Cornell University Press, 1987), 141–60. On the 1915 Chicago strike see *Chicago Day Book*, cited in Winifred Carsel, *A History of the Chicago Ladies' Garment Workers' Union* (Chicago: Normandie House, 1940), and Ricki Carole Myers Cohen, "Fannia Cohn and the International Ladies' Garment Workers' Union" (Ph.D. diss., University of Southern California, 1976).

On the Lawrence Textile Strike of 1912, which is not discussed here but represents a key example of working women's activism in that period, see Ardis Cameron, "Bread and Roses Revisited: Women's Culture and Working-Class Activism in the Lawrence Strike of 1912," in *Women, Work and Protest: A Century of U.S. Women's Labor History*, ed. Ruth Milkman (London: Routledge and Kegan Paul, 1985), 42–62.

3. Gladys Boone, *The Women's Trade Union Leagues* (New York: Columbia University Press, 1942), 112–14.

4. Mildred Moore, "A History of the Women's Trade Union League of Chicago" (M.A. thesis, University of Chicago, 1915), cited in Diane Kirkby, "The Wage-Earning Woman and the State: The National Women's Trade Union League and Protective Labor Legislation, 1903–1923," *Labor History* 28, no. 1 (Winter 1987): 54–74.

5. *New York Call*, December 29, 1909.

6. Pauline Newman, "From the Battlefield—Some Phases of the Cloakmakers' Strike in Cleveland," *Life and Labor*, October 1911.

7. Left-wing and labor movement sources have emphasized the strike's importance as a catalyst for unionizing the garment industry. It is often referred to as the "spark" that set off the strike of sixty thousand cloakmakers the following year and paved the way for "protocolism" in the industry. Such accounts have rarely placed the strike on a continuum of working-class women's activism, and they have ignored or discounted the significance of cross-class women's alliances. See Irving Howe, *World of Our Fathers* (New York: Harcourt Brace Jovanovich, 1976), 302–5; Melvyn Dubofsky, *When Workers Organize* (Amherst: University of Massachusetts Press, 1968); Levine, *Women's Garment Workers*, 144–67. As early as 1923, Levine noted about the strike that its "hundreds of leaders have remained unnamed and unrecorded" (p. 157).

More recent feminist-Socialist accounts have stressed the importance of the cross-class women's alliances forged during the strike; they have also examined conflicts of interest between middle- and upper-class allies of the strikers and those who saw the strike as an opportunity to organize for Socialism. Feminist historians of the strike have also raised the important question of the power differential between men and women in the garment unions. Men's power in the labor movement, rooted in domination both of higher-paid jobs and unions' executive boards, strongly affected the choices made by women workers during and after the strike. It also shaped much subsequent analysis of the strike and of women's labor organizing in general. See Tax, *Rising of the Women*; Buhle, *Women and American Socialism*; Nancy Schrom Dye, *As Equals and as Sisters: Feminism, Unionism, and the Women's Trade Union League of New York* (Columbia: University of Missouri Press, 1980); Charlotte Baum, Paula Hyman, and Sonya Michel, *The Jewish Woman in America* (New York: New American Library, 1977); Joan Jensen and Sue Davidson eds., *A Needle, a Bobbin, and a Strike* (Philadelphia: Temple University Press, 1984).

8. Boone, *Women's Trade Union Leagues*, 112–14.

9. Sumner, "Spirit of the Strikers."

10. NYWTUL Secretary's Report, September 15, 1909, Reel 1, NYWTUL Papers.

11. Clara Lemlich, "The Inside of a Shirtwaist Factory: An Appeal to Women Who Wear Choice and Beautiful Clothing," *Good Housekeeping* 54, no. 3 (March 1912): 367–69.

12. Levine, *Women's Garment Workers*, 150–51.

13. Sumner, "Spirit of the Strikers"; Rose Schneiderman and Leonora O'Reilly,

"Report to the NYWTUL Executive Board, October 20, 1909," Reel 1, NYWTUL Papers; *New York Call*, November 13–19, 30, December 4–8, 29, 1909; Levine, *Women's Garment Workers*, 149–54.

14. Levine, *Women's Garment Workers*, 151; Sumner, "Spirit of the Strikers."

15. Minutes of the NYWTUL Executive Board, October 20, 1909, and Report to the Executive Board, October 20, 1909, both in Reel 1, NYWTUL Papers.

16. Clara Lemlich Shavelson, "Remembering the Waistmakers General Strike, 1909," *Jewish Currents*, November 1982. *New York Call*, November 23, 1909.

17. *New York Call*, November 27, 1909.

18. Minutes of Special Meeting of the NYWTUL Executive Board, November 13, 1909, and Secretary's Report, November 17, 1909, both in Reel 1, NYWTUL Papers; *New York Call*, November 13, 1909; Levine, *Women's Garment Workers*, 153; Clara Lemlich Shavelson, interview by Martha and Joel Schaffer, Los Angeles, Calif., February 2, 1974.

19. *New York Call*, November 23, 24, 25, 27, December 3, 1909; postcard, n.d. (content indicates that it was written right after the strike's end), in the possession of Martha Schaffer.

20. *New York Call*, November 30, December 4, 5, 6, 7, 8, 29, 1909.

21. Ibid., December 5, 7, 8, 1909.

22. Ibid.

23. *New York Call*, December 29, 1909. For detailed day-to-day coverage of arrests and skirmishes at different shops, see the *New York Times*, November 5, 6, and 14, 1909, and just about daily from November 23, 1909, through January 18, 1910. Coverage then continued intermittently through February 11, 1910.

24. Minutes of the NYWTUL Membership Meeting, April 20, June 15, 1910, Reel 1, NYWTUL Papers.

25. See Tax, *Rising of the Women*, 230–40. Tax discusses the undemocratic structure of the union and the ways that the union-appointed arbitrators undermined the women workers' control over the strike.

26. See letters between Pauline Newman and Rose Schneiderman, 1909–14, File 18A, Rose Schneiderman Collection, Tamiment Institute Library, New York University (hereafter cited as Schneiderman Papers); see also articles by Pauline Newman in the WTUL publication *Life and Labor* and in *Progressive Woman*, *Socialist Woman*, and the *Ladies' Garment Worker*, 1910–14.

27. See Pauline Newman, interview by Barbara Wertheimer, New York, N.Y., November 1976; Newman-Schneiderman letters, File 18A, Schneiderman Papers; Michael Owen, telephone interview by author, September 27, 1992; Leon Stein, interview by author, Cranbury, N.J., October 19, 1988.

28. Pauline Newman to Rose Schneiderman, April 2, 21, 1910.

29. PMN to RS, August 17, September 13, 1910.

30. PMN to RS, September 20, October 19, 1910, June 27, 1911.

31. *New York Call*, March 28, 1911.

32. *New York Times*, April 3, 1911.

33. PMN to RS, March 28, April n.d., April 12, 17, 1911.

34. PMN to RS, April 12, 17, 1911.

35. Ibid.

36. Newman, interview by Wertheimer; Minutes of the NYWTUL Executive Board, February 15, 1911, NYWTUL Papers; Helen Marot, "A Woman's Strike—An Appreciation of the Shirtwaist Makers of New York," *Proceedings of the Academy of Political Science of the City of New York*, October 1910.

37. Secretary's Report to the NYWTUL Executive Board, Secretary's Report, February 15, April 27, September 10 (?), 1911, Reel 1, NYWTUL Papers.

38. Ibid.; Pauline Newman, interview by author, New York, N.Y., February 9, 1984.

39. Minutes of the NYWTUL Executive Board, June 22, 1911, Reel 1, NYWTUL Papers.

40. PMN to RS, August 9, 1911; Newman, "From the Battlefield."

41. Ibid.

42. Newman, "From the Battlefield."

43. PMN to RS, October 2, November 7, 14, December 1, 1911.

44. PMN to RS, n.d. (but, from content, likely to be fall 1911), November 9, 21, December 26, 1911, January 16, 1912.

45. PMN to RS, January 16, 1912.

46. PMN to RS, February 22, January 16, 1912.

47. PMN to RS, November 9, 1911, January 16, 1912.

48. PMN to RS, November 21, December 26, 1911.

49. PMN to RS, February 9, 1912.

50. PMN to RS, February 22, 1912.

51. PMN to RS, n.d. (probably fall 1911).

52. PMN to RS, February 22, 1912, Newman Papers. The most complete analysis of the strike can be found in Mason, "Feeling the Pinch."

53. PMN to RS, March 5, April 14, July 11, 1912, Schneiderman Papers.

54. Josephine Casey, "Letter from Prison," *Detroit Times*, May 4, 1912, reprinted in *Out of the Sweatshop*, ed. Leon Stein (New York: New York Times Book Co., 1977), 129–31.

55. See Kathy Peiss, *Cheap Amusements: Working Women and Leisure in Turn-of-the-Century New York* (Philadelphia: Temple University Press, 1986), 50–51. See also Sarah Eisenstein, *Give Us Bread But Give Us Roses: Working Women's Consciousness in the United States, 1890 to the First World War* (London: Routledge and Kegan Paul), 99–101, for her analysis of Victorian literature about work and female respectability. The quote is from Mary A. Laselle and Katherine E. Wiley, *Vocations for Girls* (New York: Houghton Mifflin, 1913), 32, cited in Eisenstein, *Give Us Bread*, 100.

56. Peiss, *Cheap Amusements*, 51. The cigar maker Peiss quotes testified before the New York State Bureau of Labor Statistics in 1885. Peiss also cites literature from the first and second decades of the twentieth century dealing with the same problem.

57. Leonora O'Reilly, *Life and Labor*, July 1912; Levine, *Women's Garment Workers*, 221–22; Pauline M. Newman, "Letters to Hugh and Michael" (1951–69), Box 1, Newman Papers; PMN to RS, April 4, June 9, July 11, 1912, Schneiderman Papers.

58. PMN to RS, July 11, 1912.

59. See Karen Mason, "Feeling the Pinch."

60. PMN to RS, February 22, March 5, 1912.

61. See PMN to RS, February 9, 1912; *Ladies' Garment Worker*, 1914–18; Newman, interview by author.

62. There is a good deal of material on the women's trades strike of 1913. See

Levine, *Women's Garment Workers*, 218–32; Rose Schneiderman, *All for One* (New York: Paul S. Eriksson, 1967), 104–10; Newman, "White Goods Workers' Strike"; *New York Times*, May 27, 1911; January 2, 6, 8–16, 18–20, 22, 29, 1913.

63. Minutes of the NYWTUL Executive Board, February 15, April 27, May 13, 25, 1913, Reel 2, NYWTUL Papers.

64. *New York Times*, January 6, 1913.

65. See Levine, *Women's Garment Workers*, 225–26; see also Minutes of the NYWTUL Executive Board, February 15, April 27, May 13, 25, 1913, Reel 2, NYWTUL Papers.

66. *New York Times*, January 19, 20, 1913.

67. Ibid.

68. Ibid. See also Baum, Hyman, and Michel, *Jewish Woman in America*, 146–48.

69. Newman, "White Goods Workers' Strike"; *New York Times*, January 9, 10, 1913.

70. *New York Times*, January 14, 16, 1913.

71. Ibid., January 29, 30, 1913.

72. Ibid., January 14, 16, 1913.

73. Ibid., January 18, 1913.

74. Ibid., January 18, 22, 1913.

75. Ibid., January 22, 1913.

76. Newman, "White Goods Workers Strike."

77. Ibid.

78. FMC to Florence Miller, April 16, 1928, Box 4, Cohn Papers.

79. *Chicago Day Book*, cited in Carsel, *A History of the Chicago Ladies' Garment Workers' Union*.

80. See Cohen, "Fannia Cohn," 96–99. Cohen's January 10, 1974 interview with Mary Goff is cited on p. 97. See also FMC to "Dear Friend," n.d., Box 5, Cohn Papers.

CHAPTER 3

1. Fannie Zinsher to Morris Schappes, February 29, 1948, *Jewish Currents*, September 1975.

2. *New York Evening Journal*, July 14, 1907.

3. Extracts from Address Delivered by Miss Rose Schneiderman before the Women's Industrial Conference, January 20, 1926, Papers of the U.S. Women's Bureau, Sophia Smith Collection, Smith College, Northampton, Mass. (hereafter cited as U.S. Women's Bureau Papers).

4. See Ellen Carol Dubois, "Working Women, Class Relations, and Suffrage Militance: Harriot Stanton Blatch and the New York Woman Suffrage Movement, 1894–1909," *Journal of American History* 74, no. 1 (June 1987): 34–58.

5. Fannia Cohn, "Vote for Woman Suffrage" and "Complete Equality between Men and Women," *Ladies' Garment Worker*, November and December 1917.

6. Olympia Brown, speech to the 1899 convention of the National American Woman Suffrage Association, quoted in Aileen Kraditor, ed., *Up from the Pedestal: Selected Writings in the History of American Feminism* (New York: Quadrangle Books, 1968), 257–59.

For further examples of racist and anti-immigrant suffrage justifications see Kraditor, *Up from the Pedestal*, 252–65. As Kraditor's selection of documents illustrates, racist and xenophobic justifications for suffrage were not restricted to regional groups but were also incorporated into the literature of the National American Woman Suffrage Association before the turn of the century.

7. Kraditor, *Up from the Pedestal*. See also Meredith Tax, *The Rising of the Women: Feminist Solidarity and Class Conflict, 1880–1917* (New York: Monthly Review Press, 1980), 168–69.

8. Proceedings of the Second Biennial National WTUL Convention, 1909, WTUL Papers, Arthur and Elizabeth Schlesinger Library, Radcliffe College, Cambridge, Mass. (hereafter cited as WTUL Papers). Given that these comments were made at an all-women's gathering, the gender of Schneiderman's language is interesting.

9. Minutes of the NYWTUL Executive Board, April 20, 1910, Reel 1, NYWTUL Papers. In *Rising of the Women*, 223–27, Meredith Tax offers one of the only analyses I've found of racial relations among black and white women in the early-twentieth-century garment trades. For information on Schneiderman's later attempts to organize black women workers, see NYWTUL Annual Reports, 1921–38, Reels 2, 3, and 4, NYWTUL Papers.

10. Clara Lemlich, "The Inside of a Shirtwaist Factory," *Good Housekeeping* 54 (March 1912): 369.

11. Mary H. Blewett, *Men, Women, and Work: Class, Gender, and Protest in the New England Shoe Industry, 1780–1910* (Urbana: University of Illinois Press, 1988), 172–79, 191–220, and Blewett, *We Will Rise in Our Might: Workingwomen's Voices from Nineteenth-Century New England* (Ithaca: Cornell University Press, 1991), 122–39. Blewett traces the ambivalent relationship between women shoe workers and middle-class suffragists/reformers in post–Civil War New England and the debate over woman suffrage among late-nineteenth-century trade unionists.

12. See Dubois, "Working Women, Class Relations, and Suffrage Militance"; Aileen Kraditor, *The Ideas of the Woman Suffrage Movement* (New York: Norton, 1965); Kraditor, *Up from the Pedestal*; William O'Neill, *Everyone Was Brave: The Rise and Fall of American Feminism* (Chicago: Quadrangle Books, 1969).

13. "Florence Kelley on Working Girls," address to the Second Annual Convention of the Massachusetts Woman Suffrage Association; see also "Working Woman's Need of the Ballot," speech delivered to the 1898 National American Woman Suffrage Association convention, both in Kraditor, *Up from the Pedestal*, 273–76. See also Kraditor, *Ideas of the Woman Suffrage Movement*. On p. 139 (text and n. 22), Kraditor quotes several of Kelley's less enlightened comments on immigrant working women.

14. Lemlich, "Inside of a Shirtwaist Factory"; Pauline Newman, interview by author, New York, N.Y., February 9, 1984.

15. Newman, interview by author; Pauline Newman, interview by Barbara Wertheimer, New York, N.Y., November 1976.

16. See Dubois, "Working Women, Class Relations, and Suffrage Militance."

17. Ibid. See also Tax, *Rising of the Women*, 170.

18. Dubois, "Working Women, Class Relations, and Suffrage Militance." See also Tax, *Rising of the Women*, 169–71, and "Miss Rose Schneiderman, Gifted Young Lecturer," leaflet of the American Suffragettes, n.d., Reel 2, Schneiderman Papers.

19. *Socialist Woman*, May 1908.

20. Dubois, "Working Women, Class Relations, and Suffrage Militance." See also Frances Squire Potter to RS, April 24, 1910, and Harriot Stanton Blatch to RS, May 2, 1910, Reel 1, Schneiderman Papers.

21. *New York Call*, November 18, 1909.

22. See *New York Call* "Women's Page" November through December 1909, particularly November 18 and 19 and December 6, 13, 14, and 20. Though there is no record of how she voted, Newman's role in organizing the December 1909 conference was noted in the introduction to her May 2, 1914 article on Socialist suffragism for the *New York Call*. Block quote is from Tax, *Rising of the Women*, 191.

23. Minutes of the Wage Earners' League for Woman Suffrage, March 22, 1911, O'Reilly Papers. In *Rising of the Women*, 171–78, Meredith Tax offers one of the only commentaries on the emergence of the Wage Earners' League.

24. Mari Jo Buhle, *Women and American Socialism, 1870–1920* (Urbana: University of Illinois Press, 1981), 233–34.

25. Jessie Ashley, "Relation of Suffragism to Working-Class Women," *Women's Journal*, June 24, 1911, excerpted in Kraditor, *Up from the Pedestal*, 278–82.

26. Paula Scheier, "Clara Lemlich Shavelson: Fifty Years in Labor's Front Line," *Jewish Life*, November 1954.

27. Mary Beard to Leonora O'Reilly, January 1, 1912, cited in Tax, *Rising of the Women*, 177.

28. Beard to O'Reilly, July 21, 1912, cited in Tax, *Rising of the Women*, 177–78.

29. Martha Schaffer, telephone interview by author, March 11, 1989.

30. Newman, interview by Wertheimer; Scheier, "Clara Lemlich Shavelson."

31. Max Fruchter to Rose Schneiderman, March 5, 1911, Reel 1, Schneiderman Papers.

32. Rose Schneiderman, *All for One* (New York: Paul S. Eriksson, 1967), 121–22.

33. Minutes of the Wage Earners' League for Woman Suffrage, March 22, 1911, O'Reilly Papers.

34. "Bill for Suffrage Week," n.d., O'Reilly Papers.

35. Ibid.

36. Newman recalled the vividness and dramatic power of O'Reilly's speaking style (Newman, interview by author); Constance D. Leupp commented on Lemlich's speaking style in her article "30,000 Girls Strike in New York City," *The Survey*, December 18, 1909.

37. "Senators vs. Working Women" (handbill of the Wage Earners' League for Woman Suffrage), Reel 12, O'Reilly Papers.

38. All quotes from this meeting were taken from a Wage Earners' League pamphlet called *Senators vs. Working Women* that contains full versions of all the "commonsense" answers to specific state senators' arguments. This pamphlet became the most popular of the league's publications. In the Wage Earners' League for Woman Suffrage collection, a subset of the O'Reilly Papers.

39. Ibid.

40. Ibid.

41. Ibid.

42. Transcript of Clara Lemlich's speech, April 22, 1912, in ibid.

43. "Senators vs. Working Women" (handbill for the April 22 meeting) and *Senators vs. Working Women* (pamphlet), both by the Wage Earners' League for Woman Suffrage, O'Reilly Papers.

44. Schneiderman, *All for One*, 121–23; PMN to RS, July 26, 1912, Schneiderman Papers.

45. Schneiderman, *All for One*, 121–23; M. Sherwood to Harriet Taylor Upton, July 15, 1912, Reel 1, Schneiderman Papers.

46. Schneiderman, *All for One*, 121–23; Nancy Schrom Dye, *As Equals and as Sisters: Feminism, Unionism, and the Women's Trade Union League of New York* (Columbia: University of Missouri Press, 1980), 122–39.

47. *New York Call*, May 2, 1914.

48. Newman, interview by Wertheimer.

49. PMN to RS, n.d., File 18A, Schneiderman Papers.

50. PMN to RS, n.d., File 18A, Schneiderman Papers; Mary Beard to Leonora O'Reilly, July 21, 1912, O'Reilly Papers. O'Reilly returned to the helm of the Industrial Section in 1915.

51. Minutes of the NYWTUL Executive Board, December 29, 1914, Reel 2, NYWTUL Papers.

52. *The Message*, December 25, 1914.

53. Pauline Newman, *New York Call*, May 2, 1914.

54. Buhle, *Women and American Socialism*, 234–35.

55. Minutes of the NYWTUL Executive Board, July 12, 1915, Reel 2, NYWTUL Papers.

56. Ibid.; ibid., November 19, 1915, Reel 2, NYWTUL Papers; Dye, *As Equals and as Sisters*, 136–38.

57. Schneiderman, *All for One*, 110–17; RS to PMN, February 6, 1916, and August 6, 1917, Newman Papers. RS to Benjamin Schlesinger, February 6, 1916, and to Abe Baroff, December 1, 1916, Reel 1, Schneiderman Papers.

58. Fannia Cohn, "Vote for Woman Suffrage" and "Complete Equality between Men and Women," *Ladies' Garment Worker*, November and December 1917.

59. Cohn, "Vote for Woman Suffrage."

60. "Suffrage Correspondence Course," Suffrage Papers, Reel 12, O'Reilly Papers.

61. "Letter Series," Suffrage Papers, Reel 12, O'Reilly Papers.

62. Schneiderman, *All for One*, 124–25.

63. "For Congress, 18th Congressional District, Vote for Pauline Newman" (campaign handbill and poster), and Newman, "Fragments toward an Autobiography, October 11, 1958," both in Box 9, Newman Papers; Newman, interview by Wertheimer; *New York Times*, July 12, 1929.

64. Rose Schneiderman, "WTUL Legislative Efforts" (typescript for a radio speech), June 1955, Reel 2, Schneiderman Papers. See also Nancy Cott, *The Grounding of Modern Feminism* (New Haven: Yale University Press, 1987). On p. 105, Cott notes that the way women voted varied from region to region, but there is some evidence that women tended to improve the chances of radical parties and candidates in New York.

65. Schneiderman, "WTUL Legislative Efforts."

66. *New York Times*, May 31, 1920; Schneiderman, *All for One*, 146–48.

67. Schneiderman, *All for One*, 146–48.

68. Ibid., 130–33; *New York Times*, March 7, 1919.

69. *New York Times*, May 31, 1920; RS to Margaret Dreier Robins, March 10, 1919, Reel 1, Schneiderman Papers; Schneiderman, *All for One*, 146–48; Cott, *Grounding of Modern Feminism*, 65.

70. See Roslyn Terborg-Penn, "Discontented Black Feminists," in *Decades of Discontent*, ed. Joan Jensen and Lois Scharf (Albuquerque: University of New Mexico Press, 1983); see also Cott, *Grounding of Modern Feminism*.

71. *New York Times*, May 30, 1920; Frank Crosswaith to RS, April 7, 1949, Schneiderman Papers; WTUL Biennial Convention Proceedings, 1909–29, WTUL Papers; NYWTUL Annual Reports, 1922–40 and 1944–49, NYWTUL Papers. Speech before Harlem Labor Committee, 1939, Box 9, Cohn Papers; correspondence with A. Philip Randolph, Boxes 3–5, Cohn Papers.

CHAPTER 4

1. See Dee Ann Montgomery, "Miller, Frieda Segelke"; Elizabeth Payne Moore, "Dreier, Mary"; Charles H. Trout, "Perkins, Frances"; and Edward T. James, "Anderson, Mary," all in *Notable American Women: The Modern Period*, ed. Barbara Sicherman and Carol Hurd Green (Cambridge: Belknap Press of Harvard University Press, 1980). See also David Brody, "Swartz, Maud O'Farrel," in *Notable American Women: A Biographical Dictionary*, ed. Edward T. James, Janet Wilson James, and Paul S. Boyer, 3 vols. (Cambridge: Belknap Press of Harvard University Press, 1971), 3:413–15. There are, of course, many sources on Eleanor Roosevelt. This account draws most heavily from two: Joseph P. Lash, *Eleanor and Franklin* (New York: Signet, 1971), and Blanche Wiesen Cook, *Eleanor Roosevelt, Volume One, 1884–1933* (New York: Viking, 1992).

2. Rose Schneiderman, "Women's Role in Labor Legislation," n.d., Reel 2, Schneiderman Papers.

3. See Nancy Schrom Dye, *As Equals and as Sisters: Feminism, the Labor Movement, and the Women's Trade Union League of New York* (Columbia: University of Missouri Press, 1980), 140–61, and Alice Kessler-Harris, *Out to Work: A History of Wage-Earning Women in the United States* (New York: Oxford University Press, 1982), 205–14, for somewhat different interpretations of the NYWTUL and the early years of its legislative activity.

There is a burgeoning literature on middle-class women's activism and the development of the early-twentieth-century American welfare state. Much of this scholarship is concerned with the way that the arguments for and the conceptualization of the state's responsibilities to dependent women and children reinforced a gendered conception of citizenship that limited American women's political power after they got the vote. See *The Politics of Social Policy in the United States*, ed. Margaret Weir, Ann Shola Orloff, and Theda Skocpol (Princeton: Princeton University Press, 1988); Mimi Abramovitz, *Regulating the Lives of Women: Social Welfare Policy from Colonial Times to the Present* (Boston: South End Press, 1988); and Carole Pateman, "The Patriarchal Welfare State," in *Democracy and the Welfare State*, ed. Amy Gutmann (Princeton: Princeton University Press, 1988), 231–61. For an overview of the new scholarship see Linda Gordon, "The New Feminist Scholarship on the Welfare State," in *Women, the State, and Welfare*, ed. Linda Gordon (Madison: University of Wisconsin Press, 1990), 9–35.

Of particular relevance to the analysis offered in this chapter is Gwendolyn Mink, "The Lady and the Tramp: Gender, Race and the Origins of the American Welfare State," in Gordon, *Women, the State, and Welfare*, 92–123. Mink argues that the early-twentieth-century U.S. welfare state can be distinguished from its European counterparts in that the European governments' social policies were targeted at a basically gender-neutral worker-citizen while U.S. policies were targeted at a citizen-mother. She points to a persistence of the idea of republican motherhood posited by Linda Kerber—the notion that "motherhood . . . held the key to vigor in the citizenry"—and argues that middle-class reformers played both on that linkage and on fear of unassimilable new immigrant groups to create a consensus for social welfare programs that "socialized motherhood." Mink concludes that "the gender-biased social welfare innovations of the pre–New Deal period tackled problems of poverty through a focus on dependent motherhood and sought solutions to dilemmas of ethnic and racial diversity in the regulation of motherhood" (114).

4. Gordon, "New Feminist Scholarship."

5. As Linda Gordon has noted, working-class women "actually gained . . . power from it, because they could use different systems against each other—for example, the welfare system against domestic male supremacy." Ibid., p. 16. Carole Pateman makes similar points in "The Patriarchal Welfare State."

6. See Mink, "Lady and the Tramp"; Virginia Sapiro, "The Gender Basis of American Social Policy"; Gordon, "New Feminist Scholarship"; and Barbara J. Nelson, "The Origins of the Two-Channel Welfare State," all in Gordon, *Women, the State, and Welfare*.

7. Diane Kirkby, "The Wage-Earning Woman and the State: The National Women's Trade Union League and Protective Labor Legislation, 1903–1923," *Labor History* 28, no. 1 (Winter 1987): 54–74. See also NYWTUL Annual Reports, 1917–55, Reels 2, 3, 4, NYWTUL Papers.

8. Mink, "Lady and the Tramp."

9. The literature on the NWP and the struggle over an Equal Rights Amendment is voluminous. The sources consulted for the ERA section of this chapter include the NYWTUL Papers, 1921–49 (Reels 8, 9, 10, 11, and 12); Elizabeth Faulkner Baker, *Protective Labor Legislation* (New York: Columbia University Press, 1925); J. Stanley Lemons, *The Woman Citizen* (Chicago: University of Illinois Press, 1973); Nancy Cott, *The Grounding of Modern Feminism* (New Haven: Yale University Press, 1987); Philip Foner, *Women and the American Labor Movement* (New York: Free Press, 1980); and Sybil Lipschultz, "Mischievous Equality: Women, Protection, and Equal Rights," paper presented at the NYU Comparative Social History Colloquium, October 30, 1986.

10. In *The Rising of the Women: Feminist Solidarity and Class Conflict, 1880–1917* (New York: Monthly Review Press, 1980), Meredith Tax argues, correctly, that "the women who built the WTUL . . . made it possible for women to do trade union organizing as a career, but with this possibility came careerism. Thus, along with the development of trade unionism among women to the point where it could sustain professional organizers, came the development of the woman labor leader—never a complete equal in the labor aristocracy because she was a woman, but nevertheless able to find her place in its ranks" (122).

That accurately describes the career trajectories of Schneiderman and Newman. But while Tax sees the conservative influence of the AFL as the determining force behind this development, I believe that the involvement of relatively powerful middle- and upper-class women in the League was what cemented their status as "women labor leaders."

11. Alice Kessler-Harris has examined some of the ways in which Schneiderman's recasting of her image in the 1930s diminished her effectiveness as a labor leader. See Kessler-Harris, "Rose Schneiderman," in *American Labor Leaders*, ed. Warren Van Tine and Melvyn Dubofksy (Urbana: University of Illinois Press, 1987). In his Ph.D.

dissertation, "Solidarity Forever: Rose Schneiderman and the Women's Trade Union League" (University of Delaware, 1978), Gary Endelman analyzed the harm that Schneiderman's waffling on the CIO did to the WTUL in the late 1930s and 1940s.

12. Rose Schneiderman to Paul, Alice, Florence, Hilda, and Maud, n.d. (obviously written after the 1914 election), Box 5, Newman Papers.

13. In *Madam Secretary, Frances Perkins* (Boston: Houghton Mifflin, 1976), George Martin recounts Perkin's experience of the fire (pp. 84–86); Leon Stein, ed., *Out of the Sweatshop: The Struggle for Industrial Democracy* (New York: New York Times Book Co., 1977), includes a series of eyewitness accounts of the fire (pp. 188–201), including Perkins's "Address, Fiftieth Anniversary Memorial Meeting, March 25, 1961" (pp. 200–201). The fiftieth anniversary meeting was held on the corner where the fire took place.

14. Frances Perkins, "Not in Vain," in Stein, *Out of the Sweatshop*, 200.

15. *The Survey*, April 8, 1911; Martin, *Madame Secretary*, 87–88; Margaret Dreier Robins to RS, June 14, 1943, Reel 1, Schneiderman Papers.

16. Frances Perkins, *The Roosevelt I Knew* (New York: Viking Press, 1946), 22.

17. Schneiderman told of her lobbying experience on the twelve-hour bill in "Senators vs. Working Women" (handbill by the Wage Earners' League), Reel 12, O'Reilly Papers.

18. Testimony of Helen Marot, *Fourth Report of the New York State Factory Investigating Commission*, vol. 5 (Albany: J. B. Lyons Printers, 1915).

19. Testimony of Miss Pauline M. Newman, ibid., 2868–71.

20. Ibid.

21. Even legislators who supported minimum-wage legislation intended, says Alice Kessler-Harris, "to preserve morality for those destined to earn but not . . . to tempt those in families to live outside them." Minimum-wage laws "limited fantasy to the price of survival and held open the door of ambition to a meager independence." Kessler-Harris, *A Woman's Wage: Historical Meanings and Social Consequences* (Lexington: University Press of Kentucky, 1990), 112–13.

22. Newman testimony, *Fourth Report*, 2868–71; Rose Schneiderman, "Women's Role in Labor Legislation," n.d., Reel 2, Schneiderman Papers; Baker, *Protective Labor Legislation*, 169–71.

23. Baker, *Protective Labor Legislation*, 154–57; Martin, *Madame Secretary*, 141–50.

24. Pauline Newman, "Of Maud Swartz" (handwritten tribute), Box 6, Newman Papers; Rose Schneiderman, *All for One* (New York: Paul S. Eriksson, 1967), 181–82.

25. Ibid.

26. Schneiderman, *All for One*, 181–82.

27. Information on Maud Swartz is scarce. See David Brody, "Swartz, Maud O'Farrel." In *All for One*, Rose Schneiderman mentions Swartz frequently. *American Federationist*, August 1929, reports on her activities surrounding the Workmen's Compensation Law of New York State. Her obituaries in the *New York Times* and *New York Herald Tribune*, February 23, 1937, summarize her major activities. Information on her personal relationship with Schneiderman is gleaned from Newman, interview by author, and from letters in the Schneiderman Papers, the Newman Papers, and the Eleanor Roosevelt Papers, Franklin Delano Roosevelt Presidential Library, Hyde Park, N.Y. (hereafter cited as Eleanor Roosevelt Papers).

28. Brody, "Swartz, Maud O'Farrel."

29. Newman, interview by Wertheimer; Newman, interview by author; Elisabeth Burger, interview by author, New York, N.Y., December 15, 1987; *Christian Science Monitor*, August 2, 1938; *New York World Telegram*, n.d., clipping file, Box 15, Frieda S. Miller Papers, Schlesinger Library, Radcliffe College, Cambridge, Mass. (hereafter cited as Miller Papers).

30. Burger, interviews by author, December 15, 1987, and December 21, 1993.

31. Newman, interview by Wertheimer.

32. RS to PMN, August 11, 1917, Box 5, Folder 78, Newman Papers.

33. Ibid., October 16, November 2, 14, 1918, Box 5, Newman Papers.

34. *First Annual Report of the Director: Women in Industry Service, Organized July 1918* (Washington, D.C.: June 30, 1919), in Box 71, Mary Van Kleeck Papers, Sophia Smith Collection, Smith College, Northampton, Mass. (hereafter cited as Van Kleeck Papers); Schneiderman, *All for One*, 126.

35. Ibid.

36. Biographical information and the seemingly authoritative spelling of Nell Swartz's last name were taken from her obituary in the *New York Times*, March 6, 1952. It is difficult to track down sure information on her. Sometimes it seems as though there are two women—one named Schwartz and the other Swartz—but there was in fact only one Nell Swartz or Schwartz. Perhaps she anglicized the spelling to hide her Jewish background.

37. *Revolutionary Radicalism Part One: Subversive Movements*, 2 vols. (Albany: J. B. Lyons Printers, 1920), 1032, 1041, 1052, 1102, 1989; Schneiderman, *All for One*, 128–29; Gladys Boone, *The Women's Trade Union Leagues* (New York: Columbia University Press, 1942), 134–35.

38. Baker, *Protective Labor Legislation*, 178. See also Schneiderman, *All for One*, 222–23; Robert Caro, *The Power Broker: Robert Moses and the Fall of New York* (New York: Vintage, 1975), 111; Elisabeth Israels Perry, *Belle Moskowitz: Feminine Politics and the Exercise of Power in the Age of Al Smith* (New York: Oxford University Press, 1987), 127.

39. See RS to PMN, November 2, 1918, Box 5, Folder 78, Newman Papers; Schneiderman supports Newman's contention that "while we welcome cooperation in other bodies, we do not, as a rule, make our actions dependent on theirs." See also Pauline Newman, "Out of the Past and into the Future," *Life and Labor*, June 1921.

40. For information on the battle over the ERA see the papers of the New York WTUL and national WTUL, 1921–49; Baker, *Protective Labor Legislation*; Lemons, *Woman Citizen*; Cott, *Grounding of Modern Feminism*; Foner, *Women and the American Labor Movement*; Lipschultz, "Mischievous Equality."

41. See Baker, *Protective Labor Legislation*, 192; Lipschultz, "Mischievous Equality"; and Lemons, *Woman Citizen*, chap. 7.

42. *Third Annual Report of the U.S. Women's Bureau* (Washington, D.C.: Government Printing Office, 1921); *Fifth Annual Report of the U.S. Women's Bureau* (Washington, D.C.: Government Printing Office, 1923); Baker, *Protective Labor Legislation*, 191–93.

43. *Adkins v. Children's Hospital* as cited in Kessler-Harris, *Woman's Wage*, 52.

44. Schneiderman's comment to the *New York Times* cited in Foner, *Women and the American Labor Movement*, 144–45.

45. NYWTUL Annual Report, 1924, Reel 2, NYWTUL Papers; Lemons, *Woman Citizen*, chap. 7.

46. Schneiderman, *All for One*, 126; Rose Schneiderman, "Women's Role in Labor

Legislation," n.d., Reel 2, Schneiderman Papers; Program of the Women's Industrial Conference Called by the Women's Bureau of the U.S. Department of Labor, January 18–21, 1926, U.S. Women's Bureau Papers; Casey quoted in the *Buffalo (New York) News*, January 21, 1926.

47. Leslie cited in the *Eighth Annual Report of the U.S. Women's Bureau* (Washington, D.C.: Government Printing Office, 1926); "Extracts from Address Delivered by Miss Rose Schneiderman before the Women's Industrial Conference," typescript released by the U.S. Department of Labor Women's Bureau, January 20, 1926, Box 71, Van Kleeck Papers.

48. Lash, *Eleanor and Franklin*, 322–23.

49. Schneiderman came to Whitney's attention during her 1920 campaign for Senate on the American Labor Party ticket. Unbeknownst to Schneiderman, Whitney made a large donation to her campaign. And when the WTUL needed money to buy a headquarters, Whitney volunteered her help and brought in wealthy friends, including Eleanor Roosevelt. Schneiderman, *All for One*, 146–47; Lash, *Eleanor and Franklin*, 378.

50. There is, unfortunately, no book-length study of Mary Dreier. However, Dreier did write a biography of her sister, *Margaret Dreier Robins: Her Life, Letters, and Work* (New York: Island Press Cooperative, 1950). Biographical information on Dreier is scattered. There is a short article about her in *Notable American Women: The Modern Period*. Her papers are at the Schlesinger Library at Radcliffe College. And there are letters from her in the Margaret Dreier Robins Papers, University of Florida Libraries, Gainesville, Fla.; the Newman Papers; the Schneiderman Papers; and the O'Reilly Papers.

51. Ellen Fitzpatrick, *Endless Crusade: Women Social Scientists and Progressive Reform* (New York: Oxford University Press, 1990), 137–46.

52. Cook, *Eleanor Roosevelt*, 321–22; Schneiderman, *All for One*, 128–29; Lash, *Eleanor and Franklin*, 415; NYWTUL Annual Reports, 1921–25, Reel 2, NYWTUL Papers.

53. See Lash, *Eleanor and Franklin*; Schneiderman, *All for One*, 150–53, 156–57, 175–84; Perkins, *Roosevelt I Knew*, 30–32; Cook, *Eleanor Roosevelt*, 329, 334, 337, 339, 358, 359, 361. See also the voluminous letters between Rose Schneiderman and Eleanor Roosevelt, 1921–62, Eleanor Roosevelt Papers.

54. Lash, *Eleanor and Franklin*, 389–91.

55. Brody, "Swartz, Maud O' Farrel"; Schneiderman, *All for One*, 167–74, 181–82. See also correspondence between Rose Schneiderman and Maud Swartz, January 1920–March 1923, Reels 7, 8, 9, 10, NYWTUL Papers.

56. Schneiderman, *All for One*, 167–73.

57. Burger, interview by author, December 21, 1993.

58. Ibid.

59. In *Odd Girls and Twilight Lovers: A History of Lesbian Life in Twentieth-Century America* (New York: Columbia University Press, 1991), Lillian Faderman discusses the ambivalent laissez-faire attitude toward lesbianism in 1920s Greenwich Village (pp. 81–88). See, too, Cook, *Eleanor Roosevelt*, 296.

60. Burger, interview by author, December 15, 1987.

61. See Dee Ann Montgomery, "Miller, Frieda Segelke."

62. Burger, interview by author, December 15, 1987.

63. In her letters to Eleanor Roosevelt between 1928 and 1945, Rose Schneiderman mentions visits to Val-Kill, Campobello, and Hyde Park on numerous occasions. See

Reels 16–17 of Research Collections in Women's Studies, Eleanor Roosevelt Papers. And in her memoir, *All for One*, Schneiderman mentions several visits to Hyde Park, including one two-week stay in 1928 (pp. 176–81). Blanche Cook says in *Eleanor Roosevelt* that ER "never dared" invite Schneiderman to Hyde Park (p. 334), but that clearly changed after 1926.

64. Perkins, *Roosevelt I Knew*, 30; Schneiderman, *All for One*, 176–81.

65. Schneiderman, *All for One*, 176.

66. Ibid.; Perkins, *Roosevelt I Knew*, 32–33.

67. RS to ER, April 30, 1931. Schneiderman's letters to Eleanor Roosevelt from 1921 to 1945 are chock full of requests for Roosevelt to write to one friend or relative or another, asking for a renewal or expansion of past gifts to the League; see letters from Schneiderman to Roosevelt, Reels 16–17 of Research Collections in Women's Studies, Eleanor Roosevelt Papers. And some of the replies to Roosevelt suggest the importance of her involvement in League fund-raising. For example, Henry Morgenthau to ER, July 2, 1930, Eleanor Roosevelt Papers: "How I can I refuse to comply with my beloved niece's annual begging letter for the WTUL. Uncle Henry."

68. *New York Times*, June 3, 9, 1929.

69. Ibid., June 3, 9, 1929; RS to FDR, June 12, 1929, Reel 1, Schneiderman Papers; Lash, *Eleanor and Franklin*, 438–39; Schneiderman, *All for One*, 175–76.

70. Schneiderman, *All for One*, 176–81; Lash, *Eleanor and Franklin*, 378–79.

71. See "Frieda Miller biography," Box 1, Miller Papers; Montgomery, "Miller, Frieda Segelke."

72. Lash, *Eleanor and Franklin*, 438; FDR to RS, January 11, September 17, 1929, May 12, August 2, 1930, October 12, 1932, and RS to FDR, March 16, November 18, 1932, Reel 2, Schneiderman Papers.

73. Maud Swartz to ER, December 18, 1930, Reel 16, Eleanor Roosevelt Papers.

74. RS to FDR, November 18, 1932, Reel 1, Schneiderman Papers.

75. *New York Times*, June 20, 1933; Reel 1, Part 1, Frames 450–661, and Part II, Frames 221–32, Schneiderman Papers; Susan Ware, *Beyond Suffrage: Women and the New Deal* (Cambridge: Harvard University Press, 1981).

76. *New York Times*, January 19, 1934.

77. Report and Proceedings of the Twenty-Second International [ILGWU] Convention, 1934, cited in Endelman, "Solidarity Forever," 192; see also pp. 234–35.

78. RS to ER, July 3, 1933, Reel 16, Eleanor Roosevelt Papers. In "Solidarity Forever," Gary Endelman argues that Schneiderman was less interested in the NRA's potential to spur unionization than in its potential to improve the lives of millions of unorganized women workers (pp. 182–83).

79. *New York Times*, August 8, 12, September 12, 1933; Ware, *Beyond Suffrage*, 91.

80. Endelman, "Solidarity Forever," 201–2; Rose Schneiderman, "Women's Role in Labor Legislation," n.d., Reel 2, Schneiderman Papers.

81. RS to ER, February 20, 1934, Eleanor Roosevelt Papers; Schneiderman, *All for One*, 204–8.

82. Endelman, "Solidarity Forever," 204–6; *New York Times*, January 18, 19, 31, May 8, 1934; Schneiderman, *All for One*, 204–8. The trip was, according to Doris Faber, supposed to be long-awaited time alone for Roosevelt and journalist Lorena Hickok to celebrate Hickok's forty-first birthday. But Roosevelt came laden with statistics on all facets of Puerto Rican life and used the opportunity to take a fact-finding tour. See

Doris Faber, *The Life of Lorena Hickok—E.R.'s Friend* (New York: Morrow and Co., 1980), 161–63.

83. Endelman, "Solidarity Forever." In *Consider the Laundry Workers* (New York: League of Women Shoppers, 1937), Jane Filley and Therese Mitchell describe numerous ways employers found to make workers pay for increased costs due to NRA regulations (p. 54).

84. NYWTUL Annual Report, April 1933–March 31, 1934, Reel 3, NYWTUL Papers.

85. NYWTUL Annual Report, March 1932–33, Reel 3, NYWTUL Papers. This report notes that Eleanor Roosevelt donated profits from all radio talks to the NYWTUL during that year, basically keeping the League going.

86. Mary Dreier to PMN, July 16, 1934, and PMN to MD, August 3, 1934, Box 5, Newman Papers.

87. MD to PMN, July 16, 1934.

88. PMN to MD, August 3, 1934.

89. "Report of the Education Committee," NYWTUL Annual Reports, 1929 and 1933–34, Reel 3, NYWTUL Papers; Schneiderman, *All for One*, 185–93.

90. "Report of the Education Committee," NYWTUL Annual Report, 1938–39, Reel 4, NYWTUL Papers.

91. ER to RS, April 26, 1933, January 7, 1936, and RS to ER, February 20, 1934, January 3, 1936, all in Eleanor Roosevelt Papers.

92. RS to ER, April 16, May 21, 1936; *New York Times*, May 1, 5, 6, 7, 1936.

93. Newman, interview by Wertheimer.

94. *New York Times*, May 1, 5, 6, 7, 1936; Charlotte Baum, Paula Hyman, and Sonya Michel, *The Jewish Woman in America* (New York: New American Library, 1977), 160.

95. Newman, interview by Wertheimer; *New York Times*, May 5, 6, 1936.

96. RS to ER, May 27, 1937, May 25, June 24, October 28, 1938, and ER to RS, June 3, 1937, June 1, 1938, all in Eleanor Roosevelt Papers; *New York Times*, June 3, 9, 1929.

97. "Organization Report," March 27, October 29, 1926, Minutes of the NYWTUL Executive Board, Reel 3, NYWTUL Papers.

98. *Daily Worker*, May 31, 1927; Minutes of the NYWTUL Executive Board, April 1, 1929, NYWTUL Papers; Filley and Mitchell, *Consider the Laundry Workers*, 46.

99. See Rose Schneiderman typescript about the Fair Wage Bill of 1932 and its effect on laundry workers, n.d., Reel 2, Schneiderman Papers. *New York Times*, May 16, 23, July 14, 25, August 24, October 2, 1933.

100. NYWTUL Annual Report, 1934, Reel 3, NYWTUL Papers.

101. Ibid.; *New York Times*, January 22, 24, February 2, 1934. According to Philip Foner, Mrs. Pinchot was a frequent visitor to picket lines in her home state of Pennsylvania, where she issued inflammatory statements to reporters who questioned the propriety of her actions. One such statement, recorded at a strike of teenage shirtmakers in Allentown, captures her sensibility. Asked whether it was ladylike to picket, she answered, "Our ancestors fought for their revolution. We must fight for our economic revolution now." Pinchot would also show up in 1937 in Flint, Michigan, as part of a delegation of prominent women who came to give support to the strikers and the members of the women's auxiliaries. Foner, *Women and the American Labor Movement*, 283.

102. NYWTUL Annual Report, 1934; *New York Times*, February 11, 12, 13, 1934.

103. *New York Times*, January 2, 1938; January 8, September 17, October 1, 4, 29, 1939; November 9, 1941; and February 8, 1942.

104. Burger, interview by author, February 9, 1984; Elisabeth Burger, Address at Pauline Newman Memorial, July 1986; Schneiderman, *All for One*, 221–29.

105. RS to ER, January 29, March 2, 1937, and ER to RS, March 4, 1937, Eleanor Roosevelt Papers.

106. RS to ER, March 2, 1937.

107. RS to ER, October 24, November 12, 1939; *All for One*, 226–28.

108. Max Zaritsky to RS, March 25, 1938, and Albert Einstein to RS, June 10, 1939, Reel 1, Schneiderman Papers.

109. RS to ER, April 14, 1937; Alex Rose to RS, March 3, 1937; letters to RS from Dorothy Bellanca, Max Zaritsky, Rebecca Kohut, Celia Gross, A. Newbold Morris, Samuel Shore, Jacob Panken, and Beatrice Bisno, all March 4, 1937, Reel 1, Schneiderman Papers; Rose Schneiderman, "Women's Role in Labor Legislation," typescript, n.d., Reel 2, Schneiderman Papers; *New York Times*, February 5, March 4, April 2, 1937.

110. Schneiderman, *All for One*, 216–17.

111. *New York Times*, January 22, March 6, 8, July 3, 1938; "Industrial Women March On" (typescript of a WEVD Radio broadcast), November 24, 1938, Reel 2, Schneiderman Papers.

112. NYWTUL Annual Reports, 1939–40 and 1941–42, Reel 4, NYWTUL Papers.

113. Ibid.

114. Schneiderman, *All for One*, 221–27; NYWTUL Annual Report, 1944, Reel 4, NYWTUL Papers; Frieda Miller, "A Christmas Message," *Labor Chronicle*, December 1940.

115. *New York Times*, September 25, October 18, 1942, March 6, October 28, November 20, 1943.

116. NYWTUL Annual Report, 1944.

117. Schneiderman, "Women's Role in Labor Legislation."

CHAPTER 5

1. ILGWU Education Department, "Announcement of Courses Given in Workers' University, 1923–1924," cited in Susan Stone Wong, "From Soul to Strawberries: The International Ladies' Garment Workers' Union and Workers' Education, 1914–1950," in *Sisterhood and Solidarity: Worker's Education for Women, 1914–1984*, ed. Joyce Kornbluh and Mary Frederickson (Philadelphia: Temple University Press, 1984), 43–44.

2. Robin Miller Jacoby, "The Women's Trade Union League Training School for Women Organizers, 1914–1926," in Kornbluh and Frederickson, *Sisterhood and Solidarity*, 5–35; NYWTUL Annual Reports, 1923–55, Reels 2–4, NYWTUL Papers; Union Health Center Papers and ILGWU Collection, New York State School for Industrial and Labor Relations, Cornell University, Ithaca, N.Y.

3. Cohn reiterated these themes in many of her writings. For example, see Fannia Cohn, "Woman's Eternal Struggle: What Worker Education Will Do for Woman," *Pioneer Woman*, January 1932. See also Cohn, "Women Workers Coming into Their Own" (typescript), n.d., Box 9, Cohn Papers.

4. Cohn, "Woman's Eternal Struggle."

5. Arthur Levine, "An Unheralded Educational Experience: Brookwood Remembered," *Change* 13 (November–December 1981): 38–42.

6. *Ladies' Garment Worker*, April 1918.

7. Fannia Cohn, "Educational Department of the International Ladies' Garment Workers' Union," cited in Wong, "From Soul to Strawberries," 46–47.

8. Benjamin Stolberg, *Tailor's Progress* (New York: Doubleday, 1944), 216.

9. Dubinsky's comments on Fannia Cohn were taken from a 1973 interview of Mark and Helen Norton Starr by historian Ricki Carole Myers Cohen, cited in Cohen, "Fannia Cohn and the International Ladies' Garment Workers' Union" (Ph.D. diss., University of Southern California, 1976); see also Stolberg, *Tailor's Progress*, 288–91. Cohn's quote is from FMC to "Dear Friend," n.d., Box 5, Cohn Papers.

10. Charles Beard to FMC, August 6, 1919, Box 1, Cohn Papers.

11. Rose Pesotta to David Dubinsky, n.d., David Dubinsky Collection, ILGWU Archives, cited in Alice Kessler-Harris, "Problems of Coalition Building: Women and Trade Unions in the 1920s," in *Women, Work, and Protest: A Century of U.S. Women's Labor History*, ed. Ruth Milkman (London: Routledge and Kegan Paul, 1985), 110–38; the citation appears in n. 45.

12. Fannia Cohn, "Complete Equality between Men and Women," *Ladies' Garment Worker*, December 1917.

13. Ibid.; Cohn, "What Can Workers' Education Do for Working Women?," *Machinists' Monthly Journal*, November 1924; Cohn, "Winning Workingwomen to Unionism" (photocopy), n.d., Cohn Papers.

14. Minutes of the NYWTUL Executive Board, June 1 and October 27, 1908, Reel 1, NYWTUL Papers; "Teaching English to our Foreign Friends" (series), *Life and Labor*, October 1911 and January 1912.

15. See Minutes of the NYWTUL Executive Board, August 22, 1907, and June 1, 1908, Reel 1, NYWTUL Papers; Colette Hyman, "Labor Organizing and Female Institution Building: The Chicago Women's Trade Union League, 1904–1924," in Milkman, *Women, Work, and Protest*, 22–42.

16. For Cohn's views on her WTUL training school experience, see FMC to Florence Miller, April 16, 1928, Cohn Papers. For more information on the WTUL training school, see Jacoby, "The Women's Trade Union League Training School."

17. Louis Levine [Lewis Lorwin], *The Women's Garment Workers: A History of the International Ladies' Garment Workers' Union* (New York: B. W. Huebsch, 1924), 486–87.

18. See Levine, *Women's Garment Workers*, 486–94, and Wong, "From Soul to Strawberries."

19. Cohn, "Winning Workingwomen to Unionism"; the "economic question" quote is cited by Alice Kessler-Harris in "Problems of Coalition Building," 119. See also Pauline M. Newman, "Difficulties with Sister: Problems of Women in Industry," n.d., Newman Papers.

20. See Report of the Ladies' Waistmakers' Union Local 25 to the Sixteenth Convention of the International Ladies' Garment Workers' Union in Cleveland, May 1922, ILGWU Collection.

21. Rose Pesotta, *Bread upon the Waters* (New York: Dodd, Mead and Co., 1944; reprint, Ithaca: Cornell University Press, 1976), 12; Proceedings of the Convention of

the American Federation of Labor, St. Paul, Minnesota, June 10–20, 1918, cited in Levine, *Women's Garment Workers*, 495; Kessler-Harris, "Problems of Coalition Building," 126–29.

22. Levine, *Women's Garment Workers*, 486–93.

23. Pauline Newman, "Unity House," *The Message*, February 23, 1917.

24. Levine, *Women's Garment Workers*, 482–505.

25. FMC to "Dear Friend," n.d., Cohn Papers. In "From Soul to Strawberries," Susan Stone Wong cites interviews with Mark and Helen Starr that allude to the tension between Poyntz and Cohn. This tension is also noted in Cohen, "Fannia Cohn." See also *New York Times*, December 18, 1937.

26. Wong, "From Soul to Strawberries"; Cohen, "Fannia Cohn," 130–31; Levine, *Women's Garment Workers*, 482–505.

27. Leon Stein, interview by author, Cranbury, N.J., October 19, 1988.

28. Gus Tyler, interview by Ricki Carole Myers Cohen, October 30, 1973, as cited in Cohen, "Fannia Cohn," 128; FMC to John Dewey, February 9, 1933, and FMC to "Dear Friend," July 28, 1937, Box 5, Cohn Papers; Levine, *Women's Garment Workers*, 488.

29. Leon Stein, interview by author.

30. Charles Beard to FMC, August 6, 1919, and B. J. R. Stolper to FMC, April 27, 1920, Box 4, Cohn Papers; Cohen, "Fannia Cohn," 131; Tyler quote cited in Cohen, "Fannia Cohn," 147.

31. Stolberg, *Tailor's Progress*, 290–91.

32. Ibid., 286.

33. Sarah Zimand to FMC, June 9, 1922, Box 1, Cohn Papers.

34. FMC to "Dear Friend," n.d., Box 5, Cohn Papers.

35. Alexander Fichandler to Abe Baroff, September 8, 1921, Box 3, Cohn Papers; see also FMC to "Dear Friend," n.d., Box 5, Cohn Papers; Wong, "From Soul to Strawberries"; Levine, *Women's Garment Workers*, 482–505; Leon Stein, interview by author.

36. Levine, *Women's Garment Workers*, 353.

37. See ibid., 354–55, and Kessler-Harris, "Problems of Coalition Building."

38. See Kessler-Harris, "Problems of Coalition Building," 127–31, and Levine, *Women's Garment Workers*, 353–59.

39. In 1920, AFL organizer William Foster founded the Trade Union Educational League (TUEL) to promote widespread discussion of union reform, coordinate insurgent activity, and lend ideological coherence to spontaneous local rebellions within the labor movement. Before long, many of the insurgents in the ILGWU had become associated with TUEL. Newly elected ILGWU president Morris Sigman warned union members that TUEL membership was unacceptable because of the TUEL's relationship to the Communist Party. Foster and other TUEL leaders belonged to the party and were pledged to follow a directive, issued in June 1921 at the International Communist Congress in Moscow, that Communist Party members should radicalize and transform conservative trade unions by "boring from within."

40. Pauline Newman, "Women's Garments and Their Makers," n.d., Box 6, Newman Papers.

41. Fannia Cohn, "Adult Worker Education: Its Aims and Goals," n.d., Box 7, Cohn Papers.

42. Leon Stein, interview by author.

43. Levine, *Women's Garment Workers*, 431; see also Kessler-Harris, "Problems of Coalition Building," 127–28. According to Levine, ILGWU records from 1924 assign no gender to an additional 7,633 members.

44. Report and Proceedings of the Seventeenth Biennial [ILGWU] Convention, 1924, cited in Kessler-Harris, "Problems of Coalition Building," 125; see also Fannia M. Cohn, "What Can Workers' Education Do for Working Women?," *Machinists Monthly Journal*, November 1924. Statistic from Kessler-Harris, ibid., 113.

45. For a full description of the dissident movement within the ILGWU, see Levine, *Women's Garment Workers*, 355–59, and Kessler-Harris, "Problems of Coalition Building." For information on the shop-floor insurgency in the ACW, see Steve Fraser, "Dress Rehearsal for the New Deal: Shop Floor Insurgents, Political Elites, and Industrial Democracy in the Amalgamated Clothing Workers," in *Working-Class America*, ed. Michael H. Frisch and Daniel Walkowitz (Urbana: University of Illinois Press, 1983).

46. Fannia Cohn, Alexander Fichandler, David J. Saposs, Henry Dana et al. to "Brother or Sister," March 1921, Box 4, Cohn Papers; FMC to Emma, May 8, 1953, Box 5, Cohn Papers; "Worker Education Conference" (typescript), Reel 2, Schneiderman Papers.

47. For information on Brookwood, see Jonathan Bloom, "Brookwood Labor College, 1921–1933" (M.A. thesis, Rutgers University, 1978); Richard J. Altenbaugh, *Education for Struggle: The American Labor Colleges of the 1920s and 1930s* (Philadelphia: Temple University Press, 1990); Altenbaugh, " 'The Children and the Instruments of a Militant Labor Progressivism': Brookwood Labor College and the American Labor Movement of the 1920s and 1930s," *History of Education Quarterly* 23, no. 4 (Winter 1983): 395–411; Levine, "An Unheralded Educational Experience"; and Sidney Jonas, interview by author, Brooklyn, N.Y., August 10, 1980.

48. FMC to Selig Perlman, December 26, 1951, and FMC to "Dear Emma," May 15, 1953, Cohn Papers.

49. Cohn was a member of the NYWTUL and was active on a variety of fronts between 1917 and 1921. She had been part of a WTUL delegation that visited President Woodrow Wilson in 1917, and she chaired the committee on labor standards and legislation the following year. Still, Cohn's relations with the League were ambivalent. League leaders never understood exactly why. A decade later, Elisabeth Christman wondered in a letter to Mary van Kleeck about "the seeming break between Fannia Cohn and our League. This seems to be the case and I am sorry about it." Christman to Van Kleeck, March 1928, Box 71, Van Kleeck Papers.

50. Mary Anderson to FMC, February 23, 1921; Ernestine Friedman to FMC, July 26, 1921; Evelyn Preston to FMC, June 13, 1922; FMC to Mary Anderson, March 4, 1921; FMC to Ethel Smith, July 23, 1929, all in Box 1, Cohn Papers. Rose Schneiderman, *All for One* (New York: Paul S. Eriksson, 1967), 141–46.

51. Levine, *Women's Garment Workers*, 499; Cohen, "Fannia Cohn," 140–42.

52. Cohen, "Fannia Cohn," 137.

53. Ibid., 140–42; Levine, *Women's Garment Workers*, 499–505; *Justice*, March 11, 25, 1921, April 1, 1921, and June 24, 1921; FMC to "Dear Friend," December 6, 1923; FMC to Perlman, December 26, 1951; FMC to "Dear Emma," May 15, 1953, all in Box 5, Cohn Papers.

54. Cohen, "Fannia Cohn," 174.

55. Miriam Stein, interview by author, Cranbury, N.J., October 19, 1988; FMC to John Frey, April 14, 1924; Cohen, "Fannia Cohn," 174.

56. Arthur Gleason to FMC, August 12, 1921, and May 17, 1922, Box 1, Cohn Papers. John Frey, who wrote Cohn frequently in those years, sent condolences on Gleason's death (January 10, 1924, Box 1, Cohn Papers). See also *New York Times*, December 31, 1923, and "Gleason, Arthur Huntington, 1878–1923," in *Who Was Who in America: Volume 1, 1897–1942* (Chicago: Marquis Who's Who, Inc., 1981).

57. See correspondence between Evelyn Preston and Fannia Cohn, 1922–35, Cohn Papers. For first contacts between them see January 28 and 31, 1922; March 29 and 31, 1922; and April 3, 1922, Boxes 1 and 4, Cohn Papers.

58. Preston to FMC, January 28, March 31, and April 3, 1922; FMC to Preston, April 1922, n.d., and October 9, [1922?], Boxes 1 and 4, Cohn Papers.

59. Alexander Fichandler to FMC, September 8, 1921; Preston to FMC, January 28 and 31, March 29 and 31, 1922; FMC to Preston, March 31 and April 10, 1922, Boxes 1 and 4, Cohn Papers.

60. Preston to FMC, March 31, April 13 and 25, 1922, Box 1, Cohn Papers; FMC to Preston, April 17, 19, and 28, 1922, Box 4, Cohn Papers.

61. Preston to FMC, December 7, 1923, Box 1, Cohn Papers.

62. Fannia M. Cohn, "Trip to Bermuda," August 11, 1923, Box 8, Cohn Papers.

63. Preston to FMC, September 1923, and FMC to Preston, n.d.

64. For information on Wolfson see Alice Kessler-Harris, "Wolfson, Theresa," in *Notable American Women: The Modern Period*, ed. Barbara Sicherman and Carol Hurd Green (Cambridge: Belknap Press of Harvard University Press, 1980), 742–44.

65. Wolfson to FMC, May 6, 1922; FMC to Wolfson, May 15, 1922; FMC to Wolfson, n.d., Cohn Papers. The two kept up a correspondence through the 1950s; see Boxes 1, 4, and 5, Cohn Papers.

66. Wolfson to FMC, November 19, 1923, Box 1, Cohn Papers.

67. See Theresa Wolfson, *The Woman Worker and the Trade Unions* (New York: International Press, 1926), 50–51; FMC to Preston, October 27, 1922, Box 4, Cohn Papers.

68. FMC to Preston, May 22, 1924, and FMC to Florence Thorne, June 24, 1926, Box 4, Cohn Papers; Cohen, "Fannia Cohn," 82, 172–80.

69. Fannia Cohn, "Can Women Lead?," *Justice*, February 15, 1936.

70. Cohen, "Fannia Cohn," 187.

71. FMC to Thorne, June 24, 1926, Box 4, Cohn Papers.

72. FMC to Marion Phillips, July 13, 1928, Box 4, Cohn Papers.

73. See FMC to Grace Klueg, May 27, 1926, January 25 and March 3, 1927; FMC to May Peake, April 20, 1927; and FMC to Marion Phillips, September 13, 1927, Cohn Papers. See also Fannia Cohn, "Can We Organize the Flapper?," *Labor Age*, December 1927, and Cohn, "Youth and the Labor Movement," *Justice*, January 27, 1928.

74. See *New York Times*, August 9 and November 10, 1928; FMC to A. J. Muste, January 10 and 21, February 5, 13, and 20, and March 4, 1929, Box 4, Cohn Papers.

75. Cohen, "Fannia Cohn," 203–11; FMC to Muste, January 10 and 21, February 5, 13, and 20, and March 4, 1929; FMC to Spencer Miller, March 28, 1929, Box 4, Cohn Papers.

76. FMC to William Andrews, August 1, 1930, and FMC to Isidore Nagler, November 5, 1930, Box 4, Cohn Papers.

77. Wolfson to FMC, April 30, 1930, Box 2, Cohn Papers.

78. FMC to "Dear Friend," n.d., Box 5, Cohn Papers; NYWTUL Organizing Report, February 1931, Reel 3, NYWTUL Papers.

79. FMC to David Dubinsky, October 12, 1932, Box 4, Cohn Papers.

80. Leon Stein, interview by author.

81. FMC to John Dewey, February 9, 1933, and FMC to Marx Lewis, May 18, 1933, Box 5, Cohn Papers; *Justice*, August 1 and September 1, 1933.

82. Fannia Cohn, "The Uprising of the Sixty Thousand: The General Strike of the Dressmakers' Union, 1933," *Justice*, September 1, 1933; Pesotta, *Bread upon the Waters*, 2.

83. Cohn, "Woman's Eternal Struggle"; Fannia Cohn, "Working Women in Action," *Worker's Education Bureau of America Quarterly*, January 1936.

84. Elizabeth Balanoff, "Interview with Maida Springer Kemp," *The Black Woman Oral History Project, from the Arthur and Elizabeth Schlesinger Library on the History of Women in America*, ed. Ruth Edmonds Hill, 10 vols. (Westport, Conn.: Meckler, 1990), 7:45–157.

85. Cohn, "Working Women in Action"; David Dubinsky, "Rebirth of the Union," *American Federationist*, December 1929.

86. FMC to "Dear Brother," n.d., Cohn Papers (though there is no date and no personal salutation, the letter clearly was written to Dubinsky after Cohn was stripped of her official title in 1935); FMC to "Dear Bertha," April 29, 1935, Box 5, Cohn Papers.

87. Leon Stein, interview by author.

88. Ibid.

89. For a good taste of Dubinsky's hard-headed approach to unionism and his militant anti-Communism, see Max Danish, *The World of David Dubinsky* (Cleveland: World Publishing Co., 1957). For a sense of the derisive attitude the new union leadership displayed toward Cohn, see Stolberg, *Tailor's Progress*, 288–91, and Mark Starr, "Education for Labor," *Forum 55*, May 1946, both cited in Wong, "From Soul to Strawberries."

90. Mark Starr, interview by Cohen, cited in Cohen, "Fannia Cohn," 247. Leon and Miriam Stein, interviews by author.

91. Mark Starr, *Training for Union Service* (New York: ILGWU, 1940), cited in Wong, "From Soul to Strawberries"; Rose Pesotta to David Dubinsky, n.d., quoted in Kessler-Harris, "Problems of Coalition Building," 137 (n. 45).

92. Leon and Miriam Stein, interviews by author.

93. FMC to "Dear Friend," July 28, 1937, Box 5, Cohn Papers.

94. See Cohn correspondence, 1932–61, Box 5, Cohn Papers, to get a sense of just how wide-ranging her activities were.

95. Leon and Miriam Stein, interviews by author.

96. A. Philip Randolph to FMC, May 23, 1944, Cohn Papers. She also won high praise from Ed Lewis of the Urban League, who called himself "for many years . . . a keen admirer" and saluted her as "one of our finest members . . . inspiring and heartwarming." Ed Lewis to FMC, August 8, 1951, and December 9, 1954, Box 3, Cohn Papers.

97. Jack Barbash to FMC, October 2, 1962, Cohn Papers. See also letters to FMC from Arthur Schlesinger, April 8, 1949; Merle Curti, June 21, 1949; Alvin Johnson, September 25, 1951; Harry J. Carman, January 27, 1953; Irwin Edman, May 22, 1954; Spencer Miller, November 23, 1955; and John Kenneth Galbraith, July 28, 1958, all in Box 3, Cohn Papers.

98. Charles Beard to FMC, July 26, 1945; Labor Day, 1945; and November 19, 1945, Box 3, Cohn Papers.

99. Beard to FMC, February 19, 1947.

100. Miriam Stein, interview by author.

101. Ibid.

102. Rose Pesotta, "Resignation from the ILGWU," Box 134, David Dubinsky Collection, ILGWU Archives, cited in Ann Schofield, introduction to Pesotta, *Bread upon the Waters*, ix.

103. See Herbert Hill, "The ILGWU Today: The Decay of a Labor Movement," *New Politics* 1, no. 4 (Summer 1962): 6–17; Michael Myerson, "ILGWU: Fighting for Lower Wages," *Ramparts* 8 (October 1969): 51–55; and Erin K. Rowland, "Black and Puerto Rican Women in the International Ladies' Garment Workers' Union, 1933–1980" (undergraduate honors thesis, Dartmouth College, 1993).

104. Leon Stein, interview by author; Pauline Newman, interview by Barbara Wertheimer, New York, N.Y., November 1976.

105. The most complete source for information on Maida Springer Kemp is Balanoff, "Interview with Maida Springer Kemp." See also Rowland, "Black and Puerto Rican Women."

106. For another example, see Laddie Saddes to FMC, July 15, 1939, Box 3, Cohn Papers. Balanoff, "Interview with Maida Springer Kemp," 73.

107. Leon Stein, interview by author; Tyler quote cited in Cohen, "Fannia Cohn," 146.

108. FMC to Perlman, December 26, 1951, Cohn Papers.

CHAPTER 6

1. Clara Lemlich Shavelson, interview by Martha and Joel Schaffer, Los Angeles, Calif., February 2, 1974. See chapter 3 for a description of Lemlich's battle with Mary Beard.

2. Shavelson, interview by Schaffers.

3. Rita and Murray Margules, Martha and Arthur Schaffer, interview by Joel Schaffer, Queens, N.Y., 1974. See also Paula Scheier, "Clara Lemlich Shavelson: Fifty Years in Labor's Front Line," *Jewish Life*, November 1954.

4. Scheier, "Clara Lemlich Shavelson." See also the prologue and chapter 2, above, for discussions of housewives' activism and the 1913 white goods strike in Brownsville.

5. Shavelson, interview by Schaffers.

6. Ibid.; Scheier, "Clara Lemlich Shavelson."

7. Martha and Arthur Schaffer, Rita and Murray Margules, interview by Schaffer; Rae Appel, interview by Joel Schaffer, Brooklyn, N.Y., 1974.

8. Appel, interview by Schaffer.

9. During the early 1920s, the NYWTUL began trying to organize a Housewives' Industrial League; see NYWTUL Annual Reports, 1922–24, Reel 12 NYWTUL Papers. By the 1920s, Fannia Cohn had also become extremely interested in worker's wives. See FMC to William Green, March 6, 1925; FMC to Grace Klueg, August 27, 1926, and January 15, 1927; and FMC to Mary Peake, April 20, 1927, Box 4, Cohn Papers. In 1926 and 1928 Schneiderman and Cohn co-sponsored two national women's auxiliary

conferences at Brookwood College to lay plans for large-scale housewives' consumer, housing, and educational campaigns.

As for the Communist Party women, historian Robert Shaffer has pointed out that during the 1920s, the party's leadership was primarily concerned with organizing workers in what they considered the "basic industries," those on which the American economy depended. Since there were few women workers in steel, mining, or automobile manufacturing, national CP officials could see little reason for putting energy into recruiting women. See Robert Shaffer, "Women and the Communist Party, USA, 1930–1940," *Socialist Review* 9, no. 3 (May–June 1979): 73–118.

10. FMC to Marion Phillips, September 13, 1927, Box 4, Cohn Papers.

11. While there is no way of knowing exactly how much money American working-class women controlled during the Great Depression, a study by the American Federation of Women's Auxiliaries of Labor estimated in 1937 that American women in union households spent $6 billion annually. *Working Woman*, March 1937.

12. *Woman Today*, April 1936.

13. Appel, interview by Schaffer.

14. Sophie Melvin Gerson, interview by author, Brooklyn, N.Y., February 17, 1989.

15. Sophie Melvin Gerson, "Memorial Address for Clara Lemlich Shavelson," October 24, 1982, notes and transcript in my possession.

16. See Dana Frank, "Housewives, Socialists, and the Politics of Food: The 1917 New York Cost of Living Protests," *Feminist Studies* 11, no. 2 (Summer 1985): 255–85. Frank emphasizes the importance of cost-of-living issues to the housewife activists of 1917. "For these housewives," she writes, "prices must have taken on a significance equivalent to or perhaps surpassing the importance of wages for those who work for pay. . . . Food price protests were these women's way of organizing at their own workplace, as workers whose occupation was shopping, preparing food, and keeping their families content" (279).

17. In an article for the *Daily Worker*, May 23, 1927, Kate Gitlow looked back on the conditions that had made possible the mass mobilization of New York housewives.

18. *New York Times*, March 22, 27, April 3, 7, May 7, 1919.

19. See *New York Times* from March to September 1919, particularly May 3, 4, 7–10, 12–15, June 17, and September 4–6, 1919. In her paper "Women's Councils in the 1930s," presented at the Sixth Berkshire Conference on the History of Women (1984), Smith College, Northampton, Mass., Meredith Tax discussed Clara Shavelson's role in these housewives' uprisings. Her information was drawn from interviews with Shavelson's daughters, Rita Margules and Martha Schaffer.

20. *New York Times*, September 4–6, 1919.

21. Shavelson, interview by Schaffers.

22. Ibid.

23. Pauline Newman, interview by author, New York, N.Y., February 9, 1984; Pauline Newman, "Letters to Hugh and Michael," Box 1, Newman Papers.

24. Gerson, "Memorial Address."

25. Ibid.; Jerry Trotter, speaking at the Shavelson memorial, October 24, 1982, transcribed from a tape in possession of Joel Schaffer.

26. Dora Smorodin, speaking at the Shavelson memorial, October 24, 1982, transcribed from a tape in possession of Joel Schaffer; *Daily Worker*, May 23, July 12, 1927;

for information on the Passaic strike see Vera Buch Weisbord, *A Radical Life* (Bloomington: Indiana University Press, 1987), 122–23; Gerson, interview by author.

27. Gerson, interview by author.

28. *Daily Worker*, May 23, July 12, 1927; *Party Organizer* 5, no. 2 (January 1932); Rose Nelson Raynes, interview by author, Brooklyn, N.Y., February 17, 1989.

29. *Daily Worker*, May 23, 1927.

30. Ibid.; ibid., July 12, 1927.

31. Raynes, interview by author, February 17, 1989; *Party Organizer*, January 1932; Shaffer, "Women and the Communist Party."

32. "Declaration of Aims and Principles of the United Council of Working-Class Women," June 22, 1929; UCWW leaflet, n.d., vertical file: United Council of Working-Class Women, Tamiment Library. Raynes, interview by author, February 17, 1989.

33. Martha Shaffer, telephone interview by author, March 11, 1989.

34. Raynes, interview by author, October 8, 1987.

35. Appel, interview by Schaffer; "Declaration of Aims and Principles of the United Council of Working-Class Women," June 22, 1929.

36. Dora Smorodin, interview by author, Maplewood, N.J., December 30, 1990.

37. "Declaration of Aims and Principles of the United Council of Working-Class Women," June 22, 1929.

38. "Who is Clara Shavelson?" (leaflet from her 1938 campaign for New York State Assembly in the Second Assembly District), courtesy of her daughter, Martha Schaffer; Martha Schaffer, telephone interview by author, March 11, 1989.

39. Rita and Murray Margules, Martha and Arthur Schaffer, interview by Joel Schaffer.

40. *Party Organizer* 10, no. 7 (July 1937): 36.

41. A *Working Woman* study conducted during the winter of 1931 reported that even among those workers who were still employed in the big cities of the United States, income had declined 33 percent while food prices had decreased only 7 percent. Thus it had become significantly more difficult for working-class families to buy food (*Working Woman*, March 1931). See also "Working-Class Women Unite against Misery and Starvation" (leaflet of the UCWW), n.d., vertical file: United Council of Working-Class Women, Tamiment, and *Working Woman*, December 1931. For a more complete accounting of the nationwide Depression-era housewives' movement, see Annelise Orleck, "'We Are That Mythical Thing Called the Public': Militant Housewives during the Great Depression," *Feminist Studies* 19, no. 1 (Spring 1993): 147–72.

42. Raynes, interview by author, October 8, 1987.

43. *Party Organizer* 11, no. 3 (March 1938).

44. Raynes, interview by author, October 8, 1987.

45. For more information the history of Jewish life in Brighton see Annelise Orleck, "Soviet Jews in Brighton Beach," in *New Immigrants in New York*, ed. Nancy Foner (New York: Columbia University Press, 1987): 273–304.

46. Walter Edberg, interview by author, Brooklyn, N.Y., May 1980.

47. Sidney Jonas, interview by author, Brooklyn, N.Y., August 1980.

48. Martha Schaffer, interview by author; Evelyn Velson, interview by author, Oakland, Calif., September 9, 1992.

49. Appel, interview by Schaffer.

50. Ibid.

51. Jack Friedman, interview by author, Brooklyn, N.Y., July 1980.

52. Appel, interview by Schaffer.

53. Friedman, interview by author.

54. Raynes, interview by author, October 8, 1987.

55. Shirley Kupferstein, interview by author, Brooklyn, N.Y., May 1980.

56. Appel, interview by Schaffer; Frances Fox Piven and Richard A. Cloward, *Poor People's Movements: Why They Succeed, How They Fail* (New York: Vintage Books, 1979), 48–60; Philip Foner, *Women and the American Labor Movement* (New York: Free Press, 1979), 307.

57. Appel, interview by Schaffer; Scheier, "Clara Lemlich Shavelson"; Clara Shavelson and Morris Schappes, "Remembering the Waistmakers' General Strike, 1909," *Jewish Currents*, November 1982.

58. Appel, interview by Schaffer.

59. *Working Woman*, December 1931; Appel, interview by Schaffer; Martha Schaffer, interview by author.

60. Martha Schaffer, interview by author.

61. Gerson, "Memorial Address."

62. Gerson, "Memorial Address."

63. *Working Woman*, October, December 1933, February, March 1935. In 1941, when Congress began putting pressure on President Roosevelt to cut spending on social programs, the women's councils had amassed a significant enough body of data that Eleanor Roosevelt called on them to testify before Congress. *New York Times*, October 6, 1941.

64. Ann Barton, "Revolt of the Housewives," *New Masses*, June 18, 1935; *Daily Worker*, June 3, 1935.

65. See *New York Times*, May 27–31, June 1, 2, 6, 10–12, 14–16, 1935. See also Mark Naison, *Communists in Harlem during the Great Depression* (New York: Grove Press, 1983), for a description of the strike in Harlem (pp. 149–50).

66. Raynes, interview by author, October 8, 1987.

67. Although it ended early, strike leaders considered the strike a success. Meat prices around the city were reduced by four to six cents a pound. And in Harlem, inflated prices were reduced by as much as 50 percent. Neighborhood councils formed permanent inspection committees, which monitored local butcher shops for violations of the strike agreement. See *Working Woman* 6, no. 7 (July 1935), and Clara Lemlich Shavelson's description of the strike in *Working Woman* 6, no. 8 (August 1935).

68. Raynes, interview by author, February 17, 1989.

69. *Working Woman*, August 1935.

70. Ibid.

71. Ibid.; *Chicago Daily Tribune*, August 18, 1935.

72. *Woman Today*, August 1936, July 1937; *Detroit Free Press*, August 6, 7, 9, 1935; *Newsweek*, August 31, 1935; *New York Times*, August 19, September 1, 5, 1935.

73. *Working Woman*, June 1935; *Woman Today*, April 1936; *New York Times*, April 10, 1936; *Party Organizer*, September 1935. Meridel Le Sueur describes the radicalization of one of those farm women—Mary Cotter—in her 1940 short story "Salute to Spring," in Le Sueur, *Salute to Spring* (New York: International Publishers, 1940).

74. Dorothy Moser, interview by author, New York, N.Y., October 8, 1987.

75. *The Nation*, June 5, 12, 1937.

76. *New Republic*, April 8, 1936.

77. *Working Woman*, March 1935.

78. See Naison, *Communists in Harlem*, 232–48, for a description of the origins of the ALP and a discussion of the participation of Communist activists in the 1936 and, particularly, the 1938 elections.

79. Appel, interview by Schaffer. The fullest treatment of Marcantonio's career can be found in Gerald Meyer, *Vito Marcantonio, Radical Politician* (Albany: State University of New York Press, 1989). See, too, the entry on the Seventy-sixth Congress in *Notable Americans: What They Did from 1620 to the Present*, ed. Linda S. Hubbard (Detroit: Gale Research, 1988), 205.

80. "Who is Clara Shavelson?" (leaflet of the Communist Party Women's Commission, Eighth District), courtesy of Martha Schaffer.

81. Mary Inman, *Thirteen Years of CPUSA Misleadership on the Woman Question* (Los Angeles: published by the author, 1949). See also *Party Organizer*, August 1937. Anna Damon, an active member of the Communist Party Women's Commission, complained bitterly about local officials' siphoning off funds from her work with St. Louis black women.

82. Avram Landy, "Marxism and the Woman Question," cited in Robert Shaffer, "Women and the Communist Party, USA, 1930–1940," *Socialist Review*, May–June 1979; and Inman, *Thirteen Years of CPUSA Misleadership*, 11–21.

83. Inman, *Thirteen Years of CPUSA Misleadership*, 14; 38–39.

84. In her memoir, *The Autobiography of an American Communist: A Personal View of a Political Life, 1925–1975* (Berkeley: Lawrence Hall and Co., 1977), and in "A Response to Ellen Kay Trimberger's Essay, 'Women in the Old and New Left,'" *Feminist Studies* 5, no. 3 (Fall 1979), Peggy Dennis analyzes in some detail the Communist Party's "culture of personal relations" as it concerned women. The Dennis quote is from "Response," 453.

85. *Woman Today*, June 1936.

86. Martha and Arthur Schaffer, Rita and Murray Margules, interview by Schaffer.

87. Appel, interview by author; Martha and Arthur Schaffer, Rita and Murray Margules, interview by Schaffer; Evelyn Velson, interview by author.

88. Evelyn Velson, interview by author; Appel, interview by Schaffer.

89. Evelyn Velson, interview by author.

90. *Jewish Currents*, November 1982; Scheier, "Clara Lemlich Shavelson"; Martha and Arthur Schaffer, Rita and Murray Margules, interview by Schaffer.

91. Appel, interview by Schaffer.

92. Ibid.; Martha Schaffer, interview by author.

93. Martha and Arthur Schaffer, Rita and Murray Margules, interview by Schaffer; Martha Schaffer, interview by author.

94. Evelyn Velson and Martha Schaffer, interviews by author. Information on Ruth Young is sketchy but there is some in Foner, *Women and the American Labor Movement*, 368, 379–80, 392. See also *New York Times*, February 5, 1943, September 27, 1944, and January 8, 1948.

95. Martha Schaffer, interview by author.

96. Ibid.; Morris Schappes mentioned Shavelson's work for the League against War and Fascism in *Jewish Currents*, November 1982; Sophie Gerson did the same in her

"Memorial Address." See also *Brooklyn Eagle*, October 22, November 5, 1932, May 28, 1933, and October 2, 1934.

97. Martha Schaffer, interview by author.

98. Martha and Arthur Schaffer, Rita and Murray Margules, interview by Schaffer.

99. Appel, interview by Schaffer.

100. Ibid.; Martha Schaffer, interview by Schaffer.

101. Smorodin, interview by author; Martha Schaffer, interview by author.

102. Appel, interview by Schaffer.

103. Martha Schaffer, interview by author.

104. Shavelson, interview by Schaffers; Scheier, "Clara Lemlich Shavelson"; Raynes, interview by author, October 8, 1987.

105. Scheier, "Clara Lemlich Shavelson."

106. *New York Times*, August 20, 24, 25, 1935; May 20, July 20, August 3–31, 1948; February 24, 26–28, May 25, 26, June 14, August 18, 1951.

CHAPTER 7

1. Estimates of these totals vary. These are taken from Frieda Miller, "What's Become of Rosie the Riveter?," *New York Times*, May 5, 1946, and Philip Foner, *Women and the American Labor Movement* (New York: Free Press, 1980), 360–67.

2. Miller, "What's Become of Rosie the Riveter?"; Foner, *Women and the American Labor Movement*. For a general analysis of the position of women workers in the post–World War II period, see also Alice Kessler-Harris, *Out to Work: A History of Wage-Earning Women in America* (New York: Oxford University Press, 1982); Barbara Wertheimer, *We Were There: The Story of Working Women in America* (New York: Pantheon, 1977); and William Chafe, *The Paradox of Change: American Women in the Twentieth Century* (New York: Oxford University Press, 1991).

3. Mary Anderson to RS, June 10, 1943, Reel 1, Schneiderman Papers; *New York Times*, October 28, November 20, December 26, 1943; Foner, *Women and the American Labor Movement*, 357–61, 370, 386; Chafe, *Paradox of Change*, 138–39.

4. Foner, *Women and the American Labor Movement*, 357–60, 386.

5. NYWTUL Annual Report, 1944, and letter to members, January 3, 1945, Reel 4, NYWTUL Papers.

6. *New York Times*, June 13, August 16, 1944; Dee Ann Montgomery, "Miller, Frieda Segelke," in *Notable American Women: The Modern Period*, ed. Barbara Sicherman and Carol Hurd Green (Cambridge: Belknap Press of Harvard University Press, 1980); Pauline Newman résumé, n.d., Box 1, Newman Papers.

7. *New York Times*, February 22, March 9, April 8, May 26, July 16, 1946. For the first scholarly assessment of the Congress of American Women, see Amy Swerdlow, "The Congress of American Women: Popular Front Peace and Sexual Politics in the Cold War," in *U.S. History as Women's History: New Feminist Essays*, ed. Linda Kerber, Alice Kessler-Harris, and Kathryn Kish Sklar (Chapel Hill: University of North Carolina Press, 1995).

8. *New York Times*, September 20, 1943; Foner, *Women and the American Labor Movement*, 360–93; Elizabeth Balanoff, "Interview with Maida Springer Kemp," *The Black Woman Oral History Project, from the Arthur and Elizabeth Schlesinger Library on the*

History of Women in America, ed. Ruth Edmonds Hill, 10 vols. (Westport, Conn.: Meckler, 1990).

9. In interviews, both Dora Smorodin and Evelyn Velson commented on the change in Ruth Young's politics after World War II. Smorodin, interview by author, Maplewood, N.J., March 12, 1991; Velson, interview by author, Oakland, Calif., September 9, 1992.

10. Miller, "What's Become of Rosie the Riveter?"

11. Ibid.

12. Frieda Miller, "Challenges of the Past and Present" (prepared for booklet of the Wisconsin State Federation of Labor Convention, August 19–24, 1946), Miller Papers.

13. NYWTUL Annual Report, 1946, Reel 4, NYWTUL Papers; Miller, "Challenges of the Past and Present."

14. NYWTUL Annual Report, 1946; Elisabeth Christman to RS, September 11, 1946, Reel 14, NYWTUL Papers. For a brief account of the 1946 strikes see Jeremy Brecher, *Strike* (Boston: South End Press, 1972), 226–30.

15. Christman to RS, June 13, September 11, 1946; RS to Christman, November 12, 19, 1946; Mary Winslow to RS, November 26, 1946, Reels 13–14, all in NYWTUL Papers.

16. PMN to Mary Dreier, August 3, 1934, Box 5, Newman Papers; Schneiderman quote cited in Gary Endelman, "Solidarity Forever: Rose Schneiderman and the Women's Trade Union League" (Ph.D. dissertation, University of Delaware, 1978), 237.

17. See Endelman, "Solidarity Forever," 236–49.

18. Reports of Work, Cara Cook, March–August 1939, and March 8, 1943, cited in ibid., 239, 245.

19. Ibid., 248.

20. RS to Christman, November 19, 1946, Reel 14, NYWTUL Papers.

21. RS to Christman, September 11, 1946, and Herbert Merril to RS, September 12, 1946, Reel 14, NYWTUL Papers.

22. Mary Murphy to Christman, October 5, 1946; Dorothy Kenyon to Blanch Freedman, November 30, 1946; Christman to RS, February 5, 14, 1947, all in Reel 14, NYWTUL Papers.

23. NYWTUL Annual Report, 1947, Reel 4, NYWTUL Papers.

24. Typescript of Rose Schneiderman's speech to the 1947 National WTUL Convention, Reel 2, Schneiderman Papers.

25. Ibid.

26. NYWTUL Annual Report, 1948, Reel 5, NYWTUL Papers.

27. RS to Christman, October 21, December 10, 1947, and Organization Report, NYWTUL Annual Report, 1947, Reels 4 and 14, NYWTUL Papers.

28. Christman to RS, October 24, 1947, Reel 14, NYWTUL Papers.

29. For general coverage of the post–World War II Red Scare see David Caute, *The Great Fear* (New York: Simon and Schuster, 1978). Victor Navasky, *Naming Names* (New York: Viking Penguin, 1980), is the most thorough study of the 1947 HUAC investigations into Communism in Hollywood. There are several studies of the Alger Hiss case, including Allister Cook, *A Generation on Trial* (New York: Knopf, 1950); John Cabot Smith, *Alger Hiss: The True Story* (New York: Holt, Rinehart, Winston,

1976); and Allen Weinstein, *Perjury: The Hiss-Chambers Case* (New York: Random House, 1979). For insight into the alienation of former Communist Whittaker Chambers, see Chambers's own memoir, *Witness* (New York: Random House, 1952).

30. See Susan M. Hartmann, "Kenyon, Dorothy," and Eleanor Midman Lewis, "Van Kleeck, Mary," in *Notable American Women: The Modern Period*, 395–96, 706–7.

31. *New York Times*, April 7, 1949.

32. Ibid.

33. Frank R. Crosswaith to RS, April 7, 1949; letters to RS from James Farley, Eleanor Roosevelt, Herbert Lehman, and Fannia M. Cohn, April 8, 1949; "Thirty-One Roses to Rose" (letters to RS from Mary Dreier, Pauline Newman, Mabel Leslie, Blanch Freedman, Bessie Engelman, Geriel Rubin et al.), April 25, 1949, Reel 2, Schneiderman Papers; *New York Times*, April 26, June 3, September 25, 26, 1949.

34. *New York Times*, June 15, 1950; NYWTUL Annual Report 1951, Reel 5, NYWTUL Papers;

35. Ibid.

36. Pauline Newman, interview by Barbara Wertheimer, New York, N.Y., November 1976.

37. Typescript of a WEVD Radio broadcast, 1955, Reel 2, Schneiderman Papers.

38. Endelman, "Solidarity Forever," 266–67; correspondence between RS and ER, 1946–62. See particularly RS to ER, January 6, 1958; n.d. [1958]; n.d. [1960]; March 14, 1960; n.d. [1961], Eleanor Roosevelt Papers.

39. *Brooklyn Eagle*, August 18, 25, November 16, 1945, January 10, 1946; *News from the* IWO, November 1947, International Worker's Order Collection, Tamiment Institute Library, New York University (hereafter cited as IWO Papers); *New York Times*, February 22, 1946, October 4, December 4, 1947; Paula Scheier, "Clara Lemlich Shavelson: Fifty Years in Labor's Front Line," *Jewish Life*, November 1954. For the first in-depth examination of the Emma Lazarus Federation see Joyce Antler, "Feminism, Judaism, and History: Rewriting the Narrative of Jewish Women's Lives," in *U.S. History as Women's History: New Feminist Essays*, ed. Linda Kerber, Alice Kessler-Harris, and Kathryn Kish Sklar (Chapel Hill: University of North Carolina Press, 1995).

40. *New York Times*, December 4, 10, 1947.

41. Ibid., August 3, 8–10, 1948.

42. Rose Nelson Raynes, interview by author, Brooklyn, N.Y., February 17, 1989; *New York Times*, August 3, 5, 8–10, 1948.

43. Sophie Melvin Gerson, interview by author, Brooklyn, N.Y., February 17, 1989; *New York Times*, August 8, 9, 11, 19, 28, 31, 1948.

44. *New York Times*, February 24, 26–28, June 14, 1951.

45. Ibid.

46. *New York Times*, October 23, November 20, 1949; *Woman Today*, March 1937; *The Nation*, June 5, 12, 1937, February 18, 1939; *Business Week*, November 11, 1939; *Forum*, October 1939; *New Republic*, January 1, 1940.

47. *New York Times*, October 23, 1949, January 7, 1950. For a more detailed account of the House investigations of CAW, see Swerdlow, "Congress of American Women."

48. Circular, from the Yiddish document "Ruben Saltzman calls a meeting" [to resolve what to do with JPFO insurance monies], April 4, 1953, IWO Papers; *New York Times*, June 26, July 2, 1952, April 24, October 20, 1953; Raynes, interview by author, February 17, 1989.

49. Raynes, interview by author, February 17, 1989. This analysis owes a great deal to Antler, "Feminism, Judaism, and History."

50. Scheier, "Clara Lemlich Shavelson."

51. Martha Schaffer, interview by Joel Schaffer, Queens, N.Y., 1974.

52. Clara Shavelson, "U.S.S.R" (typescript in possession of Joel Schaffer), 10–18.

53. Evelyn Velson, interview by author.

54. Shavelson, "U.S.S.R."; Scheier, "Clara Lemlich Shavelson."

55. Scheier, "Clara Lemlich Shavelson"; Morris Schappes, "In Memoriam: Clara Lemlich Shavelson, March 28, 1886–July 25, 1982," *Jewish Currents*, November 1982.

56. Morris Schappes notes that the last time he had seen Shavelson was at a rally to save the Rosenbergs; Schappes, "In Memoriam." See, too, Antler, "Feminism, Judaism, and History."

57. Martha Schaffer, telephone interview by author, March 11, 1989.

58. Ibid.

59. Martha Schaffer, interview by Schaffer. The Star Chamber, named for the stars painted on the ceiling, was the Westminster Palace meeting hall of the King of England's court during the fifteenth, sixteenth, and seventeenth centuries. The court was well known for its abuses of power, which led to its dismantling in 1641.

60. *New York Times*, May 7, 8, 1953; September 26, October 1, November 12, 15, 17, 1955; June 20, 22, 1956. Velson, a close aide to controversial California longshoreman's leader Harry Bridges, was a favorite target of investigative committees during the 1950s.

61. Martha Schaffer, interview by author.

62. Julia Velson, interviews by author, Brooklyn, N.Y., December 30, 1990, and Oakland, Calif., September 9, 1992.

63. Scheier, "Clara Lemlich Shavelson"; Sophie Melvin Gerson, "Memorial Address for Clara Lemlich Shavelson," October 24, 1982, notes and transcript in my possession.

64. Rita and Murray Margules, Martha and Arthur Schaffer, interview by Joel Schaffer, Queens, N.Y., 1974.

65. CLS to David Dubinsky, August 19, 1954, and Adolph Held to CLS, n.d., 1959, in possession of Shavelson's family.

66. CLS to Adolph Held and David Dubinsky, n.d., and Adolph Held to CLS, June 16, 1960, in possession of Shavelson's family.

67. FMC to "Dear Friend," n.d., Box 5, Cohn Papers.

68. Mary Goff to FMC, May 13, 1946; Matthew Woll to FMC, April 5, 1946; Charles Beard to FMC, August 21, 1946; and David Dubinsky to FMC, April 2, 1946, Box 3, Cohn Papers.

69. Arthur Schlesinger, Jr., to FMC, April 8, 1949; Merle Curti to FMC, June 21, 1949; C. M. Pierce to FMC, January 18, 1950; Herbert Lehman to FMC, December 7, 1950; Ed Lewis to FMC, August 8, 1951, Box 3, Cohn Papers.

70. Spencer Miller to FMC, August 19, 1951, Box 3, Cohn Papers.

71. Alvin Johnson to FMC, September 25, 1951; Harry J. Carman to FMC, January 27, 1953; Edwin Young to FMC, April 3, 1951, Box 3, Cohn Papers.

72. Felix Frankfurter to FMC, December 7, 1957; Herbert Lehman to FMC, April 4, 1958, Box 3, Cohn Papers.

73. Leon and Miriam Stein, interview by author, Cranbury, N.J., October 19, 1988.

74. "Educational Pioneer Fannia Cohn Retires after Five-Decade Service," *Justice*, September 1, 1962.

75. Jack Barbash to FMC, October 2, 1962; Lewis Lorwin to FMC, September 28, 1962; Dick Deverall to FMC, August 15, 1962, Box 3, Cohn Papers.

76. Leon and Miriam Stein, interviews by author.

77. Ibid.

78. PMN to RS, September 11, 1949, Box 5, Newman Papers.

79. Newman, interview by Wertheimer; Pauline Newman résumé, n.d., Box 1, Newman Papers. NYWTUL Annual Reports, 1947–48, 1949–50, 1950–51, and 1951–52, Reel 5, NYWTUL Papers.

80. Frieda S. Miller to PMN, n.d., Box 3, Newman Papers.

81. See letters from Miller to PMN, Box 3, Folders 41, 42, and 44, Newman Papers. See also *New York Times*, September 7, 1955; *Times* (London), October 23, 1955.

82. *New York Times*, September 7, 1955; *Times* (London), October 23, 1955; *Manila Times*, October 19, 1955; *Nippon Times* and *Pakistan Times*, February 27, 1956.

83. Elisabeth Burger, interview by author, New York, N.Y., December 15, 1987.

84. Ibid.; Michael Owen, telephone interview by author, September 27, 1992; *New York Evening Star*, January 21, 1940; *Christian Science Monitor*, November 22, 1940; *New York Herald*, August 18, 1944; *New York Post Weekly Magazine*, October 14, 1944.

85. Burger, interview by author, December 15, 1987; "Fragments 1958–1961," Box 9, Newman Papers.

86. Burger, interview by author, December 21, 1993.

87. Newman, "Fragments 1958–1961," entry dated October 11, 1958, Box 9, Newman Papers.

88. Newman, "Fragments 1958–1961," entry dated only 1961.

89. Burger, interview by author, December 15, 1987; Esther Peterson to PMN, n.d., February 28, 1956, July 22, 1958, September 16, 1959, June 29, 1962, August 17, 1962; Frieda Miller letters to PMN, Folder 42, Newman Papers.

90. Owen, interview by author.

91. Letters to PMN from Vera Peterson, March 30, 1968, January 20, 1969, August 10, 1973; Geriel Rubin, August 11, 1973; Bess [?], August 15, 1973; Jo Starr, July 28, 1973; Frances Doyle, July 28, 1973; Marion Hobson, July 15, 1973; Esther Peterson, July 24, 1973, all in Newman Papers.

92. Leon Stein, interview by author. Actually the young striker's speech came a week later, at the last session of the conference. Leon Stein, ed., *Out of the Sweatshop: The Struggle for Industrial Democracy* (New York: New York Times Book Co., 1977), 341–43.

93. Martha Schaffer, interview by author; Clara Lemlich Shavelson, interview by Martha and Joel Schaffer, Los Angeles, Calif., February 2, 1974.

94. Evelyn Velson, interview by author; Martha Schaffer, interview by author.

95. Martha Schaffer, interview by author.

96. Ibid.

97. Ibid.

98. Ibid.

99. Ibid.

100. Raynes, interview by author, February 17, 1989.

1. "Educational Pioneer Fannia Cohn Retires after Five-Decade Service," *Justice* September 1, 1962; *Justice*, September 10, 1962.

2. Jack Sessions to Fannia Cohn, September 4, 1962, Box 3, Cohn Papers.

3. Leon Stein, interview by author, Cranbury, N.J., October 19, 1988.

4. Ibid.; Miriam Stein, interview by author, Cranbury, N.J., October 19, 1988; *Justice*, September 1, 1962; Ricki Carole Myers Cohen, "Fannia Cohn and the International Ladies' Garment Workers' Union" (Ph.D. diss., University of Southern California, 1976), 249–50; Susan Stone Wong, "Cohn, Fannia M.," in *Notable American Women: The Modern Period*, ed. Barbara Sicherman and Carol Hurd Green (Cambridge: Belknap Press of Harvard University Press, 1980), 154–55.

5. "Fannia Cohn Dies: Pioneer Educator Was ILG Veteran," *Justice*, January 1, 1963.

6. "Fannia Cohn Dies"; Leon and Miriam Stein, interviews by author; Elizabeth Balanoff, "Interview with Maida Springer Kemp," *The Black Woman Oral History Project, from the Arthur and Elizabeth Schlesinger Library on the History of Women in America*, ed. Ruth Edmonds Hill, 10 vols. (Westport, Conn.: Meckler, 1990), 7:72; *Webster's Third New International Dictionary Unabridged*, s.v. "zealot."

7. "Fannia Cohn Dies"; Leon and Miriam Stein, interviews by author.

8. Benjamin Stolberg, *Tailor's Progress* (New York: Doubleday, 1944), 286.

9. Leon Stein, interview by author; Abraham Bisno is cited in Charlotte Baum, Paula Hyman, and Sonya Michel, *The Jewish Woman in America* (New York: New American Library, 1977), 160–61.

10. Ralph Taylor to "Aunt Rose," March 15, 1949, Reel 1, Schneiderman Papers; Gary E. Endelman, *Solidarity Forever: Rose Schneiderman and the Women's Trade Union League* (Arno Press: 1982).

11. These speculations are based on Gary Endelman's interview with Lucy Goldthwaite for "Solidarity Forever: Rose Schneiderman and the Women's Trade Union League" (Ph.D. diss., University of Delaware, 1978). He cites her on pp. 270–72.

12. RS to Eleanor Roosevelt, n.d. [1961], n.d. [1962], May 21, 1962, Eleanor Roosevelt Papers; Endelman, "Solidarity Forever," 270.

13. Endelman, "Solidarity Forever," 271; Rose Schneiderman, *All for One* (New York: Paul S. Eriksson, 1967).

14. Clara Shavelson, "The Women's Trade Union League, 1903–1955" (typescript dated only 1963), papers in possession of Martha Schaffer. See also "WTUL Notes" in Yiddish and English, in possession of Joel Schaffer.

15. Pauline Newman, interview by author, New York, N.Y., February 9, 1984; Endelman, "Solidarity Forever," 270–71.

16. *New York Times*, October 17, 1934; Dorothy Kenyon to RS, March 6, 1940, Reel 1, Schneiderman Papers.

17. RS to PMN, August 11, 1917, Newman Papers; RS to ER, March 2, 1937, Eleanor Roosevelt Papers.

18. RS to ER, March 14, 1960, Eleanor Roosevelt Papers.

19. See Harold Ginzburg to RS, March 4, 1960, Schneiderman Papers; Endelman, "Solidarity Forever," 261.

20. Pauline Newman, interview by Barbara Wertheimer, New York, N.Y., November 1976; Newman, interview by author; Leon Stein, interview by author.

21. *New York Times*, August 14, 1972.

22. Vera Peterson Joseph to PMN, August 10, 1973, Box 9, Newman Papers.

23. Philip Foner, *Women and the American Labor Movement* (New York: Free Press, 1979), 516–36.

24. Ibid., 487–89; "Text of speech to CLUW, 1978," Newman Papers.

25. "Text of speech to CLUW, 1978"; Elisabeth Burger, interview by author, New York, N.Y., December 15, 1987; Judith Freeman Clarke, *Almanac of American Women in the Twentieth Century* (New York: Prentice Hall, 1987), 204.

26. Burger, interview by author, December 15, 1987.

27. Ibid.; Leon Stein, interview by author.

28. Burger, interview by author, December 15, 1987.

29. Pauline Newman, "Maud Swartz," "Of Maud Swartz," "Maud Swartz, a Year after Her Death," "Elisabeth Christman," "Of Mary Anderson," "Agnes Nestor—A Tribute," "Rose Schneiderman," "Rose Schneiderman—A Tribute," Box 6, Newman Papers.

30. *New York Times*, September 1, 1975; September 1, 17, 1980; March 23, 1983. Pauline Newman correspondence with Barbara Wertheimer, February 11, March 27, 1975; April 20, June 10, 1976; March 28, n.d.; August 27, n.d.; January 8, May 5, June 6, 17, 1977, all in Box 9, Newman Papers. Michael Owen, telephone interview by author, September 27, 1992.

31. Newman, interview by author.

32. Martha Schaffer, telephone interview by author, March 11, 1989.

33. Ibid.

34. Clara Lemlich Shavelson, interview by Joel and Martha Schaffer, Los Angeles, Calif., February 2, 1974.

35. Martha Schaffer, interview by author.

36. Ibid.

37. Ibid.

38. Ibid.

39. Evelyn Velson, interview by author, Oakland, Calif., September 9, 1992.

40. Shavelson, interview by Schaffers.

41. Martha Schaffer, interview by author.

42. Sophie Melvin Gerson, "Memorial Address for Clara Lemlich Shavelson," October 24, 1982, notes and transcript in my possession.

43. Martha Schaffer, interview by author.

44. PMN to Patricia Miller King (director of the Schlesinger Library), n.d., Folder 157, Newman Papers.

45. Owen, interview by author.

46. Burger (December 15, 1987) and Leon Stein, interviews by author.

47. Ibid.

48. Ibid.

49. "Bid Farewell to Pauline," *Justice*, July 1986.

50. Burger, interview by author, December 15, 1987.

51. "June 23 Memorial for Pauline," *Justice*, May 1986; "Bid Farewell to Pauline," *Justice*, July 1986.

52. *Pauline Newman* (booklet produced by Health Education Resources Services, ILGWU, 1986).

53. *Jewish Currents*, September 1975.

54. Balanoff, "Interview with Maida Springer Kemp," 71.

55. Esther Peterson to PMN, November 30, 1978, Box 9, Newman Papers.

SELECTED BIBLIOGRAPHY

ARCHIVAL SOURCES

Cohn, Fannia M. Papers. Astor, Lenox, and Tilden Foundations, Rare Books and Manuscripts Division, New York Public Library.

International Ladies' Garment Workers' Union Collection. New York State School for Industrial and Labor Relations, Cornell University.

International Worker's Order Collection. Tamiment Institute Library, New York University.

Miller, Frieda S. Papers. Arthur and Elizabeth Schlesinger Library, Radcliffe College.

National Women's Trade Union League. Papers. Arthur and Elizabeth Schlesinger Library, Radcliffe College.

Newman, Pauline M. Papers. Arthur and Elizabeth Schlesinger Library, Radcliffe College.

New York Women's Trade Union League. Papers. Tamiment Institute Library, New York University.

O'Reilly, Leonora. Papers. Tamiment Institute Library, New York University.

Pesotta, Rose. Papers. Astor, Lenox, and Tilden Foundations, Rare Books and Manuscripts Division, New York Public Library.

Roosevelt, Eleanor. Papers. Franklin Delano Roosevelt Presidential Library, Hyde Park, New York.

Schneiderman, Rose. Papers. Tamiment Institute Library, New York University.

Shavelson, Clara Lemlich. Private Papers. Courtesy Martha Schaffer, San Diego, California.

Union Health Center. Papers. New York State School for Industrial and Labor Relations, Cornell University.

U.S. Women's Bureau. Papers. Sophia Smith Collection, Smith College.

Van Kleeck, Mary. Papers. Sophia Smith Collection, Smith College.

INTERVIEWS

By the Author

Elisabeth Burger. New York, N.Y., December 15, 1987, and December 21, 1993.

Walter Edberg. Brooklyn, N.Y., May 1980.

Jack Friedman. Brooklyn, N.Y., August 1980.

Sophie Melvin Gerson. Brooklyn, N.Y., February 17, 1989.

Sidney Jonas. Brooklyn, N.Y., August 10, 1980.

Shirley Kupferstein. Brooklyn, N.Y., May 1980.

Jane and Adela Margules. Brooklyn, N.Y., December 30, 1990.

Dorothy Moser. New York, N.Y., October 8, 1987.

Pauline M. Newman. New York, N.Y., February 9, 1984.

Michael Owen. By telephone, September 27, 1992.

Rose Nelson Raynes. Brooklyn, N.Y., October 8, 1987, and February 17, 1989.

Joel Schaffer. Oakland, Calif., September 9, 1992.

Martha Schaffer. By telephone, March 11, 1989.

Dora Smorodin. Maplewood, N.J., March 12, 1991.

Leon Stein. Cranbury, N.J., October 19, 1988.

Miriam Stein. Cranbury, N.J., October 19, 1988.

Evelyn Velson. Oakland, Calif., September 9, 1992.

Julia Velson. Brooklyn, N.Y., December 30, 1990, and Oakland, Calif., September 9, 1992.

By Other Individuals

Rae Appel. Interviewed by Joel Schaffer, Brooklyn, N.Y., 1974.

Murray Margules. Interviewed by Joel Schaffer, Queens, N.Y., 1974. Transcript in interviewer's possession.

Rita Margules. Interviewed by Joel Schaffer, Queens, N.Y., 1974. Transcript in interviewer's possession.

Pauline M. Newman. Interviewed by Barbara Wertheimer, New York, N.Y., November 1976. Transcript in Box 1, Newman Papers.

Arthur Schaffer. Interviewed by Joel Schaffer, Queens, N.Y., 1974. Transcript in interviewer's possession.

Martha Schaffer. Interviewed by Joel Schaffer, Queens, N.Y., 1974. Transcript in interviewer's possession.

Clara Lemlich Shavelson. Interviewed by Martha and Joel Schaffer, Los Angeles, Calif., February 2, 1974. Transcript in interviewers' possession.

PUBLISHED SOURCES

Newspapers and Magazines
American Federationist, 1925–30
Brooklyn Daily Eagle, 1930–45
Buffalo (New York) News, 1926
The Call, 1906–19
Charities and Commons, 1905
The Daily Worker, 1925–38
Equal Rights, 1923–29
Justice, 1962, 1969, 1982, 1986
Labor Age, 1925–28
Ladies' Garment Worker, 1913–18
Life and Labor, Life and Labor Bulletin, 1911–49
The Message, 1914
The Nation, 1928–40
The New Republic, 1928–37
New York Times, 1902–8, 1909–13, 1917–19, 1932–72
Party Organizer, 1925–39
People's Daily World, 1982
Progressive Woman/Socialist Woman, 1907–12
The Survey, 1909–10
Woman Today, 1936–37
Working Woman, 1929–35
The World, 1926

Government Reports

Annual Report of the Director: Women in Industry Service, 1919. Washington, D.C.: Government Printing Office, 1920.

Reports of the State of New York Factory Investigating Commission. 10 vols. Albany: J. B. Lyons Printers, 1912–15.

Report of the Joint Legislative Committee Investigating Seditious Activities, Filed April 24, 1920, in the State of New York. Albany: J. B. Lyons Printers, 1920.

U.S. Women's Bureau Annual Reports, 1918–50. Washington, D.C.: Government Printing Office.

Books and Scholarly Articles

Alpern, Sara, Joyce Antler, Elisabeth Israels Perry, and Ingrid Winther Scobie, eds. *The Challenge of Feminist Biography: Writing the Lives of American Women.* Urbana: University of Illinois Press, 1992.

Baker, Elizabeth Faulkner. *Protective Labor Legislation with Special Reference to Women in the State of New York.* New York: Columbia University Press, 1925.

Bao, Xiaolan. *Holding Up More Than Half the Sky: Chinese Women Garment Workers in New York City, 1949–1990.* Urbana: University of Illinois Press, forthcoming.

Baron, Ava, ed. *Work Engendered: Toward a New History of American Labor.* Ithaca: Cornell University Press, 1991.

Baum, Charlotte, Paula Hyman, and Sonya Michel. *The Jewish Woman in America.* New York: New American Library, 1977.

Baxandall, Rosalynn, Linda Gordon, and Susan Reverby, eds. *America's Working Women: A Documentary History.* New York: Vintage Books, 1976.

Benson, Susan Porter. *Counter Cultures: Saleswomen, Managers, and Customers in American Department Stores, 1890–1940.* Urbana: University of Illinois Press, 1986.

Bloom, Leonard. "A Successful Jewish Boycott of the New York City Public Schools, Christmas 1906." *American Jewish History* 70, no. 2 (December 1980): 180–88.

Boone, Gladys. *The Women's Trade Union Leagues.* New York: Columbia University Press, 1942.

Brecher, Jeremy. *Strike!* Boston: South End Press, 1972.

Buhle, Mari Jo. *Women and American Socialism, 1870–1920.* Urbana: University of Illinois Press, 1981.

Buhle, Paul. *Marxism in the United States from 1870 to the Present Day.* London: Verso, 1987.

Byington, Margaret F. *Homestead, the Households of a Milltown.* New York: Charities, 1910.

Cameron, Ardis. "Bread and Roses Revisited: Women's Culture and Working-Class Activism in the Lawrence Strike of 1912." In *Women, Work, and Protest: A Century of U.S. Women's Labor History,* ed. Ruth Milkman (London: Routledge and Kegan Paul, 1985).

Chafe, William. *The American Woman: Her Changing Social, Economic, and Political Roles, 1920–1970.* New York: Oxford University Press, 1972.

Chernin, Kim. *In My Mother's House: A Daughter's Story.* New York: Harper and Row, 1983.

Clark, Sue Aislie, and Edith Wyatt. *Making Both Ends Meet: The Income and Outlay of New York Working Girls.* New York: Harper's, 1911.

Cobble, Dorothy Sue. *Dishing It Out: Waitresses and Their Unions in the Twentieth Century*. Urbana: University of Illinois Press, 1991.

Cohen, Ricki Carole Myers. "Fannia Cohn and the International Ladies' Garment Workers' Union." Ph.D. diss., University of Southern California, 1976.

Cook, Blanche Wiesen. *Eleanor Roosevelt, Volume One (1884–1933)*. New York: Viking, 1992.

Cott, Nancy. *The Grounding of Modern Feminism*. New Haven: Yale University Press, 1988.

Danish, Max. *The World of David Dubinsky*. New York: World Publishing Co., 1957.

Dreier, Mary. *Margaret Dreier Robins: Her Life, Letters, and Work*. New York: Island Press Cooperative, 1950.

Dubofsky, Melvyn. *When Workers Organize*. Amherst: University of Massachusetts Press, 1968.

Dubofsky, Melvyn, and Warren Van Tine, eds. *American Labor Leaders*. Urbana: University of Illinois Press, 1987.

Dubois, Ellen Carol. "Working Women, Class Relations, and Suffrage Militance: Harriot Stanton Blatch and the New York Woman Suffrage Movement, 1894–1909." *Journal of American History* 74, no. 1 (June 1987): 34–58.

Dye, Nancy Schrom. *As Equals and as Sisters: Feminism, Unionism, and the Women's Trade Union League of New York*. Columbia: University of Missouri Press, 1980.

———. "Creating a Feminist Alliance: Sisterhood and Class Conflict in the New York Women's Trade Union League, 1903–1914." *Feminist Studies* 3, nos. 1 and 2 (Fall 1975): 111–25.

Eisenstein, Sara. *Give Us Bread But Give Us Roses: Working Women's Consciousness in the United States, 1890 to the First World War*. London: Routledge and Kegan Paul, 1983.

Endelman, Gary. *Solidarity Forever: Rose Schneiderman and the Women's Trade Union League*. New York: Arno Press, 1982.

Ettinger, S. "The Jews at the Outbreak of the Revolution." In *The Jews in Soviet Russia since 1917*, ed. Lional Kochan, 3d ed. (Oxford: Oxford University Press, 1978).

Ewen, Elizabeth. *Immigrant Women in the Land of Dollars: Life and Culture on the Lower East Side, 1890–1925*. New York: Monthly Review Press, 1985.

Faderman, Lillian. *Odd Girls and Twilight Lovers: A History of Lesbian Life in Twentieth-Century America*. New York: Columbia University Press, 1991.

Faue, Elizabeth. *Community of Suffering and Struggle: Women, Men, and the Labor Movement in Minneapolis, 1915–1945*. Chapel Hill: University of North Carolina Press, 1991.

Fitzpatrick, Ellen. *Endless Crusade: Women Social Scientists and Progressive Reform*. New York: Oxford University Press, 1990.

Foner, Philip. *Women and the American Labor Movement: From World War I to the Present*. New York: Free Press, 1980.

Frank, Dana. "Housewives, Socialists, and the Politics of Food: The 1917 Cost of Living Protests." *Feminist Studies* 11, no. 2 (Summer 1985): 255–85.

Frankel, Noralee, and Nancy Schrom Dye, eds. *Gender, Class, Race, and Reform in the Progressive Era*. Lexington: University Press of Kentucky, 1991.

Fraser, Steve. "Dress Rehearsal for the New Deal: Shop Floor Insurgents, Political Elites, and Industrial Democracy in the Amalgamated Clothing Workers." In *Working-Class America*, ed. Michael H. Frisch and Daniel J. Walkowitz (Urbana: University of Illinois Press, 1983).

Freedman, Estelle. "Separatism as Strategy: Female Institution Building and American Feminism." *Feminist Studies* 3, nos. 1 and 2 (Fall 1975): 512–29.

Gerstle, Gary. *Working-Class Americanism: The Politics of Labor in a Textile City, 1914–1960.* Cambridge: Cambridge University Press, 1989.

Glenn, Susan A. *Daughters of the Shtetl: Work and Unionism in the Immigrant Generation.* Ithaca: Cornell University Press, 1990.

Gordon, Linda. *Heroes of Their Own Lives: The Politics and History of Family Violence.* New York: Viking, 1988.

———, ed. *Women, the State, and Welfare.* Madison: University of Wisconsin Press, 1990.

Gutman, Herbert. *Work, Culture, and Society in Industrializing America.* New York: Vintage Books, 1977.

Hall, Jacquelyn Dowd, James Leloudis, Robert Korstad, Mary Murphy, Lu Ann Jones, and Christopher B. Daly. *Like a Family: The Making of a Southern Cotton Mill World.* Chapel Hill: University of North Carolina Press, 1987.

Heller, Celia. *On the Edge of Destruction.* New York: Schocken, 1980.

Henry, Alice. *Trade Union Woman.* New York: D. Appleton and Co., 1915.

———. *Women and the Labor Movement.* New York: G. H. Doran and Co., 1923.

Howe, Irving. *World of Our Fathers.* New York: Harcourt, Brace, Jovanovich, 1976.

Hyman, Colette. "Labor Organizing and Female Institution Building: The Chicago Women's Trade Union League, 1904–1924." In *Women, Work, and Protest: A Century of U.S. Women's Labor History,* ed. Ruth Milkman (London: Routledge and Kegan Paul, 1985).

Hyman, Paula. "Immigrant Women and Consumer Protest: The New York City Kosher Meat Boycott of 1902." *American Jewish History* 70, no. 1 (September 1980): 91–105.

Isserman, Maurice. *If I Had a Hammer: The Death of the Old Left and the Birth of the New Left.* New York: Basic, 1987.

———. *Which Side Are You On?: The American Communist Party during the Second World War.* Middletown: Wesleyan University Press, 1983.

Jacoby, Robin Miller. "The Women's Trade Union League and American Feminism." *Feminist Studies* 3, nos. 1 and 2 (Fall 1975): 126–40.

———. "The Women's Trade Union League Training School for Women Organizers." In *Sisterhood and Solidarity: Worker's Education for Women, 1914–1984,* ed. Joyce Kornbluh and Mary Frederickson (Philadelphia: Temple University Press, 1984).

Joselit, Jenna Weissman. "The Landlord as Czar: Pre–World War I Tenant Activity." In *The Tenant Movement in New York City, 1904–1984,* ed. Ronald Lawson and Mark Naison (New Brunswick, N.J.: Rutgers University Press, 1986).

Kenneally, James J. *Women and American Trade Unionism.* Montreal: Eden Press, 1981.

Kessler-Harris, Alice. "Organizing the Unorganizable: Three Jewish Women and Their Union." *Labor History* 17, no. 1 (Winter 1976): 5–23.

———. *Out to Work: A History of Wage-Earning Women in America.* New York: Oxford University Press, 1982.

———. "Problems of Coalition Building: Women and Trade Unions in the 1920s." In *Women, Work, and Protest: A Century of U.S. Women's Labor History,* ed. Ruth Milkman. London: Routledge and Kegan Paul, 1985.

———. "Where are the Organized Women Workers?" In *A Heritage of Her Own,* ed. Nancy Cott and Elizabeth Pleck (New York: Simon and Schuster, 1979).

——. *A Woman's Wage: Historical Meanings and Social Consequences.* Lexington: University Press of Kentucky, 1990.

Kessner, Thomas, and Betty Boyd Caroli. "New Immigrant Women at Work: Italians and Jews in New York City, 1880–1905." *Journal of Ethnic Studies* 5, no. 4 (Winter 1978): 19–31.

Kirkby, Diane. *Alice Henry: The Pen and the Sword.* Cambridge: Cambridge University Press, 1991.

——. "The Wage-Earning Woman and the State: The National Woman's Trade Union League and Protective Labor Legislation, 1903–1923." *Labor History* 28, no. 1 (Winter 1987): 54–74.

Kraditor, Aileen. *The Ideas of the Woman Suffrage Movement.* New York: Norton, 1965.

——, ed. *Up from the Pedestal: Selected Writings in the History of American Feminism.* New York: Quadrangle Books, 1968.

Lagemann, Ellen Condliffe. *A Generation of Women.* Cambridge: Harvard University Press, 1979.

Lash, Joseph. *Eleanor and Franklin.* New York: New American Library, 1971.

Lawson, Ronald. "The Rent Strike in New York City, 1904–1980: The Evolution of a Social Movement." *Journal of Urban History* 10, no. 3 (May 1984): 235–58.

Lemons, J. Stanley. *The Woman Citizen: Social Feminism in the 1920s.* Urbana: University of Illinois Press, 1973.

Le Sueur, Meridel. *Salute to Spring.* New York: International Publishers, 1940.

Levine, Louis [Lewis Lorwin]. *The Women's Garment Workers: A History of the International Ladies' Garment Workers' Union.* New York: B. W. Huebsch, 1924.

MacLean, Annie Marion. *Wage-Earning Women.* New York: Macmillan, 1910.

——. *Women Workers and Society.* Chicago: A. C. McClurg, 1919.

Martin, George. *Madam Secretary: Frances Perkins.* Boston: Houghton Mifflin, 1976.

Mason, Karen M. "Feeling the Pinch: The Kalamazoo Corset Makers Strike of 1912." In *To Toil the Livelong Day: America's Women at Work, 1780–1980,* ed. Carol Groneman and Mary Beth Norton (Ithaca: Cornell University Press, 1987).

Metzker, Isaac, ed. *A Bintel Brief: Sixty Years of Letters from the Lower East Side to the Jewish Daily Forward.* New York: Doubleday, 1971.

More, Louise Boland. *Wage Earners' Budgets: A Study of Standards and Costs of Living in New York City.* New York: H. Holt and Co., 1907.

Morrison, Joan, and Charlotte Fox Zabrisky, eds. *American Mosaic.* New York: E. P. Dutton, 1982.

Naison, Mark. *Communists in Harlem during the Depression.* New York: Grove Press, 1983.

Neidle, Cecyle S. *America's Immigrant Women.* Boston: G. K. Hall, 1975.

Nekola, Charlotte, and Paula Rabinowitz. *Writing Red: An Anthology of American Women Writers, 1930–1940.* New York: Feminist Press, 1987.

Nelson, Bruce. *Workers on the Waterfront: Seamen, Longshoremen, and Unionism in the 1930s.* Urbana: University of Illinois Press, 1990.

Odencrantz, Louise. *Italian Women in Industry: A Study of Conditions in New York City.* New York: Russell Sage Foundation, 1919.

Orleck, Annelise. "'We Are That Mythical Thing Called the Public': Militant Housewives during the Great Depression." *Feminist Studies* 19, no. 1 (Spring 1993): 147–72.

Peiss, Kathy. *Cheap Amusements: Working Women and Leisure in Turn-of-the-Century New York*. Philadelphia: Temple University Press, 1986.

Perkins, Frances. *The Roosevelt I Knew*. New York: Viking Press, 1946.

Perry, Elisabeth Israels. *Belle Moskowitz: Feminine Politics and the Exercise of Power in the Age of Al Smith*. New York: Oxford University Press, 1987.

Pesotta, Rose. *Bread upon the Waters*. New York: Dodd, Mead and Co., 1944. Reprint, Ithaca: Cornell University Press, 1976.

Piven, Frances Fox, and Richard A. Cloward. *Poor People's Movements: Why They Succeed, How They Fail*. New York: Vintage Books, 1979.

Pleck, Elizabeth. "A Mother's Wages: Income Earning among Married Black and Italian Women, 1896–1911." In *A Heritage of Her Own*, ed. Nancy Cott and Elizabeth Pleck (New York: Simon and Schuster, 1979).

Pratt, Norma Fain. "Culture and Radical Politics: Yiddish Women Writers in America, 1890–1940." *American Jewish History* 70, no. 1 (September 1980): 68–90.

———. "Transitions in Judaism: The Jewish American Woman through the 1930s." *American Quarterly* 30, no. 5 (Winter 1978): 681–702.

Rowland, Erin. "Black and Puerto Rican Women in the International Ladies' Garment Workers' Union of New York City, 1933–1980." Undergraduate honors thesis, Dartmouth College, 1993.

Scheier, Paula. "Clara Lemlich Shavelson: Fifty Years on Labor's Front Line." *Jewish Life* (November 1954).

Schneiderman, Rose. *All for One*. New York: Paul S. Eriksson, 1967.

Seller, Maxine. "The Education of Immigrant Women, 1900–1935." *Journal of Urban History* 4, no. 3 (May 1978): 307–30.

Simon, Kate. *Bronx Primitive: Portraits in a Childhood*. New York: Harper Colophon, 1982.

Smith, Judith E. *Family Connections: A History of Italian and Jewish Immigrant Lives in Providence, Rhode Island, 1900–1940*. Albany: State University of New York Press, 1985.

Stein, Leon, ed. *Out of the Sweatshop: The Struggle for Industrial Democracy*. New York: New York Times Book Co., 1977.

Stern, Elizabeth. *I am a Woman and a Jew*. 1926. Reprint, New York: Arno Press, 1969.

Stolberg, Benjamin. *Tailor's Progress: The Story of a Famous Union and the Men Who Made It*. New York: Doubleday, 1944.

Tax, Meredith. *The Rising of the Women: Feminist Solidarity and Class Conflict, 1880–1917*. New York: Monthly Review Press, 1980.

Terborg-Penn, Rosalyn. "Discontented Black Feminists." In *Decades of Discontent: American Women, 1920–1940*, ed. Lois Scharf and Joan Jensen (Albuquerque: University of New Mexico Press, 1987).

Van Kleeck, Mary. *Working Girls in Evening Schools*. New York: Russell Sage Foundation, 1914.

Ware, Susan. *Beyond Suffrage: Women in the New Deal*. Cambridge: Harvard University Press, 1981.

———. *Partner and I*. New Haven: Yale University Press, 1988.

Weber, Michael P. "Eastern Europeans in Steel Towns: A Comparative Analysis." *Journal of Urban History* 11, no. 3 (May 1985): 280–313.

Yezierska, Anzia. *Hungry Hearts and Other Stories*. New York: Viking Penguin, 1985.

Zipser, Arthur, and Pearl Zipser. *Fire and Grace: The Life of Rose Pastor Stokes*. Athens: University of Georgia Press, 1989.

by Miller and Newman, 145–46; on Miller's and Newman's relationship, 146, 282, 283, 285; on Newman, 282, 304, 310, 311, 312

Cahan, Abraham, 26
Carman, Harry J., 278
Carrigues, Madame, 77
Casey, Josephine, 72, 73, 113, 140
Catt, Carrie Chapman, 92–93, 106
Central Labor Unions Council, 111
Chambers, Whittaker, 264
Chicago, Ill.: clothing makers' strike (1910), 53; WTUL chapter, 71, 122, 144, 174
Chicago Dressmakers' Union, 54, 79
Child care, 178, 254
Children: factory laborers, 25, 32, 35–36; housewives' movement and, 217, 227; radical organizers, 223–24; public school boycott, 245; institutionalization of, 320 (n. 33)
Childs, Mrs. R. S., 161–62
Christian Science Monitor, 282
Christman, Elisabeth, 129, 163; Newman and, 8, 305; in Chicago WTUL, 122, 138, 144; as national WTUL secretary, 144, 149, 154, 260; and Schneiderman, 144, 263; and labor legislation, 261; and dissolution of WTUL, 265, 266
Civil rights movement, 271
Class struggle: industrial feminism and, 6, 49–50; housewives' movement and, 7, 218, 219, 223, 242; Eastern European Jews and, 17–18, 24; women's suffrage and, 89, 92, 99
Cleveland, Ohio: cloakmakers' strike (1911), 53, 68–69
Coalition of Labor Union Women (CLUW), 303
Coffin, Jo, 144
Cohn, Fannia M.: career as labor activist, 2, 6, 7, 8, 56, 113, 255, 288, 313, 314; mistrust of cross-class alliances, 4, 5, 118, 185; middle-class back-

ground, 4, 22, 23, 38, 185, 296–97; commitment to workers' education, 4, 118, 170–71, 172, 173–74, 175–76, 177–79, 181, 184, 185–86, 192, 197–98, 295, 297; education of, 9, 20, 22, 38, 44; as factory worker, 9, 31, 32, 37–38; Polish Jewish background, 16–17, 18; exposure to revolutionary ideas, 18, 22–23; relations with family, 22, 23, 38, 185, 186; immigration to America, 23, 38; and housewives' movement, 30, 217, 218; and feminism, 34, 173; and Jewish identity, 34, 184, 198; union organizing work, 38, 46, 47, 63, 183, 194; elected to ILGWU local executive board, 48; as ILGWU vice president, 54, 79, 109, 169, 185, 191; and labor strikes, 63, 75, 76, 79, 194, 195; and women's suffrage movement, 87, 89, 91, 109, 173; and civil rights for blacks, 112, 198; as ILGWU Education Department secretary, 117, 177–79, 180–81, 186, 192, 194–95, 196, 278; and WTUL, 118, 142, 144, 342 (n. 49); loyalty to ILGWU, 118, 172, 184, 194, 202–3, 297–98; and Jewish refugees from Nazism, 164; in ILGWU internal power struggles, 172, 183–84, 192, 193, 194, 196, 197, 203, 296, 297; nervous breakdowns, 172, 192, 276–77; conflicts with male union leaders, 172–73, 181, 184, 185, 190–91, 196, 197, 279, 296, 297, 301; feuds with Dubinsky, 172–73, 194, 196, 197, 198, 277, 278, 285, 295; friendship with Charles Beard, 173, 179, 186, 199, 277; distrust of Communist Party, 182–83, 184; and Workers Education Bureau, 184, 185–86, 193; friendship with Theresa Wolfson, 187, 189–91, 194; friendship with Evelyn Preston, 187–89; moodiness, 188, 190; complaints of union sexism, 191–92, 199, 200, 280, 296; Student Fellowship program, 198, 199, 200, 277–78, 314;

promotion of younger women leaders, 199–200, 201–2, 314; and American Labor Party, 240; and anti-Communist witch-hunts, 257, 277; *Worker's Education in a Troubled World*, 277; forced retirement, 278–79, 295–96; Dubinsky's praises for, 279, 296; death of, 296

Cold War, 273

Collegiate Equal Suffrage League, 101

Communist Party USA: and ILGWU, 5, 76, 155, 172, 182, 223, 341 (n. 39); Newman and, 5, 118, 155, 223; Shavelson's loyalty to, 113, 118, 216, 217–18, 222–23, 226–27, 240, 241, 242, 245, 307–8; Schneiderman and, 118, 128, 257; and labor movement, 118, 171–72; WTUL and, 127, 128; anti-Communist harassment, 139, 248, 264, 270, 273–74; and Roosevelt, 160; and domestic workers, 165; Cohn and, 182–83, 184; indifference to women's issues, 217–18, 345–46 (n. 9); and housewives' movement, 218, 224, 227, 232, 233, 234–35, 241–42, 245, 269–70; founding of, 222; Women's Commission, 225; in Brighton Beach, 230; Shavelson's electoral campaigns with, 234, 240; Taft-Hartley Act and, 263

Community Councils for National Defense, 221

Comparable worth laws, 167, 254

Conference for Progressive Labor Action, 193

Congress of American Women (CAW), 255, 267, 268, 270

Congress of Industrial Organizations (CIO): battle with AFL, 127, 154, 256, 260, 261; WTUL and, 127–28, 154, 156, 256–57, 260–61, 264; Communist influence in, 128; and female workers, 156, 253, 255, 256, 267

Consumer strikes, 217, 218, 255; meat boycotts, 27, 28, 220–21, 235–36, 237–38, 248, 268–69, 270, 348 (n. 67)

Continental Congress for Economic Reconstruction, 195

Contraception, 307

Cook, Cara, 166, 261

Cook, Nancy, 142, 143, 145

Corey, Louis, 200

"Crazy to Learn" (Yezierska), 39

Cross-class alliances, 34; in WTUL, 43–44, 62, 88, 129, 140, 333 (n. 10); in women's suffrage movement, 92–93, 105–6; and labor reforms, 121, 149, 162, 167–68, 325 (n. 7); and workers' education, 185

Crosswaith, Frank, 198

Curti, Merle, 198, 277, 278

Dahme, J. A. H., 35

Daily Worker, 230

Danish, Max, 200

Daughters of St. Crispin, 92

Debs, Eugene V., 42

Democratic Party, 124, 143–44, 147, 149, 159

Dennis, Peggy, 242

Detroit Times, 72

Deverall, Dick, 279

Dewey, John, 171, 195

Dewey, Thomas E., 166, 167, 270

Dewson, Molly, 145

Dickerman, Marion, 142, 143, 145

Domestic laborers, 165–66, 168, 246, 259

Domestic Workers' Compensation Law (New York, 1945), 259

Draper, Muriel, 270

Dreier, Margaret. *See* Robins, Margaret Dreier

Dreier, Mary, 149, 163; friendship with Newman, 8, 44, 122, 155, 305; as New York WTUL president, 44, 59, 142–43, 154; in shirtwaist strike of 1909, 59, 61; founding of New York WTUL, 93, 142; friendship with Schneiderman, 122, 267, 299; and labor legislation, 130, 140, 143; in New York State government, 131,

138, 143; and struggle between WTUL and AFL, 155; in federal government, 160; and dissolution of WTUL, 259, 265, 266; death of, 299

Dressmaking trade: labor strikes, 46, 79, 195; NRA code, 152, 195

Dreyfus, Alfred, 18

Dubinsky, David: as ILGWU president, 10, 152, 195–97, 201, 203, 302; respect for Schneiderman, 151, 152, 194, 285, 301–2; feuds with Cohn, 172–73, 194, 196, 197, 198, 277, 278, 295; and workers' education, 196; and Shavelson's pension dispute, 275–76; and Newman, 279, 285; praises for Cohn, 279, 296

Dulles, John Foster, 274–75

Dyche, John: and shirtwaist strike of 1909, 59; relations with Newman, 65, 66, 68, 69, 70, 72, 73–74; and white goods strike of 1913, 75

Eastern European Jews, 318 (n. 9); Russian persecution of, 17, 18, 319 (n. 12), 320 (n. 29); political radicalization, 17–18; and women's roles, 18–20; immigration to America, 23, 24, 26, 28, 320 (n. 29)

Eastland, James O., 274

Economic depression of 1907, 29

Economic depression of 1920–21, 191

Economic rights, 88, 125

Edberg, Walter, 230

Education: Jewish women and, 19–20, 38–39; working women and, 39–40, 44, 169, 233–34; and Progressive Era, 322 (n. 9). See also Workers' education

Einstein, Albert, 164

Eisenhower, Dwight D., 281

Emma Lazarus Council, 231–32

Emma Lazarus Federation of Jewish Women's Clubs (ELF), 270–71

Engelman, Bessie, 265

Equality League of Self-Supporting Women, 94, 95

Equal pay, 102, 166–67, 168, 253, 254

Equal Pay Law (New York, 1944), 167, 254

Equal Rights Amendment (ERA), 113, 139–40; working-class opposition to, 6, 95, 112, 126, 141, 256, 261–62; middle- and upper-class support of, 94–95, 112; union support for, 302–3

Ethnicity, 18, 58, 89–90

Fair Labor Standards Act (1938), 159, 165, 253

Farmer-Labor Party, 238

Federal Bureau of Investigation (FBI), 274

Feigenbaum, Benjamin, 59, 60

Feminism: working-class women and, 2–3, 6, 34–35, 49–50, 93; and labor legislation protections, 6, 125–26, 302–3; and women's suffrage, 88, 93, 173; Communism and, 226–27. See also Industrial feminism

Fichandler, Alexander, 181, 184

Flynn, Elizabeth Gurley, 242

Foster, William Z., 182, 341 (n. 39)

France, anti-Semitism in, 18

Frankfurter, Felix, 278

Freedman, Blanch, 167, 259, 265

Friedland, Louis, 181

Friedman, Jack, 231, 232

Friedman, Mollie, 176, 191

Fruchter, Max, 99

Galbraith, John Kenneth, 198, 199

Gardner, Herb, 309

Garment industry: female workers, 32, 33, 37, 41, 321–22 (n. 3); sweatshops, 32, 33–34, 38, 193; child labor, 35–36; union organizing in, 37–38, 41, 55, 57–65, 68–79, 325 (n. 7); labor strikes, 46–47, 53–54, 55, 57–63, 68–69, 72–79, 195, 325 (n. 7); ethnic workers, 47, 58; congressional investigation of, 77; racketeering in, 193

Germany, 280

Gerson, Sophie Melvin, 220, 223, 224, 234, 308

influence in, 155, 172, 184, 223;
Union Health Center, 169, 202, 313;
Education Department, 170, 172,
176, 177, 178, 181, 183, 184, 186, 192,
196–97, 202, 278; and workers' education, 171, 175, 179–81, 196, 197;
female membership, 172, 183, 201;
Local 25 education program, 175,
176, 177; Jewish influence in, 178;
Unity Centers, 178, 186; Workers'
Universities, 179–80, 186; democracy
movement in, 181–83; breakup of
Local 25, 182; struggle with TUEL,
182, 183, 341 (n. 39); financial diffi-
culties, 186–87, 193; Local 22, 200,
201; Shavelson's pension controversy,
275–76
International Longshore Workers'
Union, 245
International Women's Congress against
War and Fascism, 244
International Worker's Order (IWO),
248, 267–68, 270; Emma Lazarus
Division, 268
Israel ben Eliezer (Ba'al Shem Tov),
27–28
Italian immigrants, 47–48, 58, 76

Jacobi, Mary Putnam, 93
Jewish Currents, 313
Jewish Daily Forward, 26–27, 108
Jewish Life, 273, 274–75
Jewish People's Fraternal Order, 268
Jewish Woman in America (Baum, Hyman,
and Michel), 158
Jewish women: employment, 18–19, 24,
31; cultural roles and, 19, 20, 21; and
education, 19–20, 38–39; in housewives' movement, 26, 27, 28, 228–29;
and labor activism, 30, 34, 46, 58, 60,
67–68; Emma Lazarus Federation,
270–71
Jews: Lower East Side immigrant community, 15, 23–24, 26–27, 34; and
political radicalism, 17–18, 27, 222;
immigration to America, 23, 24, 26,

28, 39, 320 (n. 29); refugees from
Nazism, 164; Brownsville immigrant
community, 215–16; Brighton Beach
immigrant community, 229–30,
231–32
Johnson, Alvin, 278
Johnson, Hugh, 152
Joint Board of Sanitary Control, 74, 76
Jonas, Sidney, 27, 230
Joseph, Vera Peterson, 284, 303
Judaism, 17, 19, 20, 21
Justice, 275, 279, 295

Kalamazoo Corset Company, 72, 74
Kaneko, Josephine Conger, 69
Kelley, Florence, 93, 94, 132
Kellor, Frances, 143
Kennedy, John F., 267, 284
Kenyon, Dorothy, 264, 281
King, Patricia Miller, 309
Kupferstein, Shirley, 232

Labetsky, Minnie, 78
Labor legislation: women's activism and,
9, 121, 123–25, 167–68; New York
reforms, 36, 132–33, 134, 139, 150,
160, 163, 165, 167, 259; WTUL and,
125, 152, 154, 159, 160, 162–63, 167,
253, 254, 256, 259, 261, 262; conflict
with Equal Rights Amendment,
125–26, 139–40, 141, 261–62, 302;
Triangle fire and, 130, 131; minimum
wage, 132–34, 152, 161, 164–65, 259;
Supreme Court and, 140, 153–54,
165; Eleanor Roosevelt and, 143–44,
152; New Deal reforms, 152, 159–
60, 165, 168, 253, 302; post–World
War II reversals, 262–63
Labor strikes, 46, 55; New York shirtwaist makers (1909), 5, 53, 54, 57–58,
60, 61–63, 313, 325 (n. 7); capmakers
union (1905), 43; Milgrim shop
(1907), 46–47; Brooklyn white goods
workers, 47–48, 53–54; Weisen and
Goldstein shop (1907), 48; Leiserson
shop (1909), 49, 58–59; Cleveland

and poverty, 15, 23; leadership of 1907 rent strike, 16, 29–30, 31; Lithuanian background, 17, 19; reactions to anti-Semitism, 18, 68; education of, 20–21, 40; exposure to revolutionary ideas, 21, 26–27; immigration to America, 23, 25; as factory worker, 25, 31, 32, 35–36, 49; and feminism, 34; and Jewish identity, 34, 67, 184; commitment to Socialism, 40, 42, 67, 70, 96, 107, 110; electoral campaigns, 42, 93–94, 110; relations with middle- and upper-class allies, 44, 64–65, 123; friendship with Mary Dreier, 44, 122, 155, 305; friendship with Leonora O'Reilly, 44, 305–6; friendship with Shavelson, 48, 61; and 1909 shirtwaist strike, 54, 55, 56–57, 59; union organizing work, 61, 63–65, 66–67, 68–69, 72, 117, 121, 123, 154, 155; appointed first woman organizer for ILGWU, 61, 312; conflicts with male union leaders, 65, 70, 93, 99; leadership of Cleveland cloakmakers' strike, 68–69; authorship of articles on labor struggle, 69–70, 74, 78; and sexual harassment, 70, 72, 73–74; affair with Frank Bohm, 70–71; leadership of Kalamazoo corsetmakers' strike, 72, 73, 74; as factory inspector, 74, 131, 146; in women's suffrage movement, 87, 89, 93–94, 95, 96, 97, 99, 101, 105, 106, 107, 113; as ILGWU health education director, 117, 128, 146, 169, 202, 280; as vice president of national and New York WTUL, 117, 265; distrust of Communist Party, 118, 155, 223; lobbying for labor legislation for women, 121, 123, 125, 130, 132–33, 134, 150, 160, 163, 165; friendship with Frances Perkins, 122, 128; relationship with Frieda Miller, 123, 128, 136–37, 144–47, 282–85, 306, 309, 310, 311; Miller's promotion of career of, 123, 128, 146, 147, 167, 254; access to political power, 124,

126, 127, 128, 147, 158–59; and Equal Rights Amendment, 126, 262, 302–3; perceived as conservative "old guard" of WTUL, 127, 154–55, 156, 256, 261, 262; in New York State government, 131, 161, 163, 165, 167, 254; organization of Philadelphia WTUL, 136, 139, 144; relations with family, 136, 311–12; closeness to the Roosevelts, 144, 149, 158–59; rearing of Elisabeth Burger with Miller, 145–46; shift of allegiance to Democratic Party, 149, 150; and battle between AFL and CIO, 155, 256, 257, 260; in New York City government, 160; and workers' education, 169, 175, 176; on Unity House, 177; in ILGWU internal power struggles, 183–84; inspiration of younger female leaders, 201, 202, 303–4, 314; respect of male union leaders for, 202, 279–80, 285, 301; and housewives' movement, 217; as member of federal Labor Advisory Board, 254; as anti-Communist, 257, 280–81; and decline and dissolution of WTUL, 259, 265–66; investigation of German working conditions, 280–81; service on UN commissions, 281; and Miller's illness and death, 285; as symbol of ILGWU history, 285, 304, 305, 312–13; and Schneiderman's death, 302; honored by Coalition of Labor Union Women, 303; old age, 303, 305, 306, 309, 312; death of, 312–13

Newman, Sarah, 69
New Republic, 239
New York (state): child-labor laws, 36, 163; legislature, 101, 132, 139; women's suffrage referenda, 108, 110; Factory Investigating Commission (FIC), 131, 132, 133, 134; labor law reforms, 131, 150, 160, 163; women's work-hour regulation, 132; minimum-wage regulations, 132–33, 134, 161, 164–65, 259; Industrial Code, 134;

friendship with Mary Dreier, 122, 267, 299; and Equal Rights Amendment, 126, 140, 141, 261–62; access to political power, 126, 150, 152, 157–58; in New York State government, 127, 131; perceived as conservative "old guard" of WTUL, 127, 140, 154–55, 156, 256, 261–62; as member of NRA Labor Advisory Board, 127, 151–54, 161, 302; and battle between AFL and CIO, 127–28, 256, 257, 260–61; attacked by Red-baiters, 138, 139; shift of allegiance to Democratic Party, 149, 150, 265; Dubinsky's respect for, 151, 152, 194, 285, 301–2; investigation of Puerto Rican working conditions, 153; and workers' education, 156, 169, 174, 175, 184–85, 192; as New York secretary of labor, 163, 164–65, 166, 254, 302; and Swartz's death, 163–64, 301; and Jewish refugees from Nazism, 164; and American Labor Party, 240; and decline and dissolution of WTUL, 259, 260–61, 262–63, 264–65, 266–67; retirement and old age, 264–65, 266, 267, 284, 298–300; inspiration of younger female leaders, 267, 314; work for International Labor Organization, 281; writing of memoirs, 298–99, 300, 301; death of, 302; Newman's profile of, 305

Schneiderman, Samuel, 20

Schwartz, Cecilia, 27

Scott, Melinda, 106, 108, 129

Seattle, Wash.: WTUL chapter, 261

Seneca Falls Equal Rights Convention (1848), 92

Service workers, 160, 255

Sessions, Jack, 295

Sexual harassment, 70, 72–74

Shaffer, Robert, 345–46 (n. 9)

Shapiro, Feige, 158

Shavelson, Clara Lemlich, 1; career as labor activist, 2, 4–5, 6, 7, 8, 9, 16, 117, 306–7, 313; as Communist, 5,

223; support of Sandinista rebels, 7, 223, 274; Ukrainian Jewish background, 17, 18, 19, 21, 32; exposure to revolutionary ideas, 18, 22, 40, 48; education of, 20, 21–22, 39, 40, 41, 44, 48, 99, 233–34, 314; immigration to America, 23, 25; as factory worker, 25, 31, 32–33, 36, 68, 215; organization of housewives' movement, 27, 30, 216–18, 220, 221, 224, 226–28, 229, 231–32, 234, 239, 248–49; and Jewish identity, 34; and feminism, 34, 227; union organizing work, 41, 46, 48–49, 63, 97, 276, 287; as executive board member of ILGWU local, 48; friendship with Schneiderman, 48; in Socialist Party, 48; leadership of labor strikes, 48, 49; friendship with Newman, 48, 61; as leader of 1909 shirtwaist strike, 49, 53, 56, 57, 58–61; relations with male union leaders, 49, 75, 99, 215, 301; powerful personality of, 49, 247–48, 286–87; talent for public speaking, 61, 68, 97, 101, 118, 217, 220, 228, 233, 241, 246; and Triangle fire, 66; blacklisted following shirtwaist strike, 68, 97, 215; campaigns for women's suffrage, 87, 89, 91, 96, 97–98, 101, 102–3, 108; as co-founder of Wage Earners' League, 96; tensions with upper-class allies, 98, 99; fired as suffrage organizer, 98–99, 105, 106; loyalty to Communist Party, 113, 118, 216, 217–18, 222–23, 226–27, 240, 241, 242, 245, 307–8; marriage to Joe Shavelson, 118, 215, 220; politicization of marriage and motherhood, 119, 219, 240, 245, 249, 307; and workers' education, 169–70; relations with family, 215, 219–20, 227–28, 240, 242, 243–45, 246–47, 249, 307–8; home life in Brooklyn, 215–16, 220, 230, 243; birth of children to, 216, 229; leadership of rent strikes, 220, 221, 232; founding of United Council of Working Class Housewives, 223; inspiration of younger radicals, 224, 227, 245, 307, 314; founding of United Council of Working Class Women, 225, 226; health and dietary regimens, 230–31, 285–86; leadership of unemployment protests, 232–33; leadership of food boycotts, 233, 235, 236, 237, 248, 268–69, 287; style of dress, 233, 247; authorship of political articles, 234, 236, 241, 299–300; electoral campaigns, 234, 238, 240; leadership of Progressive Women's Councils, 240, 248, 255, 268; in American Labor Party, 240–41; trips to Soviet Union, 244, 272–73; support for peace campaigns, 245, 246, 273; and blacks, 246; as leader in International Worker's Order, 248, 267–68; return to garment work, 248, 271; anti-Communist harassment of, 257, 270, 273–74; and husband's death, 271–72; denunciations of U.S. imperialism, 274–75; denied pension by ILGWU, 275–76; second marriage, 286; old age, 286–88, 306–7; encounters with historians, 306; death of, 308–9

Shavelson, Irving. *See* Velson, Charlie

Shavelson, Joseph, 217, 246, 248; marriage to Clara Lemlich, 118, 215, 220; and Clara's political activism, 242, 243, 244; illness and death, 268, 271

Shavelson, Martha. *See* Schaffer, Martha Shavelson

Shavelson, Rita, 216, 245, 247

Shaw, Anna Howard, 105

Shirt and Dress Manufacturer's Association, 68

Shirtwaist makers: strike of 1909, 5, 53, 54, 57–58, 60, 61–63, 313, 325 (n. 7); union organizing, 41, 48

Sigman, Morris, 191, 341 (n. 39)

Silverman, Jenny, 200

Simkovitch, Mary, 30

"Slave markets," 165, 166, 246

Smith, Alfred E., 111, 124; investigation of factory conditions, 131–32; as governor of New York, 134, 138–39, 141

Smith, Miranda, 256

Smorodin, Dora, 224, 227

Socialism, 17; in Jewish immigrant communities, 26, 27, 34; working women and, 33, 34, 42, 48, 93; women's suffrage movement and, 93, 95–96, 99–100

Socialist Literary Society, 40

Socialist Party: support for New York rent strike, 29; and working women's education, 40; Newman's campaigns for, 42, 63–64, 70, 93–94, 110; and labor movement, 43, 171–72; and women's suffrage movement, 95, 97, 107–8; Women's Committee, 97

Social Security Act (1935), 149, 159, 168

Sojourners for Truth, 271

"Song of the Shirt" (Hood), 40

Soviet Union, 272–73

Speishandler, Miriam. *See* Stein, Miriam Speishandler

Springer, Maida, 195, 199, 200, 201–2, 256, 296, 314

Stalin, Josef V., 244, 272

Stanton, Elizabeth Cady, 92

Starr, Mark, 196, 197, 278

Stein, Leon: on Newman, 64, 202, 279, 280, 285, 304, 310, 313; on Cohn, 179, 194, 196, 198, 199, 278, 295; on Cohn and younger workers, 198; on Cohn's mentoring of young women, 199–201; marriage to Miriam Speishandler, 201; on Cohn and union sexism, 280, 296; on Schneiderman's funeral, 302

Stein, Miriam Speishandler, 198, 199–201, 280, 296

Stockholm Peace Petition, 273

Stokes, J. G. Phelps, 77

Stokes, Rose Pastor, 77

Stolberg, Benjamin, 1, 171, 180, 197, 297

Stolper, B. J. R., 179

male union leaders and, 45; and union organizing, 45, 46; and labor strikes, 59, 61, 62, 261; and Jewish women, 67; and women's suffrage movement, 88, 108, 109; and blacks, 90–91; Schneiderman as president of, 117, 127, 128, 144, 151, 166, 265; Roosevelts and, 122, 124, 147, 148, 154, 158; and labor legislation, 125, 152, 154, 159, 160, 162–63, 167, 253, 254, 256, 259, 261, 262; and Communist Party, 127, 128; and battle between AFL and CIO, 127–28, 155, 156, 256–57, 260–61; influence in federal government, 137–38, 159, 255; and Equal Rights Amendment, 139, 262; National Woman's Party and, 140; International Congress of Working Women, 141–42; Maud Swartz as president of, 144; national offices, 144; and workers' education, 174–75, 257; decline and dissolution of, 257, 259–60, 264, 265–66; Red-baiting attacks on, 264; Coalition of Labor Union Women and, 303. *See also* New York Women's Trade Union League

Workers' compensation, 168

Workers' education: Cohn and, 4, 118, 170–71, 172, 173–74, 175–76, 177–79, 180–81, 184, 185–86, 192, 197–98, 295, 297; Schneiderman and, 156, 169, 174, 175, 184–85, 192; WTUL and, 156, 169, 174–75, 257; industrial feminism and, 169, 171; Newman and, 169, 175, 176; Shavelson and, 169–70; ILGWU and, 170, 171, 172, 175–81, 186, 196–97; Workers Education Bureau and, 184, 185, 193; Brookwood Labor College, 184–85, 188, 192–93, 194

Workers Education Bureau (WEB), 184, 185, 193

Worker's Education in a Troubled World (Cohn), 277

Workers' resorts, 177

Workers' University, 179–80, 186

Working class: feminism and, 2–3, 6, 34–35, 49–50; and cross-class alliances, 4, 34; housewives' movement and, 7, 30, 219; and rent increases, 28–29; radical activism, 45; rural conditions, 70; and women's suffrage, 89, 100; legislative protections and, 124; standards of living, 217, 224–25; Communist Party and, 240. *See also* Working women

Working Woman, 236, 239

Working women, 1; and political activism, 2, 5, 9–10, 55, 297, 298; and feminism, 2–3, 6, 34–35, 49–50, 93; Schneiderman on, 6, 57, 80, 104, 140–41; labor legislation and, 6, 123–26, 160, 168, 259, 261, 262, 303; and Equal Rights Amendment, 6, 303; industrial feminism and, 6–7, 10, 54–55, 118; and Jewish culture, 8, 18–19, 24, 34; garment industry conditions, 32, 33, 37, 41, 321–22 (n. 3); and Socialism, 33, 34, 42, 48, 93; and union organizing, 33–34, 37, 41–42, 43, 45, 58, 253, 333 (n. 10); and cross-class women's alliances, 34, 44, 92–93, 129; employment discrimination against, 37, 76, 125, 167, 191, 254, 262, 267; and self-education, 39–41, 169, 233–34; and WTUL, 43, 45, 46, 129–30; difficulties in attaining labor leadership positions, 43, 65, 182, 191–92, 200–201, 267; labor strikes, 53–54, 55, 57–58, 60, 61–63, 76–77; and prostitution, 62, 103; sexual harassment of, 72–74; and suffrage movement, 80, 87–89, 90, 91–93, 99–100, 102, 109–10; and racism, 90; and "femininity," 103–4; maximum-hours laws and, 132, 139; minimum-wage laws and, 132–34, 152, 259; wages earned by, 133, 253, 254; and National Woman's Party, 140; blacks, 152–53, 161, 165–66; Roosevelt administration and, 159, 167; World

War II and, 166–67, 253–55; schools
for, 169, 171, 174–77, 179–80, 185;
and ILGWU internal power struggles,
172, 182, 183; unemployment protests, 232–33; post–World War II set-
backs, 257, 258–59, 263; and child-
rearing, 320 (n. 33); Communist Party
and, 345–46 (n. 9)
World War I, 107, 220–21
World War II, 166–67, 253–54, 258

Yezierska, Anzia, 39
Young, Ruth (Ruth Yugelson), 245, 247,
256, 257, 307
Young Women's Christian Association
(YWCA), 152
Yugelson, Ruth. *See* Young, Ruth

Zaritsky, Max, 43, 151, 164, 195
Zinsher, Fannie, 87, 313
Zola, Emile, 39